Using
Microsoft
Access
2000

Susan Sales Harkins

Tom Gerhart

Ken Hansen

A Division of Macmillan Computer Publishing, USA
201 W. 103rd Street
Indianapolis, Indiana 46290

Using Microsoft Access 2000

Copyright © 1999 by Que Corporation

International Standard Book Number: 0-7897-1604-6

Library of Congress Catalog Card Number: 98-84936

Printed in the United States of America

First Printing: April 1999

02   01   00   99   4   3   2   1

Trademarks

Warning and Disclaimer

Executive Editor
Rosemarie Graham

Acquisitions Editor
Neil Rowe

Development Editor
Susan Shaw Dunn

Managing Editor
Jodi Jensen

Project Editor
Dana Rhodes Lesh

Copy Editor
Rhonda Tinch-Mize

Indexer
Kevin Kent

Proofreaders
Mona Brown
Betsy Deeter

Technical Editor
Michel Walsh

Software Development Specialist
Andrea Duvall

Team Coordinator
Carol Ackerman

Interior Designers
Nathan Clement
Ruth Lewis

Cover Designers
Ruth Lewis
Dan Armstrong

Layout Technicians
Amy Parker
Ayanna Lacey
Heather Miller

Contents

About the Authors

Access and VBA are **Susan Sales Harkins**'s bread and butter, having written about both for *The Cobb Group* (now *ZDJournals*) for more than five years. In that capacity, it was never enough to just "know" Access—Susan had to live and breathe it because "if you print it," a reader somewhere will disagree with your solution. During Susan's seventh year at *The Cobb Group*, the publisher moved to another state, and Susan took advantage of the opportunity to return to the development world full time; that's how RabbitTracks Consulting was born. Susan gathered her best contacts—experts in their own fields—that share a common belief that computing shouldn't have to hurt to be good. You can visit RabbitTracks Consulting's Web site at `www.rabbittracks.com`.

Tom Gerhart has been an independent consultant since 1993, when he retired from IBM. His current area of specialty is the design and development of business solutions based on Microsoft Office, with a primary emphasis on Access and SQL Server. He has worked with all releases of Access, with many projects involving back-end databases (including Oracle and Microsoft SQL). He has also worked with Visual Basic, including the development of ActiveX components. Tom does some training in addition to his consulting.

Ken Hansen is a principal in HSC Consulting, Inc., specializing in developing solutions that use Access, Visual Basic, Microsoft Office, and SQL Server. He has more than 20 years' experience in the information systems area, having started his career designing mainframe financial systems in the days of removable disk drives and punch-card input. Ken has been developing applications with Access since its initial release. He started out life as more of a financial type, with an MBA in accounting and finance from Northwestern University, but decided that this computer stuff is more fun. Ken is a retired CPA and a Microsoft Certified Solutions Developer. He can be reached at `hscc@compuserve.com`. A percentage of Ken's royalties will be donated to The Race for the Cure (breast cancer research) and to The INN at Beth Israel Hospital (in appreciation for the work of Dr. Fred Epstein, one of the world's foremost pediatric neurosurgeons).

Dedications

To my husband, Bill, for encouraging me to explore.

—Susan Sales Harkins

To my Kathy and my mother, who at different periods of my life have been there with unwavering understanding, patience, and support.

—Tom Gerhart

Acknowledgments

A big thanks to Jim Blanchard and Mark McCoy for having all the answers, to Schatzi for sharing Jim with RabbitTracks, and the folks at Macmillan for their patience.

—Susan Sales Harkins

Thanks to my family and friends who gave me the confidence and encouragement to embark on this project, and to Susan, Ken, and Neil, who helped my hand along the way.

—Tom Gerhart

I want to thank my wife, Barb (please—no Barbie and Ken jokes), for holding down the fort as I run from one meeting or project to another. I never had it so good and promise that one day I will learn to say "no" and finish all my jobs around the house.

—Ken Hansen

Tell Us What You Think!

As the reader of this book, *you* are our most important critic and commentator. We value your opinion and want to know what we're doing right, what we could do better, what areas you'd like to see us publish in, and any other words of wisdom you're willing to pass our way.

As an associate publisher for Que, I welcome your comments. You can fax, email, or write me directly to let me know what you did or didn't like about this book—as well as what we can do to make our books stronger.

Please note that I cannot help you with technical problems related to the topic of this book, and that due to the high volume of mail I receive, I might not be able to reply to every message.

When you write, please be sure to include this book's title and author as well as your name and phone or fax number. I will carefully review your comments and share them with the author and editors who worked on the book.

Fax: 317-581-4666

Email: office_que@mcp.com

Mail: Associate Publisher
         Que
         201 West 103rd Street
         Indianapolis, IN 46290 USA

MICROSOFT ACCESS 2000 IS THE DESKTOP database choice of thousands of users for many reasons. Access is "at home" with home users who want to store and retrieve personal data easily. Access also works very well in business environments with multiple users.

One of the most commonly praised attributes of this data-storage and retrieval system is its easy-to-understand graphic interface for creating queries, forms, and reports—something that many larger, more complicated database systems lack. In other words, even inexperienced programmers can use Access to turn a stack of invoices, a card file of customer names, a ledger, and an inventory list into a relational database that makes entering, updating, and reporting information as easy as clicking a button.

Because of Access's ease of use and quick learning curve, learning your way around it has another appeal. Creating applications with Access has become a popular inroad for people who want to move into the field of computer development and programming. Many successful data-management consultants can tell you that they started out creating simple Access applications, eventually learned Visual Basic for Applications (VBA) and other programming skills, and moved on to professional development. Many of these experts still use Access for their clients' database needs and have pushed this flexible and powerful member of Microsoft Office to its limits.

Access 2000 offers more than just a "pretty face" for learning how to manage data. You'll find these benefits and more from using Access:

- Sample databases—Microsoft includes sample databases to help you learn about real-world tables, forms, queries, and reports, and how they are interconnected to form a data management system. The Northwind database (a fictional trading company with data of its own) offers several sample forms and reports that you can alter, and it includes code modules that you can adapt. You can even copy table structures from this database to create your own tables.

- Wizards—Microsoft makes creating an Access database very easy. You can choose from several examples of databases in the Database Wizard for such storage uses as contact information, inventory control, a ledger, and so on. You can create and then modify these databases to meet your own needs.

- Keys to understanding the structure—After you decide how to create and relate your tables, you can easily view all the relationships in your database with the graphical interface in the Relationships window. This makes one of the toughest parts of relational database design much easier and more manageable.

- Microsoft Office integration—You can use Access with Word, Excel, and other Microsoft Office applications to create mail merges, charts, and other helpful uses for your data.

- Easier programming—You can use relatively simple code with macros to automate repeated tasks, or you can try more complex and flexible code with VBA. Access provides graphical shortcuts and hints to help make writing code easier.

- Common standards—When you're ready for the big time, you can rest assured that Access uses standards that help its applications scale up to work within larger environments. Access uses objects and SQL (Structured Query Language) to make its code—and your learning—adaptable to other applications.

Why This Book?

The *Using* series of books from Que is designed with various needs in mind, but all of them aim to make using your computer application easier and more efficient. *Using Microsoft Access 2000* works well in various ways for those who are relatively new to Access but who use it regularly. Features in this edition include the following:

- An improved index to help you find information under the terms you're used to using. We've tried to anticipate alternative terms for key concepts. Finding the task you want to perform is quicker, and you can resolve your problem without extended searches for help.

- The information is presented more clearly so that you can quickly spot the answers to your problems. This information includes figures with expanded callouts, notes in the margins, and easy-to-follow steps in the text. Whether you spot a figure you want to duplicate, a note that provides helpful information, or a task heading that suits your needs, you'll be able to find the answers to solve your problems in easy and clear ways.

- This volume is designed with a dual purpose in mind: reference and tutorial. If you're new to Access or still don't understand certain concepts or procedures, you can follow the book from beginning to end to learn how to use the product. If you're already somewhat familiar with Access but want a resource for how-to solutions or information to expand your knowledge, you can look up a wide variety of tasks for concise answers or instructions.

- With *Using Microsoft Access 2000*, you get what you need for long-term use at an affordable price. You won't have to figure out what you want to know from the middle of a long course project or wade through pages of theory and high-end material. You'll be able to pick out any task now or at some point in the future to understand what you want to know.

Who Should Use This Book?

This book is for anyone who uses Access and needs to accomplish a specific task, solve a problem, or learn a technique to make data management more manageable. This book is right for you if any of the following applies:

- You have a basic understanding of Windows, such as menu and mouse operations, but Microsoft Access has been gathering dust on your system, and you're ready to put it to good use.

- You have tentatively explored Microsoft Access, playing with the wizards and maybe creating a database from the samples, but you have no idea how it all works or how to modify the database to meet your specific needs.

- You own or work for a business and want to find an easy way to manage all the information you now have on paper or in clumsy applications: invoices, records, accounting information, customer contacts, vendors, and so on. You print letters and reports that are never quite what you want or that have to be calculated and addressed by hand.

- You're ready to put up-to-date, in-depth information about your business on the Web.

- Perhaps you're fascinated by a product that can be used for a simple home business or for a large corporation's presence on the Web. You want to improve your skills and eventually create sophisticated database applications via the most direct route possible. You want a book that starts at the beginning and has an easy learning curve, but that moves you into programming concepts that more advanced books assume you already know.

How This Book Is Organized

Using Microsoft Access 2000 has task-oriented, easy-to-navigate tutorials and reference information that are presented in a logical progression, from simple to complex tasks. It covers features of the program you'll use in your daily work.

Throughout the book, you'll find examples in the figures that you can re-create by using the Northwind sample database or, where indicated, the database the author has created (which can be downloaded from the book's Web site). However, the tasks are also flexible because when you're ready to perform them on your own database, you can insert your own options, file or control names, or properties. You can work through the book lesson by lesson, or you can find specific information when you need to perform a job quickly.

Using Microsoft Access 2000 is divided into seven parts.

Part I: Learning the Access Essentials

Two of the most helpful elements in learning Access are getting started quickly and doing so with a solid foundation. If you try to get started too quickly, you will almost certainly end up with errors, confusion, or unreliable data later on. By contrast, if you get bogged down with too much theory and don't see the benefits of using Access quickly, you might think it's too difficult to learn. The chapters in this section show you some of the essentials of solid database design and how to lay a blueprint for the database you want to create.

Part II: Creating a Database and Its Objects

Access 2000 is object driven. The chapters in this section introduce you to each object. You'll learn what they are, how to create them, and how to modify them.

Part III: Storing, Controlling, and Manipulating Data

Another essential of database management is ensuring data integrity. The chapters in this section show how relationships and certain types of fields work to control data input. You'll also see how to import and export data.

Having a large storehouse of data in your computer's memory does you very little good unless you know how to retrieve the answers you're looking for. These chapters also show you how to create simple queries on a single table to retrieve just the data you want to select. You'll see how to collect specific data from various tables to create a resultset ready for generating a report or viewing onscreen. Access makes creating queries easier by using a graphical interface that writes the code for you. Then you'll find more flexible querying methods with an introduction to querying with SQL.

Part IV: Creating the Interface: Input and Output

Even if you understand all the workings of your database behind the scenes, end users responsible for inputting and changing data might not. Access makes it easy for you create a front end where your users can input data via forms. This section shows you how to create these forms and control user actions in navigating or changing data.

The other part of the front end that users care about is generating a legible, concise report. You'll see how to create reports with various controls that print the results of queries or other data sources, based on your business needs.

Part V: Automating the Database

Beyond creating the basics of a database application, you'll want to refine what you've created for the most efficient use. You might want to automate tasks that you perform frequently or create reusable dialog boxes for your user interface. The chapters in this section show you how to use macros for simple coding, and they then give you a solid foundation in VBA for customizing the uses of your application.

Part VI: Beyond the Desktop

If you're working in a multiuser environment, you have to consider such things as security and the number of simultaneous users. You might also want to present information about your company on the Web. These chapters show you how to secure and deploy your database in different ways to make it accessible on a larger scale.

The chapters in this section also deal with some of the more complex features new to Access 2000: Web scripting, pages, projects, and ADO.

Additional Elements

You'll also find a glossary of terms to refresh your memory or explain the details as you read. Terms that you find italicized in the text are defined in the glossary.

Be sure to use the book's tearout card inside the cover. Tear it out and take it with you wherever you use Access. It contains some of the most common information you'll need but might not always remember. Keep it next to your computer as a quick reference.

Web Site

Downloads for this book are available at `http://www.mcp.com/product_support`. Enter the book's ISBN into the Search box (`0789716046`—no hyphens are required) and then click the Search button to go to the book's information page, where you can find the code.

The Web site also includes the element "Sample Snippets of Useful and Common VBA Samples," which provides you with ready-to-use VBA code snippets that you can use in your application. After you learn the importance and the uses of VBA in Part V, you'll want real-world examples that you can use on your own.

Conventions Used in This Book

The commands, directions, and explanations in this book are presented in the clearest format possible. The following are some of the features that will make this book easy for you to use:

- Menu and dialog box commands and options—You can easily find the onscreen menu and dialog box commands by looking for bold text such as this: "Open the **File** menu and click **Save**."

- Combination and shortcut keystrokes—Instructions to hold down several keys simultaneously use a plus sign (+), such as **Ctrl+P**. These keystrokes are also boldfaced in the text.

- Graphical icons, with the commands they execute—Look for icons like this— —in text and in numbered steps. These indicate buttons onscreen that you can click to accomplish the procedure.

- Cross-references—If there's a topic that is a prerequisite to the current section or that builds further on your task, you'll find the cross-reference after the numbered steps or at the end of the section, like this:

SEE ALSO

➤ *Learn how to place controls on a form or report on page xx*

- Glossary terms—Items that appear in italic in the text, along with a definition, are found in the glossary in the back of the book.

- Sidebars—Information related to the task at hand—including shortcuts, alternatives, warnings, and additional explanations from the author—appears in sidebars next to the related material.

- Figures and callouts—The figures in this book often include helpful callouts and more descriptive captions than in other books. These also appear in the margin area so that you can easily spot a figure similar to your current screen. You'll be able to find a quick explanation of a certain control or element related to your problem or task.

What you see onscreen might vary slightly from some of the figures in this book. This is due to various options during installation, as well as hardware setup or Windows size and resolution options.

PART

I

Learning the Access Essentials

Starting with a Properly Normalized Design

Learn to do your homework: Design the database before you build it

Examine the rules of normalization

Review primary keys, foreign keys, and referential integrity

The Importance of a Good Design

Relational database theory is based on complex mathematical principles that are beyond the scope of this book. However, the results of these principles—normalization rules—are easy to apply, and that's what this chapter discusses. *Normalization* is the process of creating and relating tables according to a fixed set of rules. If a database is well designed—that is, normalized—even a non-developer can discern the gist of the database by reviewing its tables and their relationships to one another.

But before tackling normalization, first be sure you're familiar with a few common database terms:

- *database*   A collection of related data that pertains to a particular purpose or topic and the tools used to manipulate that data. For instance, an Access database might maintain current stock and order information for a company.

- *table*   A collection of related data stored in rows and columns, such as a table of customer addresses.

- *field*   A column within a table and the smallest unit of data in the entire database. A field might contain a customer's name, phone number, zip code, and so on.

- *record*   A row within a table. This row is comprised of fields and contains related data for one complete data unit. For instance, a record would contain all the field data for the same customer.

- *object*   An individual Access component such as a table, form, query, or report.

- *form*   An Access object that displays information stored in a table in non-table (rows and columns) format.

- *query*   An Access object that stores questions about the stored data.

- *report*   An Access object that stores the details for displaying or printing data in an organized manner.

- *recordset*   A group of records that meet specific criteria.

What's an anomaly?

A badly designed database is apt to return errors, otherwise known as anomalies. An *anomaly* is an error that occurs while adding, updating, or deleting data. For instance, if inserting a new record causes a calculated control to return incorrect data, you have what's called an *insert anomaly*. An *update anomaly* occurs when updating a single field produces a ton of additional updates. Finally, a *delete anomaly* would incorrectly delete additional data based on a single delete action. A good database design prevents anomalies, and the best design is a thoroughly normalized one.

Engaging the Rules of Normalization

The normalizing process consists of several rules, but this chapter reviews only the three most important ones. For the most part, you won't need to delve any further into the process. After reviewing the rules, you'll design a database from scratch. Here are the three rules:

- All fields should be *atomic*, meaning that the data can't be divided any further.

- All fields in a table must refer to a key field—either primary or foreign. (A *primary key* field contains a unique value for each record. A *foreign key*, discussed later in this chapter, is the result of related tables.)

- All fields must be mutually independent, meaning that there are no hidden relationships to other fields in the same table.

Along with these rules for normalizing a database, you'll also want to establish a naming convention standard that you use consistently.

SEE ALSO

➤ *Get an in-depth look at primary key fields on page 184*
➤ *For more on naming conventions, see page 31*

Planning the Database Structure

The first step to designing a database is to consider its purpose. What information will you store? Who will use it? What kind of output will you need? You can answer these questions by examining the data you'll be storing in the database and reviewing the current process for storing that data. If others will use the application, talk to them as well. Ask them how they're accomplishing the task right now, and what they expect from the application.

Dividing the Data into Tables

When you have a clear picture of the job your database will do, you're ready to tackle the second step. Simply list each piece of data you plan to store. Suppose that you want to store product

Planning for size

Remember that Access is limited to 255 concurrent users. (However, for many reasons, this is an unrealistic networking goal, which this book won't cover.) Also consider the size of the data storage and use areas—these two aspects are more along the lines of physical factors. You will need to explore the size and scale of your eventual application. This chapter concentrates on the theoretical design of a database, regardless of its size.

information for a bookstore. Your first list might resemble the one shown in Figure 1.1. It's easy to see that you have two types of information: book information and publisher information. At this point, your database will require at least two tables. The next step is to design each table.

FIGURE 1.1

List the data you might collect in a bookstore database.

Rabbit's Bookhutch #1

Book Title
Book ISBN #
Book Price
Book Author
Book Publisher
Book Category
Publisher Address

Subdividing the Tables into Fields

You now have a good idea which tables you need and the information you'll store in each. The next list (see Figure 1.2) is more specific than the first. As you can see, it breaks your data into tables and fields.

FIGURE 1.2

After breaking the data into tables, define the fields in each table.

❶ Translate regular business object names, such as an International Standard Book Number (ISBN), into succinct table and field names that comply with established standards.

Rabbit's Bookhutch #2

tbl Book   tbl Publisher ──❶
  Title   Name
  ISBN   Address
  Price   City
  Author   State
  Publisher   ZIP code
  Category

The First Rule

Here's where the normalization rules come into play. Remember, the first rule states that each field must be atomic. If you're wondering why, consider the Author field in tblBook. Now, you just show one field. You could (and should) break this data down further into two fields, one for last names and one for first names. Why does it matter? Consider how difficult it would be to sort the table by last name or to query the table for authors by their last names. You'd have to physically scan the database or write a special expression to handle this type of sort or query. On the other hard, atomic fields are easy to work with.

Another concern is repetitive data in a single field. Now, you have one field to list a book's categories. Although all books will have at least one category, many books might have more than one. For instance, *Jane Eyre* is considered a classic, but it also fits into the gothic and romance categories. Similarly, *Treasure Island* fits into the adventure and children's categories, with adventure being its primary category. You could enter all appropriate categories into one field, but how would you search for a particular category? This setup repeats the same problem discussed earlier with the Author field.

A second solution would be to have several category fields, Category1, Category2, and so on, where Category1 is the book's main category. Although this arrangement is better, it still has problems. For instance, to search for all books in a particular category, you'd have to search all the category fields, which would be awkward. Another problem is the limit imposed on the number of categories a book can have. You can have only as many categories as you have category fields.

The best solution is to create a third table, outlined in Figure 1.3. This table has no limit on the number of categories a book can have, and searching for those categories will be easy because all the categories are in one field.

FIGURE 1.3

A third table identifies each book's categories.

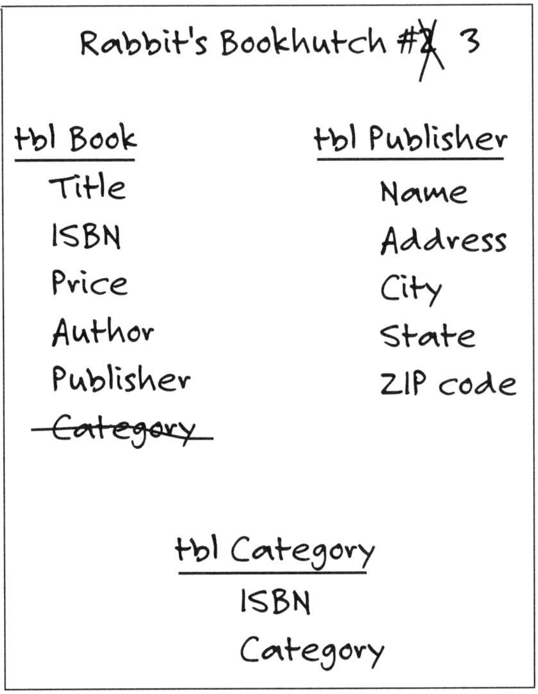

Rabbit's Bookhutch #~~2~~ 3

tbl Book
- Title
- ISBN
- Price
- Author
- Publisher
- ~~Category~~

tbl Publisher
- Name
- Address
- City
- State
- ZIP code

tbl Category
- ISBN
- Category

Multiple options

In a table like this one, you can repeatedly use a value that must be unique in another table. For example, the ISBN must be unique in the tblBook table, but in tblCategory you can repeat the ISBN for each record to list the book in multiple categories. The most important point is that the ISBN in tblCategory must match an existing book, which is taken care of in relating fields later in this chapter.

At this point, you should be able to see the advantages of having atomic fields in your tables. The table tblPublisher appears to be atomic without any further division.

The Second Rule

The second normalization rule requires each table to have a primary key. Keys are discussed in more detail later, but a normalized table should have at least one field that contains a unique entry for each record. Such a field is known as a *primary key field*.

SEE ALSO

➤ *More information on primary key fields is on page 184*

Primary key versus index

A primary key isn't an index. Access always indexes a primary key, but they aren't the same thing. An index refers to an internal Jet operation that speeds sorting. A primary key identifies a unique value field.

One of your tables, tblBook, has a natural primary key—the ISBN. In contrast, tblPublisher doesn't have a field that you can guarantee will always contain a unique value. You might think the publisher's name is a good candidate, but two publishing firms could possibly have the same name. The easiest solution is to add an AutoNumber field to `tblPublisher`. It isn't the only solution, but for now, it's the simplest.

Having a primary key isn't enough. Each field in the table must refer to the primary key. That means each piece of data must be related to the primary key in some way. The table lists in Figure 1.4 are updated so that you can review this rule further. At this point, all three tables appear to fulfill this requirement. The fields in `tblBook` all relate to the book's ISBN. Likewise, with `tblPublisher`, all the fields describe `PublisherID`. It doesn't matter that the value in `PublisherID` isn't publisher data—it matters only that you can identify the publisher and its pertinent information by a unique value. At this point, `tblCategory` doesn't have a primary key, so don't consider it just yet.

Working with AutoNumbers

AutoNumber is just what the name implies—it's a data type you can select for a field, and Access will automatically generate subsequent unique numbers for all records you enter. Using this data type is the easiest way to create a unique value for a primary field. However, if you delete a record, its AutoNumber is gone; Access won't reuse it.

FIGURE 1.4
You've identified or added primary key fields to your tables where appropriate.

The Third Rule

The third rule is that all fields must be mutually independent. Sometimes, this rule can be difficult to discern. Simply put, it means that no field depends on the information in any other field in the same table. All three of your tables fulfill this requirement.

However, that won't always be the case. The trick to finding dependent fields is to consider changing the data. If that change affects any other data in the same table, you have a problem. For instance, if an order table contains a price per unit, the quantity ordered, and a total, you have a dependent field. If you change the value in the quantity field, you must remember to update the value in the total field. You must omit dependent fields to have a normalized table. In this case, you'd omit the total field and replace it with a query expression or a calculated control.

SEE ALSO

➤ *Read about calculated controls on page 328*

Is There a Relationship Between the Tables?

Now that you've successfully divided your data into normalized tables, you can turn your focus to how that data is related. The first thing you might notice is that every book has a publisher. This means that every record in tblBook should refer to a record in tblPublisher. However, not every publisher has to have a current listing in tblBook. This arrangement is called a *one-to-many relationship*. Each record (book) in tblBook refers to only one publisher; each record (publisher) in tblPublisher might refer to many books or no books.

Now look at tblCategory. Each book will have at least one category record in tblCategory. Unlike your publisher table, where a publisher doesn't require related books, each record in tblCategory will relate to a book in tblBook. You won't have a record in tblCategory that doesn't relate to a book. This type of table doesn't fit the requirements of a one-to-many relationship because the one side doesn't require a relating record in the many side. Your current arrangement breaks this rule. For now, refer to this table as having an *associate relationship* because there's an association between the two tables, but no set rules.

Two other relationships are one-to-one and many-to-many. In a *one-to-one relationship*, each record in either table is related to only one record in the other table. In a *many-to-many relationship*, one table can contain many records for each record in the other table.

SEE ALSO

➤ *For more on relationships, see page 183*

Linking the Tables

You've done a good job of dividing and subdividing your data into tables and determining the relationships between those tables:

- tblBook and tblPublisher are related by the publisher.
- tblBook and tblCategory are related by the ISBN.
- There's no relationship between tblCategory and tblPublisher.

Figure 1.5 shows the relationships between your three tables.

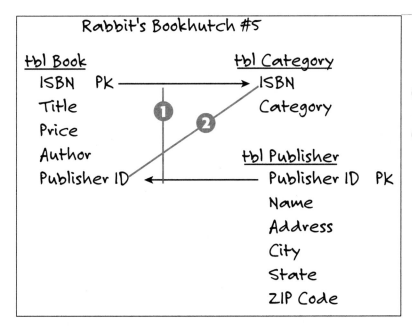

FIGURE 1.5

After you define primary key fields, it's easy to discern the relationships between your tables.

① It's a good idea to give related fields the same name.

② Putting a related field into another table creates a *foreign key*.

Relationships and Data Protection

You can use these relationships to protect your data. You see, you can't just add and delete records as you like in a properly normalized database. Just as you followed rules to create your tables, you also must follow rules to update them. For example, you don't want to delete a record from tblPublisher while a book from that publisher still resides in tblBook. Likewise, you don't want to delete a record from tblBook and leave the category records for that book in tblCategory. (This wouldn't be particularly harmful, but it would be inefficient.) What's more, you shouldn't add a new book to tblBook if there's no publisher in tblPublisher to relate that book to. As you can see, a great deal needs to be considered before you actually start adding records to your new database.

The Evolving Foreign Keys

When you relate two normalized tables, they produce an offspring field known as the *foreign key*. Specifically, you have a parent table that contains a primary key field. The related child table inherits the primary key as a foreign key. For instance, the ISBN is the primary key in tblBook. Because you linked tblBook and tblCategory by this field, the ISBN field becomes tblCategory's foreign key. Similarly, the publisher table's primary key is PublisherID, which becomes the foreign key in tblBook. The relationship between primary and foreign keys has a higher purpose. You can force referential integrity, which places constraints on the data.

Forcing Referential Integrity

Referential integrity is another set of rules that Access uses to protect the relationships between related tables. Specifically, referential integrity ensures that the relationship is valid and that you don't accidentally corrupt your data by adding or deleting records inappropriately. Access does so by making sure that there are no unmatched foreign key values; such a record is known as an *orphaned record*. You can just as easily create a *widowed record* by not providing or deleting a foreign key record when it's required. Referential integrity checks for the following conditions:

- Primary key fields must contain unique entries.

- Related fields must be the same data type, with one exception: an **AutoNumber** field can relate to a **Number** field.

- Tables must be in the same database.

- You can't enter a value in a foreign key before creating the related record (entering the primary key value) in the parent table.

- You can't delete a record from a parent table if a matching record exists in a related (child) table.

- You can't change the primary key value in the parent table if that record has related records.

If an attempt is made to delete or change a primary key value when a matching foreign key value exists, Access responds in one of three ways:

- Access disallows the change. This is generally the best option because it forces you to manually delete the related records, before Access allows you to delete the primary key value. For instance, if you want to delete a customer record when order records for that customer exist, you have to delete all the order records before Access allows you to delete the customer record.

- Access *cascades* the change. Specifically, if you're changing a primary key value, Access updates all the related foreign key values accordingly. If you're deleting a primary key value, Access deletes any related foreign key records. This option can be dangerous because you might end up deleting information you didn't mean to delete.

- Access nullifies the change by setting the related foreign key to null. Generally, you want to avoid this option because it creates orphans.

Another integrity rule

There are two integrity rules: referential integrity and entity integrity. The *entity integrity* rule states that a primary key must contain data. In other words, you can't leave a primary key field blank because a blank field can't uniquely identify a record.

Refining the Design

Believe it or not, when you reach this point, most of your design work is done. You have a good first draft of your database to evaluate. The final step is easy but crucial, so don't omit it—even if you're in a hurry to get your application up and running. This is the last chance you have to catch design errors before you include them in your database:

- Check each table for a primary or foreign key.
- Make sure that each field relates to its key field.
- Review each table's referential constraints for logical constraints.

The checklist in Table 1.1 shows that each table in your bookstore database has a key field.

Tables and keys

Remember, a normalized table doesn't require both primary and foreign keys, but it must have one or the other.

TABLE 1.1   Checking Key Fields

Table	Primary	Foreign
tblBook	ISBN	PublisherID
tblPublisher	PublisherID	
tblCategory		ISBN

A quick review of your table design in Figure 1.5 seems to confirm that each field relates to its key. The last step is to review your referential restraints. As shown in Table 1.2, all seems to be fine. You can still make changes, but at the moment, the design appears sound.

TABLE 1.2   Reviewing Referential Constraints

Primary	Foreign	Restriction
tblPublisher. PublisherID	tblBook.PublisherID	Don't add a record to tblBook if there's no relating PublisherID entry in tblPublisher. Don't delete a record from tblPublisher if there's a related record in tblBook.

Primary	Foreign	Restriction
tblBook.ISBN	tblCategory.ISBN	Don't add a record to tblCategory if there's no related ISBN entry in tblBook. Don't delete a record from tblBook if there's a related record in tblCategory.

Putting the Design to Work

The final step might seem like the easiest one to take. Refer to your final sketch to build the database, and then enter some test data and make sure that everything works as expected. You'll find that a well-designed database quickly lends itself to reliable results. Don't expect the database to be perfect because you might still find a few problems. But because of the work you've put into the design, any problems that crop up should be easy to resolve.

If you follow this simple seven-step process, I guarantee that you'll find the finished database more efficient and dependable.

When You Need to Break the Rules

For the most part, a normalized database is the best route to take. Occasionally, however, you might find that you need to break a few rules. Normalizing can, in certain circumstances, actually slow down some actions. If this happens and performance is a major priority, you can denormalize a table or two. You might also find that a normalized arrangement simply doesn't suit the solution you have in mind. (I recommend that you change your mind rather than denormalize data, but it's your application.)

If you make the decision to denormalize, do so because it's what you want to do. Not fully understanding the normalization process isn't a good reason to break the rules. Then, after you decide to denormalize, be sure to make the necessary adjustments in order to avoid the anomalies that are bound to occur. It's also a good idea to document your decision, your justification for it, and your related adjustments.

Understanding Access Objects

Learn about the Access object hierarchy

Recognize the native Access objects

Adopt and use a naming convention

What Are Objects?

A *database* is a software application that stores data. You then use specific features to query, analyze, and report that data. Access uses objects to interact with your data. These objects are probably very familiar to you as tables, forms, and reports. Form and report controls are also objects.

There's more to objects than meets the eye, however. Almost everything—except the data, of course—is an object. Even the application itself is considered an object—the Application object. The Application object is actually part of a higher structure—the Access Object Model. Off this main structure you'll also find data access objects known as Data Access Objects (DAO). Data objects allow you to directly modify and manipulate data via data objects using VBA—you don't actually interact with data objects. Chapter 29, "A Primer on ADO," has more information on ADO.

The Application object contains all the objects native to Access—the controls, forms, reports, and modules that you interact with during each session. *Native objects* are those objects that exist within a hosting application. Native objects belong to a higher order called collections. A *collection* is an object that contains related elements. For instance, the Forms collection contains all the open form objects. In turn, each form object contains a Controls collection, which contains control objects that represent all the control objects on that form.

The Application hierarchy contains the following objects: the Forms collection, the Reports collection, the Modules collection, the DataAccessPages collection (which is new to Access 2000), the Screen object, the DoCmd object, the Err object, the Debug object, and even the Application object. (The Err and Debug objects are Visual Basic objects, so this chapter won't review them.)

SEE ALSO

➤ *Learn more about the new Pages object on page 578*

Collection versus object

Because there are collections and objects of the same type, you might be wondering how you can tell them apart in a reference. A collection name is fixed; you state it in plural form using proper case letters. For example, Forms and Reports are both collections. When you refer to a generic object, control, form, or report, you do so in singular form with lowercase letters: **Forms** refers to a collection, whereas **form** refers to an object; **Reports** is a collection, **report** is an object; and **Controls** is a collection, **control** is an object. An object name is something you supply; `MyForm`, `mycontrol`, or `rptMine` are all examples of object names.

What Are Tables?

When you enter data into an Access database, Access stores that data in a table. Specifically, a *table* is a collection of related data stored in rows and columns. Each row contains a *record*—one complete unit of data. Each record consists of columns or *fields*—the smallest unit of data. Every field should relate to the table's purpose. For instance, if you create a table to store address information, you might have a field for name, street address, city, state, and zip code. A record would then consist of all these fields of information for one entity. In other words, your table would consist of many records—one for each entity and all containing address data.

As a general rule, you don't interact directly with tables too often. Instead, other Access objects—queries, forms, and reports—are attached, or *bound*, to a table. When Access needs to display or refer to your stored data, a form or report retrieves that data from its bound table or query and displays it in form or report format.

SEE ALSO

➤ *Learn more about designing and creating tables on page 62*

➤ *To learn how to manipulate data using VBA, see page 528 or page 530*

What Are Queries?

Storing data is only part of most database applications. Generally, you analyze stored data to find trends; doing so helps you make better business decisions. One way to analyze data in Access is through queries. For instance, you can use a query to return a simple telephone list or to determine the amount of your Christmas bonus. The uses are practically limitless. In fact, queries allow you to view and analyze data in many different ways:

- You can update, change, and even delete data.
- You can sort records by fields or by groups.
- You can view records that meet specific criteria.

- You can perform calculations on groups of records.
- You can combine tables and even other queries.

Technically, a *query* is a stored question or request. Access actually stores the question or request in query form—similar to the way a table stores data. You can then modify the query as your needs change. You also can execute a query as often as you like (for the most part).

Because queries are complex tools, an entire chapter is devoted to them—Chapter 6, "Creating Queries."

What Are Forms?

Forms are the objects you'll use to interact with your data, so you'll probably find yourself working with them more than any other object. A *form* retrieves data through various means:

- You can bind the form directly to the table.
- You can get to the table data via a query.
- You can create a recordset through SQL or VBA.

SEE ALSO
➤ *For more information on recordsets, see page 530*

Forms make viewing, entering, and modifying your data easier. Most of the time, you can think of a form as a screen representation of the paper forms you're already using. Instead of writing on your paper form, you're typing into your Access form. Certain tasks, such as sorting and searching, are easily handled with forms. You can also use forms as part of your application's interface—a good example of this is a switchboard form. A *switchboard* form directs users through a custom application by opening other forms and reports as they're needed. All in all, you'll find the Access form a flexible and versatile tool—a jack-of-all-trades. Chapter 7, "Creating Forms," explains how to create a form.

What's a recordset?

A *recordset* is a group of records that behave like an object, but are separate from an object. This means you don't need an object, such as a form or report, to manipulate data—you use VBA instead. However, you can and often will attach a recordset to an object.

What Are Reports?

Many of you can relate to the phrase, "I'll need that report first thing tomorrow." If you're using the wrong database, you could end up spending the night at the office. If you're using Access, you can print out the report and go home—just be ready for your boss's praise in the morning.

A *report* is a displayed or printed copy of your data presented in a particular format. For instance, you might group your records by date, or you might print a list of customers by region. The only thing that really limits the power of the Access reporting feature is your imagination. Chapter 8, "Creating Reports," contains all the information you need to create your own reports.

What Are Modules?

Looking at modules takes you beyond the interface objects you're probably most familiar with: tables, queries, forms, and reports. A *module* is an object that stores VBA code. You enter a procedure (a defined task, presented in code) into a module and then use object events (or other procedures) to execute these procedures. (See Chapter 26, "Introducing Visual Basic for Applications," for information on VBA.)

There are two types of modules: class and standard. A *class module* contains an object definition. For instance, forms and reports both have attached class modules. Any code you enter into such a module is specific to that form or report. You can even create your own definition. A *standard module* contains no object definition and contains code that's available to the entire application.

SEE ALSO

➤ *This book doesn't deal with class modules beyond forms and reports. However, for a review of the subject, see page 632*

What's an event?

An *event* is an action that's recognized by an object, such as a mouse click, opening a form, or entering data into a control.

Reviewing the Screen Object

Until now, this chapter has dealt with objects that you interact with directly. The Screen object is a bit different—it provides programmatic access to and information about the active form, report, or control. You'll use the Screen object programmatically to

- Define forms, reports, and controls
- Obtain information about forms, reports, and controls
- Set form, report, and control properties

Of course, you can perform all three programming tasks without ever using the Screen object. However, the Screen object interacts with the active object, not an object you reference. This means you don't need to know the current object's name to obtain information or modify it. The benefit is that you can write one procedure to work with any number of objects. For example, the following code will display the name of the active form in a message box, regardless of which form is active:

```
Dim frmMyForm As Form
Set frmMyForm = Screen.ActiveForm
MsgBox frmMyForm.Name & " is the name of the active form."
```

You can use this procedure with any form. (The Name property doesn't belong to the Screen object; Name is a property of the form object.)

SEE ALSO

➤ *Learn proper VBA syntax on page 469*

The Screen Object's Properties

The preceding code adds a property to the Screen object. Specifically, it uses the ActiveForm property to identify the active form. The Screen object has several properties:

Property	Description
ActiveControl	Identifies or refers to the active control.
ActiveForm	Identifies or refers to the active form.
ActiveReport	Identifies or refers to the active report.

Property	Description
PreviousControl	References the last control to have the focus. If only one control has had focus, this property returns an error.
MousePointer	Identifies or changes the mouse pointer.
ActiveDataAccessPage	Identifies or refers to the active page.
ActiveDatasheet	Identifies or refers to the active datasheet.

If the appropriate object doesn't have the focus, your code creates an error. For instance, if you use the ActiveForm property and a report has the focus instead of a form, your statement returns an error.

Reviewing the DoCmd Object

Almost anything you can do with a macro, you can do by using the DoCmd object in a VBA statement. The DoCmd object has a number of methods that mimic macro actions and menu choices. A *method* is a predefined task that belongs to a specific object; an *action* is a macro instruction. You'll use the DoCmd object to perform simple tasks such as opening or closing a form. For example, the statement

```
DoCmd.OpenForm "frmMyForm"
```

opens the form named frmMyForm; the OpenForm method belongs to the DoCmd object and mimics the OpenForm macro action.

Naming Conventions

Naming conventions are the rules you apply when naming your application's objects. You can choose an existing convention, or you can develop your own. The key is to adopt one and to consistently apply it. A good name will indicate an object's purpose and class. The examples in this book use a style of naming tables and fields designed to make identifying objects quicker and more consistent.

Other Screen properties

Technically, the Screen object has two other properties: Application and Parent. You don't need to specify the Screen object when using these properties, and frankly, you might never use them at all. The Application property (not to be confused with the Application object discussed earlier in this chapter) returns information or references the active application. The Parent property refers to the parent object. For example, if a subform or subreport is active, you can use the Parent property to return the sub's parent form or report.

Advantages of consistency

Following an accepted, widely used convention will make your application more universally understood, not to mention helping out the other developers who might work with you or inherit your application later.

Syntax for Naming Objects

You'll find that many developers use the following form:

`classObjectname`

where `class` is a prefix that identifies the type of object and `Objectname` states the object's purpose or task. The `class` argument is lowercase, and `Objectname` is always initial or proper case.

History and Logic of Naming Conventions

This method evolved from a standard convention named the *Hungarian convention*, pioneered by Charles Simonyi. To discuss the entire breath of the Hungarian convention would be overkill, so let's deal specifically with the object-level naming conventions employed in this book.

To apply this method, you need to know an object's class and purpose. The first is pretty obvious—you're naming a table, form, report, control, and so on. The object's purpose can be a little more complicated because you have creative and practical control over this component. In other words, you could name a sales report `rptRabbit`, but no one would know what it was. The one clue would be the `rpt` component, indicating it's a report. Beyond that, however, they'd just be guessing. A better name might be `rptSales`.

Table 2.1 lists several objects by purpose and class and lists the Hungarian method's result. In contrast, it also includes a name with no convention at all. As you can see, with no convention used, you can quickly run into problems. The main problem is determining which object is what. For instance, in the table, which object is the table and which is the report? (Access allows you to use identical names as long as the classes are different. However, the results are still confusing.) Nor does the name in the third column define the object. In contrast, the Hungarian method names are quite descriptive, identifying the object's class and task.

TABLE 2.1 **Example of Convention Styles**

Object	Hungarian	No Convention
Donor information	tblDonors	Donors
Donor report	rptDonors	Donors
Donations to date	tblDonations	Donations
Donations report	rptDonations	Donations

Table 2.2 lists the class prefixes used throughout this book. As you can see, this method has been extended to include controls and data types.

TABLE 2.2 **Prefixes for Various Objects**

Access Object	Access Object	Access Object	Access Object
Table	tbl	AutoNumber	lng
Query	qry	Currency	cur
Form	frm	Date/Time	dtm
Report	rpt	Memo	mem
Macro	mcr	Yes/No	ysn
Module	bas	Check box	chk
Class module	cls	Combo box	cbo
Byte	byt	Command button	cmd
Integer	int	Label	lbl
Single	sng	List box	lst
Long Integer	lng	Option button	opt
Double	dbl	Subform/subreport	sub
Text	str	Text box	txt

More tags available

The tags in Table 2.2 have been included to coincide with the discussions in this book. This list is by no means complete. For a more comprehensive look at naming conventions, read *F. Scott Barker's Microsoft Access 2000 Power Programming*, from Sams Publishing.

New User Features in Access 2000

Learn about the enhanced Database window and File dialog box

Notice improvements to the Clipboard, conditional formatting, and compacting when you close the database

Replace old add-ins with new features such as Name AutoCorrect and printing the Relationship window

Easily exchange files with Access 97

Use subdatasheets to view related records without a query

Learn the benefits of Unicode

Converting to Prior Versions

For the first time, you can save an Access database as a previous version file, so you can easily share your databases with someone that hasn't upgraded. Simply choose **Database Utilities** from the **Tools** menu. Then, select **Convert Database**, and finally, select **To Prior Access Database Version** to save the current Access 2000 database as an Access 97 file.

Announcing the New Database Window

If you've been using an older version of Access, you'll be glad to know that Access 2000 won't shock your sensibilities. Most of those familiar and convenient options that you've come to rely on are still readily available. If you're new to Access with this new release, you'll find Access easier to use than ever before.

The first enhancement old users will probably notice is the new Database window (see Figure 3.1). This window is consistent with other Office applications, specifically Outlook 2000. The tabs across the top of the Database window in older releases are replaced by the Database object bar to the left. There's a new object—Pages—in the object list. This object is actually an HTML document that you can view with Internet Explorer 5.0, a feature that won't work with earlier versions.

SEE ALSO

➤ *Learn more about the new Pages object on page 578*

You can click any item on the Database window object bar to update the contents of the Database window. For example, Figure 3.1 shows all the table objects in the Northwind database (which comes with Access 2000, but you must install it). To see all the forms, click the **Objects** button at the top of the object bar, and then click **Forms**; to see queries, click **Queries**, and so on. If you click the **Groups** button at the bottom of the object bar, Access displays a list of user-defined groups. These groups can contain any type of native object and are new to Access 2000; you'll use them to organize your objects in most any way you want.

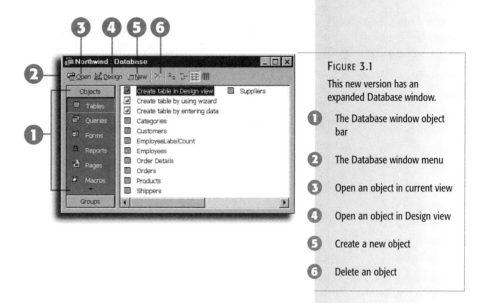

FIGURE 3.1

This new version has an expanded Database window.

1. The Database window object bar

2. The Database window menu

3. Open an object in current view

4. Open an object in Design view

5. Create a new object

6. Delete an object

Many old commands are now available from the Database window object bar. Simply right-click the object bar to display the shortcut menu in Figure 3.2. If you right-click the list area (the white background), Access displays a smaller version of this menu (see Figure 3.3). If you choose **Arrange Icons**, you can control the way Access sorts the objects. Specifically, you can sort by the object's name or type. You can also sort by the date you created or modified each object.

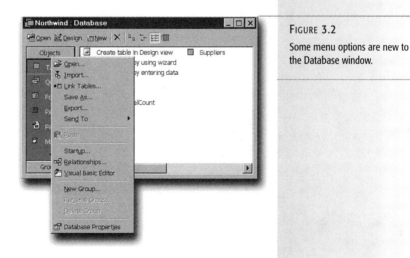

FIGURE 3.2

Some menu options are new to the Database window.

FIGURE 3.3

You can sort the listed objects.

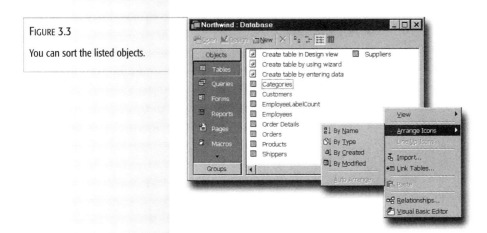

The Database window also sports a new menu bar across the top. The commands are self-explanatory.

The four icons to the right of the menu bar aren't new to Access, but they are new to the Database window. (They were on the Database object bar.) These features allow you to display the list of objects in different ways. For instance, the Large Icons button [icon] displays the objects as large icons (see Figure 3.4). Likewise, the Small Icons button [icon] displays the objects as small icons. The List button [icon] is the default display—creating a list of object names. The Details button [icon] lists information—a description, the creation date, a modified date, and the object type—about the object.

FIGURE 3.4

You can display objects as large icons.

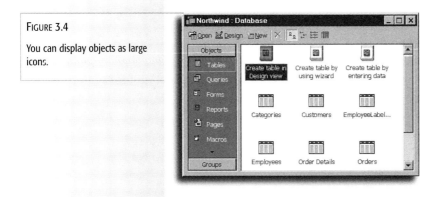

Using the File Dialog Box

The File dialog box has also had a makeover. It looks different, but you've seen most of it before. The biggest change is the toolbar on the left (see Figure 3.5). You'll find this on all the File dialog boxes (Open, Save, Import, and Export). I won't show each one because the additions are basically the same for each dialog box.

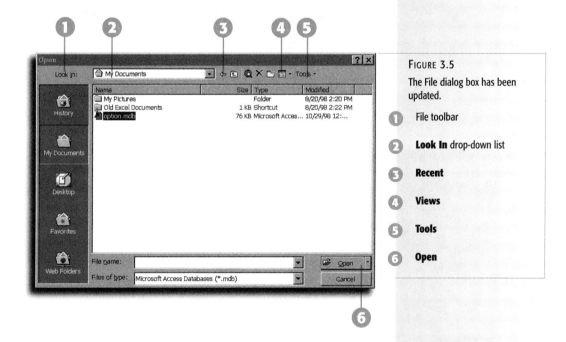

FIGURE 3.5

The File dialog box has been updated.

1 File toolbar

2 **Look In** drop-down list

3 **Recent**

4 **Views**

5 **Tools**

6 **Open**

The My Documents folder is the default. You can look for files anywhere in your system by using the Look In drop-down list, but the new toolbar quickly takes you to the Desktop and the Favorites folder. The History folder tracks the files you've worked on.

A new addition to this release is the **Recent** button, which allows you to step backward through your last few tasks in the dialog box. The **View** button replaces the Large Icons, Small Icons, List, and Details icons from the last version. The **Tools** button is actually a drop-down menu with the following commands: **Find, Delete, Rename, Add to Favorites, Map**

Network Drive, and **Properties**. The remaining buttons aren't new to this version.

Earlier versions allowed you to open a database exclusively. New with this version is the **Open** button, which gives you several new options: **Open**, **Open Read-Only**, **Open Exclusive**, and **Open Exclusive Read-Only**.

Enhancing the Windows Clipboard

One of the most useful additions is the new Clipboard menu (see Figure 3.6), which is available with Access, Excel, Word, Outlook, and PowerPoint. If you dock the Clipboard menu to the current toolbar, you'll lose the Item options.

FIGURE 3.6

A new toolbar offers greater flexibility when using the Clipboard. The toolbar is undocked in this figure.

1 Items options

An alternative way to open the Clipboard toolbar

The quickest way to open the Clipboard toolbar is to simply copy the same item to the Clipboard twice in a row. To do so, just click the **Copy** button 🖻 on the current object menu twice. Access automatically displays the Clipboard toolbar. (This feature works consistently in Design view, but not in others.)

Access doesn't display the toolbar by default; you must open it. To display the Clipboard toolbar, choose **Toolbars** from the **View** menu. Then, choose the **Clipboard** option.

The Clipboard saves up to 12 items for later recall. However, the **Paste** button 🖻 pastes the most recently copied item. By using the Clipboard toolbar, you can quickly access the other 11. (Figure 3.6 shows only four item slots. Don't worry—as you copy new items to the Clipboard, the Clipboard toolbar displays empty new slots.)

Paste from the Clipboard

1. To copy multiple items to the Clipboard, select each item individually and then click the **Copy** button 🖻 on the Clipboard toolbar or the current object menu.

2. When you're ready to start pasting, click the spot where you want to paste an item to.

3. Select the appropriate **Item** option from the Clipboard toolbar. Access copies the selected item to the current object (the object you selected earlier). Or, you can click **Paste All** to paste all the items at once.

Updating with Name AutoCorrect

In earlier versions, if you renamed an object, you had to find every reference to that object and update it as well. If you didn't, sooner or later you encountered an error. For instance, if you changed the name of a field in one of your tables but didn't update the bound controls in your data-entry form, you would certainly have trouble using that form.

Access 2000 now automatically updates references if you change an object's name. For instance, if you change a field name in one of your tables, Access 2000 updates all your bound controls so that you can continue to work without error. Name AutoCorrect also updates references in queries.

You must turn this feature on for it to work. Choose **Options** from the **Tools** menu and click the **General** tab. Next, select **Track Name AutoCorrect Info** in the **Name AutoCorrect** section. Then, turn on the feature by selecting **Perform Name AutoCorrect**. Name AutoCorrect remains enabled through this and subsequent sessions, unless you turn it off.

Improved Conditional Formatting

Conditional formatting allows you to set a value's font, styles, and color depending on set conditions. For instance, you can easily display positive values in black and negative values in red. This feature also works with values expressed as less than, greater than, between, or equal to.

To apply conditional formatting to a form or report control, while in Design view, choose **Conditional Formatting** from the

Format menu. Access displays the Conditional Formatting dialog box (see Figure 3.7). The upper portion of this dialog box displays the default format; in the lower portion, select the formats you want when a value meets conditions you specify.

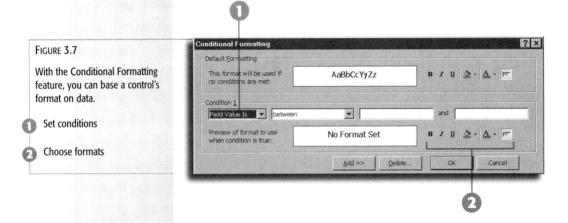

FIGURE 3.7

With the Conditional Formatting feature, you can base a control's format on data.

1 Set conditions

2 Choose formats

Reviewing Unicode

Microsoft Office relies on the Unicode standard to display documents correctly, regardless of their origin. The Unicode standard, developed by the Unicode consortium, governs character coding and provides a 16-bit international character code for information processing that covers the world's major languages. The Unicode standard defines character encoding, and the properties and algorithms used in its implementation. Simply put, if an application supports Unicode, Access can read that application's files, which makes data transfer easier and more accurate than before.

Working with Subdatasheets

Subdatasheets create a hierarchical display of your data in Datasheet view. Rather than view a single table or record, you can open a subdatasheet and view related data. For instance, if you open the Categories table in the Northwind database (which comes with Access 2000, but you must install it), you can expect to view only those records stored in that table. However, the Categories table is related to the Products table. By using a subdatasheet, you can display the category records and their related product records.

If related records exist, Access displays an additional column at the datasheet's left margin. If that column contains a plus sign, the record has related records; if the column contains a minus sign, there are no related records. To see the related records (see Figure 3.8), simply click the plus sign. For instance, the first record in the Orders table, for order 10248, has three related records.

Viewing the subdatasheet

As soon as you open a record's subdatasheet, Access displays a minus sign to indicate that all the related records are visible. To close the subdatasheet, click the resulting minus sign.

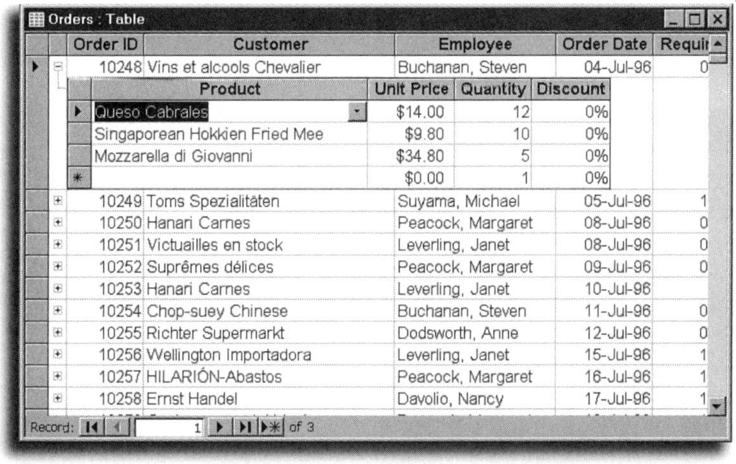

FIGURE 3.8

This subdatasheet displays three related records for order 10248.

Printing the Relationships Window

In earlier versions of Access, if you wanted to know about relationships, you had to use the Documenter Wizard or buy a third-party product. Now, you can use the Print Relationships Wizard to print the Relationships window. After you open the Relationships window, choose **Print Relationships** from the **File** menu. The wizard then creates and previews a report that you can save or print.

Compacting Access Data on Closing

Compacting an Access database has always been a manual task, unless you automated it with code. Now, you can compact your database when you close it. Doing so compresses your file each time you close it, which saves on resources. To turn on this feature, choose **Options** from the **Tools** menu. Then, on the General page, select the **Compact on Close** check box.

Creating a Database and Its Objects

Creating a Database

Create a working application with little effort

Reuse wizard-generated database objects

Leave your mark by documenting your decisions

Getting Started

You can build a database in two ways: by using the Database Wizard, or by opening an empty database and building all your objects with wizards or from scratch. There's no right or wrong decision. Basically, the wizard is quick and easy; building from scratch can take awhile. However, a non-wizard database can be more flexible and versatile than a wizard-generated database. You might find that starting with the Database Wizard and then modifying the results works well for you.

What's a Wizard?

Wizards benefit every user

Don't think that wizards are beneficial only to beginners because developers also use them—a wizard is often the fastest means to an end. For instance, if a client wants to see a prototype, you can always use the Database Wizard to quickly create a professional and easy-to-use sample application.

If you are unfamiliar with wizards, take a moment to review just what they are. Access is a complex tool, but Microsoft understands that most users simply won't get the full benefit of the program until they're well schooled in the package. In an effort to reduce the learning curve and make Access easier to use, Microsoft added wizards.

A *wizard* is a specific program that creates an object or performs a task. More specifically, a wizard presents a series of dialog boxes, with each dialog box presenting a group of options from which you can choose before continuing to the next step. Using one wizard is pretty much the same as using another. They all follow the same pattern; they just have different goals. The Database Wizard used in this chapter helps you create a turnkey application. A *turnkey* application is one that's ready to use—simply launch it and go to work.

What's an object?

Access is an object-oriented program, which means that you communicate with Access and vice versa through visual objects—tables, forms, reports, and modules. These objects contain the data and code that comprise your application. To learn more about Access objects, read Chapter 2, "Understanding Access Objects."

I encourage you to use these wizards; they speed up your work and reduce errors. However, the sooner you learn about Access objects and tasks, the sooner you'll be comfortable using the program. In fact, you must have a little knowledge of Access and its terminology to use even the wizards, so don't hesitate to try your hand at creating objects from scratch.

Launching Wizards

You'll find the object wizards in the Database window, under the appropriate tab. For instance, Figure 4.1 shows the Tables section of the Northwind database in the Database window. (Northwind comes with Access but you must install it.) The query, form, and report wizards are located in their respective sections.

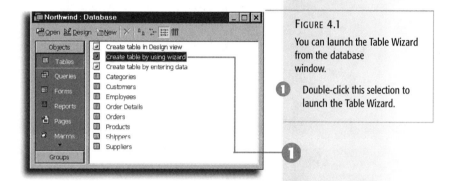

FIGURE 4.1

You can launch the Table Wizard from the database window.

❶ Double-click this selection to launch the Table Wizard.

Launching an object wizard

1. To launch an object wizard, click the appropriate icon on the object bar in the Database window: Tables, Queries, Forms, Reports, and Pages. For instance, to create a table, select the Tables icon.

2. Double-click the resulting wizard option in the list box. To create a table, choose the **Create Table by Using Wizard** option.

-OR-

1. Open the New Object button's ▦▾ drop-down list and choose the appropriate object. For instance, if you're creating a new query, you would select **Query**. (The icon on the New Object button displays the object type last chosen.)

2. In the resulting dialog box, double-click the wizard option. If you had selected **Query** from the New Object button's list, the resulting dialog box would be the New Query dialog box and you would then double-click the **Simple Query Wizard**. Three other wizards available here aren't available from the Database window.

-OR-

1. From the **Insert** menu, select the appropriate object. For instance, to create a form, select **Form**.

2. In the resulting window, double-click the wizard of your choice. If you're creating a form, you might choose the **Form Wizard** option. You can choose from six form wizards.

The Database Wizard is available when you launch Access.

Launching the Database Wizard

1. Launch Access.

2. The program displays the dialog box shown in Figure 4.2. At this point, you can choose between opening an existing database, opening a blank database, or launching the Database Wizard. To launch the Database Wizard, select the **Access Database Wizards, Pages, and Projects** option, and click **OK**.

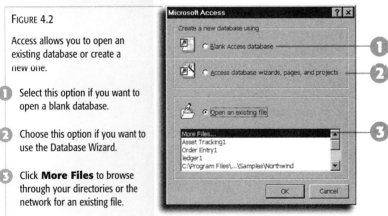

FIGURE 4.2

Access allows you to open an existing database or create a new one.

1. Select this option if you want to open a blank database.

2. Choose this option if you want to use the Database Wizard.

3. Click **More Files** to browse through your directories or the network for an existing file.

Reviewing the Database Wizard

The Database Wizard creates an application, producing all the tables, forms, and reports necessary to complete a particular function. The wizard offers several databases to choose from for personal and business uses. For a complete list, choose **New** from the **File** menu and then click the **Databases** tab.

Using the Database Wizard

1. Launch Access, select the **Access Database Wizards, Pages, and Projects** option, and click **OK**. The dialog box in Figure 4.3 appears, displaying various databases. The buttons on the right allow you to change the way the wizard displays the list. The **Large Icons** button is the default. The middle button, **List**, displays the files as a list rather than icons. The last button, **Details**, displays the list of database filenames, size, and file type, as well as the date each file was last modified.

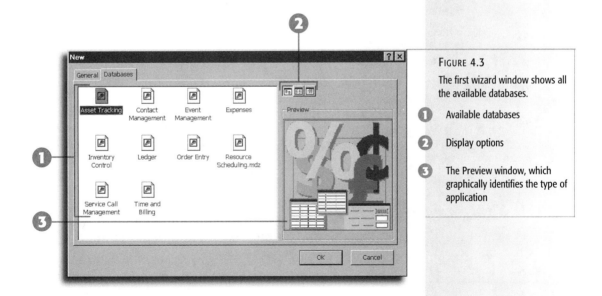

FIGURE 4.3

The first wizard window shows all the available databases.

① Available databases

② Display options

③ The Preview window, which graphically identifies the type of application

As you select each database, the wizard updates the Preview frame. The graphic in this frame helps you identify each file as a business or personal database. To choose a database, double-click it or select it and click **OK**. For the example, select Asset Tracking. After you select a database, click **OK** to continue.

2. Figure 4.4 shows the wizard's second window. This is a simple File dialog box. The wizard gives the new database you're creating a default name, but you can change it. For instance, the wizard named the database Asset Tracking1—keep that name for now. The options along the top are the same ones in the File Open and File Save dialog boxes.

3. If you change your mind, click **Cancel** to stop the process. If you're ready to continue, click the **Create** button.

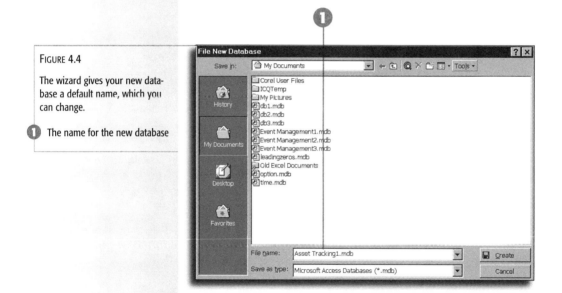

Save as file type

The **Save as Type** option lets you change the file type. Most users will never use this option. However, when you're ready to secure your database, you can learn more about this and other security-related options in Chapter 32, "Applying Security to the Database."

FIGURE 4.4

The wizard gives your new database a default name, which you can change.

1 The name for the new database

The Finish button

If the **Finish** button is enabled, you can click it. The wizard will complete the database without prompting you for any more information.

4. The wizard first displays a blank Database window and then the dialog box shown in Figure 4.5. The Asset Tracking database stores asset, depreciation, maintenance, employee, departmental, and vendor information. If you click **Finish**, the wizard opens the new application; if you click **Cancel**, the wizard deletes what you've done up to this point and closes. When you're ready to continue, click **Next**.

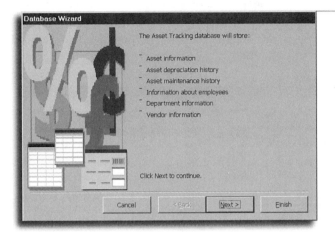

FIGURE 4.5

This dialog box identifies the type of data the new application will store.

By default, each table in the new application contains certain fields. The dialog box shown in Figure 4.6 allows you to add to or delete from the defaults.

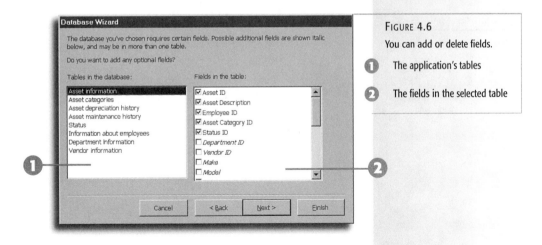

FIGURE 4.6

You can add or delete fields.

1 The application's tables

2 The fields in the selected table

The wizard includes any checked fields in the selected table. Deselect any particular field you don't want. Fields that are italicized are optional fields that you must check to include.

5. Although for the purposes of this example you don't need to change any field selections, you could make any changes you like. Click **Next** when you're ready to continue.

6. The next dialog box (see Figure 4.7) allows you to choose the display style from the listed predefined options. For this example, accept the **Blends** style default. Click **Next** to continue.

FIGURE 4.7

Choose a predefined style.

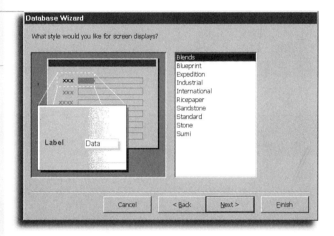

Moving through the wizard

Keep in mind that any time the wizard still displays a **Back** button, you can return to the previous dialog box to change your choices. This is helpful when you're not sure which option, fields, or appearance you want.

7. Figure 4.8 shows a dialog box that asks you to choose from the predefined report styles. For this example, specify **Bold**. When you're ready to continue, click **Next**.

8. In the next dialog box, you can change the database's title and identify a default picture to display in your reports (see Figure 4.9). This is a good way to include a company logo in your report titles. For this example, use the title Asset Tracking Example.

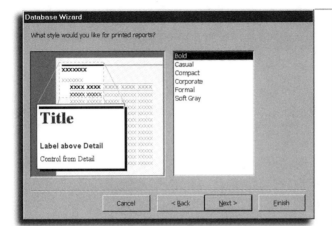

FIGURE 4.8

Choose a report style.

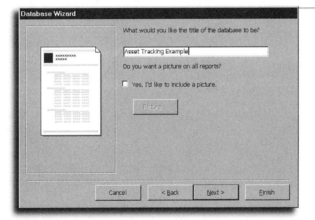

FIGURE 4.9

Change the title and identify a
picture for your reports.

This example won't use a picture in the reports, so click **Next** to continue. However, when you want to identify a picture, select **Yes, I'd Like to Include a Picture** and then click the enabled **Picture** button. In the **Insert Picture** dialog box (see Figure 4.10), use the **Look In** drop-down list to browse your folders until you find the appropriate file. You might need to adjust the **Files of Type** (the default is Graphic Files) to find the appropriate file. To continue, click **Next**.

Adding a sample graphic

To get a picture for this example, look in the Program Files\Microsoft Office\Clipart\Popular directory. (You might have installed Microsoft Office in another folder other than Program Files.) Click anything you want to see in the wizard dialog box. Click the **Picture** button again to change it.

FIGURE 4.10

Use this dialog box to locate and identify a picture file for your reports.

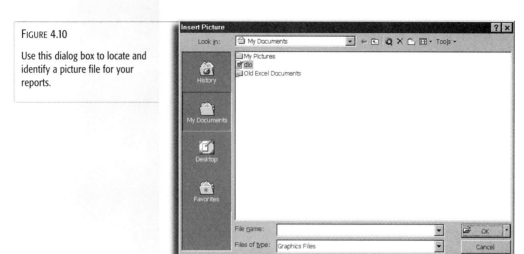

9. In the final wizard dialog box (see Figure 4.11), leave the **Yes, Start the Database** option selected because you want to open the database. (If you deselect it, Access will exit the wizard without opening the application.) The **Display Help on Using a Database** option opens the **Help** section. Click **Finish**; the wizard displays a progress bar while creating your database. When the process is complete, Access will open the new database and display its Switchboard form (see Figure 4.12).

FIGURE 4.11

The final window lets you decide whether to open the database.

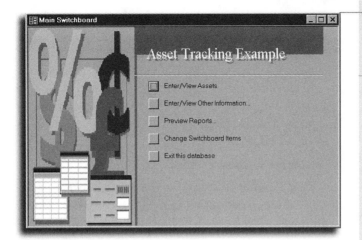

FIGURE 4.12
The wizard displays the new database's Switchboard form.

At this point, feel free to explore the database by clicking the Switchboard options and reviewing the application's tables, forms, reports, and modules. Keep in mind that this application was created in just a few minutes. To re-create the same from scratch could take hours or days, depending on your skill level.

The wizard results will seldom be exactly what you need, so you can expect to spend a little time modifying the application. To see the structure beneath the Switchboard form, double-click the minimized title bar next to it (it might be partially hidden by the form) to open the database in the Database window. You can view the objects on the various tabs for tables, forms, queries, macros, and modules.

SEE ALSO

➤ *Learn about modifying tables on page 63*
➤ *Create a form on page 105*

Documenting the Database

Often you'll need to have a hard-copy printout of a database's design. This isn't the data that's stored in the database's tables, but rather the design characteristics of the tables, queries, reports, macros, and modules contained within the database.

By using the Documenter Wizard, you can easily create a report that shows the important characteristics of any objects within a database. You can even specify which characteristics should be included in the report, making it easy to customize the information provided to various parties. The report that's produced can be printed, saved as a new table within the database, or output to an external file format, such as a Microsoft Excel spreadsheet or an HTML file.

Using the Documenter Wizard

1. Open the database that you want to document. From the **Tools** menu select **Analyze**, and then click **Documenter**. The Documenter dialog box appears (see Figure 4.13).

FIGURE 4.13

The Documenter Wizard's main dialog box enables you to customize a report to shows the important characteristics of any objects within a database.

Using the tabs across the top of the dialog box, you can select specific object types to document. On the **Current Database** page, you'll find the same entries for every database:

- The **Properties** entry will output the properties of the database file itself (which you can view and modify by choosing **Database** Properties from the **File** menu).

- The **Relationships** entry will report the relationships that exist between tables and the properties of those relationships.

On the **All Object Types** page are entries for all the objects in the database, including the two entries from the Current Database page.

2. To specify which characteristics of an object are included in the output, click the object's tab. Or, if you're on the **All Object Types** page, select an object of that type (a table, for example) and then click the **Options** button. A Print *object* Definition dialog box appears (Figure 4.14 shows the Print Table Definition dialog box). In this dialog box, you can specify exactly which information will be output for that object type. Change the options as appropriate, and click **OK** to return to the wizard's main dialog box.

FIGURE 4.14

In the Print Table Definition dialog box, you specify which characteristics of an object are documented.

3. After you select all the objects that you want to document, click **OK**. The Object Definition report is created and displayed in a Print Preview window (see Figure 4.15).

4. Now that you have the Object Definition report, you can print it, or save it:

- To print the definition, click the **Print** button 🖨 on the Database toolbar. Some objects (particularly forms and reports) can produce rather lengthy output, so you might want to scroll through the preview window before clicking this button.

- To save the definition to an external file, choose Export To from the File menu. In the dialog box that appears, specify the type of file to create (HTML, Microsoft Excel, MS-DOS Text, or Rich Text Format) and click OK. A File Save dialog box appears, allowing you to choose the folder and name for the external file.

FIGURE 4.15

The Documenter Wizard displays the Object Definition report.

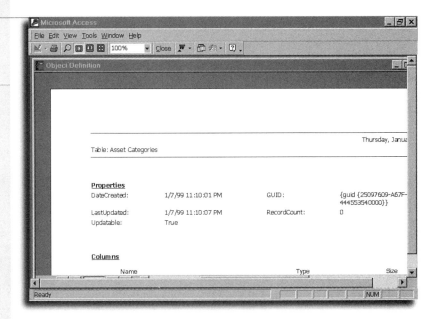

5. After you finish working with the output, close the Object Definition window.

SEE ALSO

➤ *Learn about creating data reports with a wizard on page 122*

Creating Tables

Create tables quickly and easily

Learn the basics of primary keys and relationships

Assign appropriate field and table names

How and when to use indexes

Saving time with the Table Wizard

Designing Tables

Much has been said so far about good database design, and tables are the cornerstone of a good design. Before you start working with tables, you need to know about a few things to watch for:

Duplicate information

Primary key fields must contain unique values. However, don't worry if the foreign key contains duplicate values—they're perfectly acceptable and, in fact, intentional.

- Scrutinize large tables carefully. Remember, you want fields that relate to a table's purpose, and sometimes that can be confusing. Before you know it, you might have a hodge-podge of fields in one or two tables rather than spread out over the seven or eight tables that you really need.

- Sound the alarm if you find yourself repeating data in multiple tables. This is a sure sign that the design might be less than it could be.

- Watch for blank fields. Any time you find lots of empty fields, you're looking at a potential design problem. The most likely reason for leaving a field blank is that the data simply doesn't pertain to that record. In a well-normalized table, this will seldom be the case.

SEE ALSO

➤ *More information about normalizing tables is on page 13*

In the end, remember one rule and you'll be well ahead of the game: All fields should relate to the primary key field (or the foreign key, if there isn't a primary key). You also might want to consider using the Database Wizard to get started. Then, you can modify the tables in Design view as needed.

SEE ALSO

➤ *Get more information on primary key fields on page 184*
➤ *Learn how to use the Database Wizard on page 51*

Whether you use a wizard to build your tables or build them from scratch, you need a solid understanding of *normalization*—the process of creating and relating tables according to a fixed set of rules. Beyond that, you need to know the database's purpose and each table's purpose within the database. When you determine what type of information you'll store in your tables, you must break that data into fields. As you consider your field data, you must keep two things in mind:

- The data in each field must be the smallest unit possible, meaning you can't divide the data any further. The proper way to store address data is in separate fields—one each for the street address, the city, the state, and the zip code.

- All data should be mutually independent, which means that deleting or changing the contents of one field won't affect another.

SEE ALSO
➤ For an in-depth review of normalization, see page 13

Working with the Table in Design View

Figure 5.1 shows a typical table—the Customers table from the Northwind database that comes with Access (you must install it). Figure 5.2 shows the same table in Design view. This view contains a unique toolbar with tools you'll use only in this environment, which is typical. Table 5.1 gives a short description of these buttons.

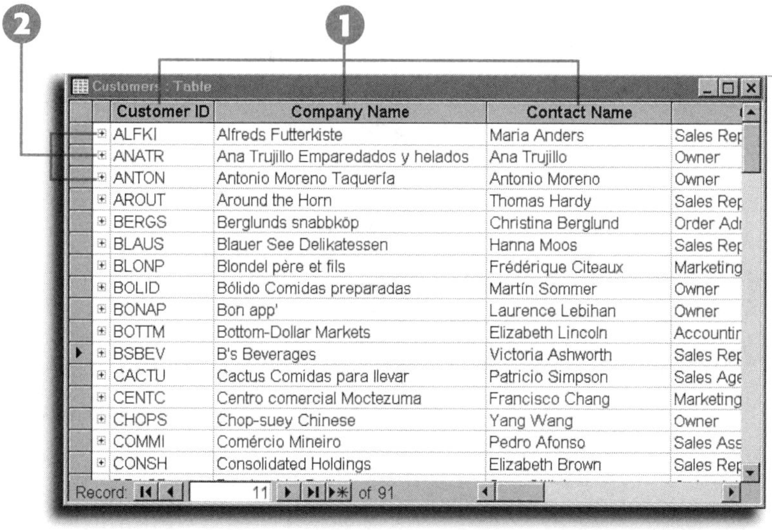

Multiple lines in a field

Just because a field must contain the smallest unit of data doesn't mean it can contain only one line. For instance, a street address often has two lines—perhaps a building address and a suite number. In this case, simply enter the building number, or the first line of the two-line address. Press **Ctrl+Enter** to move the cursor to a new line. Then, enter the suite number or second line of your street address. Multiline fields won't interfere with the normalization process. As long as the data is appropriate to that field, it breaks no rules.

FIGURE 5.1

This is a table in Datasheet view.

1. The columns are fields, each containing a single unit of data.

2. A row constitutes a record and contains all the data that relates to the primary key.

FIGURE 5.2

This is the same table in Design view.

1 View

2 Primary Key

3 Indexes

4 Insert Rows

5 Delete Rows

6 Field rows

7 Properties section

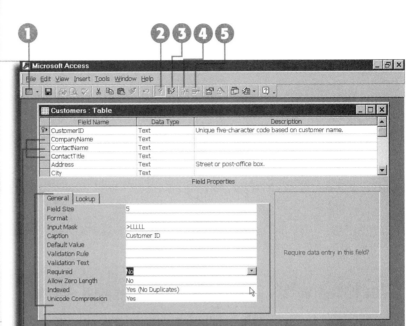

TABLE 5.1   **Table Design Toolbar Buttons**

Name	Icon	Task
View		Display table in Datasheet view
Primary Key		Assign a primary key to a field
Indexes		Define indexes
Insert Rows		Insert a field row
Delete Rows		Delete a field row

Working with Field Properties

The lower section of Design view lists all the field's properties. Several properties have drop-down lists, from which you simply choose the appropriate option. The Caption and Validation Text properties require that you select the field and type your setting.

As you select each property field, Access updates the information in the panel to the right. Table 5.2 briefly reviews most of the field properties you'll work with.

TABLE 5.2   Field Properties

Property	Explanation
Field Size	Determines the maximum number of characters you can store in this field
Format	Determines how Access displays the entry
Input Mask	Controls how you enter data
Caption	Access will display this text in a bound field's label control and as the column heading text in Datasheet view.
Default Value	Enters this value automatically for a new record/field if user doesn't input another value
Validation Rule	An expression that determines the values Access will accept
Validation Text	The custom error message Access displays when an entry doesn't conform to the Validation Rule
Required	Determines whether you can enter a null value
Allow Zero Length	Allows a zero-length string length
Indexed	Sets an index for the field and determines whether the field can contain duplicate values
Unicode Compression	Uses Unicode rules to compress the field

SEE ALSO

➤ *For more information on Unicode, which is new to Access 2000, see page 42*

Naming Fields

To add a field to a table, select a field row in Design view, enter the field's name, and choose an appropriate data type. The field name is really up to you, but it should indicate the field's purpose. Perhaps the easiest way to add a new field is to use the Field Builder.

SEE ALSO

➤ *For examples of table names that follow standard conventions, see page 31*

Zero-length strings

A *zero-length string* is an actual string that contains no characters—the equivalent of the "" string. A zero-length string isn't the same as a null value, which indicates that there's no entry or result.

Using the Field Builder

1. Open a table in Design view by selecting it in the Database window and clicking **Design** ![Design]. Or create a new table by clicking **Tables** in the Database window, clicking **New** ![New], and then double-clicking **Design View**. You're going to create a new table for this exercise.

2. Select a blank field row and click the **Builder** button ![Builder] on the Table Design toolbar.

3. The builder's first window displays a list of sample tables. As you highlight the table options in the **Sample Tables** list box, Access updates the field names in the **Sample Fields** list box. The **Business** and **Personal** options at the bottom of the window update the list of tables in the **Sample Tables** list box accordingly. You'll select a table from the **Sample Tables** list box and then choose the appropriate field name from the **Sample Fields** list box. As you can see in Figure 5.3, the **Tasks** table and the first field—**TaskID**— have been selected. Click **OK** to continue.

FIGURE 5.3

Use the Field Builder to add fields to a new table.

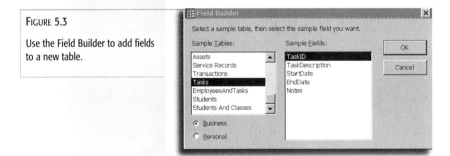

4. Access returns you to the new table in Design view, having added the chosen field for you. Figure 5.4 shows the result of selecting the **TaskID** field. The builder has made many default choices for you, which you can modify if needed. For instance, the builder assigned the Long Integer data type to your field. To change it to an AutoNumber, simply select **AutoNumber** from the **TaskID** field's **Data Type** drop-down list. If you do, Access will automatically update the field's properties accordingly. A field's properties depend heavily on its data type.

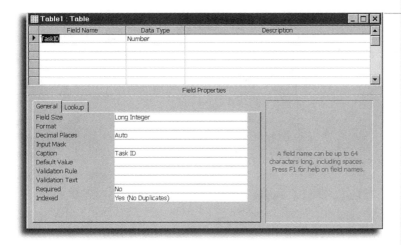

FIGURE 5.4
The Field Builder added the **TaskID** field to your new table.

5. The builder doesn't attempt to enter a description for the field, so select the **TaskID** field's Description cell and enter an appropriate explanation.

6. To make the selected field the table's primary key field, click the **Primary Key** button ⚷ on the **Table Design** toolbar. Access displays a small primary key symbol in the field's row cell. Figure 5.5 shows your table up to this point.

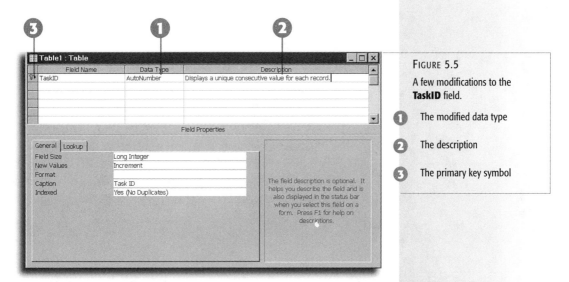

FIGURE 5.5

A few modifications to the **TaskID** field.

❶ The modified data type

❷ The description

❸ The primary key symbol

Spaces in field names

At first, you might like the idea of using spaces in field names. However, spaces can be difficult to work with sometimes, specifically in SQL statements and VBA code. (Beginning with version 6.5, SQL handles spaces fine, but earlier versions don't.) It's recommended that you don't use spaces in field names but instead use them in the field's Caption property—for example, a field named LastName and a Caption property with the text Last Name. That way, the text you see contains a space, but you don't have to deal with that space in code.

When is a number not a value?

If you're storing numbers that you won't be using in calculations, consider assigning the Text data type instead of the Number data type. For instance, because part numbers, addresses, and phone numbers aren't used in calculations, you can assign the Text data type and save memory. However, if the field is indexed, consider making it a Numeric field, because indexed strings sort more slowly than indexed numbers. If you need to sort these values numerically, you can wrap the field in a `Val()` function.

SEE ALSO

➤ *For more information on data types, see page 473*

➤ *Learn more about choosing primary key fields on page 184*

The Field Builder makes many decisions for you, and you are free to change any of them. If you add fields yourself, remember a few things:

- A field name can consist of up to 64 characters—letters, numbers, and spaces.
- Give your fields names that describe their data. For instance, you might name a field that stores a person's last name LastName or Lname.

Setting Data Types Relevant to the Data Being Stored

In the previous example, you changed the TaskID field's data type from Number to AutoNumber. When choosing a data type, you must consider the following:

- The type of data you want to accept and the type of data you want to reject
- How much memory the data type requires
- The limits that Access places on each data type

For instance, if you're entering values, you certainly don't want to accept alphabetical characters. The Number and Currency data types will accept only numerical characters. Now, the Currency data type requires 8 bytes of memory per field. The Number data type can require as few as 1 byte or as many as 8 bytes, so you'll want to use the Currency data type only when it's appropriate. Always use the most appropriate data type, but don't waste memory unnecessarily.

Finally, keep in mind that Access won't react the same way to every data type. For instance, if you apply a Text data type to a column of values, such as phone numbers or social security numbers, Access won't sort these values as you might expect.

Specifically, Access sorts them alphanumerically—meaning that the values 1, 2, 8, 10, and 18 sort as 1, 10, 18, 2, and 8. Also, you can't sort on a Memo or OLE object field.

Assigning Table Names That Describe Their Function

After you create all the fields your table requires, you need to save the table and give it a name. Simply click the **Save** button ▣ or choose **Save As** from the **File** menu. After you save the table, Access displays its name in the table's title bar. A table name can have up to 64 characters—letters, numbers, and spaces. You'll also want to give your table a name that describes its purpose—for example, you might name a customer table `Customers` or `tblCustomers`.

You can offer even more information about your table's purpose and characteristics by adding a comment to the table's `Description` property. To do so, right-click the table's name in the Database window and choose **Properties** from the resulting shortcut menu. Then simply enter the message in the Description control.

SEE ALSO
➤ *Read about naming conventions on page 31*

Reserved words

When naming any Access object, you need to remember that Access has a huge list of reserved words you can't use. For a complete list of these words, run a search in the Help section on reserved words. Also, don't use an object type—such as a field, table, form, module, macro, or report—as an object name. The same is true when naming fields: Don't use reserved words as field names.

Making Tables Efficient Objects Within the Database

Many table design features can save you time down the line. You assign them at the table level, and other objects inherit them. This means that you don't have to apply the feature more than once.

Many field properties—Format, Caption, Input Mask, Default Value, and Description—can all be inherited at the form and report level. However, you can override these properties at the form or report level by simply applying a new property setting for the form or report.

The Caption and Description properties are unique in this area because they have no real purpose at the table level. Access will display a field's Caption text in a bound control's label control. For instance, Figure 5.6 shows the Caption text—Product—for the ProductID field in the Order Details table.

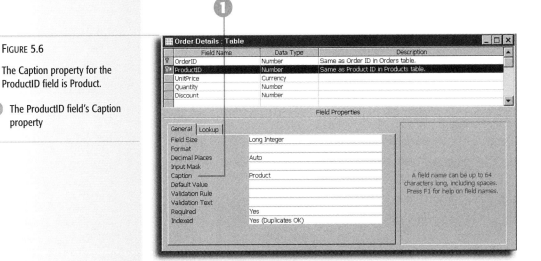

FIGURE 5.6

The Caption property for the ProductID field is Product.

The ProductID field's Caption property

As a general rule, Access displays a field's name in a bound control's label control and as a field's column heading in Datasheet view. However, Figure 5.7 shows Product instead of ProductID because the Caption property overrides the default label text. This is worth remembering if you use a field name in VBA code: Be sure not to rely on the label text of the column headings.

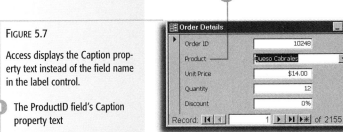

FIGURE 5.7

Access displays the Caption property text instead of the field name in the label control.

The ProductID field's Caption property text

Another useful shortcut is the field's Description property. You supply text that describes the field's purpose. For example, the description text for the ProductID field in the Order Details table is displayed in the status bar (see Figure 5.8). Even though you set the Description property at the table level, Access displays it in Form view.

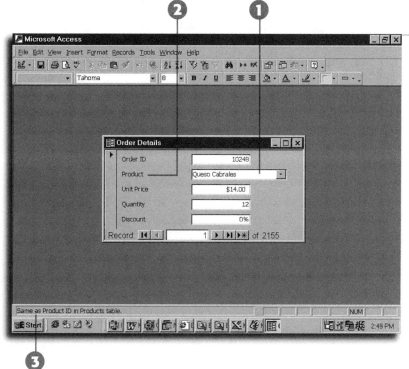

FIGURE 5.8

You set the Description property at the table design level, but Access displays it in Form view.

① The ProductID control has the focus.

② Access displays the bound field's Caption property.

③ The ProductID field's Description text appears on the status bar.

Setting Primary Keys

Primary keys are an essential component of a relational database. They're discussed throughout this book in various chapters because they're used to find data quickly and to combine data in separate tables. It's recommended that each table have a primary or foreign key. If your table doesn't have a natural primary key candidate, you can add an AutoNumber field to the table and use it as that table's primary key. A *natural primary key* is a data field (not an AutoNumber) that provides a unique entry for each record.

Field size and primary keys

The size of your primary key field can slow down your application. Choose the data type that consumes the least memory but is still adequate. Also, assign the smallest field size possible. (An AutoNumber field is automatically set to the Long Integer field size.)

When choosing a primary key field, keep a few things in mind:

- A primary key field must contain unique data.
- Access won't allow duplicate entries or a null value in a primary key field.

After you decide which field is the primary key field, you can set it by opening the table in Design View, choosing the appropriate field row, and clicking the **Primary Key** button [⚷] on the Table Design toolbar. This button acts as a toggle button, so to delete the primary key, select the primary key field row and click the [⚷] button again.

Multiple-Field Primary Keys

Until now primary keys have been discussed as though they consisted of just one field. However, you can assign a primary key to as many fields as appropriate. A multiple-field primary key performs the same as a single-field primary key. Access views the primary key—all the fields involved—as a single entity. This means that when checking for duplicate entries, Access considers all the fields.

For instance, if you include two fields in your primary key, RabbitID and RabbitName, Access will check the contents of both fields against all the existing records. If you enter the data "593" and "Maggie Rabbit" into the RabbitID and RabbitName fields, respectively, Access will reject the record only if another record contains both entries. If the RabbitID "593" already exists but the RabbitName entry isn't "Maggie Rabbit", Access will accept the record, and vice versa. An existing record must contain both "593" and "Maggie Rabbit" before Access will reject the new record.

To set a multiple-field primary key, simply select all the appropriate field rows in Design View and click the **Primary Key** button [⚷] on the Table Design toolbar.

SEE ALSO

➤ *Learn more about primary keys on page 184*

Indexes

Access indexes are a mysterious lot, and I won't attempt to explain what goes on behind the scenes between the Access objects and the Jet engine. However, you should know some things to create a quick-responding application.

Access uses an index to sort data in logical order, which is determined by the field's data type. This makes perfect sense because text and numbers are sorted differently. Unfortunately, having more than one indexed field in a table can actually slow things down. That's because Access updates the index each time you add or change a record—if you have more than one field indexed.

Access automatically indexes a primary key field. Beyond that, you should consider indexing a second field only if that field meets all the following conditions:

- The data type is Text, Number, Currency, or Date/Time.
- You will search for data or sort by this data often.
- The field will contain mostly different values.

If you do decide to assign an index, you must follow a few rules:

- Name the index.
- A primary key field is a table's primary index.
- Access won't sort records as you enter them, even if you set an index.
- Access doesn't always sort the way you expect, so don't use an index to control sort order.

The best advice is to set an index only if you're working with large amounts of data, and one or more of your fields can uniquely identify each record. If you set an index for these fields, you might increase your application's speed. Dabble with indexes any further, and you might slow things down.

To set an index, open the table in Design view and open the Indexes window, or choose **Indexes** from the **View** menu. If your table contains a primary key field, the window displays that

Do you need to index?

With the speed of today's systems, indexing probably won't significantly improve your search or sort tasks unless you have thousands of records, or your tables have many fields. In multiuser environments, you might find this situation changes and indexing significantly improves performance.

field's index. To set an index for a field other than your primary key, enter a name in the **Index Name** field, identify the field you're indexing, and then select a sort order.

Figure 5.9 shows the Products table's four indexes. Let's see if these indexes conform to the specified rules. It isn't likely that you will duplicate the product's name, but you'll probably repeat the CategoryID and SupplierID values often. What you won't see is a record that duplicates all four fields, so this table meets the test. These four fields create a unique identifier for each record. That in itself doesn't mean that the indexes are needed, but means that they are acceptable and perhaps even necessary, depending on how the data is used elsewhere in the database.

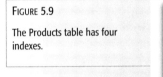

FIGURE 5.9

The Products table has four indexes.

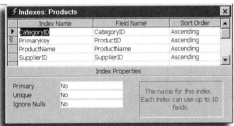

An index has properties just like fields and controls do. The Primary property refers to a field that uniquely identifies each record, similar to a primary key field. However, a primary property doesn't have to be a primary key. On the other hand, if your record contains a primary key field, it will also be the primary index. You can't modify this arrangement. The Unique property determines whether the field must contain unique data. The final property, Null, allows Access to ignore null values when sorting the table.

Like the primary key field, an index can apply to more than one field. You'll want to use this option when a sort depends on more than one field (or you need to enforce unique entries across more than one field). For instance, if you separate names into first and last name fields, you'll want to consider both fields in a sort task.

Setting a single-field and multiple-field index

1. Create a new table by selecting Tables on the Database window object bar and then double-clicking **Create Table in Design View** in the Database window.

2. Add an AutoNumber field named ID and two Text fields named LastName and FirstName.

3. Click the **Indexes** button [icon] on the Table Design toolbar to display the Indexes window. At this point, you have one single-field index on the ID field, as shown in Figure 5.10. This choice is natural because it's an AutoNumber field—a unique identifier.

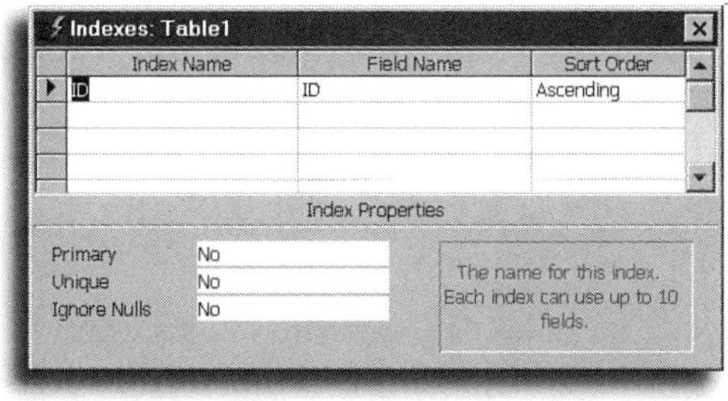

FIGURE 5.10

Access automatically sets an index to the ID field because it's an AutoNumber field.

4. To create the multiple-field index, enter an appropriate name into the **Index Name** field—in this case, **Full Name**.

5. Identify the first field in your multiple-field index. In this example, that's **LastName**.

6. Select a sort order for the specified field—**Ascending**.

7. Don't enter a new index name in the next row. Instead, select the **Field Name** column in the next row and enter the name of the second field in your multiple-field index. Then, specify a sort order for that field. This example has the FirstName field and an ascending sort. Figure 5.11 shows the completed index.

To delete an index, select the appropriate field row in the Indexes window and press the **Delete** key.

ID suffix is always indexed

Access automatically defines an index for AutoNumber fields. However, you can add the suffix ID to a field and Access will index the field, even if that field isn't an AutoNumber field. Access will do the same for three other suffixes: key, code, and num. To change this behavior, from the **Tools** menu choose **Options**, select the **Tables/Queries** tab, and modify the **AutoIndex on Import/Create** option. If you later make this field a primary key field, be sure to delete the automatic index so that you don't end up with identical indexes.

FIGURE 5.11

You added a multiple-field index to this table.

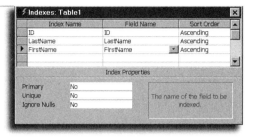

Using the Table Wizard

The Table Wizard, one of Access's many wizards, creates tables for you after you provide certain information. The wizards do a good job for the most part, and they're quick and easy to use. You can always modify a table if the wizard's choices aren't adequate. The Table Wizard does several things:

- It offers several sample tables.
- It sets a primary key for the table.
- It helps you define relationships between the table you're creating and any other existing tables.

After you launch the Table Wizard, the wizard displays a series of dialog boxes, each one soliciting clues from you regarding the type of data you'll be storing in your table. After you choose a table, select the appropriate fields. At this stage, you can even rename the fields.

Shortcut for moving fields in a wizard

When using the wizard, add a field to your table by selecting it in one control and adding it to another. To move a field from one control to the next, double-click the field or select it and then click the appropriate button (>, >>, <, or <<); these buttons are found between the two field controls. The single signs move one field at a time, the double signs move all the fields at once.

After you choose a table and its fields, the wizard helps you set a primary key field. You can accept the wizard's choice or select your own. Just remember that you must choose a field containing unique data. This is one of the Table Wizard's few limitations—you must create a primary key field. Normally, this is fine, as you'll usually want your tables to have a primary key field. But for those few times when you don't want a primary key field, you'll have to forego the Table Wizard.

SEE ALSO

➤ *Learn more about primary keys on page 184*

When you're ready to define the table's relationship, the wizard displays the current relationships. Of course, your new table won't be related to any existing tables just yet. To define a relationship, simply identify the table you want to relate the new table to and then define the type of relationship. Ordinarily, you must have a primary key and a foreign key to establish a relationship. If the table you want to relate to doesn't have a foreign key, the wizard will add one for you.

The advantages to using the Table Wizard are obvious—it's quick and easy. However, the wizard forces you to set a primary key field. Also, you might not find all the appropriate tables and fields your new table needs.

Creating Queries

Retrieve records that match specific conditions

Use the query design grid

Enter field criteria

Plan for Null values

Use the query wizards

Reviewing Queries

Storing data isn't the only goal of a database. You'll also want to manipulate and analyze your stored data. When you have questions about your data, the first place you'll want to look for answers is a query. Technically, a *query* is a stored question. To create a query, you identify the object that contains your data and the fields you want to review. Then, you use functions, expressions, and SQL statements to ask a question about that data. For instance, you might want to know which sales reps have exceeded the previous period's sales totals, or you might want to see a list of clients who haven't made purchases in a while.

The types of questions you'll need to ask depend on the type of data you store and the scope of your business. To accommodate most users, Access offers several different types of queries:

- A *Select query* is probably the most common query. Use a Select query to retrieve data that meets conditions, to group records, and to display calculations based on your data.

- A *Parameter query* prompts you for additional information before retrieving data. (Chapter 14, "Building Parameter Queries," discusses Parameter queries in more detail.)

- A *Crosstab query* summarizes your data and groups those summary values by two categories.

- An *Action query* locates data and changes it. The action queries are Delete, Update, Append, and Make-Table.

- A *SQL query* requires SQL commands to query your data. The SQL-specific queries are Union, Pass-through, Data-definition query, and Subquery.

The missing Archive Query Wizard

Access 2.0 has a wizard, the Archive Query Wizard, that copies records from an existing table to a new table and then deletes those records from the original table. If you're used to working with this wizard, you won't find it in Access 2000. Instead, run a Make-Table query to complete the same task.

SEE ALSO

➤ *Learn more about Select queries on page 213*
➤ *Find specific data about Action queries on page 217*
➤ *Read more about Crosstab queries on page 215*

You can create a query in two ways: open a blank query design grid and go to work, or launch a query wizard.

Working with the Query Design Grid

Most Access objects have two modes: view and design. A query is the same. You can create a query by adding information to a query design grid (see Figure 6.1). The *query design grid* is a graphic tool for creating a query. Specifically, you can identify tables and queries that contain the data you're querying. Then, you can specify the fields you want to query, and include criteria to restrict the query's results.

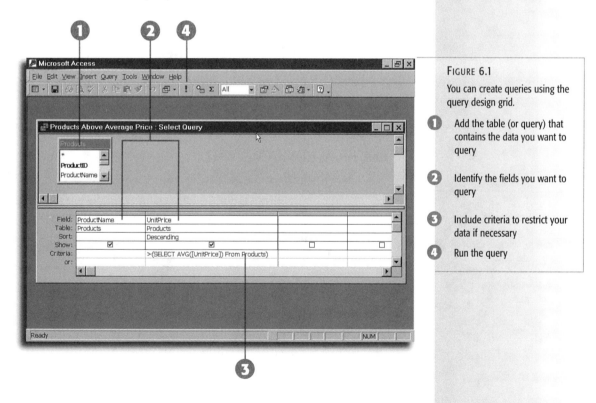

FIGURE 6.1

You can create queries using the query design grid.

1 Add the table (or query) that contains the data you want to query

2 Identify the fields you want to query

3 Include criteria to restrict your data if necessary

4 Run the query

The query design grid consists of two parts. The upper pane displays a field list for each table or query you add to the query. This area also shows relationships between any tables or queries you add. In the lower pane, identify the fields you want to review. The majority of the query design takes place in this lower grid:

- Field cells identify the fields you want to query.
- Table cells identify each field's bound table or query.
- The Sort cell specifies a sort order for that field.
- The Show cell determines whether the query displays field data.
- Criteria cells contain an expression that limits the data the query returns.
- An Or cell, an extension of the Criteria cell, allows you to include more than one condition for each field.

Adding a Table to the Query Design Grid

A query needs to reference the object that contains your data. That object can be a table, a query, or several tables or queries. You can add the necessary objects to your query in a couple ways.

Add a table to the Design View Grid

1. Select the table or query that contains your data in the Database window. For this example, choose the Customers table from the Northwind database that comes with Access.

2. Choose **Query** from the **New Object** button's 🖼️▾ drop-down list and then double-click **Design View** in the New Query dialog box.

Access displays a query design grid. The upper panel contains a field list for the table or query you selected in Step 1. The example shows the field list for the Customers table.

3. If you need to add an additional table or query, click the **Show Table** button 🖼️ on the Query Design toolbar. Access displays the Show Table dialog box (see Figure 6.2).

Opening the query design grid

You don't have to select a table or query in the Database window before opening the query design grid. To open a blank grid, select **Queries** from the Database window toolbar, and then click **New** on the Database window menu.

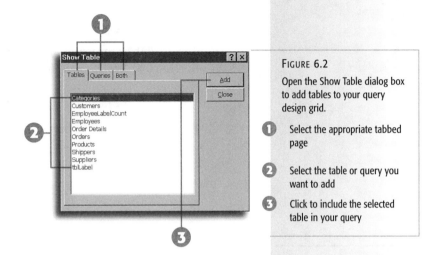

FIGURE **6.2**

Open the Show Table dialog box to add tables to your query design grid.

1 Select the appropriate tabbed page

2 Select the table or query you want to add

3 Click to include the selected table in your query

4. Use Tabbed Pages Enable to view tables, queries, or both at the same time. To add a table to your query, double-click the table in the list box. You can also select the table and then click **Add**. For this example, add the Orders table to the query and click **Close** to return to the query design grid.

Figure 6.3 shows two tables in the upper panel. Also, the join line between the two CustomerID fields indicates that a relationship exists between these two tables. You can read more about relationships in Chapter 11, "Defining and Working with Relationships."

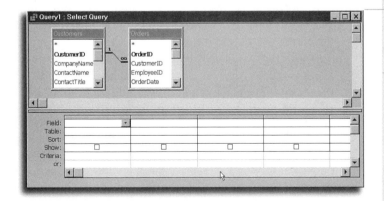

FIGURE **6.3**

The query design grid contains two related tables.

Adding Fields to the Query Design Grid

After you add the appropriate tables or queries, you need to identify the fields that contain the data you're querying. Do so by entering the name of each field in a Field cell in the lower pane. You can add a field to the query design grid in four ways:

- Drag the field name from the list box to a Field cell.
- Double-click the field in the field list. Access adds it to the first empty Field cell.
- Select a Field cell and type the name of the field.
- Select the field from a Field cell's drop-down list.

All these methods can be used to add fields one at a time. Rather than add fields in this manner, you can add all of them at once. Each field list contains an asterisk at the beginning of the list. Adding this character to a Field cell includes all the fields in your query results.

You can drag the asterisk or type it directly into a Field cell. If you choose the latter method, be sure to also specify the table in the Table cell.

When you use the asterisk, Access automatically updates the query's results if you modify the bound table or query. Unfortunately, the asterisk character also has limitations. For instance, you can't use aggregate functions with the asterisk. Also, the query result displays all the fields in the query results.

If you need a little more flexibility, double-click the field list's title bar to select all the fields in the list, and then simply drag the entire selection to the lower pane. Doing so fills the Field cells with the field names, in the same order that the fields appear in the list. When you use this method, you must update the query yourself if you add or delete fields from the bound table or query.

You might find that you need to output all the cells, but you don't need them all in the query design grid. For instance, you might want to limit an address query to only those customers that live in a certain region, but you also need their complete addresses for a letter you're going to mail them.

Using the Show control

You won't always want to display a field that you've added to the lower pane. To hide a field from the query's result, simply deselect the **Show** box. If you save this change, Access moves any hidden field to the right of the query design grid the next time you open the query–regardless of its original placement.

Output all fields in a query

1. With the query design grid open, right-click anywhere in the upper pane except on a field list. Select **Properties** from the resulting shortcut menu.

    Alternatively, you can double-click to bypass the shortcut menu and go straight to the Query Properties sheet.

2. Set the Output All Fields property to **Yes**.

Sorting Records

You can sort your query results by field data. (You can't sort a Memo, Hyperlink, or OLE Object field.) Keep in mind that any bound form or report displays the sorted query results. To select a sort order, simply select one from the Sort cell's drop-down list:

- Ascending
- Descending
- (Not Sorted)

Set a query's sort order

1. Open the Current Products List query (in the Northwind database) in Design view by selecting that table in the Database window and then clicking **Design** on the Database window menu.

2. The query contains three fields and the sort order for the ProductName is ascending, which means that the result is sorted alphabetically by product name. Change that sort order by opening the Sort field's drop-down list and choosing **Descending**.

3. Run the query by clicking the **Run** button 📍 on the Query Design toolbar. Figure 6.4 shows the results. As you can see, the query has reversed the original sort.

Specifying criteria and using Output All Fields

If you change the Output All Fields property to Yes, you must still add fields to the lower pane to specify criteria for that field. If you do so, be sure to deselect that cell's **Show** box; otherwise, the query displays that field twice.

Sorting Null values

If you run an ascending sort, Access lists any Null entries first. A descending sort lists Null values last. A *Null* field value means that the field now contains no data. This chapter discusses Null values later in the section "Planning for Null Values."

Sorting by more than one field

You can sort a query by more than one field. Consider the Current Products List query from the previous exercise. If you set the sort order for the ProductName and Discontinued fields to **Ascending**, Access sorts the records by the contents of the ProductName field first and then the Discontinued field. In this case, adding the second sort really has no effect because Access sorts from left to right. If you wanted to sort by the Discontinued field first, move that field to the left of the ProductName field.

FIGURE 6.4

This query's sort order is
reversed.

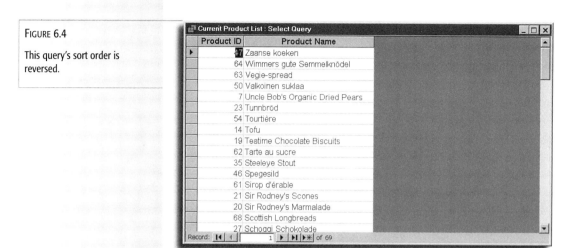

Setting Field Criteria

Often when you're constructing a query, you don't want to
return all the records in the underlying table or query in the
results. This isn't a problem if you have a small number of
records to work with. Realistically, however, this type of query
often doesn't return useful results. Fortunately, you can specify
criteria that restrict the records your query returns.

You can limit your query results by specifying certain conditions
each record must meet to be included in the results. To do so,
enter the condition as an expression in the Criteria cell. For
instance, Figure 6.5 displays the query design grid for the
Northwind query, Products Above Average Price.

You will use criteria expressions often. A criteria expression
doesn't have to be a complex mathematical equation, it can be a
simple field value, or a simple greater or lesser than comparison.
For example, it might be useful to know which customers are
located in Germany. By adding a simple string to the Criteria
cell, you can quickly produce a list of Germany-based customers.

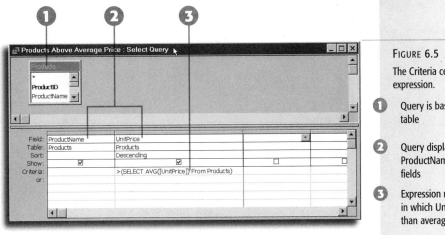

Restrict a query

1. Select the table that contains your customer data in the Database window. Select **Query** from the **New Object** button's [icon] drop-down list, and then double-click **Design View**. Use the Customers table in the Northwind database for this example.

2. Add the customer name and country fields to the lower pane of the query design grid. In the example, those fields are CompanyName and Country.

3. Select the Criteria cell for the Country field and enter "Germany", including the quotation marks (see Figure 6.6). (You don't have to type the quotation marks—Access enters them for you when you enter a string value.)

4. Click the **Run** button [icon] on the Query Design toolbar to see the results (see Figure 6.7). Only companies that contain the string Germany in the Country field are included.

FIGURE 6.6

FIGURE 6.6

The query is restricted to only the German customers.

 Type the value and enclose it in quotation marks.

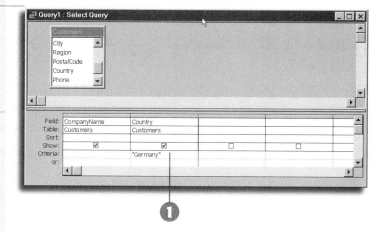

FIGURE 6.7

This query's results are restricted.

You can use much more complicated expressions. For instance, the expression "Germany" AND "Mexico" would return all the customers in Germany and Mexico (of course, there are none). The expression "Germany" OR "Mexico" would do the same (in this case, the OR operator would be effective only if another condition was being met in the same or some other field). The expression <"Germany" would return all the countries that begin with the letters *A* through *F*.

SEE ALSO

➤ *You can also use the Expression Builder to create the criteria expressions you use in your query. For more information, see page 544*

Planning for Null Values

A Null value indicates an empty field or a field filled with unknown data. Null values can be used in criteria expressions. However, a primary key field can't contain a Null value.

Null fields can affect a query's results quite strangely. The following is a list of ways Null values can affect queries:

- Access displays Null values at the beginning of an ascending sort and the ending of a descending sort. You can search for Null values by entering `IsNull` into the appropriate Criteria cell.

- If you use an arithmetic operator in an expression that you're using as a criterion and one field in the expression contains a Null value, the whole expression generally evaluates to a Null value.

Null values can catch you off guard, but if you pay attention to these points, you should be able, without a problem, to use Null values in your queries.

The difference between Null and zero

A Null field is the same thing as an empty field. Although fields that contain the value 0 or some other zero-length string appear to be empty, they aren't Null fields.

Using the Simple Query Wizard

The simplest query you can create—a *simple query*—is a type of Select query. A simple query retrieves data from specific fields, those you indicate in the query design grid. You can use aggregate functions to return totals, averages, or count records. You can calculate the minimum or maximum value in a field. You can't, however, limit the records the query retrieves by specifying criteria. For instance, you could calculate the total number of customers you have via a simple query, but you couldn't retrieve customers from a specific zip code area. After you use the Simple Query Wizard to create the basic query, you can then modify it by adding a criteria expression if needed.

Create a simple query

1. After opening the Northwind database, click the **Queries** tab; then click **New** on the Database window menu.

2. In the New Query dialog box, click **Simple Query Wizard** and then click **OK**.

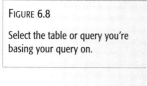

Include more than one table or query

To include more than one table or query in your query, simply change the table or query in the **Tables/Queries** list and continue to add fields to the **Selected Fields** list. The order in which you add these fields to the **Selected Fields** list determines how they appear in your query.

3. Select the table or query you want to base your query on from the **Tables/Queries** drop-down list. If you select the table or query in the Database window before executing the wizard, Access assumes that the selected table or query is the one you want to base your report on.

4. Double-click fields in the **Available Fields** list that you want to include in your query. Doing so copies the selected field to the **Selected Fields** list. As you can see in Figure 6.8, the Customers table is selected and includes only the CompanyName and Phone fields in the query. After you add all the fields you need, click **Next** to continue.

FIGURE 6.8

Select the table or query you're basing your query on.

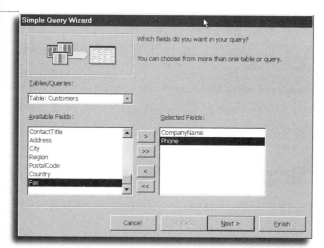

5. The next (and final) dialog box offers you the option of changing the query's name and opening the query in Datasheet view or Design view (see Figure 6.9). The default, **Open the Query to View Information**, opens the query in Datasheet view so that you can see the query's results. If you want to open the query in Design view, choose **Modify the Query Design**. The **Display Help on Working with Queries** option opens the Help section. For this example, change the query's name to Phone Numbers and retain the other defaults. After you make the appropriate choices, click **Finish**. The query returns each company and its phone number, as shown in the Datasheet view in Figure 6.10.

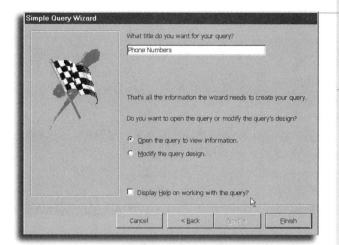

FIGURE 6.9

Choose whether the wizard opens the query in Datasheet view or Design view.

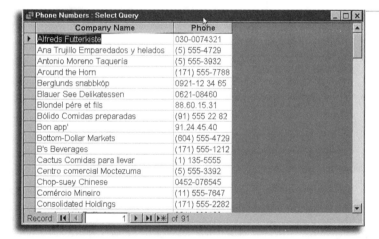

FIGURE 6.10

The query returns company names and phone numbers.

Summarizing Your Records

You learned earlier in this chapter that this wizard helps you perform calculations on your records, but the previous query returned only string data. That's because there were no value fields in the query; both fields were text fields. When the query design grid includes a Number or Currency field, the wizard displays a window with summary options.

Include summary options in a query

1. Choose a table or query in the Database window, select **Query** from the **New Object** button's 🔲▾ drop-down list, and then double-click **Simple Query Wizard**. For this example, base the query on Northwind's Order Details table.

2. Add the appropriate fields to the **Selected Fields** list in the wizard's first dialog box. For this example, add the OrderID and UnitPrice fields (see Figure 6.11). When you've selected the fields you want, click **Next** to continue.

FIGURE 6.11

Base the summary query on the Order Details table and display two of that table's fields.

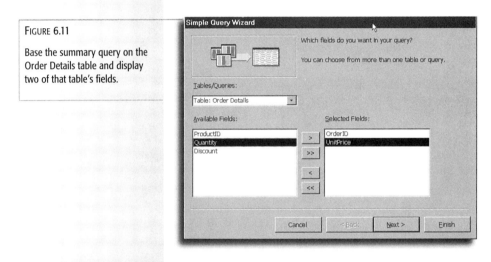

FIGURE 6.12

The wizard allows you to summarize Number and Currency fields.

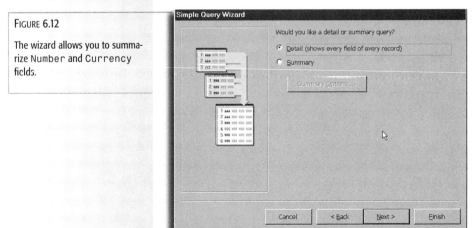

3. The wizard displays the summary window shown in Figure 6.12. The **Detail (Shows Every Field of Every Record)** option displays all the fields for every record, exactly as it claims. Click **Summary** to enable the **Summary Options** button, and then click that button.

4. The Summary Options dialog box displays each Number or Currency field you selected earlier. To return a total for each order, select the **Sum** option for the UnitPrice field (see Figure 6.13).

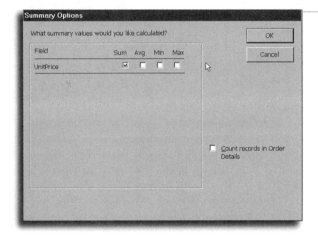

FIGURE 6.13
Return a total for each order.

The **Count Records in Order Details** check box returns the number of records that make up each total. If you select this option, the query automatically adds a new field to the query, showing the result of the count. After selecting your calculation options, click **OK** to return to the previous dialog box. Click **Next** to continue.

5. The final dialog box gives the same options as before. You can change the query's default name, determine whether to open the query in Datasheet or Design view, and display help if needed. For this example, retain all the defaults. When you finish making your selections, click **Finish**. The example query displays the results in Figure 6.14.

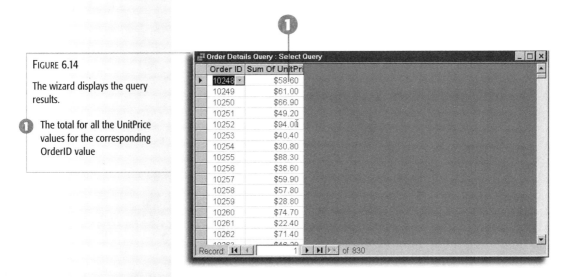

If you remember, the table contained multiple records for each
OrderID value. The OrderID field in the query contains unique
OrderID values. That's because the query combines the
UnitPrice values for each OrderID value and returns the total of
all those values in the Sum of UnitPrice field.

Figure 6.15 shows the same query with the **Count Records in
Order Details** option selected. The query in Figure 6.14 doesn't
include a count.

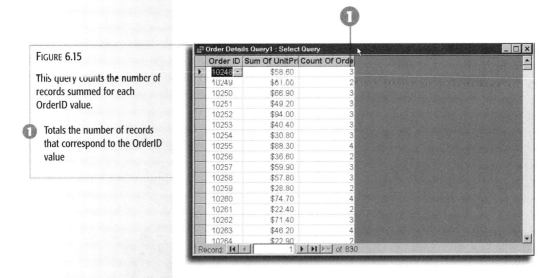

Using the Crosstab Query Wizard

The previous example, which shows the record count, is actually a Totals query. A *Totals query* performs calculations on groups of records. For instance, you can return a subtotal or the average value for a group. A Crosstab query is just a more complex Totals query. In a nutshell, a *Crosstab* query summarizes data in rows and columns (similar to a spreadsheet). A Crosstab query must contain three elements:

- A column heading
- A summary field
- A row heading

The Crosstab query shown in Figure 6.16 contains all three elements.

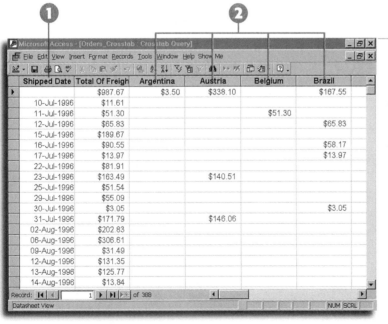

FIGURE 6.16

This Crosstab has the three essential elements.

① Shipped Date is the row heading

② Shipped Country displays the individual countries in the column heading

The Total of Freight field lists the total freight cost per day. The remaining columns break down the total freight cost by country. For instance, the freight totals for August 9, 1996, is $31.49. (We can't see the entire query in Figure 6.16, but the cost represents two shipments, one to Italy and one in the United States.) The first row is a subtotal for each country—that's why there's no date in the Shipped Date field for that record.

Creating a Crosstab query can be a complex task if you don't know what you're doing. Fortunately, the Crosstab Query Wizard makes the job considerably easier than building the query by scratch.

Create a Crosstab query with a wizard

1. Select **Query** from the **New Object** button's ![icon] drop-down list and double-click **Crosstab Query Wizard** in the New Query dialog box.

2. The wizard's first dialog box (see Figure 6.17) prompts you to select the table or query that contains the data you want to include in the query. For this example, select the Orders table. (You might need to specify whether you're querying a table, query, or both in the **View** options; the wizard updates according to the option of your choice.)

You can't use more than one query or table

Unlike some queries, you can't include more than one table or query. If you want to include fields from more than one table or query in your Crosstab query, you must create the appropriate query and then base your Crosstab query on the respective query.

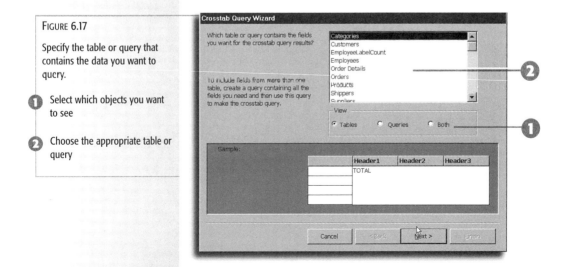

FIGURE 6.17

Specify the table or query that contains the data you want to query.

1 Select which objects you want to see

2 Choose the appropriate table or query

The Sample pane at the bottom of the dialog box shows examples of how your selections look during the wizard process as a Crosstab query. You won't see anything in this control in this first dialog box. Click **Next** to continue.

3. The wizard wants you to select a field from the Orders table to represent the Crosstab's row heading. For this example, select **ShippedDate** (see Figure 6.18). Notice that the Sample pane now displays the field in the Crosstab's row heading cells. Click **Next** after you select your row heading field.

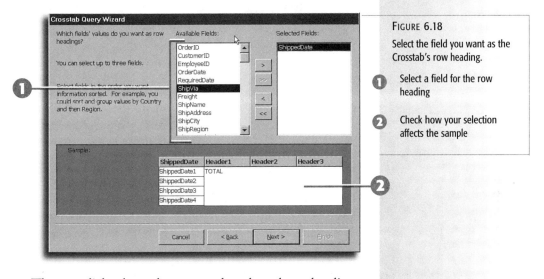

4. The next dialog box asks you to select the column heading field. **ShipCountry** is shown as selected in Figure 6.19. Also notice that the Sample pane updates to reflect this addition. After you make your selection, click **Next**.

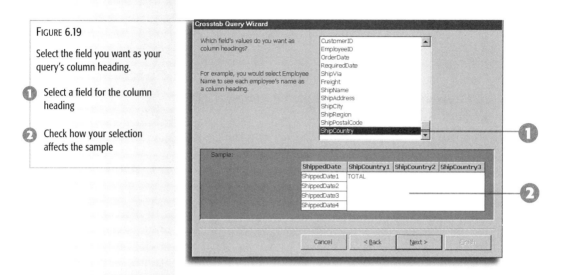

5. The wizard is ready for you to select the field you want summarized and specify how you want those values calculated. Figure 6.20 shows the Freight field and the Sum function selected. Again, the Sample pane shows an updated generic version of your selections. As you can see, this control shows a Sum function that adds the values in the Freight field, based on ShippedDate and ShipCountry. At this point, if you want to omit the summary row at the top of the query (refer to Figure 6.16), deselect the **Yes, Include Row Sums** option. After you specify the appropriate field and function, click **Next**.

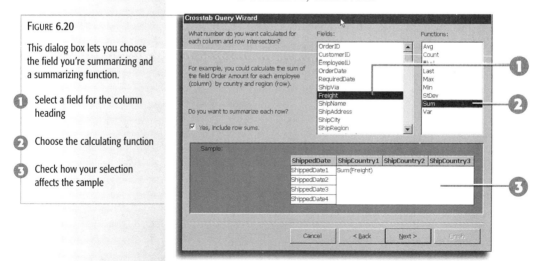

6. The final dialog box lets you change the query's default name, but don't change it for the example. You can also specify whether the wizard opens the query in Datasheet view (choose the **View the Query** option) or in Design view (choose the **Modify the Design** option). If you want to see help information on Crosstab queries, select **Display Help on Working With the Crosstab Query**. When you're ready, click **Finish** to display the query. The wizard opens it in Datasheet view, as shown earlier in Figure 6.16.

Multiple row headings

You can include more than one row heading in a Crosstab query. However, you need to modify the query design grid yourself because you can't specify more than one when using the wizard.

Using the Find Duplicates Query Wizard

Each field of every record doesn't have to be unique—in fact, you often repeat an entry. Later, however, when you want to locate data, these duplicates can cause a little trouble. For instance, if you want to query a table for a specific entry, you might use that entry in the form of a criteria expression in the query's query design grid. If, however, you want to query for only those entries that occur more than once, you need the Find Duplicates Query Wizard, which you can use to locate records that share a field entry (duplicate entries).

Suppose that you want to see if any employees have the same hire date. The easiest method is to simply check the HireDate field in the Employees table for duplicate entries.

Create a Find Duplicates query

1. Choose **Query** from the **New Object** button's drop-down list and double-click **Find Duplicates Query Wizard**.

2. In the wizard's first dialog box (see Figure 6.21), specify the table or query in which you're searching for duplicates. The **View** options, found just below the list of table or queries, update said list accordingly. For this example, select Northwind's **Employees** table and click **Next**.

FIGURE 6.21

Search for duplicates in the Employees table.

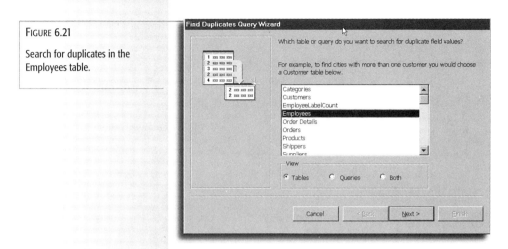

3. In the next dialog box (see Figure 6.22), select the field(s) in which you're searching for duplicates. For this example, to search for employees hired on the same date, double-click only the HireDate field to copy that field to the **Duplicate-Value Fields** list.

FIGURE 6.22

Look for duplicate dates in the HireDate field.

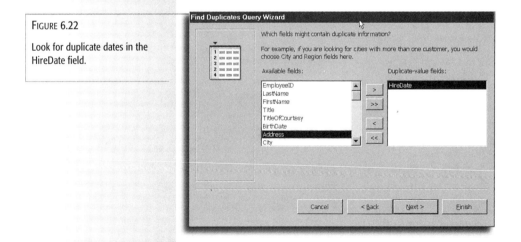

4. In the next dialog box, you can display the contents of other fields along with any duplicate entry. If the query finds any duplicate hire dates, you want to know the employees that share the same hire date. Add the LastName and FirstName fields to the **Additional Query Fields** list. When you're ready to continue, click **Next**.

5. The final dialog box is typical of most wizards' last dialog box. You can change the query's default name and decide how Access displays the query.

If you choose **View the Results**, the wizard displays the query in Datasheet view. If you select **Modify the Design**, the wizard opens the query in Design view. If you need more help, you can select **Display Help on Working with the Query**. Click **Finish** to display the results shown in Figure 6.23. As you can see, two employees, Michael Suyama and Steven Buchanan, were hired on the same date: October 17, 1993.

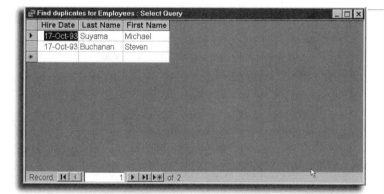

FIGURE 6.23
Two employees share the same hire date.

Using the Find Unmatched Query Wizard

One final query wizard is left to review—the Find Unmatched Query Wizard. This wizard helps you find records not related to another table in the same database. For instance, you might want to know which customers have no orders. To do so, simply compare the related field between the Customers and Orders tables. Any missing CustomerID value in the Orders table indicates customers with no orders.

Create a Find Unmatched query

1. Select **Query** from the **New Object** button's drop-down list and then double-click **Find Unmatched Query Wizard**.

2. By now, you should be pretty familiar with the wizard's dialog boxes. In the first dialog box, specify the appropriate **View** option and then select the appropriate table or query. For this example, select the Customers table because you want to find customers that don't have orders. Then click **Next**.

3. The second dialog box prompts you to identify the related table or query. As in the first dialog box, specify a **View** option and then choose the appropriate table or query. Choose Orders because this table contains order information. When you're ready, click **Next**.

4. The next dialog box (see Figure 6.24) is a little more complex. In it you must identify the related field in both tables. Fortunately, the wizard does a good job of identifying that field for you. In this example, the wizard compares the contents of the CustomerID fields in both tables for missing values in the Orders table. You can change the field in either control, if necessary. You must, however, choose fields that have the same data type. Click **Next** to continue.

SEE ALSO

➤ *Data types for fields are described on page 473*

FIGURE 6.24

The wizard selects the related field from both tables to compare.

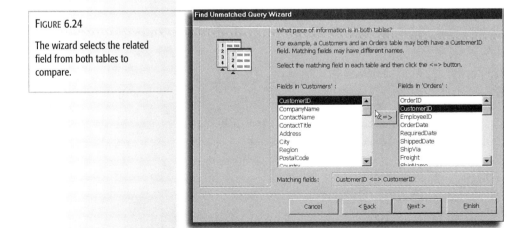

5. Specify fields you want to display in the query. For instance, you want to see the company's name, its contact, and the phone number for any customer that doesn't have an order—that way, you can make a follow-up call to the customer. Add the CompanyName, ContactName, and Phone fields to the **Selected Fields** list (see Figure 6.25). If you don't specify any fields, the wizard displays all the fields in the first table (Customers). After you specify the fields you want in your query, click **Next**.

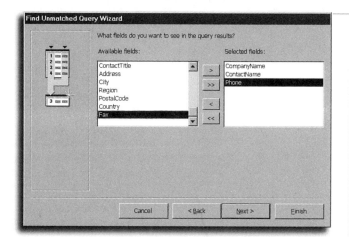

FIGURE 6.25
You want to view the company's name, contact, and phone number.

6. In the final dialog box, you can change the query's name and decide how you want to view the wizard's results. You can select **View the Results** to see the query in Datasheet view, or **Modify the Design** to open the query in Design view.

For this example, retain the defaults and then click **Finish** to display the query shown in Figure 6.26. As you can see, two customers have no orders.

FIGURE 6.26

The query show two customers without orders

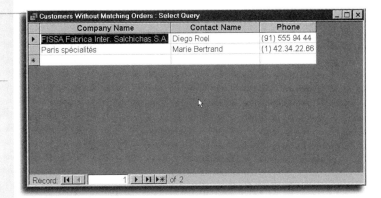

Creating Forms

Understanding Forms

Forms are the objects you use to interact with your data, so you'll probably find yourself working with them more than any other object. Forms make viewing, entering, and modifying your data easier. For the most part, you can think of a form as a screen representation of the paper forms you're already using.

Forms aren't limited to data-related tasks. Utility forms make searching and sorting data easier. You can also use forms as part of your application's *interface*—the application elements that tell Access what you want to do, such as menus and toolbars. A *switchboard* form, like the one shown in Figure 7.1, presents a menu of options. All in all, you'll find Access forms flexible and versatile—a jack-of-all-trades.

FIGURE 7.1

The Northwind switchboard guides you to several tasks.

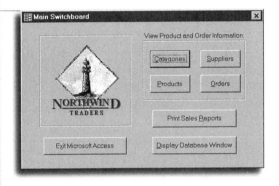

Working in Design View

Editing in Form view

You don't have to return to Design view to make property changes to your form; Access 2000 lets you make property changes while in Form view. To do so, you must change **Allow Design Changes** from **Design View Only** (the default) to **All Views**. When you do so, you can access the form's property sheet in Form view as you would in Design view. This feature is also available for reports in Access 2000.

You can use one of the many wizards to create a form, or you can create one from scratch by adding the appropriate controls and code in Design view. The wizards are quicker and give you a good start, but forms made from scratch are often more flexible and versatile. Try using the wizards whenever possible; however, you might need to tweak the results in Design view.

Create a new form

1. To create a new form from scratch, select **Forms** on the object bar in the Database window.

2. Double-click the **Create Form in Design View** option.

-OR-

1. Select the **Forms** icon on the object bar in the Database window.

2. Click **New** on the Database Window toolbar.

3. In the **New Form** dialog box, double-click **Design View**. (This dialog box also contains wizard options.)

-OR-

1. With the Database window onscreen, choose **Form** from the **Insert** menu.

2. In the **New Form** dialog box, double-click **Design View**. This dialog box also contains wizard options.

The form wizards, reviewed later in the section "Quickly Creating Forms with a Wizard," can create many useful forms. However, occasionally you might need to enhance or modify the wizard's results. Fortunately, doing so is easy. Simply open the form in Design view and go to work. You can open a closed form in Design view from the Database window. If the form is already open in Form view, simply click a button to change views.

Open a closed form in Design view

1. Choose **Forms** from the object bar in the Database window.

2. Select the form you want to modify.

3. Click **Design** [≥ Design] on the Database window toolbar.

-OR-

1. Choose **Forms** from the object bar in the Database window.

2. Right-click the form you want to modify.

3. Choose **Design** from the resulting shortcut menu.

As mentioned earlier, you can also view an open form in Design View. Simply click the **Design View** icon [≥ ▾] on the Form Design toolbar.

The New Object button

You don't have to use the Database window to create a new form. You can choose Form from the New Object button's [▦ ▾] drop-down list. In the resulting New Form dialog box, choose Design View or a form wizard. (Your New Object button might show a different icon face than the one shown.)

As you might have noticed, the View button toggles between different icons depending on which mode you are in:

The View button

In all cases where the word "View" is used, assume that this means the first button on the toolbar, no matter which icon it displays. Click the drop-down arrow to see the other available view options.

Forms	When you're viewing the design of a form, you'll see the **Form View** icon on the tool-bar. You can also click the drop down arrow to select **Datasheet View**.
Reports	A report in Design view will show the **View** icon.
Forms and Reports	A form or report in Form view or Preview, respectively, will show the **Design View** icon.

The Components of a Form in Design View

Figure 7.2 shows a blank form in Design view.

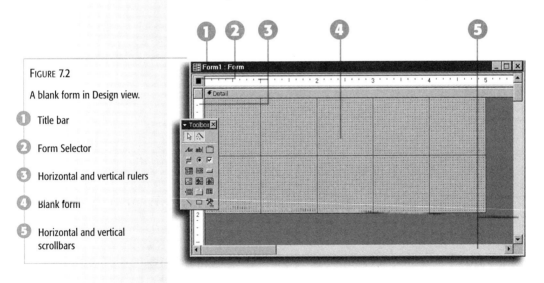

FIGURE 7.2

A blank form in Design view.

1 Title bar

2 Form Selector

3 Horizontal and vertical rulers

4 Blank form

5 Horizontal and vertical scrollbars

Each form has five components:

- The title bar displays the form's name. At the right end of the title bar, you'll find the Windows **Minimize** ▬, **Maximize** ▢, and **Close** ✖ buttons.
- You'll use the horizontal and vertical rulers to help size and position controls.

SEE ALSO

➤ *In addition to sizing and positioning controls, you can select multiple controls, as shown on page 268*

- To open the form's property sheet, simply double-click the **Form Selector** tool, the gray square at the top-left intersection of the two rulers.
- The blank form is the background where you will place the controls.
- The final component, the horizontal and vertical scrollbars, are similar to all other scrollbars. You can use the thumb or the arrows to view areas of your form that stretch beyond the Design view window.

Behind the form are the Access container window and two toolbars: Formatting and Form Design. You're probably familiar with most of the tasks these toolbar buttons offer, so this chapter won't spend any time reviewing them. Finally, there's the Toolbox, which houses all the *native* controls you'll add to your forms.

SEE ALSO

➤ *For specific information about the Toolbox, see page 256*

The Sections of a Form

When you open a blank form, it has only one data section—the Detail section (the blank form's background). Most forms need only a Detail section because it's where the actual record data is displayed. You can enhance your form by adding the following sections, shown in Figure 7.3: Form Header, Page Header, Detail, Page Footer, and Form Footer.

Other windows that open automatically

If you previously had the **Fields List** icon ▤ selected on the toolbar, the Fields List dialog box automatically opens when you open a blank form. If so, click **Close** ✖ to close it. The **Toolbox** works the same way. If you close it, you must open it. If you close a form with the **Toolbox** open, it will be open the next time you open a form in Design view.

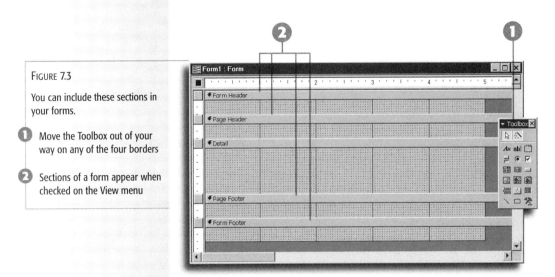

FIGURE 7.3

You can include these sections in your forms.

1 Move the Toolbox out of your way on any of the four borders

2 Sections of a form appear when checked on the View menu

Docking the Toolbox

In Figure 7.3, notice that the Toolbox has been moved to the right of the container window to get it out of the way. The Toolbox has no permanent home. You can move it using the drag-and-drop method. You can also *dock* it at any of the four borders of your container window. Simply drag it to the border as far as it will go; Access automatically docks the Toolbox for you.

The form's header and footer sections display information, such as a title. As you might expect, the header appears at the top of the form and the footer appears at the bottom. If you print the form, the header and footer information will appear once, on the first page. Don't hesitate to move task-related command buttons to the header or footer—command buttons work well in either section.

The page header and footer perform similar tasks to the form. The main difference is that the page section prints on each page; the form prints only on the first page. You also won't see the page header section or page footer when viewing the form, but Access prints this section if you print the form.

Every form has a Detail section—it's the basis of every form. You choose whether to add the header and footer sections. To add a form header or footer, choose **Form Header/Footer** from the **View** menu. Similarly, to add a page header or footer, choose **Page Header/Footer** from the **View** menu. Choosing either header/footer option adds both sections to your form. If you need just a header or a footer, you'll need to close the unneeded section yourself by clicking and dragging up the bottom border of that section.

SEE ALSO
➤ *For more information on adding controls to a form's header or footer, see page 260*

Assigning Form Properties

A form has specific attributes, called *properties*, that you can
use to modify its appearance and task. To access these properties,
open the form's property sheet (see Figure 7.4) by double-
clicking the **Form Selector** (refer to Figure 7.2) or the
Properties button on the **Form Design** toolbar.

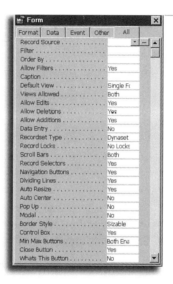

FIGURE 7.4

You can modify a form's attributes by changing its properties in
the property sheet.

After you open the form's property sheet, making changes is a
simple matter. Knowing which properties to change and which
settings to use is the trick. Many are self-explanatory; others
relate to specific tasks. For that reason, we'll refer to them as we
explore form basics and techniques in Chapter 17, "Using Forms
to Enter and Review Data," Chapter 18, "Refining Forms:
Efficient Data Entry and Beyond," and Chapter 20, "Advanced
Form Techniques." The main thing you'll want to note is that
there are properties for the whole form and properties for each
individual control you place on the form. The properties sheet
reflects the properties for the selected object.

SEE ALSO

➤ *You also can learn about some form techniques on page 632*

➤ *To understand the properties carried forward from the underlying table or query to your form properties, see page 69*

Modifying Form Properties to Create a Dialog Box

To understand the versatility of a form's properties, create a *dialog box*. A dialog box is a specific form style. It displays no navigational toolbars or record selectors, and contains a Close button in the title bar. A dialog box also has a unique border. You're constantly interacting with Access via the common dialog box, so you'll want to maintain this format when presenting a custom dialog box.

By modifying a few form properties, you can create a dialog box that looks just like the real thing. For example, the dialog box shown in Figure 7.5 is really a form. You'll learn how to create and save this form as a template. In this context, the term *template* refers to a generic form that you use as a starting point for other forms. Simply open it in Design view, add the appropriate controls and code, give it a new name, and you have a custom dialog box.

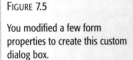

FIGURE 7.5

You modified a few form properties to create this custom dialog box.

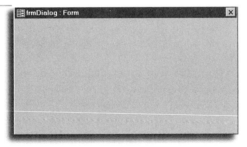

Create a custom dialog box

1. Open a blank form by clicking **Forms** on the object bar in the Database window and then clicking **New** on the Database window toolbar.

2. Double-click **Design View** in the **New Form** dialog box.

3. If Access doesn't open the form's property sheet, do so now by double-clicking the **Form Selector**, clicking the **Properties** button 🖻 on the Form Design toolbar, or double-clicking the dark background behind the blank form. (If you double-click the form, you'll open the Detail section's property sheet, which won't apply the properties to the whole form.)

4. Select the **Format** tab and the **Scroll Bars** property field, click the drop-down arrow, and select **Neither** from the resulting drop-down list.

5. Select **No** from the `Record Selectors` property drop-down list.

6. Select **No** from the `Navigation Buttons` property drop-down list.

7. Select **Dialog** from the `Border Style` property drop-down list.

8. Choose the **Other** tab and select **Yes** from the `Modal` property drop-down list. (This setting retains the focus on the form until you close it.)

9. Resize the form to approximately 4 inches by 2 inches (or any size you want).

10. Click the **Save** button 🖫 on the Form Design toolbar, enter a name such as `frmDialog`, and click **OK**.

11. Close the form.

You'll reopen this dialog box again and again to customize it and add it to your applications. Just be sure to give it a new name so you can maintain your template form.

The toggling property sheet

You can toggle the property sheet on and off just like the **Field List** and the **Toolbox**. If you leave Form view with the property sheet open, it will be open when you return to Form view. If you close the sheet before you leave Form view, it won't be open when you return.

Working in the properties sheet

Most options in the properties sheet have hidden drop-down list boxes for each property. Click anywhere on the property's name or in the selection field to make the drop-down arrow appear.

Quick access to a property field's drop-down list

Many properties have fixed settings, and Access displays those settings in a drop-down list. If you're still selecting the property field and then clicking the drop-down arrow to open the list, stop! It's more efficient to click the right edge of the property field, where the drop-down arrow is visible. Access will not only select the field, but will also open the drop-down list for you. So, what took two clicks before now requires only one. An even quicker way is to avoid the drop-down list altogether. Click to the left of the property field (in the gray area) to toggle through the property settings. Admittedly, saving one or two clicks here and there doesn't seem like a big deal. However, when you do it over and over again each day, it adds up.

SEE ALSO

➤ *Learn more about resizing controls and forms on page 267*

Learn more about resizing controls and forms on page 267

Whose standards do you use?
Everyone has their own ideas about what looks good and works well. However, it's recommended that you stick to the accepted Windows standards as much as possible. Most users are already familiar with these standards, so they'll learn how to use your custom applications more quickly. Besides, Microsoft has already done the hard part—you might as well take advantage of it. If you don't use the Windows standards, adopt your own and be consistent. Try not to be too creative—simple really is best.

Standardizing Forms

When you create a form, you want to consider the form's purpose and the user. The best advice at this point is to standardize your forms, and then apply those standards to all your forms across all your applications. This way, you'll maintain continuity in design and use, thereby reducing your development time and the user's learning curve with new applications.

You can maintain a library of standardized form types. You'll still have to add controls and code, but the basic form design and properties will already be defined. Rather than start from scratch each time, you can begin with a basic template.

Using Form Templates

Adopting a form style
It's recommended that you adopt one style for your forms and reports to create a consistent look and feel for your users. The continuity will make your applications easier to learn and use.

By default, Access's form template contains standard information that Access applies to each form, such as section size, font characteristics, and color. When you create a form from scratch, Access applies these default standards to it.

However, if you consistently change the same form properties, you should consider creating your own template, like the one shown in Figure 7.6. This form, named frmStandards, has a white background and a dialog border style. Changing your project's template won't affect any forms that already exist.

FIGURE 7.6
You can make this form your default.

Change the form template

1. After you create and save your template form, choose **Options** from the **Tools** menu.

2. On the **Forms/Reports** page, Access displays the default form template **Normal** in the **Form Template** control. Select the **Form Template** control, and replace **Normal** with the name of the form you created as your template, such as frmStandards (see Figure 7.7).

3. Click **OK**.

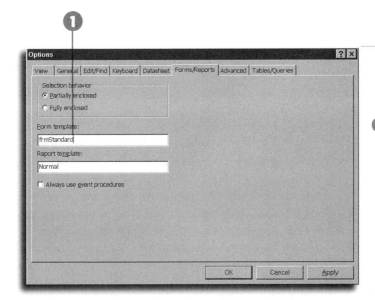

FIGURE 7.7

The Forms/Reports tab displays the current form template, **Normal**.

1 Enter the name of your own form as a template for all new forms, and Access will copy its properties.

Quickly Creating Forms with a Wizard

The Access form wizards use different defaults to generate forms based on tables and queries. There are two types of form wizards: the AutoForms and the Form Wizard. The AutoForms automatically generate a specific type of form, using all the fields in the underlying table or query. In contrast, the Form Wizard allows you to specify the fields you want to include in your form. The wizards offer four types of forms:

The form wizard terms

Throughout this chapter, similar terms are used: form wizard, Form Wizard, and AutoForms. When *form wizard* is in lower-case letters, it refers to *all* the form wizards. *Form Wizard* in uppercase is one of the many form wizards Access offers. *AutoForm* is a type of wizard that automatically generates a specific type of form. Make sure that you're clear on these terms to avoid any confusion.

- **Columnar.** You can create a form that displays data in one column, with each field on a separate line. Typically, this form displays one record at a time.

- **Tabular.** This form displays all the data from one record in the same row, in a column format. Each field is a new column. This is a good format for displaying multiple records.

- **Datasheet.** You can display data in table format on a form. It's an easy way to display your data in this format without actually opening a table.

- **Justified.** This form distributes controls evenly between the right and left margins and the top and bottom margins. This type of form is available only with the Form Wizard.

Reviewing AutoForms

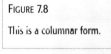

AutoForm defaults

If your AutoForm forms aren't always the same, don't worry. The columnar, tabular, and datasheet AutoForms use the settings from the last Form Wizard session as their defaults, or they will use the last format you choose from the **Format** menu's **AutoFormat** command in Design view. In contrast, the AutoForm you select from the **New Object** button relies on the form template (a columnar form is the default).

Perhaps the easiest way to create a form is to use one of the many AutoForm wizards. The default **AutoForm** is first on the **New Object** button's [icon] drop-down list.

The AutoForm wizard arranges all the fields in the underlying table in a single column and displays one record at a time. This columnar style tends to resemble typical paper forms, so it's good for viewing or entering data. The Northwind Customers form (see Figure 7.8) is a good example of a columnar form, although a few fields have been moved to create a second column.

FIGURE 7.8

This is a columnar form.

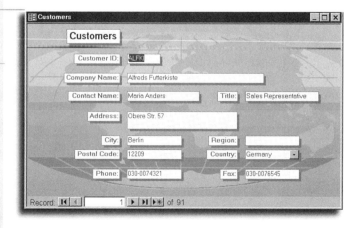

A *tabular* form is similar to Datasheet view, displaying all the fields in the same row. Generally, there isn't much resemblance between a tabular form and a corresponding paper form. However, the style works well when you display multiple records. You can use the AutoForm: Tabular wizard to quickly create a tabular form like the one shown in Figure 7.9.

Adjusting the wizard forms

Although AutoForm provides a sound start, it rarely produces exactly the form you need. You can expect to alter a few of the settings, such as label contents, text alignment, or color.

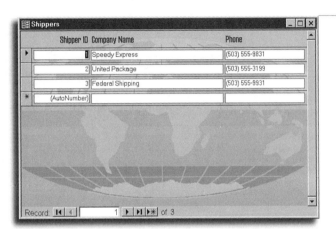

FIGURE 7.9
The AutoForm: Tabular wizard created this tabular form.

Datasheet forms also resemble Datasheet view (see Figure 7.10). This form is the Northwind Orders Subform datasheet form. These forms are a closer match to the table format than the tabular style. This style is good for viewing lots of data at the same time or displaying your data in table fashion, without actually opening your table.

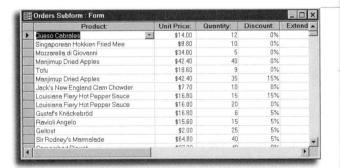

FIGURE 7.10
A datasheet form is good for viewing a lot of data.

Selecting fields in a wizard

When you select fields to include in your form by using the Form Wizard, Access keeps track of the order. When the wizard creates your form, the fields appear in the order you select them.

Shortcut for moving numerous fields

You'll have to specify the fields you want to include in your form when you use the Form Wizard. The easiest way to move all but one or two fields is to click the **>>** button when prompted to choose fields. Then, select the fields you really don't want to include and click the **<** button to exclude them from your form.

Reviewing the Form Wizard

The preceding section reviews wizards that automatically generate a form, including all the fields in the underlying table or query in that form. When an AutoForm isn't adequate, you can use the Form Wizard. This wizard offers the three previous form styles, and adds a fourth—justified.

The only difference between using an AutoForm and the Form Wizard is that you must specify certain options. When you launch the wizard, you must choose the fields you want to display on your form. The wizard also allows you to choose the form style—columnar, tabular, datasheet, and justified. You also can choose a predefined format style that specifies fonts, colors, and any special effects.

At this point, you might be wondering what a justified form is. The best way to describe it is to just show you one (see Figure 7.11). As you can see, Access has distributed the controls equally between the left and right margins and the top and bottom margins.

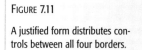

FIGURE 7.11

A justified form distributes controls between all four borders.

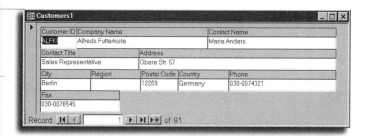

The format you select using the Form Wizard affects the AutoForms because they rely on the last Form Wizard format for their own defaults. That means the next form you create using an AutoForm will default to the same style you select when using the Form Wizard.

SEE ALSO

➤ *See how to modify the form after you create it on page 303*

Reviewing the Chart Wizard

To finish this introduction to form wizards, let's review two rather unusual form wizards: the Chart Wizard and the PivotTable Wizard. As you might expect, you use the Chart Wizard to embed a chart in a form by basing a form chart on a table or query. Or you can add a chart to an existing form or report. The PivotTable Wizard is an interactive table that performs calculations. It gets its name from its behavior—it can dynamically modify its layout to match different analysis needs.

Fortunately, the Chart Wizard is very versatile; you can choose from 20 different chart formats. The wizard also allows you to rearrange its choices. You can drag and drop controls to change the orientation, or you can change a default calculation or measurement. Specifically, the Sum(), Average(), Min(), Max(), and Count() functions are available. For instance, the chart might sum a field's value. You can modify the chart to display the average value in the field.

Access doesn't actually have charting capabilities; instead, the Chart Wizard launches Microsoft Graph 2000. After you embed the chart in a form or report, you can launch Microsoft Graph to edit the chart. Nor does Access create pivot tables on its own—the PivotTable Wizard actually relies on the same feature in Excel.

Working with the PivotTable Wizard

A *pivot table* is very powerful because it lets you produce different viewpoints of the same data. For instance, the Northwind Sales Analysis form shown in Figure 7.12 displays quarterly sales totals by employees.

FIGURE 7.12

A pivot table can vary the same data.

	Sum of Subtotal	LastName				
Years	OrderDate	Buchanan	Callahan	Davolio	Dodsworth	Fuller
1995	Qtr1	17,789	33,817	47,652	31,602	45,048
	Qtr2	210	13,921	15,543	9,502	27,691
1995 Sum		17,999	47,738	63,195	41,103	72,739
1995 Average		1,500	1,591	1,505	2,163	1,966
1994	Qtr1	2,520	15,971	7,470	2,472	5,898
	Qtr2	7,538	7,466	15,632	4,211	27,494
	Qtr3	12,086	10,800	32,605	10,222	24,354
	Qtr4	10,265	19,934	30,510	9,405	12,705
1994 Sum		32,409	54,171	86,216	26,310	70,451
1994 Average		1,706	1,003	1,627	1,385	1,677
1993	Qtr3	3,575	15,022	13,822	4,364	5,941
	Qtr4	14,809	9,932	28,874	5,530	17,408

ShipCountry (All)

Edit PivotTable

Knowing what to use for a pivot table

After you make a few pivot tables, you'll know how they work and which queries you'll want to examine. Generally, pivot tables work best when categories have multiple subheadings. For instance, displaying quarterly totals for a particular year by customer might be a good use of a pivot table. You could even add quarterly totals for other years to this arrangement.

Using pivot tables and Excel

You must have Excel installed to create a pivot table in Access. Technically, anytime you're working with a chart or pivot table, you're actually working with an ActiveX control.

The PivotTable Wizard is flexible—you can easily change the default calculations and format the fields. Also, a pivot table can display field values horizontally or vertically, calculating the total of the row or column. You can then *pivot* the existing layout to dynamically analyze the data in different ways. The Northwind database has a pivot table in the Sales Analysis form if you'd like to review it. Next you'll create one of your own.

When you launch the PivotTable Wizard, it opens Excel. At this point, by using the drag-and-drop method, add the fields you want as columns and rows. Next, add the fields for your data section.

The wizard allows you to modify data fields—you can change the function as you can with the Chart Wizard. You can also modify the format options. For instance, you might want to display your values as currency.

The PivotTable Wizard offers even more versatility than the Chart Wizard. You can modify the data source selection and the layout, and include password protection.

Creating Reports

Introducing Reports

Sooner or later in the life of your database, you'll need to create a report that shows off your data. The way you design your report determines whether it's an eye-popping presentation or a jumbled and cluttered mess. The purpose of any report should be to quickly and concisely display its data in an easily read and understood manner. When designing the report, you should consider how this report will be used and the story you want the report to tell.

You can use the Report Wizard that comes with Microsoft Access to design your report. If you want to be a little more creative, you can modify and customize the wizard's creation to better suit your needs. As with all Access objects, you can bypass the report wizards and go straight to Design view to create your own report from scratch.

Using the Report Wizards

Report wizard terms

Throughout this chapter, similar terms are used: report wizard, Report Wizard, and AutoReports. The term *report wizard* (lower case) is a generic reference to all report wizards. The proper case, *Report Wizard*, refers to only one of the many report wizards. The last term, *AutoReports*, is also a specific report wizard.

Creating a report from scratch

You don't have to use a wizard to create a report. If you want to build the report yourself, select the report's underlying table or query in the Database window. Then, select Report from the New Object button's drop-down list. Next, instead of selecting a wizard option, double-click Design View. Doing so opens a blank report, based on the table or query you selected earlier.

Access offers several different wizards that help when you're ready to generate a report. These wizards won't do everything, but they're efficient and easy to use. They also create a good solid base for most of your report needs. In a nutshell, the report wizards depend on different defaults to generate reports based on your data.

The report wizards are similar to the form wizards in that there are two types: AutoReports and the Report Wizard. The AutoReports wizard automatically generates a specific report type, using all the fields in the underlying table or query. On the other hand, the Report Wizard allows you to specify the fields you want to report on.

You can choose from three types of reports:

Columnar	Displays data in one column, with each field on a separate line
Tabular	Displays all the data from one record in the same row; each field forms a column
Justified	Distributes data evenly between the right and left margins and the top and bottom margins

Working with AutoReports

When you have few requirements, consider using the AutoReports wizard, by far the simplest choice. Simply select the table or query that you're basing your report on (in the Database window), and then choose **AutoReport** from the **New Object** button's drop-down list (see Figure 8.1).

In Chapter 7, "Creating Forms," you learned that the AutoForm wizards use the settings from the last Form Wizard session as their defaults. The AutoReport wizards are the same. Using the Report Wizard affects the defaults used by AutoReport.

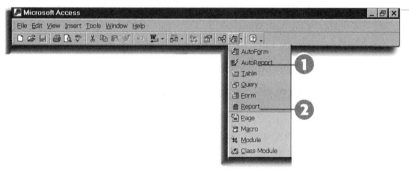

AutoReport has a few limitations. First, you can't specify a columnar, tabular, or justified report when using AutoReports. The wizard decides for you, based on the last report you created when using the Report Wizard. However, if you choose **Report** from the **New Object** button's drop-down list, Access offers two more automatic report options:

- AutoReport: Columnar
- AutoReport: Tabular

Choosing either option automatically generates the appropriate report.

AutoReports also includes all the fields from the bound table or query in your report. Consider this a limitation because often you'll want to report on only a few selected fields, rather than all the fields in the underlying table or query.

Using the New Object button

When you use the **New Object** button [icon], be sure to click the drop-down arrow rather than the object that appears on the toolbar. This icon might change to the object last selected. Then, if you're creating several reports in a row, you'll see the **Report** button [icon] appear automatically on the toolbar. Access changes the toolbar intuitively to save you an extra mouse click.

FIGURE 8.1

The New Object button offers many wizard options.

① Generates a report automatically, using all the fields in the underlying table or query

② Offers more wizard choices

Watch the changing button

The **New Object** button remembers your last choice and updates the button's picture accordingly. The next time you need this button, you can repeat the last choice by clicking the button instead of opening the drop-down list and making the same selection. If you don't want to repeat the last action, you must open the drop-down list and make a new selection.

Using the Report Wizard

As you recently learned, AutoReports has a few limitations. Fortunately, the Report Wizard is a little more flexible. It offers a third style—justified—and you can choose the fields you want to include in your report. You can't create a justified report with AutoReport.

The main difference between using AutoReport and the Report Wizard is the amount of information you must supply. You saw in the preceding section that the AutoReports require little from you. The Report Wizard asks you to

- Identify the fields you want to include in your report
- Specify a grouping field
- Determine which field to sort each group by
- Summarize numerical data
- Choose from several predefined layout and orientation options

Each step is self-explanatory. However, the grouping, sorting, and summarizing options offer many choices.

Report wizards display your data in the order that the bound table or query presents it. Fortunately, you can easily specify a grouping field and sort each group. You can even summarize Numeric fields by using the Report Wizard.

SEE ALSO

➤ *Learn more about sorting on page 81*

Specify grouping options

1. In the Database window, select the Employees table from the sample Northwind database that ships with Access.

2. Choose **Report** from the **New Object** button's drop-down list, and then double-click **Report Wizard** in the New Report dialog box.

3. In the wizard's first dialog box, move the fields you want to include in your report from the **Available Fields** list to the **Selected Fields** list (double-click the field in the **Available Fields** list, or select the field and click the **>** button between the two lists). For this example, report on the LastName,

The Finish button

If the wizard's **Finish** button is enabled, you can click it and the wizard completes the report without prompting you for further information.

FirstName, BirthDate, and ReportsTo fields. When you're ready to continue, click **Next**.

4. The second dialog box (see Figure 8.2) gives you the opportunity to group your data. For this example, group by the BirthDate field. To do so, select the field in the list box on the left and click the **>** button to update the layout of the generic form on the right (see Figure 8.3).

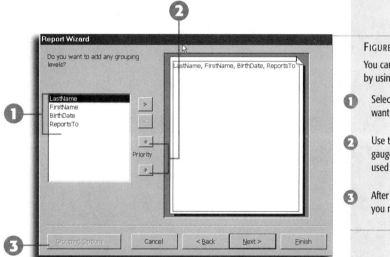

FIGURE 8.2

You can add groups to a report by using the Report Wizard.

1 Select the field by which you want to group your data

2 Use the Priority buttons to gauge which criteria is the first used to sort data

3 After you set a grouping field, you need to set the interval

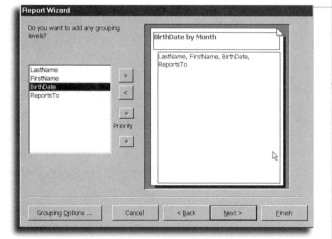

FIGURE 8.3

BirthDate is now the top level and the additional fields are shown indented below.

Now your report groups the employees by their birth dates. More specifically, the report groups by the month component of each birth date.

Grouping by Numeric fields

If you group by a Numeric field, Access offers a list of numeric groupings: 10s, 50s, 100s, 500s, 1,000s, 5,000s, and 10,000s. A text field offers still a different group: 1st letter, 2 Initial Letters, 3 Initial Letters, 4 Initial Letters, and 5 Initial Letters. If you choose 1st, Access groups by the first letter in the field; if you choose 2 Initial Letters, Access groups by the first two letters in the field, and so on.

5. You can change the grouping interval by clicking the **Grouping Options** button. The resulting dialog box (see Figure 8.4) offers options based on the field's data type. For instance, because BirthDate is a Date/Time field, the drop-down list offers date and time intervals. The default for the BirthDate field is Month. As a result, the report sorts the data by the employees' birth dates.

If you want to change the grouping interval, do so now and click **OK** to return to the wizard. Click **Next** in the wizard when you're ready to continue.

FIGURE 8.4

The grouping interval options depend on the field's data type.

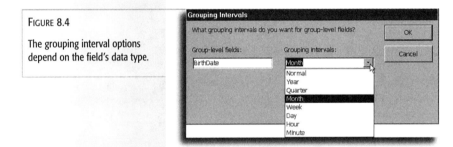

6. Specify a sort field by selecting a field from the first drop-down list (see Figure 8.5). For this example, sort by the LastName field. An Ascending sort is the default. To change that, click the Sort button to the right of the sort control.

After you set the first sort field, Access enables the second sort control. If you assign a second sort field, Access enables the third sort control, and so on. You can specify up to four sort fields.

7. To summarize data, click the **Summary Options** button. The wizard lists the Numeric fields and offers four summary options: Sum, Avg, Min, and Max. For this example, the wizard displays the only Numeric field, ReportsTo (see Figure 8.6). Because this field is simply an identifying value, you really don't want to summarize its contents. However, merely to show the report results, select the Sum option to return the total for each group's ReportsTo field. Also select the **Calculate Percent of Total for Sums** option, so you can see the result in the finished report.

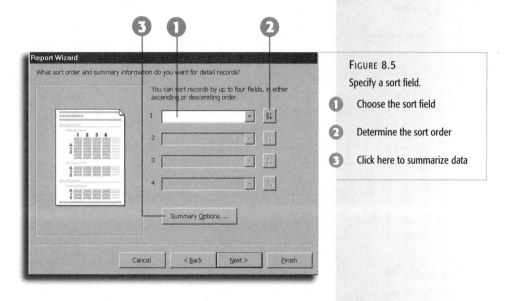

FIGURE 8.5

Specify a sort field.

1️⃣ Choose the sort field

2️⃣ Determine the sort order

3️⃣ Click here to summarize data

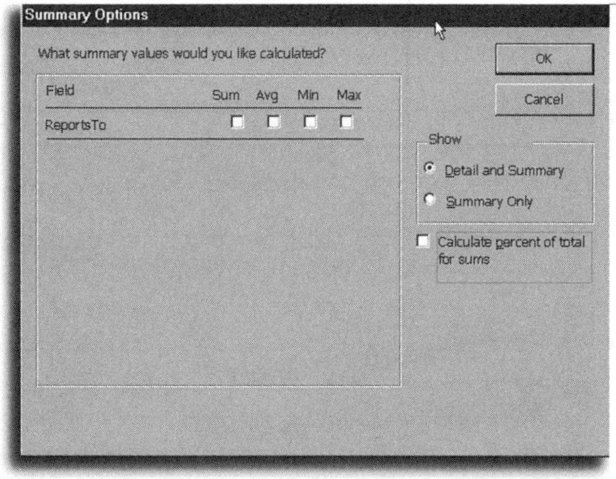

FIGURE 8.6

The wizard will help you summarize Numeric fields.

The Show option default is **Detail and Summary**, which displays all records and a summary line. If you select **Summary Only**, the wizard displays only the summary line.

After you make your selections, click **OK**. Then click **Next** to continue.

8. In the next dialog box, choose the **Block** and **Portrait** options. You can also select the self-explanatory **Adjust the Field Width So All Fields Fit on a Page** option. Click **Next** when you're ready to continue.

9. The next dialog box lets you select a report style from a list of predefined options. The default is **Bold**; don't change this option. Click **Next** when you're ready to continue.

10. The final dialog box prompts you to name the report; you can accept the default, but for this example use rptBirthDates. You can also choose between viewing the complete report in Print Preview or opening the report in Design view for further modifications. Click **Finish**. The Report Wizard generates the report (see Figure 8.7).

Adjusting fields to fit a report

The **Adjust the Field Width So All Fields Fit on a Page** option might truncate field values if you have to fit many fields between the left and right margins. Use this option wisely, or change the direction of your page layout to accommodate numerous fields.

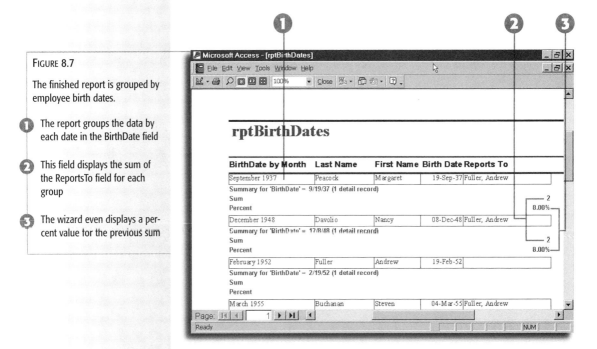

FIGURE 8.7

The finished report is grouped by employee birth dates.

❶ The report groups the data by each date in the BirthDate field

❷ This field displays the sum of the ReportsTo field for each group

❸ The wizard even displays a percent value for the previous sum

Designing a Report

Trying to get the right look for your report can be a challenge. Ultimately it comes down to two important points:

- How will your report be used?
- How much data do you want on each page?

If you plan to bind the report, try the portrait orientation with a larger left or book-style margin. This compensates for a three-hole punch or spine in the left margin. Likewise, it might be acceptable to spread your data out to occupy the entire sheet, reducing your margins to next to nothing. Be careful to consider your header and footer needs when doing this.

Select the layout of your report by choosing **Page Setup** from the **File** menu. From the Page Setup dialog box (see Figure 8.8), you can select your page margins, page orientation, paper size and source, printer designation, and layout settings.

Always preview first

As with documents you've used in other applications such as Microsoft Word, you should always preview the report before you print it. Use the **View** button to check the layout and readability of your report throughout the design process.

FIGURE 8.8

Use the Page Setup to choose layout specifics.

1. Use this page to set your report's margins.

2. This page offers report orientation, paper size, and default printer options.

3. You can manipulate report columns on this page.

When deciding margins, headers, and footers, keep in mind how each affects the actual report data. For example, if you're creating a report in portrait mode and have your left and right margins set at 1 inch, any item that extends beyond the 6.5-inch mark on the vertical ruler is printed on a new page. This is important to remember when you're resizing lines, borders, and fields. If you end up with just one object that extends past the report's right margin limit, Access prints twice as many pages as you expect—the report page and the extra page that shows only the offending object.

Viewing Reports in Design View

Regardless of how you create reports, you can always enter Design view (as with forms) to edit a report's properties and layout. To open a report in Design view, you have two options:

- Right-click a report name in the Database window, and then choose **Design** from the resulting shortcut menu.
- Highlight the report name and choose **Design** on the Database window menu.

Notice right away that Design view displays your report in sections and that your report contains no data (see Figure 8.9). Design view contains only layout, control, and property information.

The sections normally consist of a report header, a page header, a detail section, a page footer, and a report footer. A report that's being grouped or sorted has additional sections. Every section tells you which type of data is placed on your report, and where:

- A report header appears only once, at the very beginning of the report.
- A page header appears at the beginning of every new page.
- Items in the Detail section constitute the "meat" of your report. This is where the data is displayed.

Viewing the report with data

To view how your report looks with data, click the **View** button on the **Report Design** toolbar.

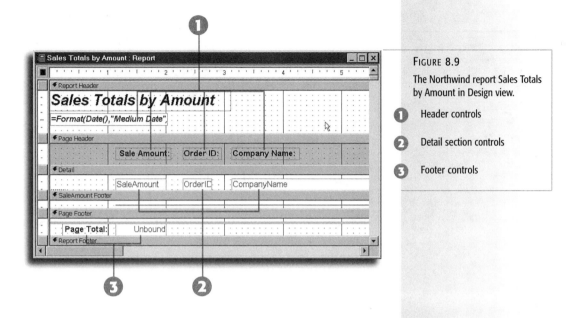

FIGURE **8.9**

The Northwind report Sales Totals by Amount in Design view.

1 Header controls

2 Detail section controls

3 Footer controls

- The page footer displayed at the bottom of each page is commonly used for page numbering, "privileged and confidential" tags, and the document name.

- The report footer appears only once, at the very end of the report.

In Design view, you also have a choice of many toolbars to use. The Report Design, Toolbox, and Formatting (Form/Report/Design) toolbars are the most commonly used. By right-clicking any toolbar, you can see which toolbars are now open; to add or remove any toolbars, use this pop-up menu or choose **Toolbars** from the **View** menu.

Setting Report Properties

Every section and control in your report—even the report itself—has properties, listed in a properties sheet. You can change the properties of the entire report, a single section, or a specific control. You can also attach an event to a report section or control, or insert an image into your report.

Getting to the properties you want

The properties sheet operates as a toggle object, meaning that it's always open or closed. Clicking the **Properties** button opens or closes it, depending on its current state. If a properties sheet is now open, the easiest way to see another object's properties is to select that object; the properties sheet automatically updates. At any time, you can select the Report Selector to see the report's properties. The Report Selector is similar to the Form Selector—it's the small gray square at the intersection of the two Design view rulers.

You can open an object's properties sheet in more than one way:

- Double-click that item.

- The **Object** drop-down list to the left of the Formatting toolbar is especially helpful when dealing with hard-to-grab items such as lines, borders, or overlapping fields. However, this works only to change the property sheet from object to object. Choosing this option alone won't open the properties sheet—it must already be open.

- Click the **Properties** button on the Report Design toolbar.

Setting report properties is easy. After you open the report's property sheet, locate the appropriate property, and change the setting. As with forms, you need to enter some settings, whereas other properties offer choices in a drop-down list. If the property sheet is already open but is displaying the properties for an object other than the one you want to modify, simply select the object you want to modify. Access automatically updates the contents of the property sheet accordingly.

Standardizing Reports

Have you ever wondered what the paintbrush icon on the Standard toolbar does? It's the **Format Painter**. It copies the *style* of a selection, rather than its content, and applies it to another selection. This is useful in Access because a person considers many stylistic changes before deciding on a final design. The Format Painter is a timesaver when you decide to use the same style or styles throughout a form or report.

Use the Format Painter to copy styles

1. Select the object that contains the attributes you want to copy to another.

2. Click **Format Painter** , which remembers all the former object's formats.

3. Click the object you want to format.

Creating a Report Template

If you find yourself using the same report styles over and over, consider making your own templates. Most likely, you've been using the copy-and-paste method. Find a report you want, copy it, paste it, rename it, enter the design of the new report, and revise. This can be a tedious chore. You can have the same layout, font selection, embedded objects, and other report properties saved as a template you can use to construct your new reports.

Create a report template

1. Create a report that has all the ingredients (style, format, structure) you know you'll need on a regular basis.

2. From the **Tools** menu, choose **Options**. In the Options dialog box, display the **Forms/Reports** page (see Figure 8.10).

3. In the **Report Template** text box, give the template a name you'll recognize later on.

Using an existing report

If your application contains a report you can use as a template, open it in Design view. Then, repeat steps 2 and 3. Access copies that report's styles to your new template.

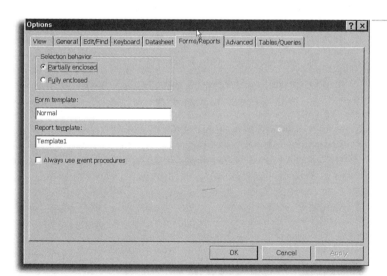

FIGURE 8.10

Saving your report template.

SEE ALSO

➤ *Find an explanation for the Options dialog box's Selection Behavior section on page 275*

You can change the template at any time, without affecting existing reports based on an earlier template. Also, Access uses your template when you create a report from scratch. The template doesn't affect the report wizards—the wizards use your last wizard settings.

Inserting a Chart into a Report with the Chart Wizard

Charting limitations

Unlike the form and report wizards, the Chart Wizard doesn't let you select fields from more than one table or query. If you want to base a chart on multiple table sources, create a query that pulls all these tables together and base your chart on that query.

In Chapter 7, "Creating Forms," you learned how to insert a chart into a form. You can use the same basic routine to insert a chart into a report. You're actually embedding an ActiveX control, because Access doesn't generate charts; instead, Access relies on Microsoft Graph 97 to create charts based on your Access data.

You can create a chart report in two ways:

- Base your report on the query that contains the data you want to chart. Then run the Chart Wizard by selecting **Report** from the **New Object** button's [icon] ▾ drop-down list and then selecting **Chart Wizard**.

- Open an existing report and choose **Chart** from the **Insert** menu to execute the Chart Wizard.

The wizard features and options you learned about in Chapter 7 are available for reports as well; creating the chart is essentially the same. The only difference is the object you're embedding the chart in—a form versus a report.

SEE ALSO

➤ *For more information on the Chart Wizard, see page 119*

Printing Your Report

You can print your report using a number of methods. Whether you are in Print Preview or the Database window, clicking **Print** [icon] prints the report. Likewise, from within Preview or the Database window, you can choose **Print** from the **File** menu (or press **Ctrl+P**) for further print options (see Figure 8.11).

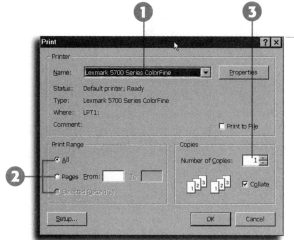

FIGURE 8.11

The Print dialog box offers further options.

1 Select from all available printers.

2 Print all or only a section of your report.

3 You can print more than one copy.

Creating Controls and Setting Properties

Offer choices with list and combo boxes

Complete tasks with the click of a button

Use option groups to limit choices

Report controls

Just because you can place most controls on a report doesn't mean you'll want to. For instance, how would you use a list box in a report? That's why this chapter concentrates on placing controls in forms. Feel free to experiment, but the average user will find few uses for report controls beyond displaying and calculating data in text controls.

Reviewing Control Wizards

Wizards do a good job of producing usable forms and reports. However, you might find that a wizard's final product often needs a tweak or two before you can use it. For instance, you might change a control's formatting or assign the form a unique task. Often, you might need to add controls that the wizard can't quite anticipate. Fortunately, Access includes five wizards for adding controls to your forms and reports:

- Option Group Wizard
- Combo Box Wizard
- List Box Wizard
- Command Button Wizard
- Subform/Subreport Wizard

Reviewing Control Properties

Most Access objects have *properties*, which you use to set an object's characteristics. For instance, a property setting determines a form's background color, a control's contents, a field's format, and so on. In a nutshell, properties determine the way an object appears and performs.

Controls have universal properties and unique properties that support their functions. For instance, all controls have a name property. If the control is bound to a table or query, the control inherits the bound field's name. If the control isn't bound, Access gives the control a name that consists of the control's type and a number. For instance, an unbound text box might have a default name of Text02. However, only the list box control offers a Multi Select property. This property controls the way you select items.

SEE ALSO

➤ *For a time-saving technique that lets you set multiple properties, see page 276*

Setting Control Properties

All controls have properties, and each property has a default setting that Access applies when you create the control. To modify a control's property, open the control's property sheet, locate the appropriate property, and change the setting.

Change a control property

  1. Open the Products form in Design view by selecting it in the Database window and clicking the **Design** button ![Design] on the window's toolbar.

  2. If Access doesn't open the property sheet, click the **Properties** button ![icon] on the Form Design toolbar. (If the Toolbox is open, you can close it.)

  3. If necessary, move the open property sheet so that you can select the **ProductID** text box control.

  4. Find the **Back Style** property and select **Transparent** from its drop-down list. Next, locate the **Border Style** property field and also choose **Transparent** from its drop-down list.

Changing these two properties inhibits the display of the control. As a result, Access displays only the control's contents in Form View.

The List Box Control

The control of choice is by far the text box, which simply displays or accepts data. Text boxes can be bound or unbound. Although they're extremely functional, they're not always adequate. For instance, to display a list of items, you might use a list box control. Displaying a list of items makes things simpler and easier for users. Rather than remember all the possible responses and then type one, users select the appropriate choice from the list box. From a development standpoint, offering a list of items reduces the chances for errors because users can't enter an inappropriate response. (Users can, however, select the wrong item from the list—nothing is totally foolproof.)

SEE ALSO

➤ *An explanation of bound and unbound controls is on page 278*

The form used in this example

In this example, you'll modify the Products form's Product ID control. You can find this form in the Northwind database that comes with Access. (You must install the database.)

Understanding bound controls

A *bound control* is one that's attached to a data source—specifically, a field. The field can be in a table or a query. For instance, if you bind a form to a table or query, you can then also bind almost any control you add to that form to a field in the bound table or query.

The list box and combo box examples

For the most part, the list box and combo box properties are the same. Rather than repeat yourself in the later combo box section, the examples are varied to discuss several display possibilities. Remember that the example is appropriate for a list box or a combo box, unless otherwise noted.

Most list boxes consist of a simple column of choices (see Figure 9.1). Technically, you can include all the fields that comprise an entire record (if you're working with a bound list box.) But you can control which column or columns the control displays. A drop-down list box adds a text box control to the top of the list box, which displays a default value or the selected value for that control.

FIGURE 9.1

A list box can display one column or several.

① This list box displays one column of choices.

Using the List Box Wizard

After you decide you need a list box, you can create the control yourself or use the List Box Wizard. The wizard walks you through the process of defining an unbound or bound control's list of choices. It's a good way to learn about a list box if you're unfamiliar with that control.

Create an unbound list box with the List Box Wizard

1. Click **Forms** on the Database object bar and then select **New** from the Database window menu. Then double-click **Design View** in the New Forms dialog box.

2. If Access doesn't open the Toolbox, click the Toolbox button on the Form Design toolbar.

3. To turn on the Control Wizards, make sure that the Control Wizards icon is selected in the Toolbox.

At this point, you can click any control that has a wizard—list box, combo box, command button, and option group—to launch the control's wizard.

4. Click the List Box tool 🔳 in the Toolbox and then click inside the blank form. In response, Access launches the wizard and displays the first dialog box (see Figure 9.2).

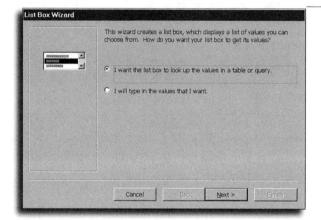

FIGURE 9.2
You can create your own list or use the data from a table or query.

5. Choose between creating your own list of items or tying your list to the data in a table or query. If you're creating your own list, choose **I Will Type in the Values That I Want**. If you're relying on a table or query, choose the default setting, **I Want the List Box to Look Up the Values in a Table or Query**.

Choose the **I Will Type in the Values I Want** option if you want to follow this example. Click **Next** to continue.

6. The next dialog box prompts you for the list box values (or items). If you want to display more than one column of items, enter the number of columns you need in the **Number of Columns** text box. Then, enter the appropriate values in the provided columns. So that the values are in sequence, enter one item in each column cell, in the order you want them to be displayed, as shown in Figure 9.3. Don't press **Enter** after typing each item; that takes you to the next wizard dialog box. Instead, type the item, and then press **Tab**. When you're finished, click **Next** to continue.

Sizing columns to see text

If a column isn't wide enough to completely display all the items, drag out the column's right edge until the column is wide enough. Or, double-click the column's heading cell to apply the Best Fit property.

FIGURE 9.3

Enter three values for your list box.

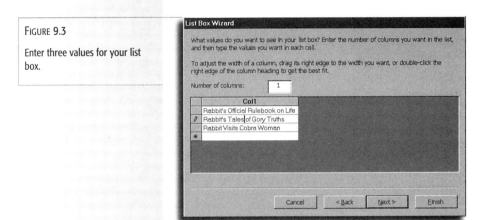

7. The final dialog box prompts you for a descriptive label—the example uses the title **Books**. If you need more help, you can select the **Display Help on Customizing the List Box** option. Click **Finish** to display the completed list box in Design view.

8. To see the list box shown in Figure 9.4, click the **View** button 🔳▾ on the Form Design toolbar. As you can see, the list box offers three choices; to choose one, select it. (You might need to increase the width of the control's label or the list box.)

FIGURE 9.4

This list box displays all the options for users to select. You can stretch the size of the text area in Deslgn view.

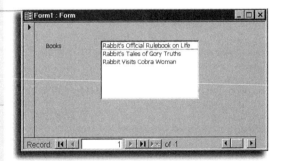

SEE ALSO
➤ *For more details on the Toolbox, see page 256*
➤ *See how to resize the label control in this example on page 268*

Creating the List Box from Scratch

You don't have to use a wizard to create a list box (or any other control); you can set the appropriate properties yourself. Figure 9.5 shows the list box from the previous example and its property sheet. The **Row Source Type** property is set to **Value List**, which is a list you provide by entering each item, as you did earlier. To create this list without the wizard, choose **Value List** from the **Row Source Type** property's drop-down list. Then, enter the appropriate values as the **Row Source** property, separating each with a semicolon.

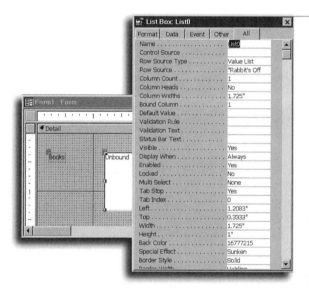

FIGURE 9.5
This property sheet shows the list box properties you must modify to display a list of values.

Create a list box without using a wizard

1. Click **Forms** and then **New** in the Database window, or use the form from the previous example. Then double-click **Design View** in the New Forms dialog box.

2. If Access doesn't open the Toolbox, open it.

3. Deselect the **Control Wizard** tool in the Toolbox if it's selected.

4. Click the **List Box** tool in the Toolbox and then click inside the blank form.

5. Click the **Properties** tool on the Form Design toolbar.

6. Set the **Row Source Type** property to **Value List**.

7. Select the **Row Source** property and enter the string The Pow Wow Trail;Orega and I on the Breadcrumb Trail.

8. Click the **View** button to see the results (shown in Figure 9.6). This list box behaves the same as the one you created earlier using the wizard.

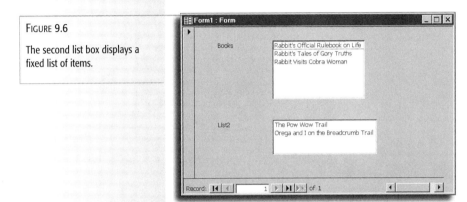

FIGURE 9.6

The second list box displays a fixed list of items.

Creating a Multiple-Column List Box

Now, suppose that you want to display a set of items but don't want to store the displayed items. Instead, you want to store a corresponding value in another field. Or, perhaps you want to return a corresponding value in some other control. Either situation is easily handled by binding your list box to more than one column—that is, by using a multiple-column list box.

Create a multiple-column bound list box

1. Open a blank form, or open the form from the last example in Design view.

2. Open the **Toolbox** if necessary and make sure that the **Control Wizards** tool is selected.

3. Click the **List Box** tool in the Toolbox and then click inside the form.

4. Access launches the List Box Wizard and displays the first dialog box. This time, select **I Want the List Box To Look Up the Values in a Table or Query** because you're creating a bound list box. Then click **Next** to continue.

5. In the next dialog box, choose between a table or query by selecting an option from the **View** section at the bottom of the dialog box (see Figure 9.7). The default option, **Tables**, displays the tables that are in your application in the list box. If you select **Queries**, Access updates the list box with all the queries in your application. As you might expect, the **Both** option displays all tables and queries. For this example, leave the default at Tables and then select the Categories table from the Northwind database. Click **Next** to continue.

FIGURE 9.7
Select the list box's data source in this dialog box.

6. The wizard displays the bound object's fields. Move the field that contains the values you want to display to the **Selected Fields** list (see Figure 9.8). For this example, choose to display the values from both fields in this list box. After making your selections, click **Next** to continue.

7. The wizard gives you the opportunity to modify the default control's display settings. If you retain the defaults, the wizard displays only the contents of the CategoryName field. However, you have access to the contents of the CategoryID field. To display all the bound columns in the list box, deselect the **Hide Key Column (Recommended)** option (see Figure 9.9).

At this point, you can resize the width of either column. When you're ready, click **Next** to continue.

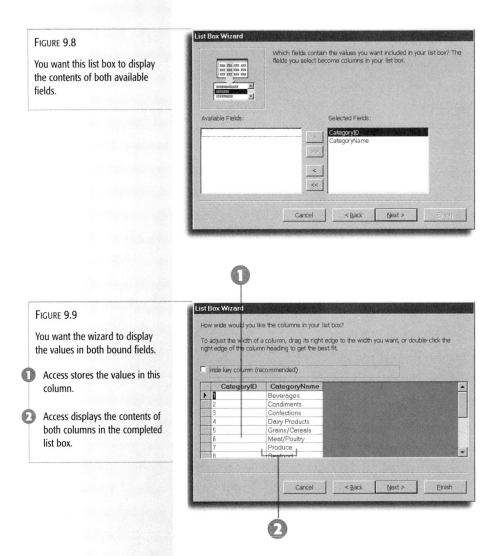

FIGURE 9.8

You want this list box to display the contents of both available fields.

FIGURE 9.9

You want the wizard to display the values in both bound fields.

1 Access stores the values in this column.

2 Access displays the contents of both columns in the completed list box.

8. The next dialog box (see Figure 9.10) lets you specify which value the list box stores when you select an item. You can choose either field. There's no right or wrong in this decision, but values are the favored choice when possible. As a result of your choice, when you select **Beverages** from the control's list (which displays items from the CategoryName field), that control actually stores the value 1 (the Beverages corresponding value from the CategoryID field), not the string "Beverages." Click **Next** to continue.

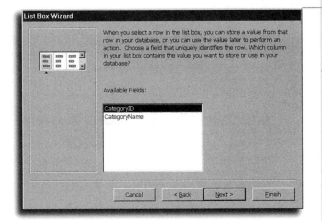

FIGURE 9.10

The default setting stores the contents of CategoryID.

9. The last dialog box prompts you to enter a descriptive label for the list box. For this example, enter Categories. Click **Finish**, and then click the **View** button 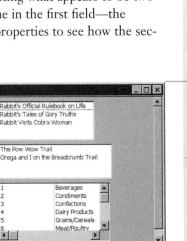 on the Form Design toolbar to display the form in Form view, as shown in Figure 9.11.

This list box is a little different from the one in the first example. You see, although you're selecting what appears to be two items, you're storing only the value in the first field—the CategoryID value. Now, look at properties to see how the second list box works.

Choosing the right data to store

In this example, you display data from one field while storing a corresponding value in another. Why? If your table contains an AutoNumber field or a primary key, that value is really the best choice for storing because of its uniqueness. Furthermore, most AutoNumber and primary key fields are almost always values, and values are easier to work with in VBA code because they don't require any special treatment. If you store a string, you'll have to enclose it in delimiters when you're ready to actually use it. That's easily done, but you might as well avoid the extra step if you can.

FIGURE 9.11

The bottom list box is bound to the Categories table and displays the contents of two fields.

What's a Table/Query List Box?

The wizard selected a table/query row source type. (The first control was a value list box.) A *table/query list box* refers to a table or query for its list. You simply specify the appropriate table or query in the Row Source property. If you add or delete an item in the bound table or query, Access updates the contents of the list box accordingly. That means you can add or delete a category to the Categories table and the list box reflects that change.

What About That *Row Source* Property?

Rather than specify the name of a table or query, the wizard enters the SQL statement

```
SELECT Categories.CategoryID, Categories.CategoryName
FROM Categories;
```

as the Row Source property. Used in this way, a SQL statement performs similar to a Select query. The list box displays the contents of the CategoryName and CategoryID fields from the Categories table.

SEE ALSO

➤ *Read more about Select queries on page 213*

Modifying the Wizard's SQL Statement

If a wizard creates a SQL statement that doesn't quite fit your needs, you can always alter it.

Change a query's SQL statement

1. To change a SQL statement when it's used as a property setting, open the appropriate form in Design View. For this exercise, work with the list box you created in the last exercise.

2. Be sure to open the property sheet if it isn't open.

3. Click the **Builder** button ▦ next to the Row Source property to launch the Query Builder. (Click the Row Source property field to make the button visible.)

4. The Query Builder displays the current settings in a query design grid (see Figure 9.12), which you can easily modify. For instance, to change the field's sort order, choose one option—Ascending, Descending, and [not sorted]—from that field's **Sort** drop-down list.

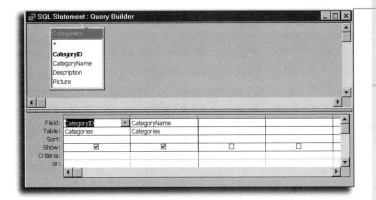

FIGURE 9.12
You can modify the default SQL statement by launching the Query Builder.

5. Suppose that you want to limit the items in the list box to only those that have a CategoryID value of 5 or less. You can easily do so by changing the SQL statement. Choose **SQL View** from the **View** button ⊞ ▾ on the Query Design toolbar to display the query's SQL statement. In this example, that statement is

```
SELECT Categories.CategoryID, Categories.CategoryName
FROM Categories;
```

To modify this statement, add a WHERE clause in the form

```
SELECT Categories.CategoryID, Categories.CategoryName
FROM Categories WHERE Categories.CategoryID <= 5;
```

Of course, you could just as easily add the expression <=5 to the query design grid.

6. To close the query design grid, click the **Close** button ✖ on the window's title bar. If you want to save the change, click **Yes**. When you return to Form View, the list box displays only those items that contain the value 5 or less in the CategoryID field.

SEE ALSO
➤ For more information on working in the query design grid, see page 81

The *Column Count* Property

The next property to review is the Column Count property. When you created the two-column list box in the section "Creating a Multiple-Column List Box," the List Box Wizard entered the value 2 as the control's Column Count setting so that the list box

Avoid a common `Column`
`Count` error

If you're tempted to use the
`Column Count` property to
hide a column, don't; you can't control the columns that the list box
displays. To hide a column, set that
column's width to 0 in the
`Column Widths` property box.
For instance, the sample list box displays two columns, and the default
width for both columns is 1". To
hide the first column, CategoryID,
change the control's **Column
Widths** property to 0"; 1". To
hide the second column,
CategoryName, use the setting
1";0". Hiding a column doesn't
mean it's off limits. To the contrary,
hiding a column in this manner is
similar to selecting the wizard's
Hide Key Column option.
However, you can hide any column,
and the wizard enables you to hide
just the primary key column.
Regardless of how you hide the column, you can still store that column's value.

The `Column Heads` property

If you set the `Column Heads`
property to **Yes**, the control will use
the first supplied item as the header.
In this case, the first item will have no
index value. The second line will
equal the index value of 0; the third
will equal 1, and so on.

displays two columns. This property must contain an integer
between 1 and the total number of fields in the bound table,
query, or—as is the case with the example—the `Row Source` property's SQL statement.

The *Column Heads* Property

The `Column Heads` property, when set to `Yes`, displays a single
row of column headings in your list box. Specifically, the property displays the bound field's `Caption` text. If the field has no
`Caption` text, the property defaults to the field name. The default
is `No`, which displays no headings.

The *Bound Column* Property

Remember the earlier discussion of which value the list box
stores? That quality is determined by the `Bound Column` property.
The default value is 1, which means the list box stores the value
from the first column—in the case of the list box example, the
CategoryID data. If you change that setting to the value 2, the
list box stores the value from the CategoryName column. Keep
in mind that this setting has nothing to do with the columns you
choose to display.

So, where does the list box store the selected value? In the example, which is an unbound control, Access stores the value internally. If your list box has a `Control Source`, the list box stores the
selected value in the bound field.

SEE ALSO

➤ *For more information on VBA and variables, see page 471*

If you set the `Bound Column` property to 0, the list box won't store
the selected item. Instead, the list box stores the selected item's
position as an integer within the list. This value is known as the
list index value. Furthermore, the list index values begin with 0,
not 1. For instance, in the first example in which the list box displays the book titles *Rabbit's Official Rulebook on Life*, *Rabbit's Tales
of Gory Truths*, and *Rabbit Visits Cobra Woman*, selecting *Rabbit's
Official Rulebook on Life* stores the value 0, selecting *Rabbit's Tables
of Gory Truths* stores 1, and selecting *Rabbit Visits Cobra Woman*
stores 2.

Working with Combo Box Controls

The combo box control is similar to the list box in most respects. Both controls display a list of items and can store your selections. However, there are a few differences. A combo box is a combination of a list box and a text box. You can select an item in the list or enter a value in the text box component. The combo box control also has a property that the list box control doesn't. That property, Limit to List, can limit the combo box text to only those items in the list.

Like the list box example shown earlier, the combo box can be bound to more than one column. If there's only one column, the value of the combo box equals the contents of the text box. If there's more than one column, the combo box equals the corresponding value from the bound column (see the Bound Column property).

Using the Combo Box Wizard

The earlier examples apply to both list boxes and combo boxes, so I won't repeat that information. Instead, create a combo box using the Combo Box Wizard and explore that control's Limit to List property.

Create a combo box with the Combo Box Wizard

1. Click **Forms** on the object bar in the Database window and then click **New** ⊞New on the Database window menu. Next, double-click **Design View** in the New Forms dialog box.

2. If Access doesn't open the Toolbox, click the **Toolbox** button ⚒ on the Form Design toolbar. To turn on the Control Wizards, click the **Control Wizards** icon ⬉ in the Toolbox.

3. Click the **Combo Box** tool ▦ in the Toolbox and then click inside the blank form. Select **I Want the Combo Box to Look Up the Values in a Table or Query** and click **Next**.

4. In the second dialog box, select the **Categories** table and click **Next**.

5. Move both fields to the **Selected Fields** list box and click **Next** twice.

6. In the final dialog box, click **Finish**.

7. Click the **View** button ⊞▾ on the Form Design toolbar to display the finished control. Click the control's arrow to display the list of categories shown in Figure 9.13. To return an item, select it from the list, and Access copies it to the text box component.

Automatically Opening the Drop-Down List

You can save yourself a keystroke by having Access automatically open a combo box's drop-down list when that control gets the focus. To accomplish this, attach a VBA procedure to the control's GotFocus event.

Automatically open a drop-down list

1. Open the form that contains your combo box in Design view.

2. Click the **Code** button 🔲 on the Form Design toolbar.

3. In the Visual Basic Editor, select the combo box from the module's Object drop-down list and the GotFocus event from the Procedure drop-down list. Be sure to use the combo box's correct name—the example uses Combo0.

4. Enter the following procedure. Your module should resemble the one in Figure 9.14.

```
Private Sub Combo0_GotFocus()
  Me![Combo0].Dropdown
End Sub
```

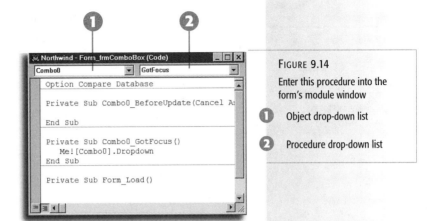

FIGURE 9.14

Enter this procedure into the form's module window

1 Object drop-down list

2 Procedure drop-down list

5. Return to the form and click the **View** button on the Form Design toolbar. (Click the VBE window's **Close** button to close the window.) As soon as the control receives the focus, VBA opens the drop-down list for you. If the control in question isn't the first control to receive focus, tabbing to that control opens its list.

SEE ALSO

➤ *Not familiar with VBA and its terms? See page 489*

The *Limit to List* Property

By default, the Limit to List property is Yes, which means you can't enter an item in the text box component of your combo box unless that entry exists in the same control's value list. If you try to enter an item not in the list, Access displays the error message shown in Figure 9.15. If you receive this message, click **OK** to clear it and then press **Esc** to delete the invalid entry.

FIGURE 9.15

Access won't let you enter an item not in the value list when the Limit to List property is set to Yes.

Displaying constants

A *constant* represents a value that doesn't change. You use *symbolic constants* in code when you want to refer to a variable that doesn't change. Although you can change a symbolic constant anytime you choose, you probably won't change them too often. To declare a symbolic constant, use the **Const** keyword instead of **Dim**.

Intrinsic constants

Access offers a number of constants, known as *intrinsic constants*. These words are reserved and, for the most part, ensure compatibility with other VBA-enabled applications. VBA intrinsic constants always start with letters, such as **ac**. (In earlier versions, the constants started with **A**.) These constants always represent a value that doesn't change. For instance, the **acDataErrContinue** constant in these steps is an example of an intrinsic constant. The last kind of constant is a *system-defined constant*—values such as **True**, **False**, and **Null**.

You don't have to contend with this error message if you don't want to. You can easily suppress it by using the control's **NotInList** event and the **acDataErrContinue** constant.

Suppress the *Limit to List* error message

1. Open in Design view any form that contains a combo box control—for this example, you can use the form you created in the last example.

2. Open the form's module by clicking the **Code** button on the Form Design toolbar.

3. Select the appropriate combo box from the Object drop-down list—continue to work with **Combo0**. Then, select **NotInList** from the Procedure drop-down list.

4. Enter the following procedure and close the Visual Basic Editor:

```
Private Sub Combo0_NotInList(NewData As String, _
                              Response As Integer)
  Response = acDataErrContinue
End Sub
```

5. Return to Form view by clicking the **View** button ⊞▾ on the Form Design toolbar.

6. Type test into the text box and press **Enter**. This time, Access doesn't display the error message—nor does it accept your value because you haven't supplied any further instruction. However, you can add code that displays a more descriptive message, deletes the inappropriate entry, or even accepts it and adds it to the value list. Press **Esc** to clear your entry.

If you try to enter a value that's not in the list, the Response argument equals 1. To override that constant in the procedure shown in Step 4, you applied the acDataErrContinue constant to the Response argument. To display a list of constants, open any module in Design View and click **Object Browser** 🔧 on the current toolbar (or press **Ctrl+J** or **F2**). After you display the browser, select the appropriate library.

The *Field List* Setting

The wizards can't create one final type of list and combo box control—a field list control. This control type lists the bound object's field names rather than the contents of the bound field. If you change a field name, or add or delete a field name, Access automatically updates the bound control accordingly. To create this type of list, set the control's Row Source Type property to Field List. Then, choose the appropriate object from the Row Source property.

Using Command Button Controls

A command button is one of the less complicated controls—it simply executes a task. For example, you can open a form or print a report by clicking a command button. Almost any task you can define with a macro or event procedure can be executed with the click of a command button. Fortunately, the Command Button Wizard anticipates quite a few of the possibilities—more than 30 of them, in fact.

Use the Command Button Wizard

1. Open a blank form, display the **Toolbox** ![toolbox icon], and make sure that the **Control Wizards** button ![control wizards icon] is selected.

2. Click the **Command Button** tool ![command button icon] in the Toolbox and then click inside the blank form.

3. Access launches the Command Button Wizard and displays its first dialog box (see Figure 9.16). The **Categories** list box displays a number of tasks the wizard can automate for you. The **Actions** list box displays the different choices for the selected **Categories** item. For this example, select **Report Operations** in the **Categories** list box and **Print Report** in the **Actions** list box. Click **Next** to continue.

Command button tasks

When you click items in the **Categories** list box, the wizard updates the list in the **Actions** list box accordingly. To familiarize yourself with all the wizard has to offer, select each item in the **Categories** list box.

FIGURE 9.16

The Command Button Wizard offers a variety of task possibilities.

1 Displays various tasks

2 Displays the appropriate choices for the selected task in the **Categories** list box

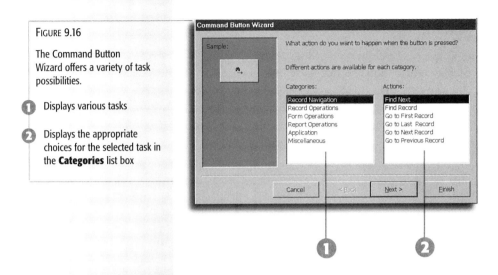

4. The next dialog box (see Figure 9.17) lists all the reports in the current application. For this example, choose **Invoice** and click **Next**.

FIGURE 9.17

The wizard lets you choose from the application's current reports.

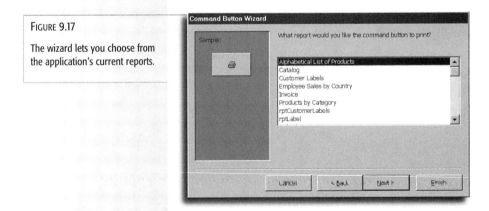

5. The following dialog box enables you to define the button's caption. Specifically, you can display descriptive text or an icon. The default option displays a Printer icon. However, for this example, you want to display text, so choose that option and then enter Print Invoice (see Figure 9.18). When you're finished, click **Next** to continue.

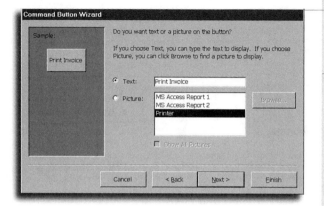

6. The final dialog box prompts you to give the button a meaningful name. For this example, use the name cmdPrintInvoice and click **Finish**.

7. You have a new command button on your blank form in Design view. If you open the form's module by clicking the **Code** button 🔧 , the code that the wizard entered appears (see Figure 9.19). This code prints the Invoice report when you click cmdPrintInvoice in Form view.

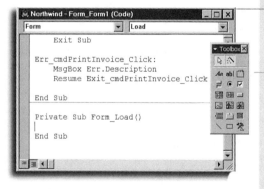

8. To see the button in Form view (see Figure 9.20), click the **View** button 🔳 ▾ on the Form Design toolbar.

FIGURE 9.20

The **Print Invoice** button prints
the Invoice report.

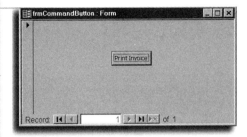

Working with the Option Group Control

An option group displays a set of choices, but it's different from
a list or combo box because you can select only one option from
the group. It's also a bit easier to use because you simply click
the appropriate choice. The group returns the value of the
selected item.

An option group consists of a group frame and a set of check
boxes, option buttons, or toggle buttons. When an option group
is bound to a field, only the group frame is bound to the field.
The Option Value property for each check box, toggle button, or
option button equals a unique value. When you select an option
in an option group, the option group returns the Option Value
setting of the selected item.

Using the Option Group Wizard

You can create a bound or unbound option group. If the group is
bound, the control returns the group's value to the bound field
(specified in the Control Source property). When the control
isn't bound, you'll want to store the group's value in a variable by
using VBA code.

The following example uses an unbound option group control to
change the mouse pointer. Specifically, it uses an option group to
offer a set of mouse pointer icons. When you choose an option,
the control returns your choice's value as the control's value.
Then, an event procedure uses that value to update the mouse
pointer.

Create an option group

1. Open a blank form, display the **Toolbox** 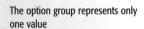, and make sure that the **Control Wizards** tool is selected.

2. Click the **Option Group** tool in the Toolbox and click inside the blank form. Access displays the wizard's first dialog box.

3. Enter a descriptive caption for each option. If you want to follow the example, enter the labels Select Arrow, I-Beam, NS Size, WE Size, and Hourglass (see Figure 9.21). After entering all the necessary labels, click **Next** to continue.

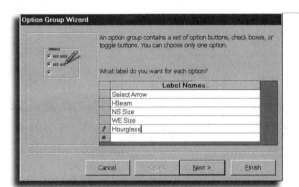

4. In the next dialog box, choose a default value (see Figure 9.22). For the example, select **Select Arrow** from the **Yes, the Default Choice Is** drop-down list. If you choose **No, I Don't Want a Default**, Access selects none of the options by default. Click **Next** to continue.

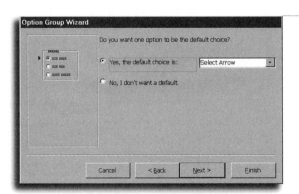

> **The option group represents only one value**
>
> Remember, the different options aren't bound to a particular field—only the completed control can be bound. For this reason, you need to enter descriptive labels for each option. Remember to press **Tab** and not **Enter** between each entry.

> **FIGURE 9.21**
> Enter descriptive labels for each option in the option group control.

> **FIGURE 9.22**
> You can specify a default option for the group.

5. The next dialog box displays default values for each option, which the wizard then applies as that option's `Option Value` property. Each value must be unique to the set. As you can see in Figure 9.23, new default values are entered rather than the wizard's. The values equal each option's designated `MousePointer` setting. (For more information on the `MousePointer` property and its settings, search on `MousePointer` in Help.) When you're done with these settings, click **Next** to continue.

FIGURE 9.23

You can accept the wizard's default value for each option, or assign your own.

1 The option button's descriptive labels

2 The option returns these values when you choose an option.

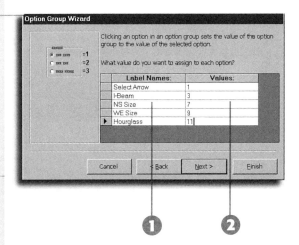

6. The following dialog box gives you several display options. The sample control shown in the left side of the dialog box updates accordingly as you select different options in each category. The example uses the **Option Buttons** and the **Raised** settings (see Figure 9.24). After you make your selections, click **Next** to continue.

7. In the final dialog box, enter a descriptive label, click **Finish**, and return to Design view.

8. Open the frame group's property sheet and enter `grpMouseSettings` as the name. (Make sure that the property sheet title bar reads Option Group.)

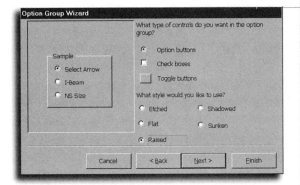

FIGURE 9.24
Select the appropriate display options.

9. Click the **Code** button [⬚] on the Form Design toolbar. Choose **grpMouseSettings** from the Object drop-down list and **AfterUpdate** from the Procedure drop-down list. Then, enter the following procedure:

```
Private Sub grpMouseSettings_AfterUpdate()
  Screen.MousePointer = Me!grpMouseSettings
End Sub
```

10. Close the Visual Basic Editor and click the **View** button [⬚ ▾] on the Form Design toolbar to open the form in Form view.

11. When you click an option, VBA updates the mouse pointer accordingly (see Figure 9.25, which shows the **Hourglass** option selected). To return the mouse pointer to its default state, click the **Select Arrow** option.

FIGURE 9.25
Select the **Hourglass** option.

Storing, Controlling, and Manipulating Data

Looking Up Values and Lists

Learn how lookup fields store one thing and display another

Use *DLookUp()* to return a value from a specific set of records

What's a Lookup?

The nature of a database—in which storage is done in rows and columns—lends itself to lookup tasks. A *lookup* task is one that returns a value or list by referring to coordinates. Those coordinates can be index values or matching criteria. For example, if you fill a combo box with three columns from a table or query, you can use the Column property to return data from any of the three columns. Or, you can use a DLookUp() function to find the first record that matches specific criteria and then return data from another field in that same record.

SEE ALSO

➤ *See an interesting use of the* Column *property on page 364*

What's a Lookup Field?

One drawback of a normalized table is that you sometimes get stuck viewing identifying values rather than a customer's name or a product's name. For instance, if you're tracking orders, it makes more sense to list the product's identifying value—perhaps a product number—than to list the product's name. That's because the value field is more likely to be the primary or foreign key than the field that contains the product's name. However, seeing the product's identification number probably isn't all that helpful because most of you won't readily relate a field of numbers to the product.

The Northwind database that comes with Access uses the lookup field feature in the Order Details table (see Figure 10.1). You can't tell by looking, but the Product field is actually a lookup field. This field is actually a Number data type that stores a unique value for each product.

Figure 10.2 shows the same table without the Product field's lookup capability. Rather than display the product's name, the Product field displays the ProductID number. Unfortunately, these values aren't all that helpful in identifying the actual product. To remedy that, you can make the Product field a lookup field by running the Lookup Wizard.

Order Details : Table

Order ID	Product	Unit Price	Quantity	Discount
10248	Queso Cabrales	$14.00	12	0%
10248	Singaporean Hokkien Fried Mee	$9.80	10	0%
10248	Mozzarella di Giovanni	$34.80	5	0%
10249	Tofu	$18.60	9	0%
10249	Manjimup Dried Apples	$42.40	40	0%
10250	Jack's New England Clam Chowder	$7.70	10	0%
10250	Manjimup Dried Apples	$42.40	35	15%
10250	Louisiana Fiery Hot Pepper Sauce	$16.80	15	15%
10251	Gustaf's Knäckebröd	$16.80	6	5%
10251	Ravioli Angelo	$15.60	15	5%
10251	Louisiana Fiery Hot Pepper Sauce	$16.80	20	0%
10252	Sir Rodney's Marmalade	$64.80	40	5%
10252	Geitost	$2.00	25	5%
10252	Camembert Pierrot	$27.20	40	0%
10253	Gorgonzola Telino	$10.00	20	0%
10253	Chartreuse verte	$14.40	42	0%

Record: 1 of 2155

FIGURE 10.1
The Product field displays product names, even though it's actually a Number field that stores unique values.

Order Details : Table

Order ID	Product	Unit Price	Quantity	Discount
10248	11	$14.00	12	0%
10248	42	$9.80	10	0%
10248	72	$34.80	5	0%
10249	14	$18.60	9	0%
10249	51	$42.40	40	0%
10250	41	$7.70	10	0%
10250	51	$42.40	35	15%
10250	65	$16.80	15	15%
10251	22	$16.80	6	5%
10251	57	$15.60	15	5%
10251	65	$16.80	20	0%
10252	20	$64.80	40	5%
10252	33	$2.00	25	5%
10252	60	$27.20	40	0%
10253	31	$10.00	20	0%
10253	39	$14.40	42	0%

Record: 1 of 2155

FIGURE 10.2
The Product field displays a value, which doesn't readily identify the product for you.

Deleting a lookup field

The Product field's lookup capability was deleted in Figure 10.2. The easiest way to do so is to open the table in Design view, click the Lookup tab in the table's Properties section, and then change the Display Control from Combo Box to Text Box.

Exploring the Lookup Wizard

The Lookup Wizard creates a field that displays one of two types of lists:

- **Lookup list**—An updatable list based on the contents of a particular field in another table or query.
- **Value list**—A fixed list of items that you enter.

As you saw in the earlier example, displaying the appropriate product's name is much more beneficial than displaying the same product's ProductID value. However, you need to maintain the value field because ProductID is a foreign key. The primary key is in the Products table. In this table, ProductID is an AutoNumber data type.

There seems to be a conflict: You need to store each product's corresponding ProductID value from the Product table, but you want to see the product's name. Fortunately, by using the Lookup Wizard, you can tell Access to do just that.

Create a lookup field in Datasheet view

1. Open the table to which you're adding the lookup field in Datasheet view by double-clicking that table in the Database window. Or, select that table in the Database window and then click **Open**. For this example, use the Order Details table.

2. Select the field to which you're adding the lookup capability by clicking that column's header cell (the gray cell that contains the field's name). In this case, it's the Product field. (The field's name is really ProductID, but the header shows just Product.)

3. Choose **Lookup Column** from the **Insert** menu to display the Lookup Wizard's first dialog box (see Figure 10.3). The first option, **I Want the Lookup Column to Look Up the Values in a Table or Query**, creates a dynamic lookup list. This means that you can add new items to or delete existing items from the associated table, and the list automatically reflects those changes. The second option, **I Will Type in the Values That I Want,** allows you to create a fixed list for the lookup column. In this case, you want the lookup column to look up the values in a table or query option, so retain the wizard's default. Click **Next** when you're ready to continue.

4. The second window prompts you for the table that contains the items you want to display. The View options at the bottom of the window update the list box with the appropriate objects: tables, queries, or both. Remember, the table or query you choose must contain the primary key that matches the current table's foreign key. To continue with the example, select the Products table (see Figure 10.4). After you choose a table, a query, or both, click **Next**.

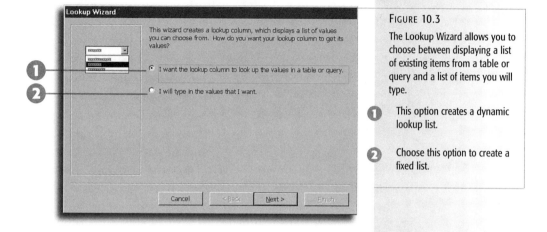

FIGURE 10.3

The Lookup Wizard allows you to choose between displaying a list of existing items from a table or query and a list of items you will type.

1 This option creates a dynamic lookup list.

2 Choose this option to create a fixed list.

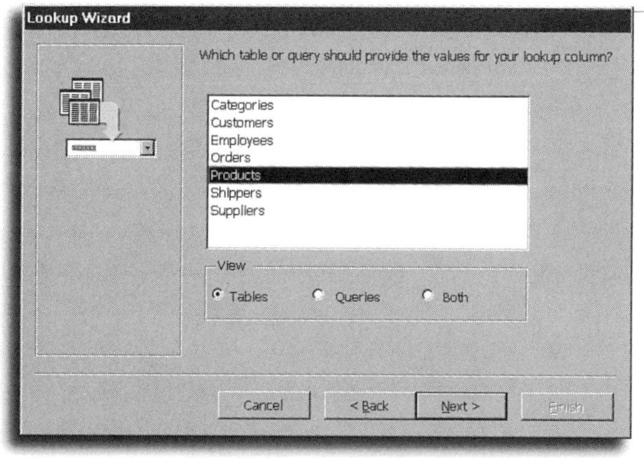

FIGURE 10.4

Display the contents of a field in the Products table.

5. In the next dialog box, identify the field that contains the items you want to display in your lookup list (see Figure 10.5). The **Available Fields** list displays the fields in the table or query you selected in the previous table. Simply double-click the appropriate field in the **Available Fields** list box to move it to the **Selected Fields** list. Click **Next** to continue.

FIGURE 10.5

Select the field that contains the items you want to display in your lookup field's list.

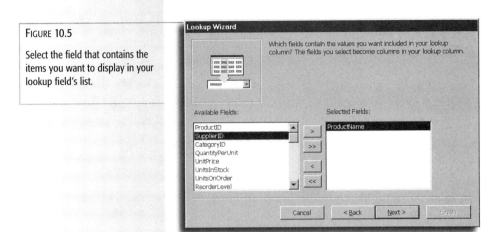

6. The next dialog box gives you the opportunity to change the column's width and to display the primary key field. You can apply the Best Fit property (which increases the width of the field to accommodate the longest item) by double-clicking the heading field's right border. The heading field is the gray cell that contains the field name. Or, you can simply expand that border until you're satisfied with the column's width.

The **Hide Key Column (Recommended)** option allows you to hide or display the primary key field that matches your current table's foreign key. You'll probably want to hide the primary key field, which is why the option is selected by default. If you want to display it, simply deselect this option. You don't want to display the primary key field, as shown in Figure 10.6. Click **Next** to continue.

7. The final dialog box allows you to enter descriptive text for your lookup field, such as the string "Product Name". You can also display more information on customizing the lookup field by selecting the **Display Help on Customizing the Lookup Column** option. For now, skip this option and click **Finish**. If you're asked to save the table, do so.

Figure 10.7 displays the results. The Product field now displays the corresponding product name from the Products table instead of a value. The table still remembers that value, but it doesn't display it.

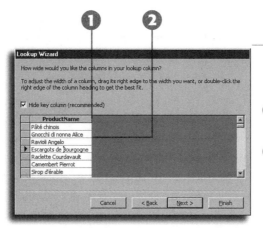

Now when you add a new record, you can choose an item from the Product field's lookup list rather than try to remember its identification number. This works because Access stores the product's identification number (the value from the ProductID field), not the product's name. Access simply displays the product name because it's more convenient.

You can also create a lookup field in Design view. The resulting lookup field is the same as the field you create in Datasheet view.

A lookup field is an inherited property

Access treats a lookup field as any other table property. If you base a form on a table that contains a lookup field, Access will pass on the lookup field's behavior and properties to the field's corresponding bound control.

In this next example, you'll create a lookup field in Design view and type your own list items rather than display a list from a table or query.

Create a lookup field in Design view

1. Open the table to which you want to add the lookup field in Design view by selecting that table in the Database window (this example uses **Order Details**) and then clicking **Design**.

2. Open the appropriate field's **Data Type** drop-down list. Figure 10.8 shows the ProductID field's drop-down list. Select the **Lookup Wizard** option.

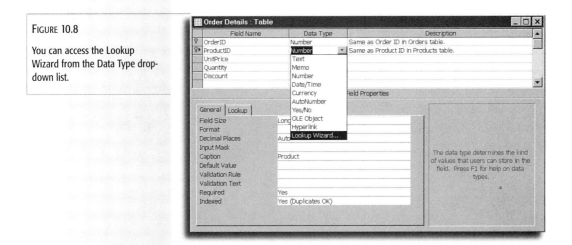

FIGURE 10.8

You can access the Lookup Wizard from the Data Type drop-down list.

3. After you launch the lookup wizard, Access displays the first dialog box (refer to Figure 10.3). This time, choose **I Will Type in the Values That I Want** and click **Next**.

4. The second dialog box for this example is different from the second dialog box in the preceding steps. This time, the wizard wants you to enter the lookup items. You also can

change the number of columns the lookup field displays. Retain the default, which is 1. Figure 10.9 shows the items you've entered for your lookup list. After you make the appropriate entries, click **Next**.

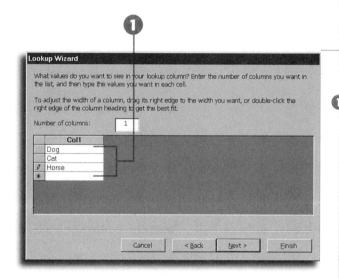

FIGURE 10.9

You can enter your own list items.

❶ Access displays the items you've entered in the field's lookup list.

5. In the final dialog box, enter descriptive text for your lookup field—such as Product Name—and click **Finish**.

6. Display the table in Datasheet view by clicking the **Datasheet View** button 🖽 ▾ on the Table Design toolbar. When Access asks you if you want to save the table, click **Yes**.

This time, there's a big difference. Access didn't write over the existing values with a corresponding item from the lookup list, which makes sense because there's no way for Access to relate an item to a value. You can choose an item from the lookup list, as shown in Figure 10.10, or you can leave it as is and use the list for new records you enter.

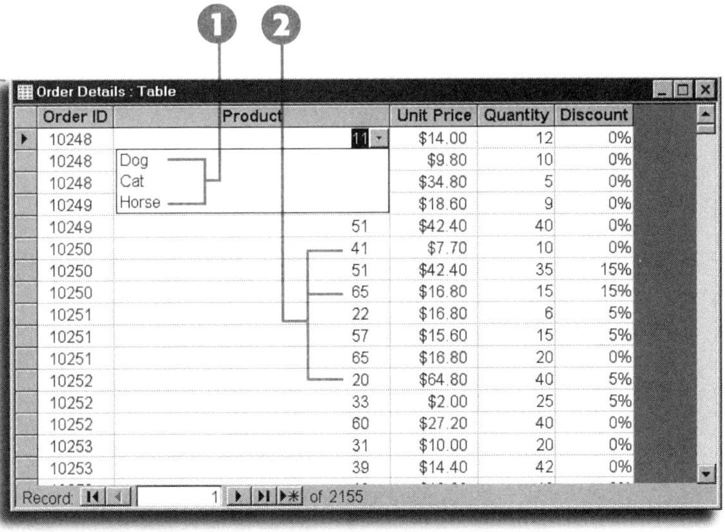

FIGURE 10.10

The new lookup field's drop-down list displays the items you've entered.

1 The lookup list contains the items you entered by using the wizard.

2 The table retains the original values; you can keep them or choose an item from the lookup list to overwrite them.

Order ID	Product	Unit Price	Quantity	Discount
10248	11	$14.00	12	0%
10248	Dog	$9.80	10	0%
10248	Cat	$34.80	5	0%
10249	Horse	$18.60	9	0%
10249	51	$42.40	40	0%
10250	41	$7.70	10	0%
10250	51	$42.40	35	15%
10250	65	$16.80	15	15%
10251	22	$16.80	6	5%
10251	57	$15.60	15	5%
10251	65	$16.80	20	0%
10252	20	$64.80	40	5%
10252	33	$2.00	25	5%
10252	60	$27.20	40	0%
10253	31	$10.00	20	0%
10253	39	$14.40	42	0%

Record: 1 of 2155

Using the *DLookUp()* Function

One of Access's built-in functions, DLookUp(), has long been a staple in many applications. You use this function to return a value from a specific field in a set domain. (A *domain* is a defined set of records.) This versatile function can be used most any-where—in a macro, a procedure, a query expression, or even a calculated control.

You'll use DLookUp() to return (or display) data that's out of the current scope. In this sense, *scope* refers to the active source, which can be a bound field. For instance, in a bound combo box, you might use DLookUp() to return a corresponding field entry from the current record. On the other hand, you can also use DLookUp() to look up data in another table or query. Suppose that the current recordset contains identification numbers that relate to a specific company name in another table. Rather than work with identification values that mean nothing, you could use DLookUp() to return the corresponding company's name.

SEE ALSO

➤ *For a broader definition of scope, see page 478*

You'll use this function with the following syntax:

DLookUp(*expression*, *domain*[, *criteria*])

expression identifies the field that contains the value you want to return. This argument is pretty versatile—it can be a simple reference to a field, or it can perform a calculation. However, this argument can't include another domain aggregate or SQL aggregate function.

What's a Domain or SQL Aggregate?

Aggregate functions return information about a set of records. DLookUp() is a domain aggregate because it considers a specific set of records in its search (the *domain* argument). There are two types of aggregate functions: domain and SQL. Both do the same thing, but you use them in different ways. Domain aggregates can be used in a VBA module but not a SQL statement. SQL aggregates are used within a SQL statement but can't be called in a VBA module. However, you can use both in a calculated control. The aggregate functions are as follows:

Function	Description
DAvg()	Returns the average from a specific field within a specific set of records.
DCount()	Counts the number of records within a specific set.
DLookUp()	Returns a value from a specific field in a set of records.
DMin() and DMax()	Return the minimum or maximum value in a specific field within a specific set of records.
DStDev() and DStDevP()	Estimate the standard deviation in a specific field of values within a specific set of records. Use DStDevP() to evaluate a population and DStDev() to evaluate a population sample.
DSum()	Returns the total of the values in a specific field within a specific set of records.

continues…

DLookUp( ) results

If DLookUp( ) finds an appropriate value, it returns that value. If the function finds more than one possible value, DLookUp( ) returns the first value it encounters. If the function finds nothing, it returns null. Therefore, it's a good idea to check the results of a DLookUp( ) for a null value in the form IsNull(DLookUp(*expression, domain, criteria*)) before proceeding with the results. Another solution is to use the Nz( ) function to return a default when no value is found. For instance, the expression Nz(DLookUp(*expression, domain, criteria*), DefaultValue) returns DefaultValue instead of null if the DLookUp( ) function doesn't find a matching value.

...continued

Function	Description
DVar() and DVarP()	Estimate variance across a specific field in a specific set of records. Use DVarP() to evaluate population and DVar() to evaluate a population sample.
DFirst()	Returns the first value in a specific field within a specific set of records.
Dlast()	Finds the last value in a specific field within a specific set of records.

The second argument for DLookUp(), *domain*, is a string expression that identifies the set of records. The optional string expression *criteria* restricts the range of data. If you're familiar with SQL, you can compare the *criteria* argument to a SQL WHERE clause (but you don't include the word WHERE). If you omit the *criteria* argument, DLookUp() will consider all the records specified in *domain*. When you refer to a field by using *criteria*, that field must be within *domain*.

Now, suppose that you have a form based on the Order Details table, similar to the one shown in Figure 10.11. (The lookup field from the Order Details table was deleted before this example was created with the AutoForm Wizard.) As you can see, the Product value of 11 doesn't tell you very much.

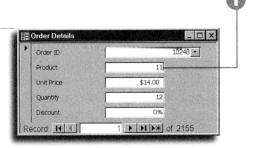

FIGURE 10.11

The form displays the real contents of the ProductID field—a value, not the corresponding product's name.

❶ The ProductID value isn't particularly helpful

SEE ALSO
➤ *For help in creating the form in this example, see page 118*

In the previous example, you created a lookup field to display the record's product name. As is usually the case with Access, there's more than one way to get the job done. You'll need to decide which solution best fits the situation at hand. This time, you see how to use DLookUp()to do this. Although the lookup field might seem easier to create, the DLookUp() function affects only the form.

Use *DLookUp()*

1. Open the object to which you're adding the function in Design view. You're going to add a function to the Orders form to return the customer's phone number, so open that form.

2. Add a text box below the City field in the upper-left corner. To delete the control's label component, click anywhere in the form's background to cancel the current selection; click the label's top-left selection handle to select just the label; and then press the **Delete** key. (See Chapter 16, "Adding Controls to Forms and Reports," to learn how to add a control to a form.)

3. Open the text box's property sheet by double-clicking the control or by selecting the control and clicking the **Properties** button 🖼 on the **Form Design** toolbar. Select the **Control Source** property and enter the expression
   ```
   =DLookUp("[Phone]","Customers","[CustomerID]='" &
   [Forms]![Orders]![CustomerID] & "'")
   ```

   You want to return the phone number, [Phone], from the Customers table, where the table's CustomerID equals the current record's CustomerID value.

4. To see the results, click the **Form View** button 📧▾ on the **Form Design** toolbar. As you can see in Figure 10.12, the additional text box displays the current customer's phone number.

FIGURE 10.12

The text box you added displays the result of a DLookUp() function—the customer's phone number.

1 A DLookUp() function is added to this text box.

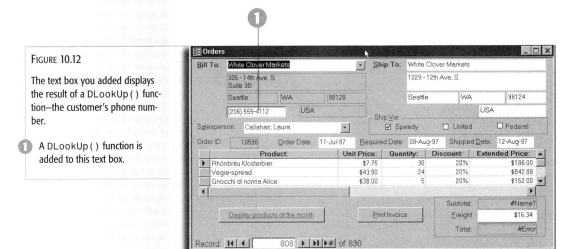

About Those Delimiters

You might have noticed that the DLookUp() function contains a few extra characters—specifically, the single and double quotation characters (' and "). Used in this manner, these characters are known as *delimiters*, predefined characters that separate one component from another. Specifically, you included a pair of single quotes (') within the criteria argument because the *reference* argument refers to a text field. You must delimit a string in a WHERE clause by using the following syntax:

```
"[field you're matching]=' " & reference & " ' "
```

Don't include the spaces between the different delimiters—double and single quotes. They've been added to this example so that it's easier to discern which characters you've used and in what order.

SEE ALSO

➤ *If you're not familiar with the concatenation operator (&), read about it on page 328*

A SQL WHERE clause also requires delimiters. Simply substitute the *reference* argument with the variable. However, if the variable contains a value, it requires no delimiters.

If your variable contains a date or time value, use the # delimiter in the following syntax:

```
"[control you're matching]=# " & variable & " # "
```

SEE ALSO

➤ *For an example of using a SQL* WHERE *clause, see page 363*

For an example of using a SQL WHERE *clause, see page 363*

Replacing delimiters with the Chr() function

Working with delimiters—especially the string delimiters—can be difficult. You can easily avoid problems by replacing delimiters with a Chr() function. Chr(34) returns double quotes, so you can concatenate double quotes in the form
```
"[control you're
matching]=" &
Chr(34) & variable
& Chr(34).
```

Defining and Working with Relationships

Understand why you need relationships

See how to create, modify, and delete relationships

Understand the types of joins available

Bringing Your Information Together

When you normalize your tables, you can begin entering data and then manipulating, analyzing, and reporting that data. To interact with your database, you'll base forms and reports on your tables (you can also base forms and reports on queries). However, all the data you want to work with won't always reside in one table.

This is where relationships come into play. For your purposes, a *relationship* is an association (link) between two related fields in different tables. In this sense, *related* means *the same*. In other words, a relationship can exist between two tables that share the same data. For instance, if you assign a product number to each product, you'll also use that number to identify each product in an order table, an invoice table, a shipping table, and so on. Therefore, the data type would be the same, and that's the critical issue. The field name doesn't have to match, but the data type does, except when the primary key is an AutoNumber. Then Access relates the AutoNumber field to a Number field.

What's a recordset?

A *recordset* is the collection of records that's attached to an object at any given time. A query's record-set depends on the tables you add to the query. A form's recordset is determined by its **Record Source** setting (the same is true with reports). You also can use VBA to create or modify an object's recordset.

Benefits of Using Relationships

Access automatically joins related fields between tables if you create a relationship between them. As a result, you can easily base queries, forms, and reports on more than one table. Using multitable queries for forms or reports increases your application's flexibility by allowing you to work with one recordset that's based on more than one table.

Subforms and subreports also benefit from relationships. If a relationship exists between the main form and the subform, Access automatically displays records in the subform that relate to the main form's record.

Another benefit is the ability to enforce *referential integrity*, a set of rules that determine when you can add, modify, and delete records. If there's no relationship, you can't enforce these rules.

SEE ALSO

➤ *Learn more about the normalizing process on page 13*

How Relationships Between Objects Work

At this point, you might be wondering exactly what a relationship does. It pulls associated (related) data together. For instance, if you try to run a query on two unrelated tables, you'll get a mishmash of data that means absolutely nothing to anybody. If you create a relationship between those tables, however, the query is more discriminating about which records to include in the results. The same is true with subforms and subreports. Without a relationship, a subform or a subreport displays all its attached records, not just those that pertain to the record in the main form. The great part is that Access accomplishes all this with very little help from you.

Now look at the three different types of relationships.

One-to-One Relationships

Suppose that you have two tables. Each record in one table is related to only one record in the other table. That's a *one-to-one relationship*, probably the least common type. There doesn't have to be a related record, but there can be no more than one. Also, a subform based on this arrangement would probably be overkill because there's no data to weed out. You might as well display the matching records from both tables together in the main form.

One-to-Many Relationships

A *one-to-many relationship* is probably the most common relationship between two tables. With this arrangement, the "many" table can contain more than one record for each record in the "one" table. Furthermore, the many table doesn't have to contain a related record for each record in the one table. However, every record in the many table must relate to only one record in the one table.

For instance, your supplier table contains only one record for each supplier. Furthermore, each record in your product table relates to a particular supplier. Either you can have many records in the product table for each supplier, or you can have no records in the product table for a supplier. You can't, however, have a record in the products table from a supplier that doesn't exist in the supplier table.

Resolving many-to-many
duplications

If you end up with a many-to-many
relationship, you should create a
third table whose primary key is
based on the original tables' primary key fields (the primary key
from both tables) to create a
multiple-field primary key. This table
has a one-to-many relationship with
both tables. Each record in the first
table can have many related records
in the new table, but each record in
the new table relates to only one
record in the first table—likewise
with the second table.

Many-to-Many Relationships

The *many-to-many relationship* is the problem child of the group
because it requires a third table. In a many-to-many relationship,
one table can contain many records for each record in the other
table. For example, a specific order in an orders table can relate
to many products in a products table. Also, a product in the
products table can appear in any number of orders in the orders
table.

Ordinarily, you'd have only one record for each product in the
products table, and only one record in the orders table for each
order. However, to maintain the relationship, you'd actually end
up with several records for each order—a record for each product in each order.

Primary Keys and Relationships

The easiest way to define a relationship is to make the related
field a *primary key*. You won't just pick a field at random. Rather,
a primary key contains unique values—many developers use the
AutoNumber data type to ensure that each table has a field of
unique entries. For instance, the preceding example uses a table
for product numbers, orders, invoices, and shipping data. Often
your data, such as a product or employee number, provides a
natural primary key. Beyond containing a unique value, each
field in your table must be related to the primary key field. In
other words, all other data must describe or enhance the primary
key field.

Don't want an automatic
relationship?

Access automatically creates a relationship between two tables when
both tables contain the same field
data type and field size, and one of
those fields is a primary key. If you
don't want Access to create these
relationships automatically, turn off
this feature by choosing **Options**
from the **Tools** menu. Then, on the
Tables/Queries page, deselect the
Enable AutoJoin option in the
Query Design section.

In this example, the product number table would be the parent
table because it contains the primary key field. When you make
the product number field a primary key, Access automatically
relates any other tables that contain the same field. These related
tables will be *child* tables, otherwise known as a *foreign key*.
Access doesn't mark a foreign key as it does a primary key, so
don't look for foreign keys in Design view.

You should also know a few other things about relationships:

- Access won't automatically relate tables that don't have a primary key.

- Even if a primary key and foreign key exist, Access won't
  create a relationship if the field names don't match.

- You can manually relate fields when a primary key doesn't exist.

- You can't create a relationship between two fields of differing data types or field size, except to join an AutoNumber to a Number field.

SEE ALSO

➤ *Learn more about primary and foreign keys on pages 19*

➤ *For a definition of the* AutoNumber *data type, see page 68*

Using the Relationships Window

You can view relationships between tables and queries in the Relationships window (see Figure 11.1, which shows the Northwind database's Relationships window). You'll also see the main toolbar buttons you need to use for this window.

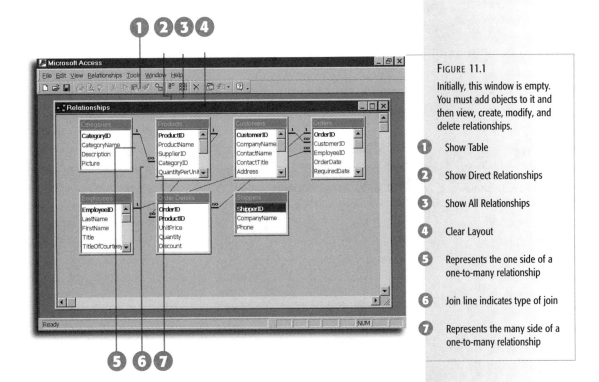

FIGURE 11.1

Initially, this window is empty. You must add objects to it and then view, create, modify, and delete relationships.

1 Show Table

2 Show Direct Relationships

3 Show All Relationships

4 Clear Layout

5 Represents the one side of a one-to-many relationship

6 Join line indicates type of join

7 Represents the many side of a one-to-many relationship

Explore the Relationships window

1. Open the Northwind sample database that comes with Access.

2. Choose **Relationships** from the **Tools** menu (press **Alt+T+R**). Access displays the database's Relationships window (refer to Figure 11.1). This database already has several established relationships. (Until you add objects to the window, Access opens the Show Table dialog box along with the window.)

3. To clear the current layout, click the **Clear Layout** button ⊠ on the Relationship toolbar. Confirm your request by clicking **Yes** in the resulting warning message box. (It's not recommended that you actually clear the Relationships window if you're working in an established application.)

To add a table or query, click the **Show Table** button ⬚ or press **Alt+R+T**. The Show Table dialog box appears (see Figure 11.2), containing three tabbed pages: **Tables**, **Queries**, and **Both**. As you click each tab, Access updates the contents of that page accordingly. For instance, if you click the **Tables** tab, Access displays all the tables in the database. The **Queries** tab displays all the queries, and the **Both** tab displays all tables and queries.

FIGURE 11.2

The Show Table dialog box gives you access to the database's tables and queries.

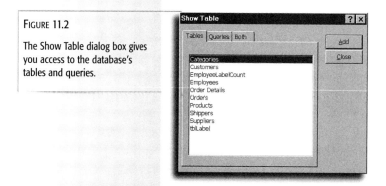

4. Double-click an object in the Show Table dialog box. When you've added all the objects you want to add, click the **Close** button.

Access displays a join line to indicate a relationship between two tables or queries. Most relationships are based on an *inner join*, which means that Access selects only those records from both tables that have a matching value in the related field. In other words, if the Categories table has a value in the CategoryID field that doesn't exist in the Products table (and vice versa), that record isn't included in any query results.

The 1 and the infinity sign (∞) tell you that the relationship is a one-to-many relationship. More specifically, the Categories table is the one side, and the Products table is the many side. The Products table can have many records related to any one record in the Categories table. The presence of the 1 and the infinity sign also tells you that the relationship forces *referential integrity*, rules that protect your data by restricting when you can add and delete records. If the relationship doesn't force referential integrity, Access displays the join line but no symbols.

SEE ALSO
➤ *For another look at relationships, see page 18*

Deleting Relationships

You can delete a relationship at any time. Select the join line and press **Delete**. If you delete a table from the Relationships window, Access deletes the table and the join line from the window. However, Access doesn't delete the table from the database or delete the relationship.

Delete and add objects and relationships

1. Open the Northwind database or any database that has related objects. From the **Tools** menu, choose **Relationships**. (You can also click the **Relationships** icon ⊞ or press **Alt+T+R**.)

Adding objects to the Relationships window

You can select objects in the Show Table dialog box and then add them to the Relationships window in several ways: by selecting an object and clicking the **Add** button; by double-clicking an object; by selecting an object and pressing **Enter**; or by using the arrow keys to highlight an object, and then pressing **Alt+A**.

Resizing the field lists

In the Relationships window, Access displays the Products table with a scrollbar. To eliminate the scrollbar and increase the depth of this field table to see all the fields at once, position the mouse pointer on the lower border of the field list and left-click—but don't release. Then pull that border down until you can see all the field names and the scrollbar disappears.

An alternative way to add an object to the Relationships window

In this exercise, you've deleted a table from the Relationships window and then used the Show Tables dialog box to display it again. You can also use the **Show Direct Relationships** button [8°] or the **Show All Relationships** button [🏛] on the Relationships toolbar. The **Show Direct Relationships** button displays all the objects related to the current object; the **Show All Relationships** button shows all the related objects in the database. However, using either button displays not only the table you deleted, but also any others related to it.

2. If the window is empty, click the **Show Table** button [🔳] on the Relationship toolbar and add two or more related objects to the window. Use the Products and Categories tables from the previous exercise.

3. Click a table list box (it doesn't matter which one) and press **Delete** to remove it from the workspace.

4. Remember, you didn't delete the table or the relationship from the database; you only deleted those objects from the window. To prove this, add the Categories table back to the window by clicking the **Show Table** button [🔳] and double-clicking the Categories table in the Show Table dialog box. Then click the **Close** button to return to the Relationships window. The window is the same as it was before you deleted the field list box.

5. To delete the relationship, select the join line between the two field list boxes and press **Delete**. When Access asks you to confirm the choice, click **Yes**. Access deletes the join line but leaves the field list boxes, as shown in Figure 11.3.

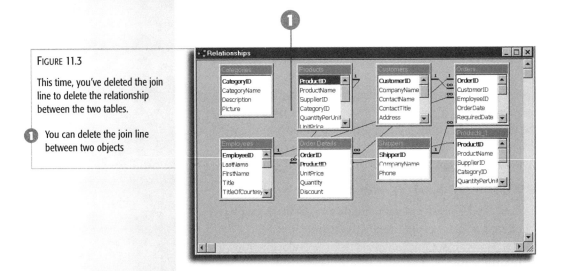

FIGURE 11.3

This time, you've deleted the join line to delete the relationship between the two tables.

① You can delete the join line between two objects

Creating a Relationship

Adding a primary key is only one way to create a relationship. In the Relationships window, you can create a relationship by dragging the related field from one field list to the same field in another table.

Create a relationship—an alternative way

1. Use the last window from the previous exercise, or open the Relationships window and delete a join line.

2. To join (or rejoin) the two tables, click the related field in one list—but don't release the mouse button. Then, drag that field to the other table list and drop it on top of the same field. In this case, the CategoryID field is dragged from the Categories table to the Products table.

3. When you release the mouse button to drop the field, Access displays the dialog box shown in Figure 11.4. The **Table/Query** and **Related Table/Query** drop-down lists display the two objects you're relating (joining). You can change the related field by selecting another field from either drop-down list. You probably won't use this option very often.

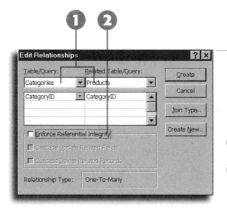

Creating relationships in the query design grid

If a relationship doesn't exist between two tables and you create one in a query's query design grid by dragging a primary key field from one table to another, you create a temporary relationship for that object. This relationship affects only that query. Similarly, if a permanent relationship does exist and you delete a join line between two tables or queries in a query design grid, you don't permanently delete the relationship—you delete the relationship for that query only. To create or delete a permanent and global relationship, you must use the Relationships window.

FIGURE 11.4

Use this dialog box to define the relationship you're creating between the Products and Categories tables.

1. The related tables and fields

2. This option protects the integrity of your data

- The **Enforce Referential Integrity** option lets you protect your data. Specifically, this feature keeps you from adding or deleting records inappropriately:

  - You can't add to the many table if there's no related record in the one table.

  - You can't delete a record from the one table if related records exist in the many table.

- If you choose **Enforce Referential Integrity**, you can then choose from the Cascade options, but it isn't necessary to do so. The **Cascade Update Related Fields** option affects your updates:

- If you select this option and then update a primary key field in the one table, Access updates any corresponding foreign key values in the many table.

- If you leave this feature turned off, Access won't allow you to change a primary key value in the one table if the many table contains related records.

  The **Cascade Deleted Related Records** option is similar to **Cascade Update Related Fields**, except that it affects the way you delete records:

  - When this option is selected, Access deletes related records from the many table if you delete the corresponding primary key record in the one table.

  - If you don't select this option, Access won't allow you to delete a primary key record in the one table if the many table contains related records.

4. Click the **Join Type** button to display the dialog box in Figure 11.5. This dialog box allows you to define the type of join the relationship produces. A *join* determines how the relationship between two tables affects the result of a bound query. Specifically, the join decides which records are selected or acted on. There are two types of joins:

    Inner join   The default join type, which selects only those records from both tables that have a matching value in the related field

Outer join	Includes all the records from one table and only those records in the second that match the value in the related field

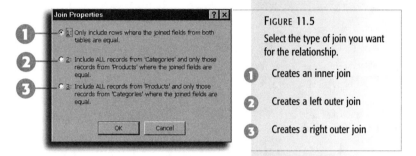

FIGURE 11.5

Select the type of join you want for the relationship.

1. Creates an inner join

2. Creates a left outer join

3. Creates a right outer join

5. You don't want to change the default join type, so click **OK** to return to the Relationships dialog box. Select the **Enforce Referential Integrity** option, and then click the **Create** button. The resulting join line appears similar to the original one you saw in Figure 11.1. It displays the 1 beside the Categories table and the infinity sign beside the Products table.

Understanding Joins

Try not to let joins frustrate you—they are really simple. For instance, Figure 11.6 displays the logic behind a simple inner join. Viewed this way, the concept is easy to grasp. If an inner join relationship exists between the Categories and Products tables, a bound query returns only those records from both tables that have a matching value in the related field, which is CategoryID. Most multitable queries rely on an inner join relationship.

FIGURE 11.6

An inner join is easy to understand if you think of the result as the intersection of two circles.

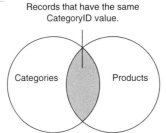

Records that have the same CategoryID value.

Categories   Products

Why left and right?

The terms *left* and *right* in an outer join come from traditional database design, in which the one table is always drawn to the left of the many table.

An outer join is a bit more complex because it includes all the records from one table and only those records from the second table that match the related field's value. You're probably wondering which table is which, right? Either table is correct. You see, there are two types of outer joins: a *left outer join* and a *right outer join*. A left outer join includes all the records from the one table and only the matching records from the many table (see Figure 11.7). A right outer join includes all the records from the many table and only the matching records from the one table (see Figure 11.8).

FIGURE 11.7

A left outer join includes the entire one table, but only records from the many table that match the primary key value.

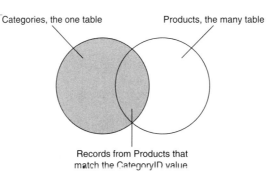

Categories, the one table   Products, the many table

Records from Products that match the CategoryID value

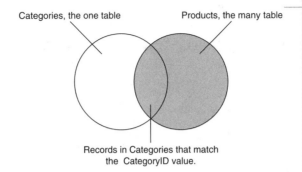

Categories, the one table

Products, the many table

Records in Categories that match
the CategoryID value.

FIGURE 11.8
A right outer join includes the entire many table but only records from the one table that match the primary key value.

You're not stuck with relationships after they're created. You can modify them at anytime, but do so with caution. Relationships can have far-reaching fingers, and you might not anticipate all the effects of changing one.

Modify a join

1. Right-click the join line and select **Edit Relationship** to display the Edit Relationships dialog box.

2. Click the **Join Type** button.

3. Select the appropriate option and click **OK**.

   If you select a left outer join (option **2**), the join line points a small arrow at the many table (see Figure 11.9). A right outer join (option **3**) points to the one table (see Figure 11.10).

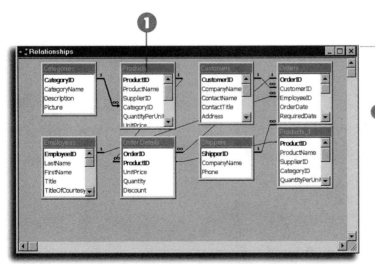

FIGURE 11.9
A left join points to the many table.

①   The many table

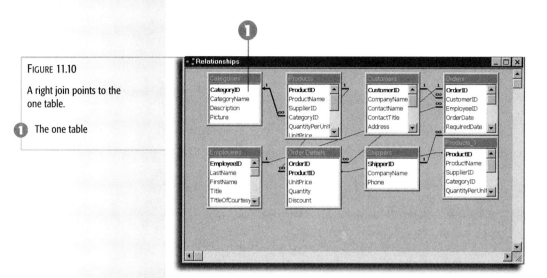

If you actually changed a relationship in an existing database,
consider returning that relationship to its original state before
continuing.

Printing the Relationships Window

Unlike earlier versions, Access 2000 can create a printable
report of the Relationships window. With that window open,
simply choose **Print Relationships** from the **File** menu. Access
responds by creating a report that looks just like your
Relationships window. You can save, print, and even send this
report to someone through email.

Managing External Data

Import text and spreadsheet data with ease using the Import Wizard

Use the Link Wizard to link to spreadsheet data

Link to text data by using the Link Wizard

Importing and Linking

At one time or another, you might need to access data stored outside your own database. You can access external data in three ways:

- Import the external table into your application
- Link your application to the external table
- Open the external table from your application

When you import data, you're creating a copy of that data, but rather than the copy be in the same format as the original, the new copy is converted to the format of a table in your Access application. For example, if you import an Excel spreadsheet, the data contained in the original spreadsheet is contained in a table within your Access application. You can use this data in any way you chose; the source data won't be affected in any way.

Linking to external data is a bit different from importing the data. Although the data appears in your application as an Access table in both cases, linking to data doesn't create a separate and disconnected copy of the data as it does when you import data. When you're working with the data in a linked table, any and all changes you make to the data are made to the original data source. If, for example, the external data represented by a linked table is an Excel spreadsheet, the data in the linked spreadsheet itself is altered to reflect any changes you make when you edit the data, add new rows, or delete rows. Access uses a different icon in the database window to distinguish between a linked table and local table (see Figure 12.1). The linked data remains available to your application until you either delete the linked table or move or delete the source data. If you no longer need the data in the linked table, you can easily delete it by using the **Delete** button in the Database window. This won't delete the source, only the link to the source.

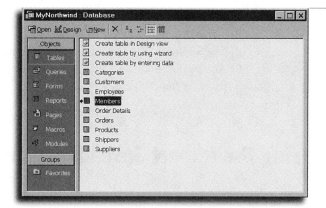

FIGURE 12.1
The table named Members is a
linked table.

SEE ALSO

➤ *See how to deal with your linked tables on page 552*

Your Access application can import or link to data from any of
the following external data sources:

- Other Microsoft Access databases (.adp, .mdb, .mdw, .mda,
  .mde)

- Excel (.xls)

- dBASE III, dBASE IV, and dBASE V (.dbf)

- Paradox 3.x, 4.x, and 5.x (.db)

- Lotus 1-2-3 (.wk*)

- Delimited and fixed-width text files in tabular format (.txt,
  .csv, .tab, .asc)

- Exchange data

- Tabular data in Hypertext Markup Language (HTML) files
  (.html, .htm)

- Open Database Connectivity (ODBC) databases, such as
  Microsoft SQL Server versions 4.2 and later

Files available on the Web

You can find Ch35_Samples.mdb on this book's related Web site (www.mcp.com/product_su pport/). Enter the book's ISBN in the **Search** box and then click the **Search** button to go to the book's information page, where you can find the code.

Importing selections of data

Access imports an entire spreadsheet or areas known as *named ranges*. A named range in a spreadsheet is a section of the spreadsheet that you've given a specific name to. The spreadsheet recognizes this named range and enables you to work with it in specific ways. You can use a named range to import partial data from a spreadsheet, instead of the entire worksheet. Open the spreadsheet in its native application, apply the name to the range of the data to be imported, save, and then close the spreadsheet. When you import the data, Access enables you to specify whether you're importing the entire spreadsheet or a named range.

You also can use data outside the current database without importing it or linking to it. This can be accomplished by using ADO objects within a VBA procedure. The database named Ch35_Samples.mdb (discussed in more detail in Chapter 35, "Taking the Next Step") includes an example of accessing data in this manner.

Using the Import Spreadsheet Wizard

Importing a spreadsheet is fairly easy because the data is already tabular. When Access imports the data, it knows where one field starts and the next begins without your having to provide this information.

In the following example, you'll work with the Common.xls sample Excel spreadsheet that comes with Microsoft Office 2000. You should find this file in the *x*:\Program Files\Microsoft Office\Office\Library folder (or in the \Pfiles\MSOffice\Library directory on the CD). You can use another Excel or a Lotus 1-2-3 spreadsheet if you want.

Import a spreadsheet

1. In Access, from the **File** menu choose **Get External Data** and then **Import**. Access displays the Import dialog box (similar to the Open dialog box). Navigate through your system's folders until you locate the spreadsheet file that contains the data you want to import. Be sure to choose the correct application from the **Files of Type** drop-down list. Highlight the file and click **Import.**

2. The wizard's first window asks you to choose the worksheet or named range you want to import. Notice that Common.xls has two worksheets named Employee Info and Product and Service Catalog. When you select a worksheet from the list in the upper right of the dialog box, the wizard updates the sample data at the bottom of the wizard window. For this example, select **Show Worksheets** and then the **Employee Info** worksheet (see Figure 12.2). After making the appropriate selections, click **Next** to continue.

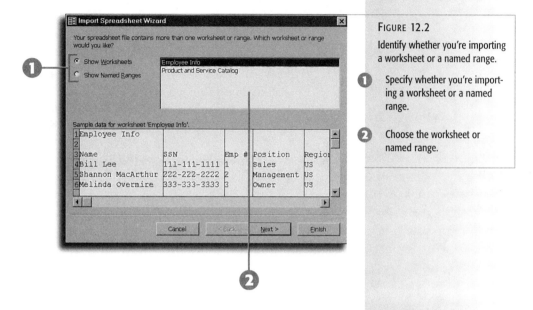

FIGURE 12.2

Identify whether you're importing a worksheet or a named range.

❶ Specify whether you're importing a worksheet or a named range.

❷ Choose the worksheet or named range.

3. You can ask Access to use the worksheet's column headings as field names or the imported data. Click the **First Row Contains Column Headings** option. Access warns you that it can't use some headings and that the wizard will name those fields for you (see Figure 12.3). Click **OK** to close the warning dialog box, and click **Next** to continue.

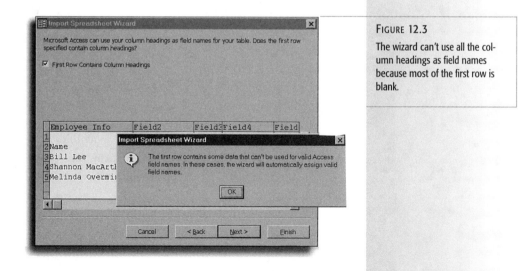

FIGURE 12.3

The wizard can't use all the column headings as field names because most of the first row is blank.

4. The wizard asks you to decide where to store the data imported from the spreadsheet. You can store it in a new table or an existing table. When you select **In a New Table**, the wizard creates a new table for the data. If you select **In an Existing Table**, you must select the table from the drop-down list. For this example, save the data to a new table (see Figure 12.4). When you've made your choices, click **Next**.

FIGURE 12.4

Specify the table for storing the imported data.

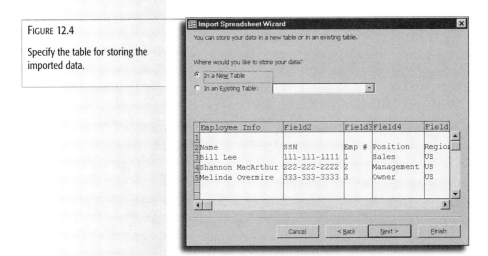

5. The next dialog box focuses on each field in the worksheet or named range, one at a time. You can specify a new field name, change the data type (sometimes), create an index, and even exclude a field from the import process. To change a particular field, click anywhere within that field, make your change(s), and select the next field.

For this example, you want to change the field names. Remember the warning message back in step 3 (refer to Figure 12.3)? You now have an opportunity to deal with it. Change the field names to match the data in row 2 of the spreadsheet. The result should resemble Figure 12.5. Click **Next** to continue.

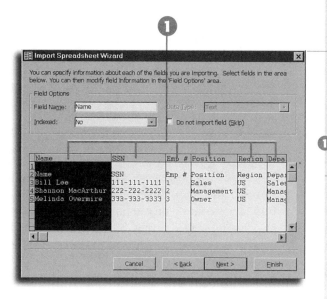

FIGURE 12.5

The wizard gives you the opportunity to change its default settings, and the field names are changed.

1 Change wizard-generated column names for clarity.

6. The wizard helps you choose a primary key field for the new table. The default option, **Let Access Add Primary Key**, adds the ID field shown in Figure 12.6. You can choose your own by selecting **Choose My Own Primary Key**. When you do, select a field from that option's drop-down list. You can also select the **No Primary Key** option if you don't want to apply a primary key. Click **Next** when you're ready to continue.

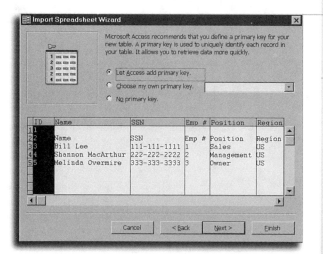

FIGURE 12.6

You're allowing Access to select the table's primary key.

Use tools built into Access to improve your database design

The Table Analyzer is one of several tools available in Access 2000 to help you document and improve the efficiency of your database design. These tools are available by choosing **Analyze** from the **Tools** menu while the database window is displayed. The Table Analyzer (choose **Table** from the **Analyze** submenu) examines your tables and suggests design improvements. Optionally, it can even split a table into two or more tables to improve database performance.

7. The final dialog box lets you change the wizard's default target table. For this example, accept the default. You also can choose to run the Table Analyzer or display help information after the wizard finishes importing the data, but for now, don't select either option. Click **Finish** when you're ready to import the spreadsheet data.

8. Access notifies you when it's finished. Click **OK** to clear the message.

Figure 12.7 shows the new table. The first row in the Excel worksheet contains only one column heading string—Employee Info. The wizard didn't import this row because you said to use its contents as field names. The second row in the worksheet is blank, which is the first row of the table. The third row of the spreadsheet contains the real column headings, which the wizard imports as the data you see as row 2 of the table. The real data starts at row 3 of the table. If you were going to use this imported data in your application, you would delete the first two rows of the table.

FIGURE 12.7

The table shows the column names you entered and a primary key.

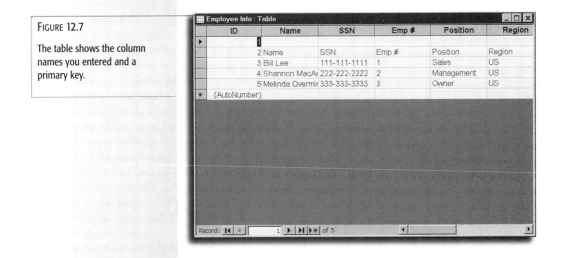

Linking Spreadsheets

You don't have to import the data. In fact, in many situations, linking to the spreadsheet is preferable. For instance, you might need to work with the most recent data, or you might want to update the data from within your Access application.

Link spreadsheets

1. In Access, choose **Get External Data** from the **File** menu, and then choose **Link Tables**.

2. The Link dialog box is basically the same as the Import dialog box. Find the spreadsheet you want to link to, select it, and click **Link**.

3. Identify the worksheet or named range you want to import and click **Next**.

4. Decide whether to use the column headings as field names and click **Next** or **Finish**. If you click **Next**, you can change the linked table's default name. If you click **Finish**, the wizard creates the link by using the default name. Click **Tables** in the Database window.

As you can see, a linked table has a different icon, usually representative of its native application—in this case, Excel.

Using the Import Text Wizard

Few differences exist between importing spreadsheet data and text. In fact, the import and linking wizards make the task extremely easy. This doesn't mean you won't run into problems—it just means that the process for importing and linking data is basically the same as using a wizard, regardless of the data's format.

There are two types of text files: *delimited* and *fixed-width*. A delimited file uses a defined character to separate data fields. The fields in the sample text file are all separated with a tab character. You can use almost any character, but the tab, comma, semicolon, and space are the established delimiters. In a fixed-width file, the fields are aligned in columns, and space characters—not tabs—are used to arrange the data.

Before you try to import a text file, make sure that the fields contain similar data and that the delimiters are consistent in number. The wizard interprets each delimiter as a new field. If your first row has five tabs, that row has five fields. If the second one has an additional tab somewhere, you'll end up with six fields and have to fix it manually after you import. If your original text file is delimited correctly, you won't have this problem.

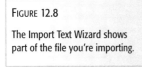

Exporting a table to a delimited text file

You need a text file to follow this example. In this case, I created a file named Employee Info.txt by exporting the Employee Info table created in the previous example. To do this, I selected the Employee Info table in the database window, chose **Export** from the **File** menu, and chose **Microsoft Word Merge (*.txt)** as the **Save as Type**.

Import a text file

1. From the **File** menu, choose **Get External Data** and then **Import**.

2. Navigate your system's structure until you find the file you're importing. Remember to select **Text Files** as the file type in the **Files of Type** drop-down list. After you find your file, select it and click **Import**, or double-click the filename to import it.

3. Access launches the Import Text Wizard. The first dialog box (see Figure 12.8) tries to identify the type of text file—delimited or fixed-width. You can change the wizard's selection if you like, although I didn't. The list at the bottom of the dialog box gives you a reasonable view of the data in the text file. After you make the appropriate choices for your text file, click **Next** to continue.

FIGURE 12.8

The Import Text Wizard shows part of the file you're importing.

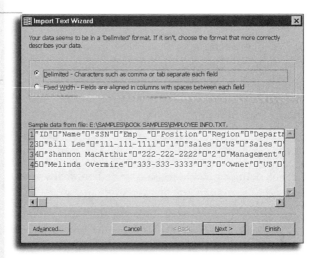

4. The next dialog box (see Figure 12.9) prompts you to identify the delimiting character. The wizard attempts a guess,
but you can change it. In this case, the wizard has correctly
chosen the **Tab** option. As you can see, the first row of the
text file used for this example contains the field names, so I
selected the **First Row Contains Field Names** check box.
You can change this option if your file doesn't contain field
names. The **Text Qualifier** option allows the wizard to
distinguish between text fields and other types of data. You'll
need to know ahead of time what, if any, character your text
file is using. I'm not using any qualifier in the example (see
Figure 12.9). The list at the bottom of the dialog box shows
the wizard's attempt to separate data into fields. The wizard
has done a great job with this example. Click **Next** when
you're ready to continue.

5. You must choose between importing the data into a new
table or an existing table. The wizard chooses **In a New
Table** by default. For this example, don't change the selection. However, if you select **In an Existing Table**, you must
also choose which table you want from the drop-down list.
When you're ready to continue, click **Next**.

Formats used for delimited text files

You might encounter delimited
text data stored in formats different from that used in this
example. Regardless of the format used, it must denote where
one field ends and the next
begins, but it can also include a
text qualifier. The text qualifier
might be used to indicate if the
data in a field is numeric or
alphabetic. For example, the following is a common format
used for a text file:
110,"AB",10,"5". This line contains four fields, separated by
commas. The second and
fourth fields can contain alphabetic characters. An alphabetic
character in the first or third
field causes an error if
imported.

FIGURE 12.9

The wizard attempts to separate
data into fields.

6. You can give each field a meaningful field name, assign a specific data type, and even exclude the field from the import process. For this example, rename your fields accordingly. Click **Next** when you're ready to continue.

7. Assign a primary key field. You can accept the wizard's choice, name your own primary key, or not add a primary key at this time. For this example, I chose to use the existing ID field as the primary key. Click **Next** to continue.

8. In the last dialog box, the wizard names the new table. You can retain this name or enter your own. You also can run the Analyze Table Wizard on the new table and display Help. Then click **Finish**.

9. The Import Wizard lets you know when it's finished importing the data. Click **OK** to clear the message.

Linking Text Files

In the first part of this chapter, you created a link from Northwind to an Excel spreadsheet. You can do the same thing with the tab-delimited text file.

Link a delimited text file

1. From the **File** menu, choose **Get External Data** and then **Link Tables**.

2. In the Link dialog box, find the text file you're linking to, select it, and then click **Link** (or double-click the filename). Be sure to change the **Files of Type** option to **.txt** so that Access can find your file.

3. Repeat steps 3, 4, and 5 from the preceding steps. To summarize, specify whether you're linking to a delimited or a fixed-width field. If you choose delimited, identify the type of delimiter and then modify the field names or omit a field. When you finish, the wizard creates the link.

   Access displays a different icon next to the linked table (see Figure 12.10). This icon indicates that the linked object is a text file.

Check your table

It's recommended that you choose to run the Analyze Table Wizard to make sure that your table is normalized. After the Import Text Wizard finishes importing the text, it asks if you're ready to proceed with the analysis. Click **Yes** to continue or **No** if you changed your mind.

Text files and spreadsheets are tables?

Because Access stores its data in tables, it considers all linked objects as tables. What's more, Access works with these objects as though they were tables. However, there are some limitations. For example, a table linked to a text file cannot be updated.

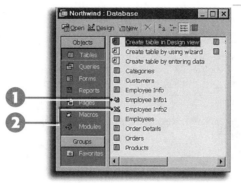

FIGURE 12.10

The icon shows that table Employee Info1 is a linked text file, and Employee Info2 is a linked spreadsheet.

1 This linked table is a text file.

2 This linked table is an Excel spreadsheet.

Importing a Fixed-Width Text File

Until now, you've worked exclusively with tab-delimited fields when working with text files. However, you can also import fixed-width text files. The process is very similar after you define the fields. Linking a fixed-width text file is the same as linking a delimited text file.

Import a fixed-width text file

1. In Access, from the **File** menu choose **Get External Data** and **Import**. Select the fixed-width text file to be imported.

2. The Import Wizard automatically chooses the **Fixed Width** option because space characters—not a delimiting charac-ter—separate the data (see Figure 12.11). Click **Next** to continue.

3. In the next dialog box, you can redraw the fields. Specifically, the wizard displays a ruler and adjustable break lines between each field. Click the break line and move it to the left or right to adjust the field size. To add a new break line, click at the desired position; to delete a delete link, double-click it. For this example, the wizard has done a great job, so no adjustments are required.

Exporting a table to a fixed-width text file

You need a text file to follow this example. In this case, I created a file named Employee Info_Fixed.txt by exporting the Employee Info table created previously. To do this, I selected the Employee Info table in the database window, chose **Export** from the **File** menu, and then selected **Text (*.txt, *.csv, *.tab, *.asc)** as the **Save as Type**.

FIGURE 12.11

This time, the wizard selects the **Fixed Width** option.

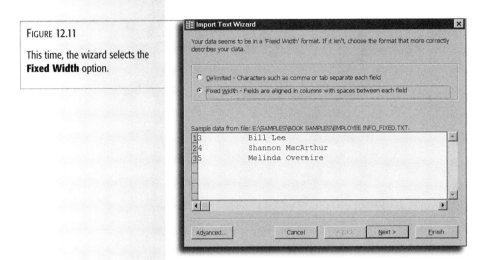

Other uses for an import specification

An import specification saved here also becomes available for use as an argument in a TransferText action of a macro or the DoCmd.TransferText method in VBA.

If you click the **Advanced** button (available in every wizard dialog box), the wizard displays the dialog box shown in Figure 12.12. The File Format options have already been discussed. The **Dates, Times, and Numbers** section enables you to specify the different delimiters for each data type. The **Field Information** section enables you to actually change the field's data type, size, and index; you can even omit the field from the import if you like. You can click the **Save As** button to save the import setup, called an *import specification*, so you can use it again; this is helpful when you import the same file often. Finally, the **Specs** button allows you to recall an import specification you previously saved. Click **OK** to return to the preceding dialog box and then click **Next** when you're ready to continue.

4. The next three dialog boxes are similar to the ones you've seen in each exercise. First, specify whether you're saving the imported data to a new table or an existing table.

5. Modify the wizard's default settings. Specifically, you can modify the field name and data type, set an index, or even omit the field from the import process.

6. Set a primary key. Choose between the wizard's choice, choosing your own, or not adding a primary key field.

7. In the final dialog box, name the new table and click **Finish**.

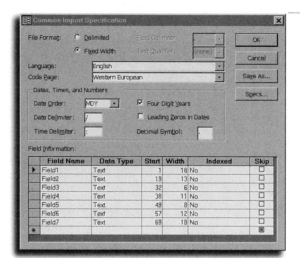

Designing and Using Queries

Retrieve data from one or more tables with a Select query

Group data and perform calculations with a Crosstab query

Use a Make-Table query to create a new table with selected data

Update fields within a table by using an Update query

Add records to an existing table with an Append query

Delete selected records from a table with a Delete query

Creating a Sample Database for This Chapter

You saw in Chapter 6, "Creating Queries," how to create simple Select queries by using a wizard. This chapter expands on that information by showing you how to create a number of different queries by using the query design grid, where you create or modify your query.

For this chapter, you need a database with data and relationships. You can create a database from a wizard or create a new database from another database. The sample database you use for this chapter should be named CHAP13.MDB. If you want, import the Customers and Orders tables from the Northwind sample database that comes with Access (the tables the examples in this chapter use). Because you'll want to import some or all of a database into another database a number of times, start by importing tables into a database you can use for this chapter's exercises.

Import existing tables into a new database

1. Create a new, blank database and name it CHAP13.MDB.
2. Select **Tables** on the Database window object bar.
3. Right-click and select **Import** from the pop-up menu. (As an alternative, from the **File** menu choose **Get External Data** and then **Import**.)
4. Locate and select the Northwind database in the Import dialog box.
5. Click the **Tables** tab and select the **Customers** and the **Orders** tables.
6. Click the **Options** button to expose the extended option available. Make sure that you've selected all the options shown in Figure 13.1.

Importing versus Exporting

Access allows you to import or export database objects. We used the import facility because it has more versatility—you can import more than one object in a single step and can automatically import any table relationships. If you want to use the export facility, it's available by choosing **Export** from the **File** menu.

Using this sample in other chapters

You will use this same database in the next few chapters, so you might want to copy it and rename it. That way, you don't have to go through the export process to make a "clean" copy if you save the queries you make here.

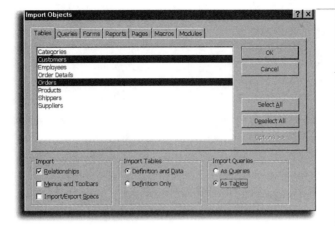

FIGURE 13.1

Importing tables into
CHAP13.MDB.

7. Click **OK** to copy the Customers and Orders tables into the
blank database you created in step 1.

You should now have a clean database with only two tables that
you can use to practice the art of querying your database.

Creating a Select Query Without Using a
Wizard

A Select query is the query you likely will use most often. A
Select query is used to retrieve rows of data from one or more
tables or queries and to display the results of the data retrieval in
a datasheet or in a form (by using it as the form's Record
Source). Access makes it very simple to create a query without
using a wizard.

Use the query design grid to create a simple query

1. Open a sample database (CHAP13.MDB) or your own sample database. Click **Queries** on the Database window object
bar.

2. Click the **New** button, select **Design View**, and then click
OK. Your query opens in Design view, and the Show Table
dialog box appears (see Figure 13.2).

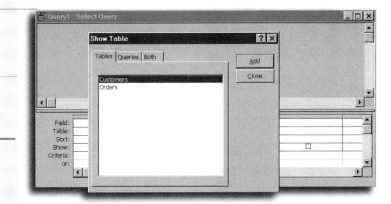

Selecting more than one table at a time

You can select more than one table or query at a time by holding down the CTL key while clicking the items you want to select in the dialog box. You can also select a range of items by clicking the first item in the range and then holding down the Shift key while clicking the last item in the range.

Selecting all the fields in a table

You can add all the fields from a table or query to your query by dragging the asterisk from the field list to the design grid. Doing so can be convenient; if you add fields to a table later, they are automatically added to the query. However, you should use this technique only when you really need to display all the fields in a table or query (such as when you want to use the query as a form's Record Source). Otherwise, if the table has a large number of fields, selecting/display-ing unnecessary fields can slow down your query. Another way to select all the fields is to double-click the table title to highlight all the fields. Then drag the highlighted fields to the grid. This method is convenient if you want all the fields except for one or two (which you can delete from the grid). Keep in mind that this method doesn't auto-matically add new table fields to the query, like the first method does.

3. From the dialog box, select one or more tables and click the **Add** button. For this example, select only the Customers table.

4. Click the **Close** button to close the Show Table dialog box.

5. To add fields to your query in Design view, drag the field name from the field list down to the design grid. For this example, drag the CompanyName and ContactName fields to the design grid. Your query should resemble the example in Figure 13.3.

You could save this query as is and generate a simple select query. Or you can enter criteria for the query or add a sort order to further refine your query. For this example, add a sort order so that the resultset is sorted alphabetically on the CompanyName field.

6. Click in the **Sort** row of the design grid under the CompanyName field. You can choose to sort the query by Ascending or Descending order.

7. Click the **Save** icon 💾 on the toolbar to save the query. A dialog box prompts you to name the query before saving it.

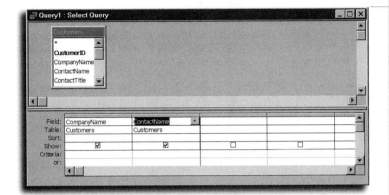

FIGURE 13.3
Add fields to the query.

Grouping Data and Performing Calculations with Crosstab Queries

Crosstab queries are used to calculate a total for data arranged in two groups of information. One group is arranged down the left side of the datasheet as a set of rows; the other is arranged across the top of the datasheet as a set of columns. The types of totals that can be calculated with a Crosstab query include sums, averages, and counts.

You saw in Chapter 6 how to use the wizard to create a Crosstab query. In this section, you see how to create a Crosstab query from scratch by using the query design grid.

SEE ALSO

➤ Turn to page 95 to see how to create a Crosstab query with the wizard

Use the query design grid to create a crosstab query

1. Open your practice database. Click the **Queries** tab in the Database window.

2. Double-click **Create Query in Design View** in the Database window.

3. With your query open in Design view, double-click the Orders table in the Show Tables dialog box to add it to the Crosstab query. Click the **Close** button to close the dialog box.

4. Add fields to the Crosstab query by dragging them from the field list box to the query design grid (as in step 5 of the preceding example). For this example, use the EmployeeID and ShipCity fields from the Orders table.

5. Click the **Query Type** icon on the toolbar and select **Crosstab Query**.

6. This adds two new rows to the query design grid, called Crosstab and Totals. For the fields that you want to appear in the final query as rows of data, click the Crosstab row and select **Row Heading**. For this example, let the ShipCity field appear as the rows in the query.

7. Click in the Crosstab row of the EmployeeID field and select **Column Heading**. This sets up the query so that the employee IDs are used for column headings in the resulting datasheet.

8. Because you must have a value for the datasheet, you need to add the EmployeeID field to the query design grid again so that it shows up twice. Drag the EmployeeID field down to the design grid, click in the Crosstab row and select **Value**, and then click in the Totals row and select **Count**.

Your Crosstab query should resemble Figure 13.4.

Crosstab query fields

When you create a crosstab query, you must designate one field as a Row Heading, one field as a Column Heading, and one field as a Value. You can have more than one Row Heading, but only one Column Heading and one Value.

FIGURE 13.4

The final crosstab query is ready to run.

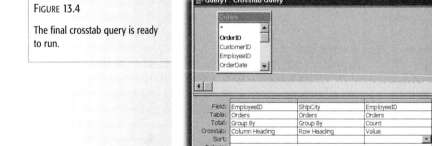

9. Click the **Run** icon ▮ to run this query. The resultset shows the ship cities as rows down the left side of the datasheet and employee IDs as columns across the top of the datasheet. This query shows the number of sales each employee made for each ship city.

10. Save your query by clicking the **Save** icon 🖫 on the toolbar.

Working with Action Queries

In Access, four types of queries are collectively known as *action queries*. An action query is so named because, unlike Select or Crosstab queries, which simply display your selected data, an action query changes—that is, performs an action on—your data. The following types of action queries are available:

- Make-Table query
- Update query
- Append query
- Delete query

Using Make-Table Queries to Create New Tables with Selected Data

You can easily create a new table and populate it with data from one or more existing tables by using a Make-Table query. You can store this table in the current database or specify another database you want to add the table to.

Create a table with a query

1. Open the CHAP13.MDB or your own sample database. Click **Queries** in the Database window object bar.

2. Click the **New** button. When the dialog box appears, select **Design View** and click **OK**.

3. Double-click the **Customers** table in the Show Table dialog box and click the **Close** button. You should now be in the Design view of a new query, with the Customers table showing in the top section of the query design grid.

Make-Table queries versus Select queries

The example here—creating a new table in the existing database, which duplicates data already in an existing table—is intended only to show you the techniques involved. If you actually wanted to show the information selected, it would be more logical to simply create a Select query. A Make-Table query can be very useful, however, for creating tables in another database or for making temporary tables to aid in complex reporting requirements.

4. Create a query by dragging the fields that you want to include in your new table down to the query design grid. For this example, build the new table by using the CustomerID, CompanyName, Phone, and Fax fields from the Customers table. When the new table is completed, it can be used as a type of phone book for the customers.

5. Click the **Query Type** icon on the toolbar and select **Make-Table Query**. The Make Table dialog box appears (see Figure 13.5).

FIGURE 13.5

Enter the new table name in the Make Table dialog box.

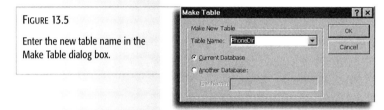

Running a Make-Table query when a table already exists

If you've already run a Make-Table query or have created the target table manually, Access deletes any records that already exist in the table. A message box asks if you really want to delete all the existing entries. If you want to add records to an existing table, you should use an Append query.

6. Enter the name that you want to call your new table in the space provided, and then click **Current Database** or **Another Database**. If you decide to save the table into another database, you need to indicate the name of that database in the **File Name** text box. If this other database isn't located in the same directory as the current database, you must enter the full path to the other database. For this example, name the table PhoneDir and save it to the current database.

7. In query design view, save the query to your database or click the **Run** icon on the toolbar to generate the new table right away. Whenever you decide to run the query, after it finishes processing, you are prompted with a dialog box similar to that shown in Figure 13.6. This dialog box tells you how many rows of data are being pasted into your new table and asks if you really want to generate a new table. Click the **Yes** button. If you click **No**, the whole process is canceled.

The new table PhoneDir should now be part of your database. If you've assigned any field properties or primary keys to the data that's used to create your new table in a Make-Table query, you must reconstruct these properties and reassign a primary key. Field properties and primary keys aren't transferred with the data in a Make-Table query. Regardless, the Make-Table query is a very useful component of Access. You can use a Make-Table query to archive old records from your current database or make backups of the data in your database, among other things.

Previewing a table before you create it

If you have a Make-Table query open in Design view, you can preview the table that is created without actually running the query. Click the **View** icon on the toolbar and select **Datasheet View**.

Updating Fields Within Tables with Update Queries

Generally, Update queries are used to update a broad range of records that reside in one or more tables. If you have only a few records to update in a single table, you can update those records directly in the datasheet. This becomes much more daunting when you're faced with changing a large amount of data that could be spread out over more than one table.

For the following example, you'll build an Update query to run against the Orders table. The Orders table has an EmployeeID column, which lists the ID of the employee responsible for each order. Assume that the employee that used ID number 1 was promoted to regional sales manager and that employee 2 will assume the first employee's responsibilities. Because the Orders table has 830 records, it would clearly take too long to attempt to reassign all the employee 1 orders to employee 2. This is a perfect scenario for using an Update query.

Use an Update query

1. Open the CHAP13.MDB or your own sample database. Click **Queries** in the Database window object bar.

2. Click the **New** button, select **Design View**, and then click **OK**.

3. Double-click the Orders table in the Show Table dialog box and then click the **Close** button.

4. Drag the EmployeeID field from the field list box down to the query design grid. Click the **Query Type** icon and select **Update Query**.

5. A new row, Update To, has been added to your query design grid. This is where you will add the value that you want to change the employee ID to. Click in this field and enter 2.

   If you ran this Update query as is, you would change *all* the employee IDs to 2. Because you obviously don't want to do this, you need to add criteria to the query that helps the Update query know which records to update.

6. Right-click in the Criteria row of the query design grid and select **Build**.

7. The Expression Builder dialog box appears (see Figure 13.7). This very complicated looking dialog box helps you perform intricate expressions rather than type the code. (This exercise only scratches the surface of the Expression Builder's capabilities, however.)

SEE ALSO

➤ *More information on the Expression Builder is available on page 542*

8. Double-click the small + sign inside the Tables folder. This opens up a listing of all the tables now in your database.

9. Because you're trying to update the Orders table, double-click this table to list all its columns.

10. Select the EmployeeID column from this list, and double-click **<Value>** in the next box. This starts writing the code for the criteria in the text box above.

11. Click the = button directly beneath the text box and then type 1. The dialog box should resemble Figure 13.8.

A criteria shortcut

Because the criteria for the update query applies to the field that you're updating, you don't really need to use the Expression Builder. You can enter 1 in the criteria row in the EmployeeID column, and Access knows that the criteria applies to that field. However, it's a good idea to learn how to use the Expression Builder.

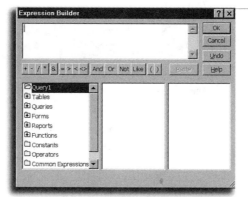

FIGURE 13.7

Use the Expression Builder to write an intricate expression.

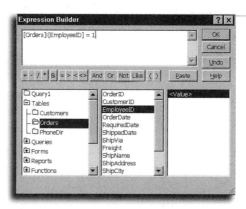

FIGURE 13.8

You've completed the criteria for the Update query.

12. Click **OK** to add this newly created criteria to the query design grid.

13. Either save this Update query to run at a later time, or click the **Run** icon [■] to run the query right away.

In either case, when you run this query, it processes and then prompts you with a dialog box similar to Figure 13.9. This dialog box tells you how many records will be updated and asks if you want to update the records. You can't undo this command by using the **Edit** menu's **Undo** command.

With a simple Update query, you've just updated 123 records and saved yourself a large chunk of editing time. The time savings becomes even more apparent when you're dealing with an update that runs many thousands of records.

Adding Records to Existing Tables with Append Queries

Another built-in action query that's a real time saver is the Append query, which you use to add records to an existing table (or tables) in a database. Append queries can be very useful for combining databases without having to retype all the information in the existing tables.

You can also use an Append query to add records to a table when all the fields of the two tables don't match. Suppose that you have a table with 22 fields, and have another table with only 10 fields that match any of those 22 fields. You can use an Append query to append the records in the table with 10 fields to the table with 22 fields and have the query ignore the 12 fields that don't match the first table.

For the following example, use the PhoneDir table that you created earlier. Because this table contains the phone and fax numbers of all your customers, this Append query would be useful if you drove the competitors out of business and acquired their customers. You are going to append the PhoneDir table to itself, but this query would work just as well if you appended the contents of the competitors' phone directories to yours.

Add records to a table with an Append query

1. Open the CHAP13.MDB or your own sample database. Click **Queries** on the Database window object bar.

2. Click the **New** button and select **Design View** from the dialog box that appears. Click **OK**.

3. Double-click the PhoneDir table in the Show Table dialog box and then click the **Close** button.

4. Drag all the fields in the field listing down to the query design grid. Click the **Query Type** icon and select **Append Query**.

5. A dialog box appears that asks for the name of the table that you want to append to. Select **PhoneDir** from the drop-down list and make sure that the **Current Database** option is selected.

6. A new Append To row appears in your query design grid. This row shows the fields in the new table to which you append the fields in the old table. By default, Access matches fields in the two tables with the same name. If your source table's field names don't match those in the append-to table, you have to indicate which field is the append target.

7. You can save the query to your database, or click the **Run** icon ![Run icon] to execute the query immediately.

Whenever you decide to run an Append query, it processes and then prompts you with a dialog box such as that shown in Figure 13.10. Click **Yes** to continue with the append process.

Ending a query before it's done

You can stop a running query by pressing **Ctrl+Break**.

FIGURE 13.10
The Append query confirms that you want to continue.

The Append query that you recently ran added duplicate records to the PhoneDir table. Normally that wouldn't happen because you would have a primary key set up on the table to not allow duplicates. Because you built the PhoneDir table with a Make-Table query, however, the table doesn't have a field designated as a unique index.

Deleting Selected Records from Tables with Delete Queries

You can use the last type of action query, the Delete query, to delete records from one or more tables. The Delete query can be used to delete old sales records from a table or to update a table that lists inventory items. Remember, though, that when you use a Delete query, it isn't possible to delete the contents of only one field in a record—the Delete query always deletes whole records.

The Delete query should be used when you need to delete a large number of records, or search through a large number of records to find the items to delete. Assume that your company has been forbidden by the government of Brazil to continue business in that country. Because you no longer need the Brazilian entries in the database, you can use a Delete query to make sure that they're deleted correctly. Because the Brazilian entries show up in all your tables, you need to delete them from all the tables.

Ensuring Relationships for a Delete Query

This example also highlights a benefit of a well-designed database. To enable this kind of transaction with the Delete query, you have to ensure that the tables have the right relationship. The tables must be able to support cascading updates and deletes (when you delete a record in the primary table and the related records in the secondary tables are also deleted). In this case, this is necessary because you not only need to delete the Brazilian customers' references in the Customers table, but also delete their orders in the Orders table and their phone information in the PhoneDir table. Rather than hunt through several records in both tables and try to cross-reference them yourself, you can remove all references to your previous customers in Brazil from all your tables with only one Delete query—assuming that your database is well designed and has the proper relationships.

When you imported the tables from the Northwind database to create the CHAP13.MDB database, you chose a number of extended options. One option was to import the relationships associated with the tables you were importing. Now, check those relationships to ensure that the tables in the database have the necessary relationships to enable cascading updates and deletes.

Check relationships for a Delete query

1. Open the CHAP13.MDB or your own sample database. Click **Tables** in the Database window object bar.

2. Click the **Relationships** icon ⬚. A blank window appears, unless you previously defined relationships in your database. Because the Northwind database has defined a relationship between the Customers and Orders tables, those two tables appear in the window (see Figure 13.11).

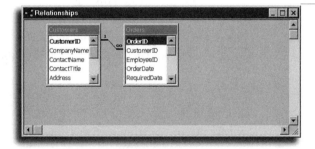

FIGURE 13.11
The Customers and Orders tables have a defined relationship.

3. Double-click the relationship line between the two tables to display the Edit Relationships dialog (see Figure 13.12).

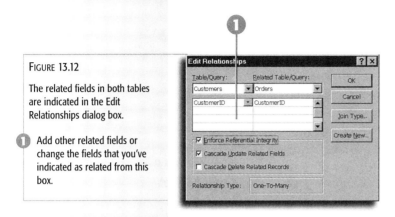

①

FIGURE 13.12

The related fields in both tables are indicated in the Edit Relationships dialog box.

① Add other related fields or change the fields that you've indicated as related from this box.

4. The **Enforce Referential Integrity** and **Cascade Update Related Fields** check boxes are selected. The existing relationship is good but needs one more thing. Select the **Cascade Delete Related Fields** check box to ensure that the delete query works as you want it to.

5. Click **OK** to close the dialog.

6. Notice that the PhoneDir table doesn't appear in the window because you created this table and never created any relationships. Right-click the blank window and select **Show Table**. Double-click the **PhoneDir** table to add it to the window, and then click **Close** to close the Show Table dialog box.

7. Arrange the tables so that you can clearly view them by clicking in the title bar of the table list and dragging the table list to the location of your choice.

8. Because you built the PhoneDir table from the Customers table, you need to create a relationship between these tables. Click the **CustomerID** field in the Customers table and drag it over to the CustomerID field in the PhoneDir table.

9. An Edit Relationships dialog box appears (refer to Figure 13.12), but none of the necessary relationship attributes are selected. Select the **Enforce Referential Integrity** check box to enable the two boxes marked **Cascade Update Related Fields** and **Cascade Delete Related Fields**. Select both options to enable cascading updates and deletes.

10. Click the **Create** button to create a one-to-many join, indicated by a line connecting the two fields in their respective tables. Your Relationships window should now resemble Figure 13.13.

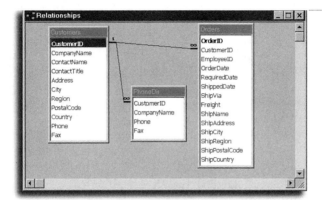

FIGURE 13.13
View the completed relationships in the Relationships window.

11. Close the Relationships window and answer **Yes** when prompted to save the window's layout.

SEE ALSO

➤ More details on one-to-many joins are on page 183

Deleting Records with a Query

You learned that the tables can support what you need from the Delete query, so now you can begin constructing the query.

Use a Delete Query to remove records

1. Open the CHAP13.MDB or your own sample database. Click **Queries** in the Database window object bar.

2. Click the **New** button and select **Design View** from the dialog box that appears. Click **OK**.

3. Add the Customers table to the query design grid by double-clicking it in the Show Table dialog box. Close this dialog box by clicking the **Close** button.

4. Add all the fields in the Customers table to the query design grid by double-clicking the asterisk in the field listing for the Customers table. You can also drag the asterisk down to the query design grid.

5. Drag the Country field to the query design grid; use this field to determine which records need to be deleted from the database. (If the Country field isn't visible in the field listing for the Customers table, scroll down the listing until you can click it.)

6. Click the **Query Type** icon and select **Delete Query**.

   A new Delete row is added to your query design grid. This row contains a From or a Where. The From is used to indicate which records you want to delete from; the Where indicates that the field is being used as a criteria field for the delete action.

7. Enter `"Brazil"` (including the quotation marks) in the Criteria row of the Country field. This tells the query to delete all records whose country matches Brazil. Your query design grid should now resemble Figure 13.14.

FIGURE 13.14

The Delete query is ready to run.

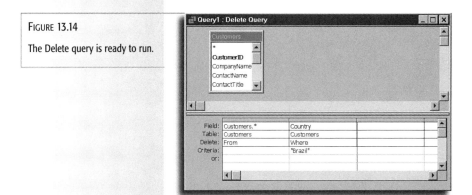

8. You can choose to save this Delete Query to your database, or click the **Run** icon to activate the query immediately. Regardless of which you choose, after the query is run and processes, a dialog box informs you of the number of records to be deleted from the primary table. The dialog box asks for confirmation of this action. Click **Yes** to continue the delete action.

Even though the Delete query deletes far more than nine records from all the tables, the dialog box that appears when you ran the Delete query shows only nine records deleted. That's because the Delete query action shows only the number of records that have been deleted from the primary table in the relationships. If you check your database after running the Delete query, you find no mention of Brazil in any of your tables.

Building Parameter Queries

Set parameters in the criteria section of the query design grid

Set parameters in the Parameter dialog box

Create an input box for user-requested criteria

Use wildcards in parameters

Setting Parameters in the Query Design Grid's Criteria Section

A *parameter query* isn't really a query different from those you've seen up to now. Using a parameter for a query merely allows you to prompt the user for information that will help you construct the query interactively. For example, you can prompt users for a range of dates and use that range to build your query against the database. If you use a parameter for your queries, the parameter prompts users for the criteria it needs to complete the query every time that it's run.

Building a Simple Parameter Query

When you build a parameter query via the query design grid, you set up the parameters directly in the criteria row of the column for which you want to set criteria.

Build a parameter query in the query design grid

1. Open the sample database and click **Queries** on the Database window's object bar.

2. Double-click the **Create Query in Design View** line.

3. Double-click the **Orders** table to add it to your query; then click the **Close** button to close the Show Table dialog box.

4. Build a query to find the orders required by a certain date and to prompt your query's user to provide this date. Drag the OrderID and RequiredDate fields from the field listing to the query design grid.

5. Add a parameter to your query. Enclose the parameter in square brackets and enter it in the Criteria row under the column for which you want to set criteria. For this simple example, enter the following line into the **Criteria** row of the RequiredDate field:

    ```
    [Enter the Required Date]
    ```

Your query design grid should resemble the one in Figure 14.1. You can preview the resultset of this query by clicking the **View** icon .

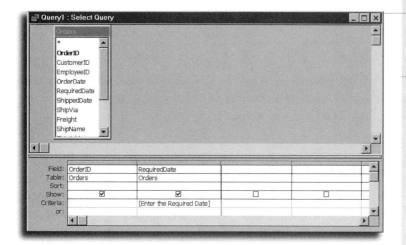

FIGURE 14.1
Creating a parameter for the select query.

When you run this query by clicking the **View** icon, a dialog box similar to the one in Figure 14.2 appears, prompting users to enter a required date. To see a valid resultset, enter 6/2/1998 into the dialog box and click **OK**. The resultset from this query should resemble Figure 14.3.

FIGURE 14.2
The dialog box that prompts the query users.

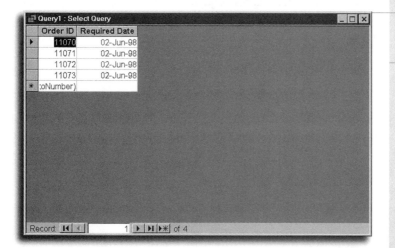

FIGURE 14.3
The parameter query's resultset.

Now save the query with any name that you want, and then close it.

This very simple example introduces you to parameter queries, but you can set up some advanced queries by prompting users for one or more criteria to use in your query. The rest of this chapter shows you the process of using parameters within your queries.

Building a More Complex Parameter Query

For this example, you will create a more functional parameter query. You'll prompt users for a range of dates, between which the required date must fall.

Build a query that prompts users for a date range

1. Open the sample database and click **Queries** on the Database window's object bar.

2. Select the query that you created in the preceding steps and click the **Design** button to open this query in Design view.

3. Select the **Criteria** row of the RequiredDate column; press **Delete** to clear the value from the previous example. Then enter the following into the RequiredDate column's **Criteria** row:
```
Between [Enter the beginning date:] And
[Enter the ending date:]
```
This tells Access that you want to set up a range of parameters. The first parameter is used for the beginning date of the range; the second parameter is used for the ending date of the range

4. Right-click within the RequiredDate column's **Criteria** row and select **Zoom** (or press **Shift+F2**) to see the query's newly added parameters (see Figure 14.4).

5. Close the Zoom dialog box, and then click the **View** icon 🖼️ ▾ to preview this query. You're prompted by two dialog boxes: The first asks you to enter a beginning date, the second asks for an ending date.

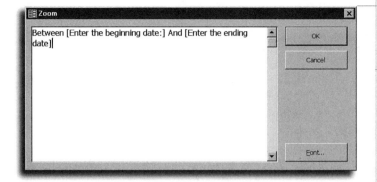

FIGURE 14.4

Add parameters that prompt for a date range from users.

6. Enter the requested parameters to see the results of your query. I suggest that you use 6/1/98 and 6/5/98.

7. Close the query and save your changes when prompted.

Setting a Parameter's Data Type

When you're setting a parameter for a query, you can also set the data type of that parameter. You must set the data type of the parameters you need if you're building a crosstab query and setting parameters for that query.

Set the data types for parameters

1. Open the sample database and click **Queries** on the Database window's object bar.

2. Select the query that you created in the preceding section and click the **Design** button to open this query in Design view.

3. From the **Query** menu, choose **Parameters**.

4. Enter the parameter that you typed in the RequiredDate field's Criteria row into the Parameter column of the Query Parameters dialog box. Type each parameter (that is, Enter the beginning date: and Enter the ending date:) on separate rows, without the square brackets.

5. In the Data Type column, select the **Date/Time** data type (see Figure 14.5).

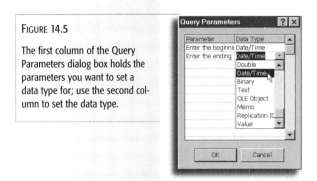

6. Close the Query Parameter dialog and run the query.

7. When the first parameter dialog appears, try entering something other than a date and see what happens. You should
   get an error message (see Figure 14.6).

8. Click **OK** to close the error dialog, and then enter an
   appropriate date for both requested dates. Close and save
   the query.

You also can create a custom input box for use in your queries.

Creating an Input Box for User-Requested Criteria

If you want to create a custom input box for your parameter
query in Access, simply construct a form that's used within your
application to gather information from your application's user.

Access allows you to create a *pop-up form*. This means that the
form stays on top of the other forms present in your application
when it's displayed. One property of a pop-up form in Access is

Modal. If the form's Modal property is No, the form is known as a pop-up form; you can access other forms in your application while it's displayed, but it always remains on top. If the form's Modal property is Yes, the form is known as a *custom dialog box*, and you can't access other forms in your application until you close the form or hide it from view.

Build a custom dialog box so users can enter the date range

1. In the sample database, click **Forms** on the Database window's object bar.

2. Click the **New** button; the New Form dialog box appears.

3. Select the **Design View** option in the New Form dialog box.

4. Resize the form so that it's an appropriate size for your custom input box. Because the query to which you're attaching needs to return a date range to the query, you need to add the following controls to the form, dragging the appropriate controls from the Toolbox:

- A label and a text box for the beginning date, named txtBeginningDate

- A label and a text box for the ending date, named txtEndingDate

- A Run Query command button, named cmdRunQuery

- A Cancel command button, named cmdCancel

5. After you place the controls on the form, change the following form properties in the properties sheet:

Tab	Property	Value
Format	Caption	Enter Date Range
	Scroll Bars	Neither
	Record Selectors	No
	Navigation Buttons	No
	Auto Center	Yes
	Border Style	Dialog

Pop-up form versus custom dialog box

Generally speaking, when you build a pop-up form, set your border style to Thin, whereas a custom dialog has a border style of Dialog. When you set up a form to be a custom dialog, all toolbars and menus will also be disabled. Therefore, you must make sure that you either place a command button on the form to close it, or don't remove the close button—otherwise, your user can't close the form without closing Access itself.

Tab	Property	Value
	Control Box	No
	Min Max Buttons	None
	Close Button	No
Other	Pop Up	Yes
	Modal	Yes

6. Save the form as frmQueryParameters and close it. Don't click the **View** button. Because you've removed the Close button from the form and haven't put any action behind the command button yet, you can't close the form.

For the form to be useful, you must now make the two command buttons functional. You'll do this by creating two macros and assigning them to the Click events of the command buttons.

Create a macro to run the parameter query

1. In the sample database, click **Macro** on the Database window's object bar.

2. Click the **New** button; the Macro window appears.

3. For the first action you want to run the query, so select the **OpenQuery** macro action from the drop-down list.

4. In the bottom half of the Macro window are the required arguments for the selected macro action. Select the name of the query that you previously created from the drop-down list that appears when you click in the **Query Name** field.

5. For the second action you want to close the form, so select the **Close** macro action from the drop-down list.

6. In the bottom half of the Macro window, select **Form** as the **Object Type**, and then select the custom dialog form that you just created for the **Object Name**.

7. Save this macro as macRunQuery and close the Macro window.

SEE ALSO

➤ *Learn how to use the macro window on page 422*

Alternative ways to close a form

You can close the form in two ways, even if you've removed the built-in Close X button and haven't placed your own Close button on the form. If the form isn't modal, use **Ctrl+F3** to close the form; if it's modal, use **Ctrl+F4**. (If you use **Ctrl+F4**, make sure that your form is modal; otherwise, you will close your application.) Another trick you can use doesn't exactly close the form but can be helpful in the right circumstances. Right-click the form's title bar, and—if you haven't disabled the default shortcut menus—you can select **Form Design** from the pop-up menu.

Create a macro to close the custom dialog form

1. Click the **New** button; the Macro window appears.

2. You want to close the form if you change your mind about running the query, so select the Close macro action from the drop-down list.

3. In the bottom half of the Macro window, select **Form** as the **Object Type** and select the custom dialog form for the **Object Name**.

4. Save this macro as macCloseForm and close the Macro window.

Link the macros to the command buttons

1. Click **Form** on the Database window object bar.

2. Select the custom dialog form and click the **Design** button.

3. Double-click the **Run Query** button to display the properties sheet.

4. Select the **Event** tab and then the On Click event.

5. From the drop-down list, select macRunQuery. Your screen should resemble Figure 14.7.

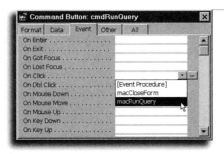

FIGURE 14.7
Assign a macro to a command button's Click event.

6. Click **Cancel**, select the Click event for this button, and select macCloseForm from the drop-down list.

7. Close and save your form.

Change the query to get the form's parameters

1. Click **Queries** on the Database window's object bar.

2. Select the parameter query created earlier and click the **Design** button; this opens the query in Design view.

3. Click the **Criteria** row of the RequiredDate field; press **Delete** to clear this field and then type the following:
```
Between forms!frmQueryParameters!txtBeginningDate
And forms!frmQueryParameters!txtEndingDate
```

This criteria tells the query that the necessary information can be found in the referenced text boxes on the frmQueryParameters form.

4. While the query is still in Design view, choose **Parameters** from the **Query** menu bar.

5. Select the query parameters that you inserted earlier in this chapter and press **Delete** to remove them. Click **OK** to close the Query Parameters dialog box.

See the custom dialog form in action

1. Click **Forms** on the Database window's object bar and double-click frmQueryParameters to open the form.

2. Enter 1/1/98 in the **Beginning Date** text box and 6/5/98 in the **Ending Date** text box (see Figure 14.8).

FIGURE 14.8

Enter a date range in the custom dialog form.

3. Click the **Run Query** command button. The query runs, the form closes, and you should see results similar to Figure 14.9.

If you open the form again and click the **Cancel** button, the form simply closes.

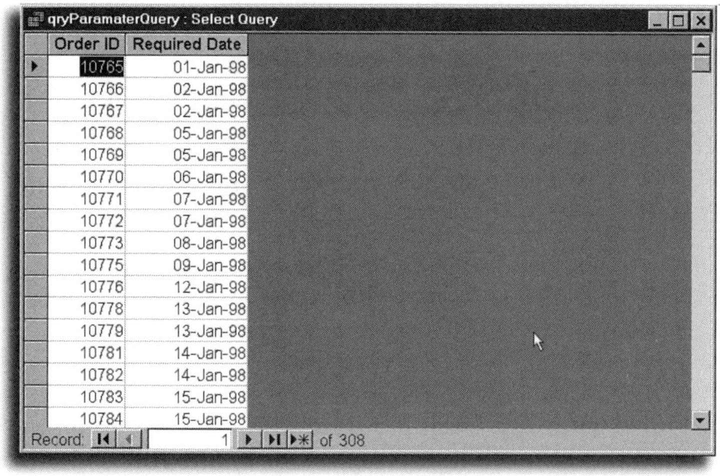

FIGURE 14.9

The result of the parameter query that uses the custom dialog form to enter the parameters.

Using Wildcards in Parameters

You can use wildcards to set your query's parameters. *Wildcards* are typically used in Access as placeholders for unknown values or to cover a range of possible values. Wildcard characters are to be used only with Text data types.

You can use the wildcards in Table 14.1 with Access. The wildcard itself is given here, along with a brief description of how to use the wildcard.

TABLE 14.1   Usage of Wildcards in Queries

Wildcard	Description/Reason for Using
Asterisk (*)	Matches any character or any number of any character. You can construct a query that uses the asterisk in the criteria of a field. Name = tr*, for example, searches for all names that begin with a *tr*. You can also use the asterisk at the beginning of a string if you know the end of the string.
Question mark (?)	Matches any single alphabetic character. You can use this wildcard to search for words where you know the beginning and end of the word, but the middle characters could be different.

continues…

Using wildcards with non-Access data sources

If you're running your parameter query against a data source other than an Access table, different criteria rules might apply when using wildcards. Refer to the documentation that came with the data source you're using to determine the correct usage of wildcards in the context of that data source.

TABLE 14.1   **Continued**

Wildcard	Description/Reason for Using
Square brackets ([ ])	Returns any character inside the brackets. This is similar to using the question mark, but with this wildcard you know the range of characters that you're looking for. Using `Name = Jo[he][ny]` in a criteria row of a Name field to return `'John or Joey'` is an example.
Exclamation point (!)	Indicates that you're looking for any character that's not in the square brackets. Using `Name = Jo[!he][!ne]`, for example, returns all names that start with *Jo*, but don't contain an *h* or an *e* in the next position or an *n* or an *e* in the last position.
Hyphen (-)	Indicates a range of characters: `Name = Jo[a-r][b-o]`.
Pound sign (#)	Matches any single numeric character. An often-used example is matching to a range of zip codes. For example, `Zip = 36###`

Advanced Uses for Queries

Query another query

Use the query design grid to create an SQL statement for a *RunSQL* macro action

Use the query design grid to create an SQL statement for use in VBA

Querying Another Query

Examples in this chapter

For the examples in this chapter, you need an existing database to run your queries. If you need a sample database to test, follow the convention of the previous chapters by exporting the Customers and the Orders tables from the Northwind sample database that comes with Access. Follow the steps at the beginning of Chapter 13, "Designing and Using Queries," to create this database and name it chap15.mdb, or rename the copy you made of your clean database from Chapter 13.

One interesting thing that you can do with Access is generate a query that uses another query as its data source. This can be very useful for such things as building a drilldown query application, which starts with a huge general database. With each iteration users go through, the resultset's contents narrow until they are looking at a small subset of the original mass of data. This small subset could be constructed to provide the data that users were looking for in the first place. You might also create different branches leading from each step to narrow the query, depending on the options or the direction you want to offer your users.

The following example walks you through the construction of such a series of queries. You won't try to build the user interface for your drilldown query machine in this chapter, but you should be able to translate the work you do in this section into a useful series of forms for your Access database application.

Build the first in a series of complex queries

1. Open your newly created chap15.mdb database and click the **Queries** tab of the Database window.

2. Click the **New** button and select **Design View**. Click **OK**.

3. Because you're going to build a series of queries in this example, you want to start with a base table. Double-click the **Customers** table listed in the Show Table dialog box to add it to the query design grid, and then click the **Close** button.

4. Double-click the asterisk at the top of the field listing for the Customers table to add all the fields in this table to the query design grid. This is your first query in the drilldown hierarchy, and you want it to include as much information as possible.

5. Close this query and save it as Drill_1 when prompted. Make sure that the **Queries** tab of the Database window is still selected, and click the **New** button. Select **Design View**, and click **OK**.

6. Because you are in the process of building the second query in your drilldown hierarchy, you won't be adding a table to the query design grid as you have in almost every previous example. Instead, on the **Queries** page of the Show Table dialog box, double-click the **Drill_1** query that you just created. This adds the query to your new query as a data source. Your application should resemble the one shown in Figure 15.1.

7. Click the **Close** button to close the Show Table dialog box. Drag the CustomerID, CompanyName, ContactName, and Phone fields from the Drill_1 query field listing to the query design grid.

What to do with the second query

This query will be step 2 in your query hierarchy. In step 1, the query resultset returns every bit of data stored in the Customers table of your database. The second query narrows this data down to the customer names and phone numbers, along with the contact names and the IDs stored in the Customers table of your database.

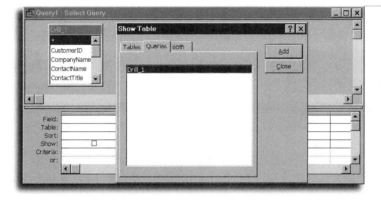

FIGURE 15.1

Creating the second query in your drilldown hierarchy.

8. Close this query and save it as `Drill_2` when prompted.

9. Make sure that the **Queries** tab of the Database window is still selected, and click the **New** button. Select **Design View** and click **OK**. This next query is the last query in your example query hierarchy.

10. Because you're using a query as the data source, select the **Queries** tab of the Show Table dialog box and double-click the **Drill_2** query to add it to the query design grid as a data source. Your database application should resemble the one in Figure 15.2. Click the **Close** button to close the Show Table dialog box.

FIGURE 15.2

Creating the third query in your drilldown hierarchy.

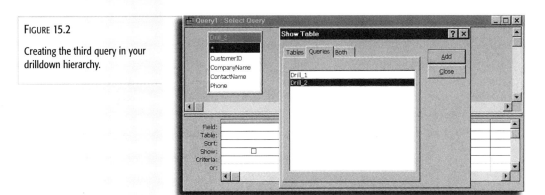

11. Drag the CompanyName field from the Drill_2 query field listing to the query design grid. Click in the **Criteria** row of the CompanyName field and enter "c*" as the criteria for the row. Your query should now resemble the one in Figure 15.3. Notice that Access automatically adds the word Like because you have used a wildcard character (the asterisk).

FIGURE 15.3

The third and final table of your drilldown hierarchy.

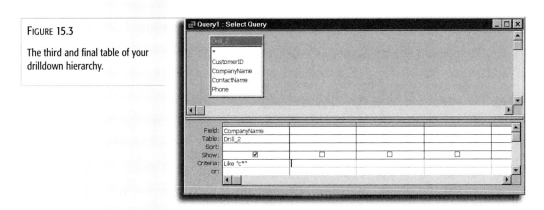

12. Close this query and save it as Drill_3 when prompted. While the query is still selected, click the **Run** button to view the results of the drilldown query that you just created.

This example was kept very simple so as not to confuse the procedure that you used. You can use this same approach and build a very complex Access application that implements several forms and user prompts to drill up and down through a large data set. If you allow your users to specify which fields they want to have returned out of each level of the drilldown hierarchy, chances are good that they will end up with the exact resultset they're looking for, even if your original database was made up of several very large tables.

Creating a SQL Statement for a Macro *RunSQL* Action

You can use a macro in your Access application to run an action query or a data definition query. An action query, as you learned in Chapter 13, is one that changes data and includes Append, Delete, Make-table, and Update queries. You can use a data definition query to create tables or indexes on tables, or to delete tables and indexes. You can also edit an existing table's properties. Data definition queries, however, are beyond the scope of this book.

When you use the query design grid to create a query, you're actually creating a SQL statement, even if you don't realize it. Access interprets the query that you construct in the design grid and constructs the required SQL statement for you. You can view the SQL statement constructed by Access by choosing **SQL View** from the **View** menu when you're in the query design grid.

Query too complex?

Sometimes when you try to run a query, you will get the message Query too complex. This often happens when you specify a number of related tables in your query. This message could indicate that you've made a mistake in your query design and should review your design to ensure that it's accurate; however, the message might also mean exactly what it says. If this is the case, you can simplify your query by breaking it into multiple queries, where the first query is used as a source for the second query, and so on. When you run the last query, it automatically runs all the queries necessary. You can use this same technique if your query complains about ambiguous joins.

What is SQL?

SQL (pronounced as "sequel" or said as the letters S-Q-L) is an acronym that stands for Structured Query Language. SQL was developed to provide a computer language that was close to English yet would allow for standardized ways to get data from a database. It was originally developed at IBM in the 1970s, and was known as SEQUEL (which stood for Structured English Query Language). Although there are standards for the SQL language, each database often has its own implementation of the language.

To run a SQL statement within a macro in your Access application, use the RunSQL action, which has two arguments:

- The text of the SQL statement that you want to run
- A Yes or No to indicate whether you want to run your SQL statement within the context of a transaction

SEE ALSO

➤ *Other events you can use with macros are on page 434*

If you don't run your SQL statement within a transaction, the transaction might run faster. However, the default value for this argument is Yes because it's safer to run a SQL statement within a transaction. ·

The text of the SQL statement that you use within your macro can't be longer than 256 characters. If you need to run a longer SQL statement, you should run it from within VBA. The last section of this chapter shows you how to generate a SQL statement and then run it inside VBA.

You should use to the following Access query types to accomplish an equivalent SQL action:

SQL Action	Access Query Type
SELECT	Select
INSERT INTO	Append
SELECT INTO	Make-table
DELETE	Delete
UPDATE	Update

In the following example, you create a simple query in the query design grid of your Access database application. You then use that query to build a macro that uses the RunSQL action to execute the query.

Build a macro that uses the *RunSQL* action

1. Open a sample database (such as chap15.mdb) and click the **Queries** tab of the Database window.

2. Click the **New** button and select **Design View** from the New Query dialog box. Click **OK**.

Using a transaction for a query

A transaction uses three different statements to ensure that changes to the data in your database are secure. The first statement, BeginTrans, is used to mark the beginning of a transaction. After the query in the transaction safely runs, you can use the second statement, CommitTrans, to commit the changes to the data in your database. And if a problem arises, you can cancel all changes to the data in your database by using the third statement, Rollback.

3. Because you're building a simple example to demonstrate using a macro to run a SQL statement, double-click the **Customers** table in the Show Table dialog box. Click the **Close** button to close the Show Table dialog box.

4. Now that you have a table with which to build a query, drag the CustomerID, CompanyName, ContactName, and Phone fields to the query design grid from the field listing (see Figure 15.4).

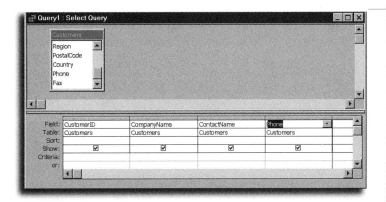

FIGURE 15.4

Creating the query for your RunSQL macro.

5. From the **Query** menu choose **Make-Table**. Enter `CustPhoneBook` into the **Table Name** field of the Make Table dialog box. This is the name of the new table that's created.

6. Click the **View** icon 🔲▾ on the toolbar and select **SQL View** to see the SQL statement that Access has created (see Figure 15.5).

Using the Make-Table option for an action query

Because you need this query to be an action query, you will change the query type to a Make-Table query. This builds a table that you can use as a customer phone book.

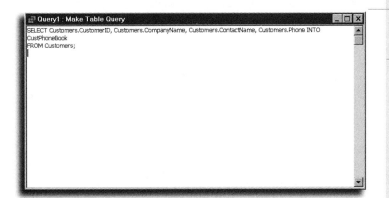

FIGURE 15.5

Viewing your query in SQL view.

7. If the SQL statement isn't selected, select it now (with your mouse). Press **Ctrl+C** to copy this query to the Clipboard.

8. Close the query design grid and save the query as RunSQL_Test when prompted.

9. Select the **Macros** tab of the Database window and click the **New** button. A blank macro window should appear.

10. In the **Action** column of the macro window, click the drop-down list and select **RunSQL**. The arguments for this type of action appear at the bottom of the macro window.

11. In the **SQL Statement** argument field, press **Ctrl+V** to paste the SQL statement that you created in the query design grid.

12. In the **Use Transaction** argument field, select **Yes** or **No**, depending on your preference.

The macro window in your application should now resemble the one in Figure 15.6.

FIGURE 15.6

The finished macro as it appears in your application.

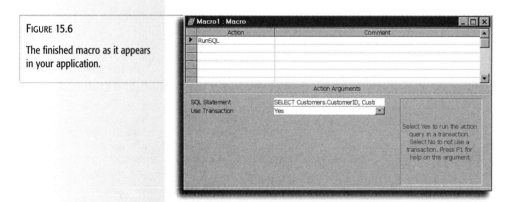

13. Close the macro sheet and save this new macro to your database application as RunSQL when prompted.

14. With the **Macros** tab of the Database window still selected, click the macro that you just created and then click the **Run** button or the **Run Macro** icon ![icon]. You should get a message box informing you that you are about to paste 91 records into a new table. Click **Yes**.

15. Select the **Tables** tab of the Database window to view the
new table that you just created by using the RunSQL action
within a macro.

SEE ALSO
➤ *Learn how to use the macro window on page 422*

This simple query example gives you a feel for the steps
involved. You can use this method to run action queries and data
definition queries from macros within your Access application.
Remember, though, that if the SQL statement that you want to
run is longer than 256 characters, you need to use the RunSQL
method of the DoCmd object in VBA, as shown in the following
section.

Creating a SQL Statement for Use in VBA

You can also use the RunSQL method to accomplish the same task
that you just completed by using the RunSQL action. The main
difference is that the RunSQL method is called from within Visual
Basic or VBA, and the RunSQL action is used as a macro action in
Access. Also, through the RunSQL method, VBA lets you use up to
32,768 characters in your SQL statement, rather than be limited
to 256 characters with the RunSQL action. (VBA coverage begins
in Chapter 26, "Introducing Visual Basic for Applications.")

The RunSQL method is a method of the DoCmd object in Visual
Basic. The DoCmd object is used to accomplish Access actions
from within the VBA. The syntax for using the DoCmd object is

```
[application.]DoCmd.method [arg1, arg2, ...]
```

where *application* is the application object itself, which is an
optional part of calling the DoCmd object, and *method* is one that's
supported by the DoCmd object. The arguments vary depending
on which method you're using.

For this example, use the DoCmd object with the RunSQL method.
The syntax for calling the RunSQL method of the DoCmd object is

```
DoCmd.RunSQL sqlstatement[, usetransaction]
```

The required *sqlstatement* argument is a string expression that's the SQL statement that you want to run. The SQL statement must be an action query or a data definition query. The *usetransaction* argument is used to indicate whether you want to enclose your query in a transaction. The default value for this argument is True, so if you omit this argument, Access assumes that you want to use a transaction.

SEE ALSO

➤ *For another examples that uses* DoCmd, *see page 356*

Creating the Interface: Input and Output

Adding Controls to Forms and Reports

Add, align, and modify controls

Work with the grid

Select and work with multiple controls

Working with the Toolbox

As you learned in Chapters 7 and 8, the wizards do a good job of creating forms and reports for you. However, wizards seldom generate the perfect form or report—you can expect to fine-tune a wizard's results. They might need only a simple touch, such as a new label caption, or a new text alignment setting. Or, they might need more heavy duty modifications, such as a calculated control. Fortunately, Access provides easy access to its controls through the Toolbox (see Figure 16.1).

FIGURE 16.1

The Toolbox offers the Access native controls.

Some displayed controls might not be usable

Although all controls installed on your system will appear when you click the **More Controls** button, you might not be able to use all of them in your application. You can use only those controls for which you have a proper development license file. Controls installed by other software might have a run-time license that allows their use only in the applicable software but prohibits their use in a development environment. Controls are available for purchase from Microsoft as well as third-party vendors.

The Toolbox houses all native Access controls. (By *native*, I mean all the controls that come with Access.) To display other available controls (see Figure 16.2), click the **More Controls** button in the Toolbox. The controls offered will depend on which software packages you might have installed on your system, so don't worry if your list doesn't match mine.

When you open your form or report in Design view, Access generally displays the Toolbox and the form or report's property sheet. If the Toolbox isn't available, you can click the **Toolbox** button on the appropriate design toolbar, choose **Toolbox** from the **View** menu, or choose **Toolbars** and then **Toolbox** from the **View** menu.

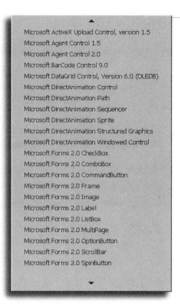

FIGURE 16.2
You can display all the controls by clicking the **More Controls** button in the Toolbox.

Working with the Grid

You might have noticed that forms and reports in Design view are covered with lines and dots (see Figure 16.3). These lines crisscross to create sections; the dots fill each section. These lines and dots form the *grid*, which helps you position controls more easily. Positioning controls is a simple process, really: You select a control and use the drag-and-drop method to align it to a grid point or grid line.

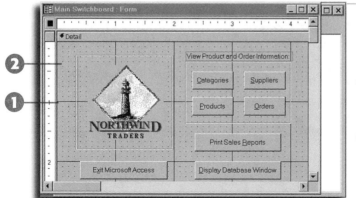

FIGURE 16.3
If your form isn't displaying the grid, choose **Grid** from the **View** menu.

❶ Using grid lines enables proportional placement across the larger form.

❷ With smaller grid points, you can more accurately and closely place your controls.

Altering the Grid

By default, the grid presents 24 dots per inch. If you find the distance between grid points too small or too large, you can adjust the distance between them by altering the form's GridX and GridY properties. The lower the setting, the greater the distance between the dots.

Alter the distance between grid points

1. Open a blank form in Design view by clicking **Forms** and then **New** in the Database window. Then, double-click **Design View** in the New Form dialog box.

2. If Access fails to open the form's property sheet, double-click the **Form Selector** or click the **Properties** icon on the Form Design toolbar.

3. Select the **Format** tab of the property sheet (if it's not already selected).

4. Select the GridX property (near the bottom of the list) and change the current setting of 24 to 12. (24 is the default, but yours might be different.)

5. Repeat step 4, using the GridY property instead.

As you can see in Figure 16.4, the dots have twice the space between them as before.

Working in the background

The blank palette you're working on is referred to as the *background* of a form or report. It acts something like the Windows desktop. If you've started to select an icon on the desktop and change your mind, you can click a blank space of the desktop. The same thing applies to the background of the form and starting to select or deselect a control—click the background to deselect it.

FIGURE 16.4

I doubled the distance between each grid point (compared to the default setting); the maximum resolution is 64. When you select a number larger than 24, the grid points won't be viewable, although the grid lines will still be displayed (the actual number might be different depending on your video driver or screen resolution).

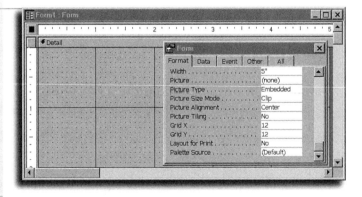

Aligning Controls to the Grid

Access automatically aligns controls to the nearest grid point or line as you create or move them when the Snap to Grid feature is on. (The default is on.) When the feature is off, Access enables you to position or move a control as you like.

Use Snap to Grid to align controls

1. On your open form, add a command button by clicking the **Command Button** tool ⬚ in the Toolbox and then clicking between two grid points on the form. Access automatically aligns the top-left corner of the new button to the nearest grid point.

2. Try to move the control by positioning the top-left corner of the button between two grid points. Notice that Access won't enable you to do so; instead, Access always aligns the top-left corner to the nearest intersecting grid points.

3. Turn off the Snap to Grid feature by choosing **Snap to Grid** from the **Format** menu in Design view.

4. Insert a second command button—be sure to click between the dots to get the full effect of the change you just made. This time, Access leaves the control where you place it.

5. Try moving the control. Notice that Access doesn't care where you release the button.

Turning Off the Grid

If you find the grid as a whole annoying or you simply don't need it, you can turn it off.

Turn off the grid

1. Open a blank form in Design view by clicking the **Forms** tab and then the **New** button in the Database window. Then, double-click **Design View**, or select **Design View** and click **OK** in the New Form dialog box.

2. From the **View** menu, deselect **Grid** (you might need to click the down-pointing arrows at the bottom of the **View**

> **Temporarily suspending the Snap to Grid feature**
>
> You don't have to turn off the Snap to Grid feature to suspend its behavior. Instead, hold down the **Ctrl** key while you move a control to temporarily turn off the feature. When you release the **Ctrl** key, Access turns the feature back on. You can use the same technique with the **Shift** key to resize a control.

menu to make this choice available). The resulting form displays no grid lines or dots (see Figure 16.5).

FIGURE 16.5

You can turn off the grid display.

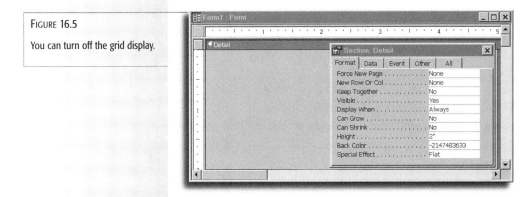

Inserting Controls

The exercises in this section help you practice or review inserting controls. To do so, simply click a control tool in the Toolbox and then click inside the form or report. To see how it's done, add a few controls to a blank form. (You'll follow the same procedure when adding controls to a report.)

Add controls to a form

The Control Wizards

By default, the **Control Wizards** control in the Toolbox is enabled. When you add certain controls to a form, the wizard is invoked and steps you through creating a control. If you don't want to use the wizard, click the wizard's **Cancel** button. You can also deselect the **Control Wizards** control to turn off the wizards. The Control Wizards are discussed in Chapter 9, "Creating Controls and Setting Properties."

1. Open a blank form by selecting **Forms**, clicking **New** in the Database window, and then double-clicking **Design View** in the New Form dialog box.

2. If Access doesn't launch the Toolbox, click the Toolbox tool on the Form Design toolbar (or choose **Toolbox** from the **View** menu). Make sure that the **Control Wizards** control is deselected.

3. Click the **Text Box** tool in the Toolbox and then click anywhere inside the form. Access adds a text box to the form (see Figure 16.6). By default, Access includes a label control to the left of each text box. Select the label control by clicking it, and double-click it to type the text you want for your text box.

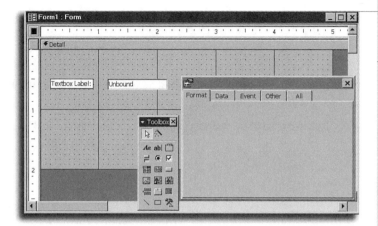

FIGURE 16.6
Add a text box to the blank form.

4. Click the **Label** tool Aa in the Toolbox and then click inside the form to add a label control. Access inserts the control in Edit mode, so you can immediately type your descriptive text (if you don't type any text, the label control disappears). At this point, type the text you want for the label control (see Figure 16.7). Both label controls are for displaying descriptive text; one label control is attached to the text box and the other is purely standalone.

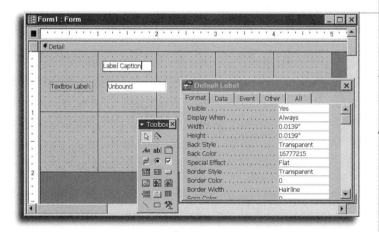

FIGURE 16.7

Add descriptive text to your label control.

Setting default properties for a control

With the properties sheet visible and without selecting a control, select any control on the Toolbox. The properties sheet displays those properties that can be set as defaults for the selected control. Some, such as the Add Colon and Add Label properties, don't appear when an existing control is selected because they apply only to new controls.

When you create a text box control, a semicolon is automatically included at the end of the label text. However, when you create a label control, the semicolon isn't included.

Adding or Changing a Control Label

Occasionally, you won't want to use the label that Access includes with each text box. When this is the case, you can easily delete it. To see how this simple procedure works, you'll modify a text box.

Delete the text box control's label

1. With the form still in Design view, click the form's background to deselect any controls.

2. Position the mouse pointer over the top-left corner of the label and click. Access selects the label control and displays the hand icon over the top-left handle (see Figure 16.8).

FIGURE 16.8

The hand pointer indicates that you've selected the label portion of this text box.

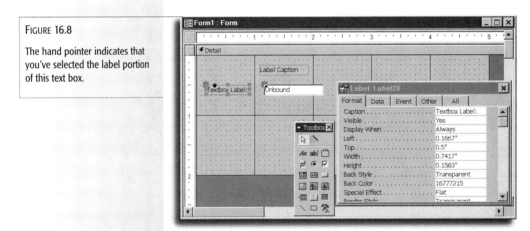

Deleting the control

To delete a control, all you have to do is click it and press **Delete**, or choose **Delete** from the **Edit** menu.

3. After the hand-shaped mouse pointer appears over the top-left handle, press **Delete**. Access deletes only the label portion of the text box.

What happens if you deleted a text box control's label and later decide that you really want a label associated with the text box? You could delete the text box and start from scratch, but that could be a lot of work if you've changed the properties of the text box. You could also create a new label control and position it so it looks like it's associated with the text box, but then if you move the text box, the label won't move with it. There is, however, a better way.

Add a label to an existing control

1. Add a new label control to the form or select an existing label control.

2. With the label control selected, right-click to display the pop-up menu. Select **Copy** if you want the selected label control to remain on the form or **Cut** if you don't.

3. Select the text box with which you want to associate the label, and then right-click and select **Paste**. The label appears and is associated with the text box. You might need to resize or position the label.

You'll learn more about resizing controls later in the section "Sizing Controls," and more about positioning controls in the section "Positioning Controls."

Adding Several Controls of the Same Type

If you want to add the same type of control to your form or report, you have two options: the copy-and-paste method and the lock option.

Copying Controls

When you want to create several controls that share the same properties, create the first control, change its properties, copy it, and then paste it as many times as you need. That way, each copied control shares the modified property settings of the first control.

Copy and paste to add several controls

1. Open a new blank form by selecting **Forms** and then **New** in the Database window. (You also can continue to work with the open form you used in the last example.) Make sure that the **Control Wizards** tool in the Toolbox is deselected.

2. Click the **Command Button** tool in the Toolbox and then click the form's background. Access adds a command button to the form.

Shortcut for adding similar controls

Using cut and paste to add several controls to a form can save time even if the properties aren't all the same. If you want the same type of controls with only minor differences in the properties, use this method to add several and then vary the properties accordingly.

3. With the command button still selected, choose **Copy** from the **Edit** menu.

4. Choose **Paste** from the **Edit** menu. Access adds a second command button to the form (see Figure 16.9). Paste a third button by again selecting **Paste** from the **Edit** menu.

FIGURE 16.9

After copying the command button, you pasted a copy of the button to your form.

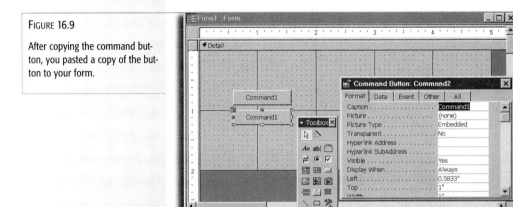

SEE ALSO

➤ *Learn more about setting properties and the time this shortcut will save for numerous settings on page 350*

Locking the Toolbox Control

An alternative to the copy-and-paste method is to lock the control type at the Toolbox. Then, you can select the type of control you want to add and simply click inside the form or report once for each control you want to add. This solution is good when the default properties are adequate, or when you'll be applying different property settings to each control.

Lock the Toolbox to add several of the same control

1. Make sure that the **Control Wizards** tool is deselected. Then, double-click the **Command Button** tool in the Toolbox. The mouse pointer changes to a box with a plus sign to indicate that you've locked the control (see Figure 16.10).

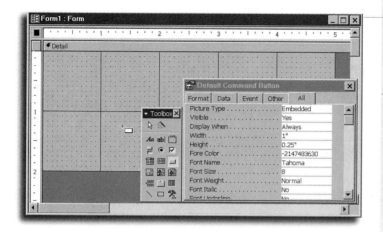

2. Click inside the form to add a command button.

3. Click inside the form to add a second command button. Continue clicking inside the form to insert as many buttons as you need.

4. To unlock the control, click the **Select Objects** tool ![select objects icon] in the Toolbox.

Positioning Controls

Working with controls is easy after you get the hang of it, but adding controls to a form or object is just the beginning. The next step is to position and align your controls. For the most part, you depend on the horizontal and vertical rulers, in conjunction with your grid settings, to position the controls you insert.

Position a control

1. Open a blank form in Design view.

2. Make sure that the **Control Wizards** tool ![control wizards icon] is deselected in the Toolbox.

3. Click the **Command Button** tool ![command button icon] in the Toolbox and click anywhere inside the blank form.

How Access names multiple controls

Access assigns a default name to a control, which you're free to change. The default name consists of the control's type and a number. If the control contains a label, Access applies consecutive even numbers to the control and consecutive odd numbers to the attached label control. For example, if the first control is a text box, that text box has the name Text0, and its label has the name Label1. When there's no label control, Access assigns consecutive numbers—not consecutive odd or even numbers.

4. By using the drag-and-drop method, drag the control to the 1-inch horizontal position (see Figure 16.11).

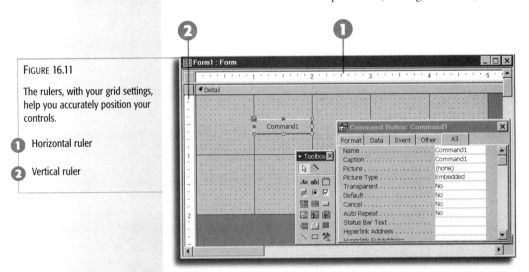

5. Maintaining the new horizontal position, drag the control to the 1-inch vertical position.

When you finish, the control should be at the intersection of both 1-inch lines (see Figure 16.12).

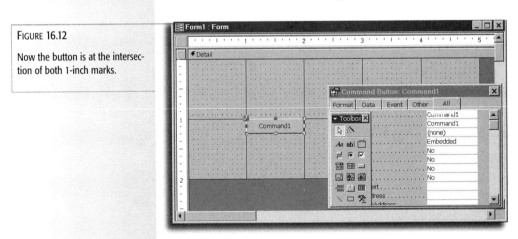

Sizing Controls

Placing your controls where you want them won't always be enough. Occasionally, you might have to change the size of a control. You might want to make all your controls the same size, or a control might be too small to completely display the contents of a field.

Directly size a control

1. Open an existing form in Design view by selecting that form in the Database window and then clicking **Design View**.

2. Select a control, especially one where the text runs past the end of a text box, and position the mouse pointer over the center-right handle. Access displays the double-arrow mouse pointer (see Figure 16.13), to indicate that you can change the size of the selected control.

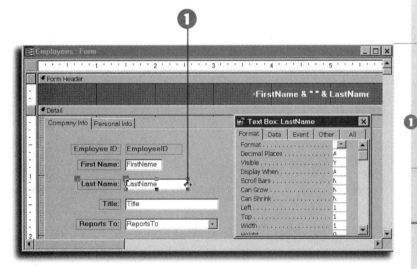

3. Drag the sizing handle to the right (or away from an adjacent label or control on an empty background) to the length you want.

You can also resize a control to match that of another control on a form. This works well if you want the size of controls to be

The database for this example

The figures in this example use the Employees form of the Northwind database. The same principles apply to any other controls you create.

FIGURE 16.13

When the double-arrow mouse pointer appears, you can resize the selected control.

1️⃣ Make sure that the double-arrow appears or you will move the control rather than resize.

Sizing by mouse

The same mouse actions you've used in other Windows applications apply with controls. If you want to expand a control up and to the right, hover the mouse pointer over the upper-right corner handle. The cursor changes to the diagonal, bidirectional arrow. The arrows over each handle show which way the control will expand.

Sizing options

Access offers several formatting options for resizing your controls. For the most part, they are self-explanatory. (Access matches the size of all controls you select to the tallest, shortest, widest, or narrowest control in the selection—whichever option you choose.) The **To Fit** option is especially worth noting—it sets the control size to adjust to the largest data entry in that field. The **To Tallest**, **To Shortest**, **To Widest**, and **To Narrowest** options are enabled only if you have two or more controls selected because Access compares and matches the sizes.

even along one edge, or if you know the values are of similar lengths. By matching the size of your controls, you also standardize the look of your forms and help reduce unused space.

Match existing control sizes

1. Select the control you want to resize.

2. Hold down the **Shift** key and select the control with the length you want to match. Both controls are now selected.

3. From the **Format** menu, choose **Size** and then **To Widest**. Access increases the size of the smaller control to match the wider control, as shown in Figure 16.14.

SEE ALSO

➤ *See more methods for standardizing the look of your forms on page 114*

FIGURE 16.14

Use the **Format** menu's **Size** command to resize the CustomerID control.

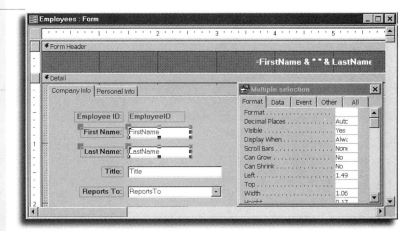

Selecting Multiple Controls

You might find yourself repeating tasks with several controls. Fortunately, Access lets you select more than one control at a time. Then, you can move, resize, or modify the whole group of controls at one time. Before you can make any changes, however, you must select the controls.

Selecting with the Shift Key

Of the several selection methods, perhaps the simplest is to select a control, hold down the **Shift** key, and then select another. You continue in this manner until you've added all the controls you want to modify in some way. This method enables you to be very specific about which controls you want to select, but it's also a little time consuming. To deselect multiple controls, simply click the form's background.

Use Shift to select multiple controls

1. Open an existing form in Design view by clicking the **Forms** tab, selecting the form, and then clicking **Design View** in the Database window. For this example, use the Northwind database's Employees form.

2. Select the first of the controls you want. (Be sure not to inadvertently select the control's label instead of the text box control.)

3. Press and hold down the **Shift** key, and then click the remaining controls. Access selects all the controls at the same time (see Figure 16.15).

Selecting with Shift

You can add as many controls as you like, as long as you continue to hold down the **Shift** key while clicking controls.

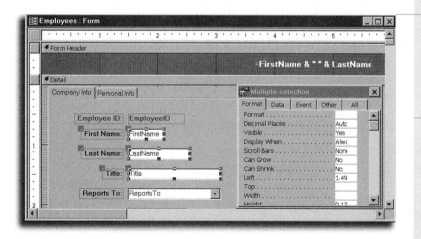

FIGURE 16.15

Selecting more than one control is easy—simply hold down the **Shift** key and click each control you want to include in your selection.

4. Select any additional controls, even if they aren't next to the ones you've selected thus far.

To see the scope of using the **Shift** key, try selecting the second, third, and sixth controls on the form. Access adds only these controls to your selection without affecting any control in between (see Figure 16.16).

FIGURE 16.16

You can add as many controls to your selection as you like.

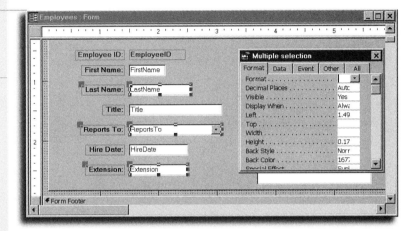

Using Rulers to Select Multiple Controls

You can also use the rulers to select controls. The outcome is a bit different, as everything below or to the right of the area you select in the ruler is also selected. Using the ruler method is less specific than the **Shift** key method, but it's quicker.

Select by simply pointing and clicking

1. With an existing form open in Design view, click the form's background to clear any previous selection. For this example, use the Northwind database's Employees form.

2. Click a mark on the horizontal or vertical ruler in line with the control(s) you want to select. Access will select control(s) directly below or across from that inch mark. Figure 16.17 shows an example of two controls selected by clicking the vertical ruler.

When you're selecting by the point-and-click method, note where the guideline falls among your controls. In Figure 16.18, Access excludes the FirstName control from the selection; because the control is shorter than the others, clicking just to the right of it missed this control.

Proximity guidelines for the ruler

If you click a mark on either ruler, a line from the ruler across the form/report appears. If any part of a control falls on that line, the control is selected.

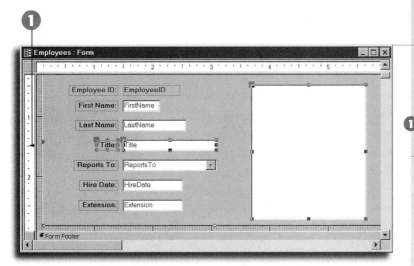

FIGURE 16.17

Access selected both controls to the right of the 1 1/2 inch mark on the vertical ruler

① 1 1/2 inch on the vertical ruler. Both controls are on this line.

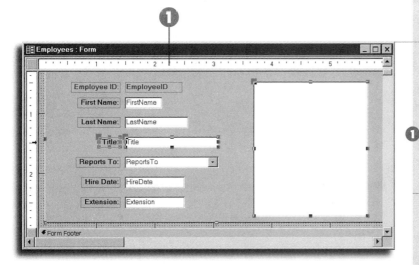

FIGURE 16.18

Access excluded the FirstName control from the multiple selection because it isn't directly below the 2 1/4 inch mark.

① 2 1/4 inch on the horizontal ruler. This line is just to the right of one control, so that control isn't included.

Access responds to more than a simple click on either ruler. You can also drag the mouse pointer along the ruler, and Access selects any control that falls under or to the right of the range that you drag the mouse across.

Drag across the ruler to select multiple controls

  1. With a form open in Design view, click the form's background to deselect all controls, if necessary.

2. Gauge the approximate edge of the range of controls you want to select. Click the ruler but don't release the mouse button. This creates the guideline straight from the ruler across the form.

3. Drag the mouse pointer across the ruler to include the controls you want.

Figure 16.19 illustrates this by showing the controls selected in the 3–4 inch range on the horizontal ruler. Access selects the Title, ReportsTo, and Photo controls because only these three controls lie in this range of the form.

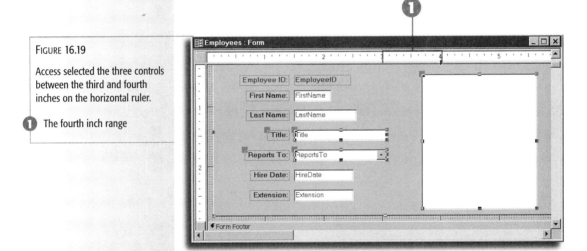

FIGURE **16.19**

Access selected the three controls between the third and fourth inches on the horizontal ruler.

❶ The fourth inch range

Similarly, Figure 16.20 shows the controls selected in a drag range on the vertical ruler. Access selects the three text box controls to the right of the 1–2 inch range: LastName, Title, and ReportsTo. However, Access also selects the Photo control because it's also to the right of this area.

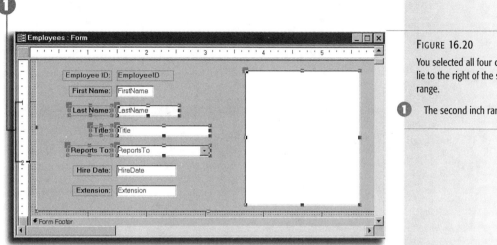

FIGURE 16.20
You selected all four controls that lie to the right of the second inch range.

1 The second inch range

Selecting Multiple Controls with the Mouse

You might be surprised to learn that there are still two more multiple selection techniques. First, you can select controls by creating an imaginary border around them with the mouse pointer.

Drag across controls to select them

1. With the form open in Design view, click the form's background to clear any previous selection, if necessary.
2. Place the pointer over the corner of the first control in an adjacent range of control.
3. Click the corner edge of the first control and drag the mouse across the control in the direction of the range you want to select.(You'll usually drag in a diagonal direction to form the loop.) As long as you continue in one fluid motion while holding the mouse button down, you can drag over any controls to select them.

Limitations of this method

If you've often used the mouse to drag across objects or lines of text, you might be familiar with these limitations. You can select only adjacent controls within a loop. You can't bend the loop to select or deselect objects that don't form an exact rectangle. You might have trouble controlling the roll of the mouse to get the exact number included if you're selecting a large range.

Figures 16.21 and 16.22 show the beginning and ending points of dragging the mouse to form a border around two text box controls and their respective label controls.

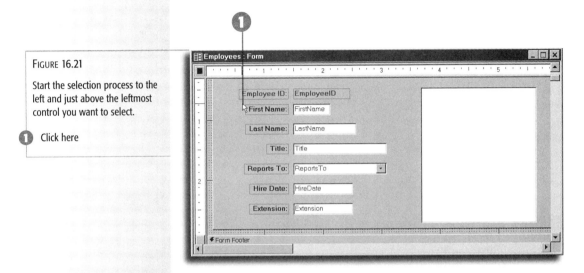

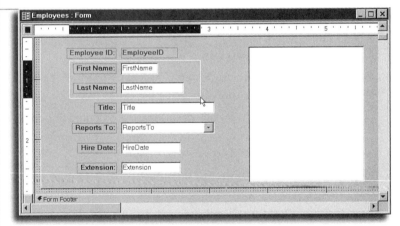

Selecting Most of Your Controls

As you can see, you can select multiple controls in several ways, each having its advantages and drawbacks. To select several controls but not all, it can sometimes be quicker and easier to select them all and then deselect the few you don't want to include. After you select all the controls, hold down the **Shift** key as you click the controls you don't want to include in the selection.

You can also use a combination of selection methods—you can select a group of adjacent controls by drawing a box with the mouse, and then select the remaining controls by holding down the **Shift** key and clicking.

Selecting multiple controls from the menu

To select all the controls in the form, choose **Select All** from the **Edit** menu.

Changing Selection Behavior Defaults

Selecting only the controls you want can sometimes be awkward because, by default, Access selects a control if you enclose any part of it in a selection process. If this presents a problem, you should adjust the way Access selects multiple controls.

Access offers two selection options: **Partially Enclosed** (the default) and **Fully Enclosed**. With the default setting, you need enclose only a small portion of a control to include it in the selection. In contrast, the **Fully Enclosed** option includes a control only if you completely enclose it.

Use the default Partially Enclosed setting

1. With a form open in Design view, click the form's background to clear the selection as necessary. (As with the other examples in this chapter, use the Employees form from the Northwind database.)

2. Click above and to the left of a control, such as the **LastName** label.

3. Without releasing the mouse button, drag the mouse pointer to a point in the middle of the controls you want to select and release the mouse button. For example, if you dragged to the 1 1/2 vertical inch mark and 2 3/4 horizontal inch mark on the Employees form, Access selects the **LastName** and **Title** controls (see Figure 16.23), even though you didn't contain them all in your drag loop.

To require Access to select only those controls completely enclosed in your drag loop, you need to adjust the selection behavior.

FIGURE 16.23

Access selects both the LastName and Title controls.

1 Dragging the mouse partially across controls selects all of them with the Partially Enclosed option.

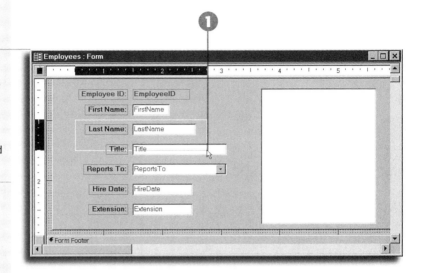

Use the Fully Enclosed setting

1. Choose the **Options** command from the **Tools** menu, and then select the **Forms/Reports** tab.

2. From the **Selection Behavior** options, choose **Fully Enclosed**. Click **OK** to return to the form.

3. Repeat the steps for using the Partially Enclosed setting. This time, Access selects only the controls that you completely enclose.

Changing the Properties of Multiple Controls

Don't forget the Undo feature

You're probably familiar with the **Edit** menu's **Undo** command. This feature enables you to change your mind after making an entry or modification. You can use **Undo** on a multiple selection as well. After changing a property setting, you can choose **Undo Property Setting** from the **Edit** menu (or press **Ctrl+Z**). You can also use the **Undo** button on the toolbar.

Multiple-selection techniques come in handy when you want to make the same modification to several controls at the same time—for example, if you want the text of all your controls to be a certain font or color. Simply create your multiple selection and then make the change once; Access applies the same modification to every control in the selection.

Modify properties in a multiple selection

1. With an existing form, such as Employees, open in Design view, click the background to clear any unwanted selections.

2. Use one of the methods described earlier in this chapter to select the controls you want to change. For example, click a

horizontal rule mark over a stack of controls to select all the text box controls on one side of the form.

3. Open a multiselection property sheet by clicking the **Properties** button 🖼 on the Form Design toolbar. Select the tab with the property you want to change, such as the Format tab.

4. Change the property, such as the Font Size, from 8 to 10. Access automatically updates the controls in the current selection (see Figure 16.24).

Missing the toolbar?

If you can't find the Form Design toolbar, it might be docked beside the Formatting toolbar. If so, drag it down and place it beneath the Formatting toolbar. If you still can't find it, choose **Toolbars** from the **View** menu to make sure that the **Form Design** option is selected.

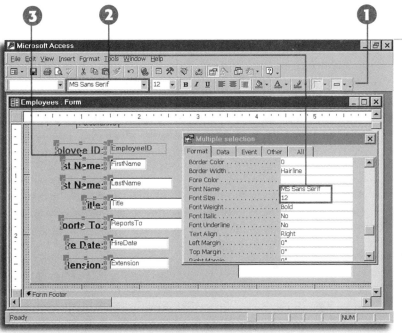

FIGURE 16.24

You increased the size of the font in several controls at one time.

1. If you're formatting multiple controls, you can use the Formatting toolbar to change font style or size and other attributes. Changes made in the properties sheet automatically appear here.

2. The change in the properties sheet shows the same style or font size as the toolbar. You can change more options with the properties sheet, but the toolbar can be a shortcut for some changes.

3. Double-click to automatically adjust the labels to fit the captions.

This example changes a property from the formatting list in the property sheet. You can also change several of these properties by clicking the corresponding option on the Formatting toolbar. For example, after you select multiple controls, click the drop-down list box on the toolbar and change the font size. The change in one location automatically updates the information in the other.

Automatically sizing controls

In Figure 16.24, you can see that when you increased the font size, the labels for the text boxes are now too small. If you position the mouse pointer as shown (with the two-headed arrow) and double-click, the labels automatically adjust their size to fit all of the label caption.

Don't worry about inadvertently affecting a stray property. When working with a multiple selection, Access displays only those properties that all the controls have in common.

Working with Bound Controls

Access provides the ability to use *bound controls*, or more generically *bound objects*. This built-in capability is one thing that makes Access so easy to use (many other database packages don't have this capability).

Table properties that affect your form

When you create a bound control, certain field properties that were set when you created the table are automatically assigned to the control. One of these is the `Caption` property. If you haven't assigned a `Caption` property, the field Name is used for the control's Label text. Other table properties carried through to the form are `Format`, `Input Mask`, `Default Value`, and `Description`. Access displays the `Description` property's text in the status bar for each control, when that control has focus. It's an easy way to display a bit of information about the control to your users.

A bound object is one that's attached to a data source. That object can be a form, a report, or a control. The underlying record source can be a table or query. For instance, a form bound to a table named `tblMyTable` displays the data in `tblMyTable`. You also can use that form to enter new data into `tblMyTable`. Actually, you can even use the form to modify the existing data in `tblMyTable`. In contrast, an unbound object has no data source. For instance, a calculated control displays data—the result of its expression—but that control isn't bound to a table or query. In other words, it displays data but doesn't store it.

A bound form or report's underlying table or query is the form's *record source*. A bound control's underlying field is the control's *control source*. Both the form's record source and the control's control source are available through the respective object's property sheet.

The Quarterly Orders form in the Northwind database is bound to the Quarterly Orders query (see Figure 16.25). This form also contains several bound controls and a calculated control (the Total control). A *calculated control* uses an expression as its data source instead of a bound field.

SEE ALSO

➤ *For more information on calculated controls, see page 328*

You can use a wizard to create bound fields, but most likely you will need to create them from scratch. The following example adds a bound control to the Quarterly Orders form in Design view.

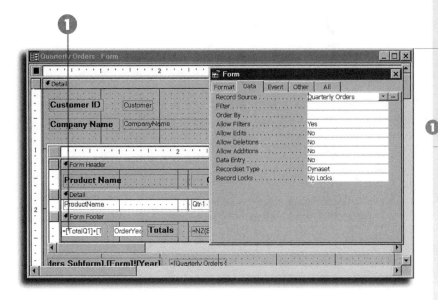

FIGURE 16.25

The Quarterly Orders form is bound to the Quarterly Orders query.

❶ A calculated control

Create a bound control

1. With your form open in Design view, click the **Field List** button 🔲 on the Form Design toolbar or choose **Field List** from the **View** menu. The Field List contains all the fields in the form's row source (bound table or query).

   If Access opens the Field List in an awkward spot, move it by clicking its title bar and dragging it someplace else.

2. Drag the field, such as CustomerID, from the Field List to the form (see Figure 16.26). Access adds a bound text box control to your form.

Adding one bound control at a time might prove time-consuming, so Access enables you to select multiple fields in the Field List. To choose a contiguous list of fields, hold down the **Shift** key and then click the first and last field. Or, hold down the **Ctrl** key and click each field to create a non-contiguous list. After you create a multiple-field selection, simply drag the lot of them to the form at the same time. Access sizes the controls to fit the data type of the field's property. For example, if you drag a smaller field (such as an ID field), a description, or image field to the form, Access automatically creates a larger display area for the larger fields.

Field names versus control names

You can have the same bound field on a form or report as many times as you like, although the situations in which this would be useful are limited. However, you can't duplicate a control name on a form or report.

Changing a bound control's default

By default, Access creates a bound text box control when you add a field by using the Field List window. If you want a different bound control type, you can temporarily change the control default by clicking another control on the Toolbox *before* you select the field from the Field List. If you've already created a control and decide that you want to change the control's type, select the control and then, from the **Format** menu, select **Change To**; you will see a list of controls that the selected control can be changed to.

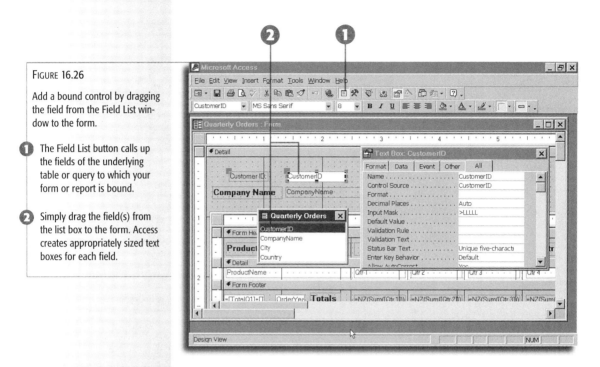

FIGURE 16.26

Add a bound control by dragging the field from the Field List window to the form.

① The Field List button calls up the fields of the underlying table or query to which your form or report is bound.

② Simply drag the field(s) from the list box to the form. Access creates appropriately sized text boxes for each field.

If you've already placed a control on a form and want to change its bound field, select the control and change its Control Source in the properties sheet. This capability is very useful if, after creating a form, you change the name of a field in the underlying table. Access won't automatically change the Control Source for all existing objects—you need to manually change it for all affected objects. This is one reason that it's so important to make sure that your database design and table structures are carefully constructed before you start creating your forms and reports.

Using Forms to Enter and Review Data

Working in Form View

Most of you use forms as though you are reading a book—you turn the page to see more information, or you turn back to review a previous page. Most forms display one record (page) at a time, but you can't turn the pages. Instead, forms contain several navigational features that you can use to view records (turn the page).

Single Form

A form that displays one record at a time is known as a single form. The Northwind Employees form (see Figure 17.1) is a good example of the Single Form setting. I'll talk about two other display settings, Continuous Form and Datasheet, later.

FIGURE 17.1

The Employees form uses the Single Form display setting.

1 Current record number

2 Record count

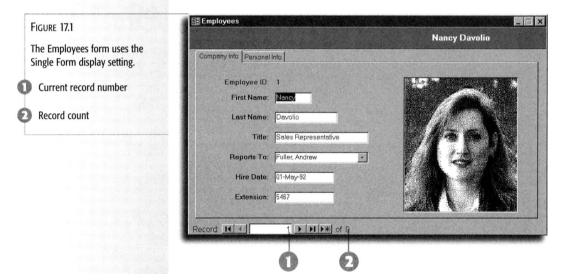

When you first open a bound form, Access displays the first record in the form's underlying *recordset* (a group of records). As you can see in Figure 17.1, the form hosts several navigational buttons at the bottom. Table 17.1 lists each button and a brief description for each.

SEE ALSO

➤ *For more on bound forms, see page 278*

TABLE 17.1   The Navigational Buttons on a Single Form

Button	Name	Description
|◀	First	Select the first record
◀	Previous	Select the previous record
▶	Next	Select the next record
▶|	Last	Select the last record
▶✳	New	Select a new record—creates a blank record for a new entry

At this point, you might want to take a few minutes to familiarize yourself with these five directional buttons. Click each a few times, making note of where that action takes you—note how the record number changes as you use the directional buttons.

When you first open a form, this toolbar indicates that you're viewing the first record and also indicates the total number of records. Access updates the record number as you browse the form's records.

Display the current record number

1. With an existing form open in Form view at the first record, click the **Next** ▶ button. Access selects the second record in the recordset and updates the current record number to reflect that change (see Figure 17.2).

2. Click the **Last** ▶| button to display the last record. As you can see in Figure 17.3, the form has 77 records.

3. Click the **Previous** ◀ button to select the preceding record—in this case, record 76.

4. Click the **First** |◀ button to return to where you started—at the first record.

Example for this task

This task uses the Products form from Northwind, but the principles apply to any form.

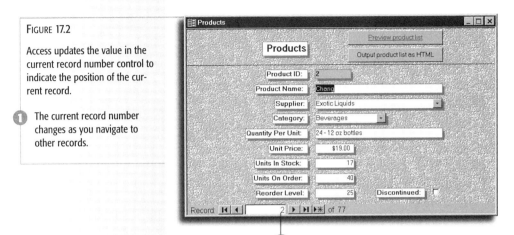

FIGURE 17.2

Access updates the value in the current record number control to indicate the position of the current record.

❶ The current record number changes as you navigate to other records.

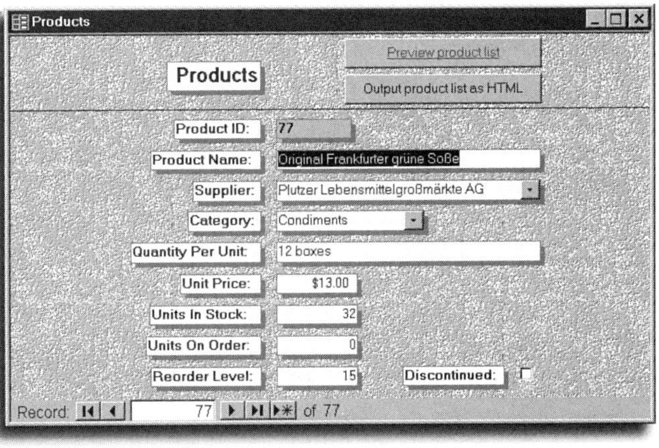

FIGURE 17.3

After clicking the last button, the current record number control displays the value 77.

Numbers probably won't match

Although the record number and the Product ID number happen to agree in this example, they will generally be different. The use of an AutoNumber data type in a field like Product ID is intended solely to provide a unique identifier for a record. Good database design will never rely on these two numbers being equal.

Using the alphabetized buttons

You might have noticed in this form that additional buttons from A–Z appear for easier navigation. Access doesn't provide the alphabetic buttons—those were added and programmed by the developer. This isn't an automatic form feature.

Continuous Form and Datasheet View

Viewing one record at a time won't always be the best choice for your data, so Access provides Continuous Form and Datasheet view. A few wizards will create a continuous form, such as the Customers Phone List form from Northwind (see Figure 17.4). Right away you can see a difference—this form displays all the records on one page. If there are more records than can be displayed on the current page, use the scrollbar to browse the records that are temporarily out of sight. You can adjust a form's display by resetting its Default View property.

FIGURE 17.4

The Continuous Forms setting displays all the records at the same time.

Change a form's display

1. With a continuous form, such as the Customers Phone List form, open in Form view, click the **View** button on the Form View toolbar to open the form in Design view.

2. If Access doesn't launch the form's property sheet, click the **Properties** button on the Form Design toolbar.

3. Open the Default View property's drop-down list to display the three possible settings: Single Form, Continuous Form, and Datasheet. The Customers Phone List's setting is Continuous Form; select **Single Form**.

4. For the result shown in Figure 17.5, click the **View** button on the Form Design toolbar. (Don't save the change.) Access doesn't change the form's layout, but the form displays only one record.

5. Return to Design view. From the properties sheet, select Datasheet View—the last setting. Then, click **View** on the Form Design toolbar to see the result (in Figure 17.6). As you can see, the form resembles a table.

SEE ALSO

➤ *For more information about limiting a form's display, see page 327*

Datasheet view without the work

If you want to get a table's-eye view of your form without altering the form's properties, you can choose **Datasheet View** from the **Design View** button . When you're done, choose **Form View** to return to the original display mode.l

FIGURE 17.5

You changed the form's
Default View property to
Continuous Form.

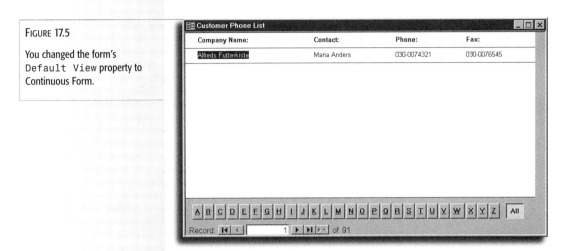

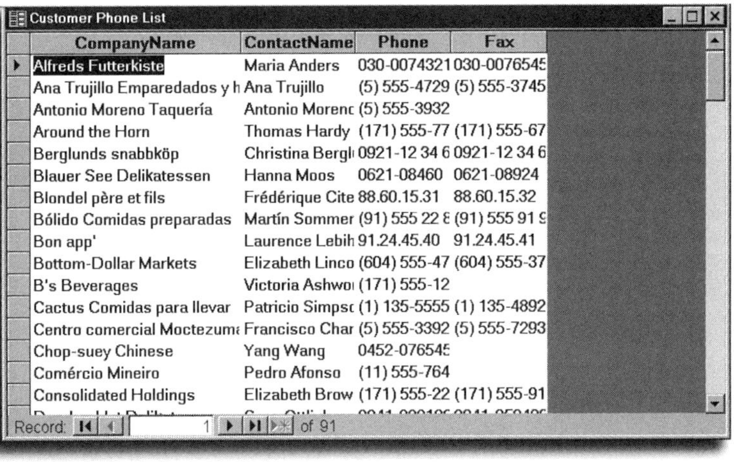

FIGURE 17.6

The Customers Phone List form
resembles a table after switching
the Default View property
to Datasheet view.

Viewing Subdatasheets

Subdatasheets allow you to view related data in a hierarchical
fashion. Apply this technique to your forms under the following
conditions:

- Your form contains a subform.
- The tables underlying the record source of the form and
  subform have some sort of hierarchical relationship that has
  been set in the tables' Subdatasheet Name property.
- The Views Allowed property of the form is set to either
  Datasheet or Both, but not Form.

Viewing a form with subdatasheets

1. With the Categories form open in Form view, click the **View** button 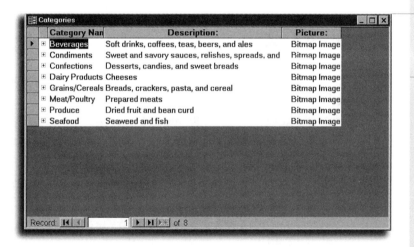 on the Form View toolbar to open the form in Design view.

2. If Access doesn't launch the form's property sheet, click the **Properties** button on the Form Design toolbar.

3. Open the Views Allowed property's drop-down list. The **Categories** setting is **Form**. Select **Both**.

4. Click the **View** button on the Form Design toolbar.

5. To see the result (in Figure 17.7), from the **View** menu choose **Datasheet**.

Automatically expanding subdatasheets

To have the form display with the subdatasheet automatically expanded, set the underlying table's **Subdatasheet Expanded** property to Yes (in Table Design view).

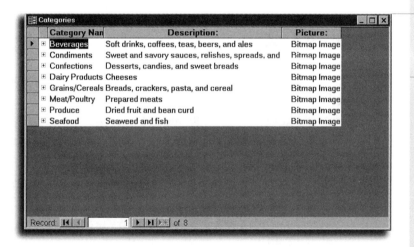

Category Nam	Description:	Picture:
⊞ Beverages	Soft drinks, coffees, teas, beers, and ales	Bitmap Image
⊞ Condiments	Sweet and savory sauces, relishes, spreads, and	Bitmap Image
⊞ Confections	Desserts, candies, and sweet breads	Bitmap Image
⊞ Dairy Products	Cheeses	Bitmap Image
⊞ Grains/Cereals	Breads, crackers, pasta, and cereal	Bitmap Image
⊞ Meat/Poultry	Prepared meats	Bitmap Image
⊞ Produce	Dried fruit and bean curd	Bitmap Image
⊞ Seafood	Seaweed and fish	Bitmap Image

Record: ◄ ◄ 1 ► ►► ►* of 8

FIGURE 17.7

Viewing the Categories form in Datasheet mode.

6. To show the subdatasheet (see Figure 17.8), click the plus sign next to the first record.

As an exercise to try on your own, use the Form Wizard to create a form based on the Categories table without a subform for the Product information. When you view this new form in Datasheet view, the records won't have a plus sign next to them, and you can't view the Product information in subdatasheets.

FIGURE 17.8

Using subdatasheets in the Categories form to display the related Products information.

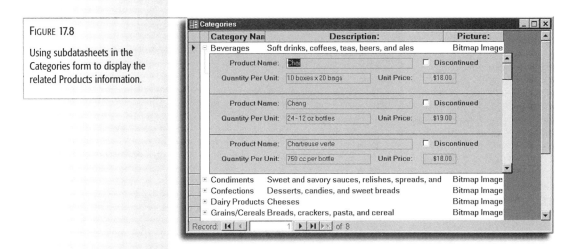

Navigating Records

Working with record numbers

Unlike some other desktop database systems, a record number doesn't have any internal significance in Access—it simply represents a record's relative position in the underlying recordset, and is displayed purely as a matter of convenience. The record number of any given record will continually change as data is added or deleted, or as the underlying recordset is sorted or filtered.

Earlier in the section "Working in Form View," I mentioned the navigational toolbar, which hosts five directional buttons: First, Previous, Next, Last, and New. This toolbar and its buttons appear on all forms, unless you inhibit them. However, these buttons provide just one way to jump from record to record. Another method is to choose **Go To** from the **Edit** menu. Doing so opens a submenu with the following choices: **First**, **Last**, **Next**, **Previous**, and **New Record**. This method is a little tedious but useful if your form doesn't have a navigational toolbar. If you know the number of the record you want to display, you can use the **F5** key.

Display a specific record

1. With the Customers Phone List form in Form view, press **F5**.

2. Enter a record number and Access will select that number. For instance, if you enter the value 3, Access will select the third record.

   So to select record number 10, press **F5**, type 10, and press **Enter**. You can use this shortcut to select any record, as long as you know the record's number.

-OR-

1. Select the value in the current record number control.
2. Enter the value that equals the number you want to view.
3. Press **Enter** and close the form without saving any changes.

Controlling Navigation in Forms

Now that you know how to get from record to record, look at a few techniques for moving between the controls on your form. For the most part, you'll press **Tab** or **Enter** to select the next control on the current form. When the last control has focus, you can press **Enter** to select the next record. If the current record is the last record when you press **Enter**, Access will display a new record, which contains empty controls so that you can enter new data.

SEE ALSO

➤ *To learn more about data-entry form properties, see page 327*

Changing the Tab Order

At this point, you might be wondering how Access knows which control is the next control. That's determined when you create the form using each control's Tab Stop and Tab Index properties. The Tab Stop property determines whether Access gives focus to a particular control. If the property is set to No, Access won't select it. When the setting is Yes, Access looks to the Tab Index value to determine where that control falls into the selection order. These values are consecutive and begin with the value 0: the first control Access will select has a Tab Index value of 0, the second control in the cycle will have a Tab Index value of 1, and so on. Access can automatically set these properties in three ways:

- If you use an AutoForms Wizard to create a form, Access will set the Tab Index values to match the order of the fields in the underlying table or query.

Properties that affect navigation

Each form has a few data-entry properties that can affect navigation. For instance, if the form's Allow Additions property is set to No, Access won't display a new record, regardless of the buttons you press or click. The New Record navigation button is actually grayed out so you can't click it.

Changing the tab order after moving controls

Regardless of the way you initially create your form, the final arrangement of the controls has no bearing on the tab order. Access won't update the Tab Index values if you rearrange the controls—you will have to do that yourself. Fortunately, you can easily change the order in which Access selects the controls on a form. You simply change the Tab Stop or the Tab Index property.

- If you use the Form Wizard, Access will set the properties to follow the order of the fields as you move them from the **Available Fields** list to the **Selected Fields** list in the wizard's dialog box.

- When you create a form, Access assigns the values in the order you add each control.

Protecting a Field by Using the *Tab Stop* Property

One reason you might want to change the Tab Stop property is to protect the data in that field while still enabling users to view the data. For example, in an **Employees** table, you might want to be able to view the Social Security number but not allow the viewer to change it easily. Setting the Tab Stop property to No means that the cursor never enters the field to update or change it.

Remove a control from the selection order

1. Double-click a form in the Database window to open it in Form view.

2. Press **Tab** enough times to run through the current selection cycle. Access will select each control. If you can reach each field, its Tab Stop property is set to Yes.

3. Press **Shift+Tab** enough times to return to the first control in the current record.

4. To begin changing the current selection order, click **Design View** 🖉 on the Form View toolbar.

5. In Design view, select the control you want. Then, double-click the control to open its property sheet. You can also click the **Properties** button 🛅 on the Form Design toolbar.

6. From the **Other** or the **All** page, open the Tab Stop property's drop-down list and change the current setting from Yes to No.

7. Return to Form view by clicking **View** 🖃 on the Form Design toolbar.

Prohibiting data entry with Tab Stop

If you use the **Tab Stop** property to prohibit data entry, also consider grouping those controls on one side or at the bottom of the screen. You might also want to set their **Enabled** property to No so that they can't be changed even if your user clicks them with the mouse.

8. Cycle through the controls until you select the control just before the one you changed. Now, press **Enter** or **Tab** one more time. Rather than select the next control, Access skips to the following control. That's the result of changing the Tab Stop property.

Changing the Selection Order

After you create and modify the controls on your form, you won't want to jump back and forth between fields if you've rearranged them. Correcting the selection order helps data entry flow smoothly with the reading order on the form.

Change the selection order

1. If the selected form is in Form view, click the **Design View** icon ⊠ ▾ to open the form in Design view.

2. Select the controls one at a time beginning with the first one (upper left, if appropriate).

3. Change each control's Tab Index to match its physical order.

4. Click the **Form View** icon ⊞ ▾ to return to Form view.

5. Press **Enter** or **Tab** to cycle through the controls as a test.

How the *Cycle* Property Affects Selection Order

Forms have another property that affects navigation: Cycle. This property controls the selection behavior when the last control on a bound form has the focus. The default is the All Records setting, which selects the first control in the next record when the last control has the focus and you press **Enter** or **Tab**.

There are two other settings:

- The Current Record setting selects the first control on the current record rather than access the next record. If you press **Shift+Tab** while the focus is on the first control, Access will select the last control for the current record.

- The Current Page setting is similar to Current Record, except that Current Page keeps the focus on the current page. (A record can require many pages.)

Selection order and control placement

Although Access will accept any selection order you determine, be sure that the order you use follows a logical left-to-right and top-to-bottom order. If you're going to set any Tab Stop properties to No but might make them available later, include the field in the numbering order as though you were going to use it. This way, when you do enable its selection, the field will be highlighted in a logical order rather than receive selection at the end.

A shortcut to changing tab order

Access has a convenient built-in feature that's much easier to use. Select **Tab Order** from the **View** menu to open the Tab Order dialog box, which lists all the controls and enables you to arrange them in the order you like. As you do so, Access automatically updates their selection order. If you really want to save time, click the **Auto Order** button, which automatically resets all tab order values to match each control's relative position. Specifically, Access sets the tab order from left to right and then from the top to the bottom.

Cycling turns the page

In keeping with the book analogy of navigating records, setting the Cycle property to All Records is the factor for helping you turn the page to the next record as you finish entering or viewing the last control of a record.

Unfortunately, you can't depend on this property to inhibit a user's access to other records. The Page Up and Page Down keys and the Previous and Next buttons will give focus to the previous or next page, respectively, regardless of the Cycle property's setting.

Limiting Access to the Previous and Next Record

If you must limit access to the previous or next record, you can attach the VBA code shown in Listing 17.1 to your form's KeyDown event. Then, set the form's Cycle property to Current Record or Current Page, appropriately.

Use code to prevent paging through records

1. Select the form and then click **Design View** in the Database window to open that form in Design view.

2. Click the **Code** button 🔲 on the Form Design toolbar to open the form's module.

3. Select **Form** in the module's Object control and KeyDown in the module's Procedure control.

4. Enter the code in Listing 17.1. (VBA will supply the opening and ending statements.) Your screen should resemble Figure 17.9.

LISTING 17.1   **Limiting Access to the Previous and Next Record**

```
1 Private Sub Form_KeyDown(KeyCode As Integer, _
  Shift As Integer)
2 Select Case KeyCode
3     Case vbKeyPageUp
4         KeyCode = 0
5     Case vbKeyPageDown
6         KeyCode = 0
7     Case Else
8 End Select
9 End Sub
```

Saving changes

You can make this alteration to the Customers form, but don't save your modifications when you're finished.

Accessing the module window

If you prefer, you can go through the properties sheet to open the form's module window. Select the appropriate **On** property, choose **Event Procedure** from the property's drop-down list, and then click the **Builder** button 🔲 to the right of the property field. Access will respond by opening the form's module and supplying the event's first and last statement (the Private Sub and End Sub statements).

Numbering of code lines

Listing 17.1 and other code listings throughout the book include line numbers to make discussion about this code easier to reference. The numbers should not be included as part of any VBA programs.

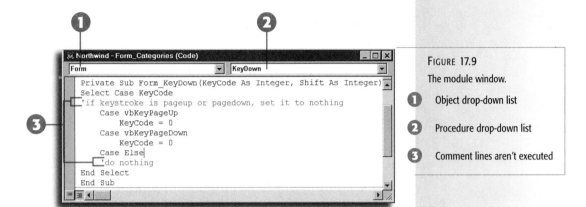

FIGURE 17.9
The module window.
1 Object drop-down list
2 Procedure drop-down list
3 Comment lines aren't executed

5. Close the module window.

6. Select **Current Record** from the Cycle property's drop-down list. (Double-click the Form Selector to select the form's property sheet.)

7. Change the Key Preview property from No to Yes. This setting sends your keystrokes to the Form event before sending it to the control.

8. Click **View** to display the form in Form view.

9. Press **Page Down**. Rather than select the next record, Access seems to do nothing. Actually, Access executes the form's KeyDown event, which checks your keystroke. Because that keystroke equals vbKeyPageDown, Access returns the KeyCode 0, which does nothing. The same thing happens if you press **Page Up**.

This exercise doesn't inhibit the form's navigational toolbar. If you want to prohibit access to other records, be sure to turn the navigational toolbar off by changing that form's Record Selectors and Navigational Toolbars properties to No.

SEE ALSO
➤ *To become oriented with the code-entry environment, see page 448*
➤ *For more information about the code you're entering, see page 469*

A shortcut to Design view

To open a closed object in Design view, select that form and then click **Design** in the Database window. You can also right-click the form in the Database window and select **Design** from the pop-up menu.

Sorting in a Form

Access doesn't sort records when it opens a form, unless you set a sort order in the underlying bound table or query, or with some event. A form uses the same order as the bound object.

You can sort records in the form environment in several ways. Perhaps the easiest method is to select the field you want to sort by and then click one of the sort buttons on the Form view toolbar: **Sort Ascending** [↓] or **Sort Descending** [↓].

You'll be using the Products form from the Northwind database in the following example. However, you can use most any form.

An easy sorting solution

1. Open a form in Form view.

2. Select the field you want to sort your records by.

3. Click **Sort Ascending** [↓] on the Form View toolbar to sort the records in ascending order by the selected field. I sorted the product records by the product names (see Figure 17.10) by selecting the Product Name field and then clicking the **Sort Ascending** button.

FIGURE 17.10

The Products form sorts by the Product ID field, but you re-sorted the records by the Product Name field.

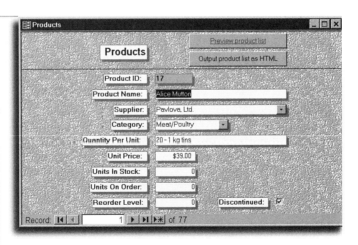

For a descending sort, click the appropriate field and then click **Sort Descending** [↓] (see Figure 17.11).

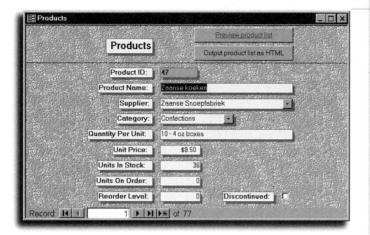

FIGURE 17.11
This time you sorted the records in descending order.

In addition to the preceding method, you have three other methods to choose from:

- Set a primary key
- Sort a query to be used as your form's record source
- Use the Order By property

Primary key fields are discussed a great deal throughout this book. Basically, a primary key requires a unique entry for each record. However, a primary key also sorts records by the contents of the primary key field. The preceding example sorted by the Product ID field because it's the primary key. Unfortunately, setting a primary key isn't appropriate for every sort because primary keys allow only unique entries and don't allow empty fields.

Because a form's record source can be a query as well as a table, you can create a sorted query and use that as your form's record source. Using a query has the additional benefit of allowing you to use a selection criteria for the records shown in your form.

When a primary key or a sorted query isn't the best solution, consider the form's Order By property. For more in-depth information on queries, see Chapter 13, "Designing and Using Queries."

SEE ALSO

➤ *For more information on primary keys, see page 71*

When things don't sort properly

A field's data type can affect the resulting sort order because numbers entered into a text field won't sort in numerical order–they will sort alphanumerically. For example, the values 1, 2, 8, 10, 11, and 15 sort in that same order numerically, but alphanumerically they sort as 1, 10, 11, 15, 2, and 8. If this is a problem, use the Val() function to return the field's contents as a value instead of text.

Working with the *Order By* Property

A multifield sort

If you want to sort by more than one field, simply add the field to the Order By property and separate each field with a semicolon (;). For instance, if you want to sort by the Employees form by the LastName and then the FirstName fields, you'd set Order By to LastName;FirstName. You also can add the strings DESC or ASC to specify a descending or ascending sort. For example, use the setting FirstName DESC to produce a descending sort by the FirstName field, or LastName ASC;FirstName DESC to force a descending sort of the FirstName field within an ascending sort by the LastName field. (Ascending is actually the default, so you won't need ASC for the most part, but including it is helpful for documentation purposes.)

The Order By property enables you to specify a sort order for the form. It's a quick solution, but it isn't dynamic. This means Access won't sort records as you enter them. Instead, this property will sort existing records when you open the form. For normal data-entry tasks, this is a good arrangement; waiting for your recordset to re-sort each time you enter a new record can be a nuisance.

For the following example, you'll work with the Employees form from Northwind. As usual, you can use most any form you like—just make sure that the form isn't already using the Order By property.

Use the *Order By* property to sort

1. Open a form in Form view. The form might already be sorting by a field—look for a good primary key candidate. The Employees form appears to sort by the EmployeeID field.

2. Click the **Design View** button ![icon] on the Form View toolbar to open the form in Design view.

3. Click the **Properties** button ![icon] on the Form Design toolbar to open the form's property sheet.

4. Select the Order By property field and enter the field you want to sort by. For the example, enter LastName (see Figure 17.12).

FIGURE 17.12

Sorting records by the LastName field.

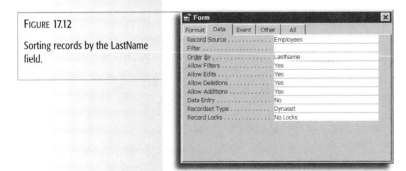

5. Return to Form view by clicking the **View** button ![icon] on the Form Design toolbar. As you can see in Figure 17.13, Access has sorted the records by the contents of the LastName field.

FIGURE 17.13
By specifying an Order By
property, you changed the sort
order.

Searching in a Form

You can find records that match specific criteria in Form view in
three quick and easy ways:

- The Find feature
- Filter By Selection
- Filter By Form

The Find Feature

The Find feature is as easy to use as the Sort feature discussed
earlier in the section "Sorting in a Form." Choose **Find** from the
Edit menu to open the Find and Replace dialog box (see Figure
17.14). If Access finds matching data, it displays the first occurrence. You can then click **Find Next** to find all the subsequent
matching entries. If no matching records exist, Access displays a
message to let you know that there are no records. You can just
click OK to clear this message box.

FIGURE 17.14

The Find command enables you to search for specific data in Form view.

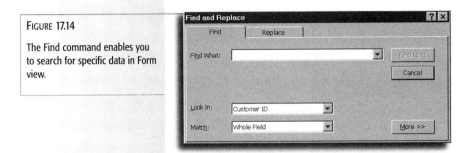

For the following example, the Northwind Customers form is used to demonstrate how to use the Find feature. You can use most any form you like; just be sure to search for appropriate data.

Use the Find feature to search for data

1. With the Customers form open in Form view, choose the City field. Then, choose **Find** from the **Edit** menu.

2. Enter Madrid in the Find What text box (see Figure 17.15); then click the **Find Next** button. Access displays the first record that contains the entry Madrid.

FIGURE 17.15

Access displays the first record where City is equal to Madrid.

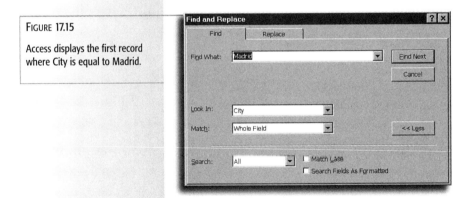

3. Click the **Find Next** button to find the next matching record. Because there are none, Access displays a message to let you know that there are no records.

The Find feature has several other options:

- **Look In** enables you to select which field you want to search on. By default, the field on which you've placed your cursor is the field you search. The drop-down list shows the name of the form's record source and gives you the option of searching through all the fields in the record source.

- **Match** enables you to specify a whole field or parts of a field. Whole Field searches the entire field and returns a match only when the search criteria matches the contents of the entire field. Any Part of Field returns a match if the search criteria is found anywhere in the field. Start of Field returns entries where the first part of the entry matches the search criteria.

- **Search** specifies a search order: **Up**, **Down**, and **All**. This way, you can search backward or forward through your records beginning with the current record. For instance, if the current record is number 14 and you choose **Down**, Access searches records 15 through the last record, but not records 1 through 13. Similarly, if you choose **Up**, Access searches only records 1 through 14. **All**, of course, searches all the records.

- **Match Case** returns entries that share the same case as the search criteria.

- **Search Fields as Formatted** matches fields that share the same display format as the search criteria.

The Filter By Selection Feature

The Filter By Selection feature combines the sort method I talked about in the section "Sorting in a Form" and the Find feature from the preceding section. Select a field, click the **Filter By Selection** button , and Access will create a temporary recordset that consists of all the records that contain matching data in the current field.

Continue to use the Customers form in the examples.

Use Filter By Selection

1. With your form open in Form view, select a field that contains the criteria you want to search for.

2. Click the **Filter By Selection** button 🔽 on the Form View toolbar. As you can see in Figure 17.16, I searched for all the records that contain Berlin in the City field. The resulting recordset contains only one record. To remove the current filter, click the **Remove Filter** button 🔽 on the Form View toolbar.

FIGURE 17.16

The Filter By Selection search turns up only one record.

① You have only one matching record.

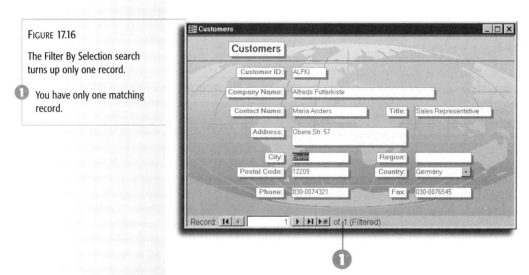

The Filter By Form Feature

This final search feature adds a bit of flexibility to the search process by enabling you to enter your own text rather than rely on the current entry.

Use the Filter By Form feature

1. With your form open in Form view, click the **Remove Filter** button 🔽 on the Form View toolbar to delete any existing filters.

2. Click the **Filter By Form** 🔽 button on the Form View toolbar.

Access displays a search template similar to the one shown in Figure 17.17. The previous filter of Berlin is still active;

that's why Access displays Berlin in the City field. You see, the **Remove Filter** button ⧩ removes the filter from the current recordset. It doesn't delete it from the form's properties.

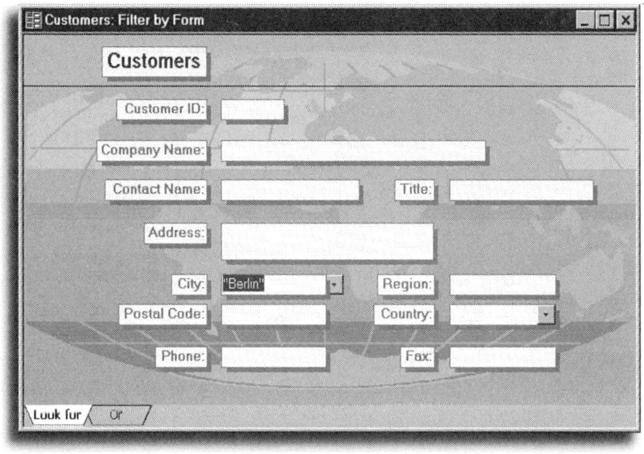

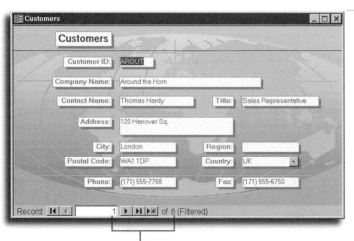

FIGURE 17.17
The Filter By Form feature displays a search template.

3. You can choose search criteria from one of the combo boxes, or you can enter your own criteria in the appropriate field. Figure 17.18 is the result of choosing **London** from the City field's drop-down list and then clicking the **Apply Filter** button ⧩ on the Filter/Sort toolbar.

Similar but different

The Remove Filter and Apply Filter icons are very similar. The Remove Filter icon is the Apply Filter icon in a *selected* state, to show that a filter has been applied.

FIGURE 17.18
Using the Apply Filter option.

① The first of six records that match the search criteria of London

The Filter/Sort toolbar (open during Filter By Form) offers two more options you might want to know about:

- **Load From Query** enables you to load an existing query into Filter By Form rather than create it.
- **Save As Query** is how you'll save a Filter By Form selection to query, so you can reload it at another time.

After you create a Filter By Form query that you know you might repeat from time to time, click the **Save As Query** button on the Filter/Sort toolbar to save it. Then, click **Load From Query** on the Filter/Sort toolbar when you want to reuse it.

Refining Forms: Efficient Data Entry and Beyond

Use the *Validation Rule*, *Format*, *Required*, and *Input Mask* properties to control the type of data your application will accept

Use formats and colors to visually convey information

Control access to your data

Use expressions to display additional information

Learn how to register and insert ActiveX controls

Verifying Data

Face it—getting users to enter data the way your application expects it is an uphill battle. A user's failure to enter the correct data can produce erroneous data or even crash your system. The more work you can get Access to do, the less your users must remember and the less you'll worry about your application.

If an application requires a lot of data entry, you'll want to take advantage of several built-in features which ensure that your users enter the type of data your application expects. You'll save your users time, and you'll avoid errors.

The best place to start is with data validation. By that I mean Access checks an entry and rejects it when that entry doesn't match the criteria you've defined for that field. Setting data types is one way to do this. If a field accepts only numbers and you enter 2a4, you'll want Access to reject that entry. This feature is built in and you need to apply only the appropriate data type to your fields to get help from Access. When the data type isn't enough, you can set stricter or more complex rules with a field's Validation Rule property.

SEE ALSO

➤ *Learn all the specific data types and their entry criteria on page 68*

Using the *Validation Rule* Property

You already know that you can limit the type of data a control accepts by assigning a data type to the bound field. A data type, however, won't always offer enough control. For instance, you can limit a control to accept only number characters. The Number data type won't limit that same entry to a particular range of values, however. If you might want users to enter only values from 1 to 10, the Number data type keeps them from entering abc but it won't keep them from entering 12.

More restriction using data types

An easy way to restrict an entry is to limit the number of characters a field can accept. Simply set the field's Field Size property at the table level to the appropriate number of characters. Suppose that you're storing alphanumeric part numbers that consist of seven characters. If you limit the field's size to 7, Access won't accept more than 7 characters in that field. Limiting the size of your field won't guarantee against typos, but it's a start. Besides, you'll save memory.

To restrict entries to particular values, use the Validation Rule property to check an entry *before* users leave the field. For the most part, you'll enter simple expressions to limit your entries with this property. An example is the problem of limiting an entry to the values 1 through 10. In this situation, you'd enter the simple expression >=1 AND <=10 as the field's Validation Rule property setting. After entering a value, Access would then evaluate the entry to see that it conforms to the limitations defined by the expression. If the value conforms, Access would accept your entry; if not, Access would display a warning message.

To see how this property works, you'll restrict the ReorderLevel field in the Products table of the Northwind database to the values 0 through 30.

Set the *Validation Rule* property

1. Select the table you want to use and then click **Design View** in the Database window.

2. Select the field in the upper pane of the Design view window by clicking the far left button next to that field.

   As you can see in Figure 18.1, some fields in the table already have restrictions. The ReorderLevel field already restricts entries to positive values.

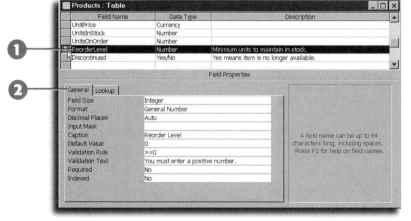

Working with nulls

If you apply a validation rule to a field, Access won't allow you to leave the field blank unless you set the field's Required property to No and add Is Null to the validation rule. To allow only Y, N, or nothing, the validation rule would be "Y" or "N" or Is Null.

FIGURE 18.1

The existing Validation Rule expression expects a positive value.

❶ Click here to select the entire field.

❷ The **General** tab shows the current validation rules and text.

3. Add to the current expression the component for your limitation, such as AND <=30.

4. Enter the warning message you want to display, such as Enter a value between 0 and 30, for the Validation Text property (see Figure 18.2).

FIGURE 18.2

You updated the Validation Rule expression so that it forces a value between 0 and 30.

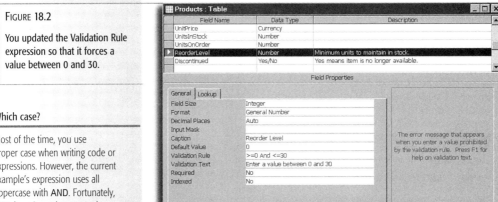

Which case?

Most of the time, you use proper case when writing code or expressions. However, the current example's expression uses all uppercase with AND. Fortunately, VBA doesn't restrict case and accepts AND, And, or and.

Applying validation rules to existing text

In this example, you're changing a validation rule for a table that already contains data. When you do this, Access tries to apply the rule to the existing data and warns you when the table contains data that doesn't conform to the new rule. Access won't destroy the non-conforming data, but it applies the new rule to that field just the same, which means you can't overwrite one non-conforming entry with another.

5. Click **Datasheet View** on the Datasheet Design toolbar to display the table. Access warns you about the possible affects of changing the existing Validation Rule property. Don't worry about that right now; just click **Yes** twice.

6. Select the first new record and test an entry that "breaks" your validation rule. Your incorrect entry should trigger a warning message box with the text you entered.

For the example, try to enter the value 40 in the ReorderLevel field. Because 40 is greater than 30, Access should reject the entry and display the message in Figure 18.3. That message is the string you entered for the Validation Text property. Press **Esc** to clear the entry.

Try entering 25. Because 25 falls between 0 and 30, Access accepts this value.

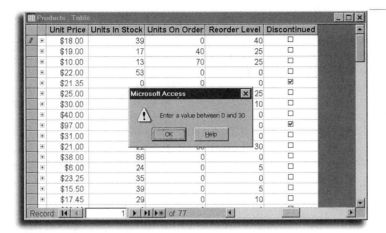

FIGURE 18.3
The value 40 doesn't conform to the new Validation Rule property and triggers an error with the message defined for the field.

Testing the Related Form

To finish testing the validation rule, you need to check any existing forms bound to the table whose field you've changed.

Use the *Validation Rule* in a form

1. Double-click the form in the Database window to open it in Form view.

2. Display a new record by clicking the **New Record** button ▶✳ on the navigational toolbar, or choose **New Record** from the **Insert** menu.

3. Enter a value beyond or outside the restrictions you created into the field you're checking and press **Enter** or **Tab**. For the example, try 31 in the ReorderLevel field. Because 31 is greater than 30, Access rejects the entry, with the same message that you saw when you tried to enter an invalid number into the table directly.

Benefits of the Validation Text property

In this example, the Validation Text is displayed when you try to enter a value that doesn't meet the Validation Rule. If you didn't enter your message in the Validation Text property, Access displays its own internal error message—one that might not be clear and often includes technical phrases that users might not find meaningful.

Changing Northwind

You might want to close the forms and tables from the Northwind examples without changing them. This keeps the database with the same data and restrictions as its queries and other design aspects expect.

Table-level validation

When you set a validation rule for a field, you can't reference other fields in the validation rule. If you need to validate one field with another, you need to set a table-level validation rule. You do this by displaying the Table properties dialog box (right-click the table in Design view and select **Properties**) and entering your validation rule.

4. Press **Esc** to clear the entry. Close the form and save your changes.

For the most part, you'll want to define a field's `Validation Rule` and `Validation Text` in the table design because any bound control inherits these properties from the table. This behavior saves you time because you need to set the property only once. When you look at the properties for the control, you won't see the entries for the table, even though they're in effect. This is because you can still use these properties for controls on your forms and reports. However, any `Validation Rule` you set for the bound control must work within the scope of the table `Validation Rule`; if the table rule limits entries to A, B, or C, you can change the control's property to allow only B or C, but you can't add D as a valid entry because it will fail the table-level validation.

SEE ALSO

➤ *For more information on applying data types, see page 475*

Forcing an Entry

One of the most important things you can do to protect your application is to force an entry. Although you won't always need to do this, sometimes it's mandatory to protect your application. For instance, if a future calculation depends on a value in a particular field, that field needs to contain something, even if it's 0. The easiest way to force users to make an entry is to enable the field's `Required` property.

The `Required` property determines whether a field can remain blank. A bound control in a form or a report inherits the bound table's setting. There are two settings: `No` (the default), which enables blank fields, and `Yes`, which forces users to make an entry before they can continue with data entry. If they try to leave the field empty, Access displays a warning message, with which they can make an entry and continue, or delete the incomplete record.

Although you'll most often benefit from this setting at the form level, you set it at the table level.

Set the *Required* property

1. Open Northwind's Products table in Design view.

2. Select the ReorderLevel field in the upper pane of the Design View window.

3. Find the Required property in the **Field Properties** section in the lower pane. Select **Yes** from the property's drop-down list.

4. Click the **View** button  on the Table Design toolbar, and then click **Yes** twice to save the change.

5. To test the enforcement of the new rule, first select a **New Record** ▶✳. Then try to enter data in all fields but the required field and see if Access accepts a blank field. When you try to leave the field blank, Access should display a warning message (see Figure 18.4). You don't get the warning message if you've set a default value because Access automatically supplies the default.

Microsoft Access

⚠ The field 'Products.ReorderLevel' can't contain a Null value because the Required property for this field is set to True. Enter a value in this field.

　　OK　　　　Help

6. Click **OK** to clear the message and press **Esc** to delete the incomplete record.

7. If you want to save your changes, close and save the table.

After you set a field's Required property to Yes, all bound controls in forms and reports also require an entry. If you try to leave the related control blank, Access displays the same warning message.

Although the Required property forces you to make an entry, Access won't display the warning message until after you try to bypass the field. It would be more efficient if you knew beforehand when an entry is mandatory—that way, you can avoid the situation altogether. Fortunately, you can visually inform users

---

Sometimes the Required property isn't effective

Setting the Required property to Yes won't always have the effect that it does in this example. For example, a Number data type field enters 0 if you fail to enter a value yourself and didn't changed the table level Default Value, which is 0 for numeric fields. This completely negates the purpose of the Required property because Access finds the value 0, even if you didn't enter it.

FIGURE 18.4

Access displays this message if you try to leave a required field blank.

Timing events

Some developers prefer to attach validation expressions to control events (generally a control's Before Update event, rather than the control's Validation Rule property). If you venture into this area, be sure to keep event timing in mind; otherwise, you could create a conflict between controls. Also, if you open the table directly or use another programming tool that can read Access databases, your form control validation isn't triggered.

by displaying required fields in a different color from all the others. Use the Color Picker to select the color you want to reflect a required field as the control's Back Color or Fore Color (not both) property. When using colors, try to stay with the Windows 16 basic colors, the only colors you can rely on to look the same on all monitors.

SEE ALSO

➤ *Get more information on event timing on page 355*

Formatting Data with the *Format Property*

Formatting data is a wide-open topic, and I could probably write several chapters on that subject alone. Instead, I will discuss some basic issues and then show you some techniques you might not think of.

Like many properties, you can apply the Format property at the table or control (form or report) level. If you apply a format at the table level, a bound control inherits that format. If you apply a format at the control level in a form or report, Access overrides the table format. If no format is defined at the table level, however, the control format won't affect the data stored in that table. The format you assign to a field or control depends on the field's data type. Actually applying the formats is easy.

Apply formats at the table level

1. Select the table and click **Design View** in the Database window.

2. Select the field you want to format in the upper pane of the Design View window. Notice what data type this field is. For example, if the data type is Number, open the **Data Type** drop-down list to display the formats you can apply to the current field (see Figure 18.5).

When are table-level properties not table-level properties?

When you set a table-level Validation Rule, that rule is always in effect. If you change the table-level Validation Rule, all existing forms will reflect the changed rule. Some properties, such as a field's Format property, aren't updated in existing forms. Always use caution when you change an existing table's design. This is only one of many reasons that you should make sure that your table structure is correct before you proceed with the development of an application.

Using the Format Painter

The Format property offers only a few formats. Others (such as font face, size, and weight, alignment, and so on) are available on the Formatting toolbar and as properties themselves. If you want to copy a particular control's formats, click that control and then click the **Format Painter** button on the Form Design toolbar. Next, select the control you want to assign those same formats to. The Format Painter applies all the first control's formats to the second.

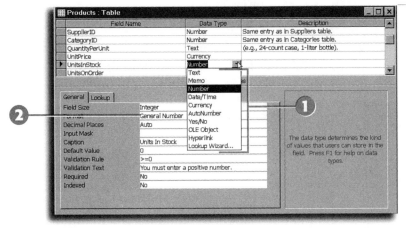

FIGURE 18.5

This field has a Number data type.

➊ Many data types have predefined formats, such as the Number data type

➋ The current setting for this Number data type

3. Select the Format property on the **General** tab. Open the property's drop-down list to see the format choices available to a Number data type (see Figure 18.6).

Quick navigation in the table design window

You can quickly move between the upper and lower panes of the table design window by pressing **F6**.

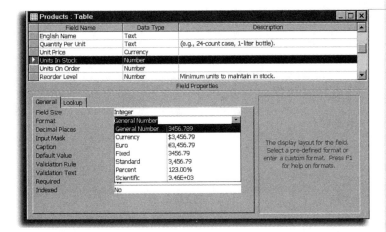

FIGURE 18.6

These formats are available to a Number field.

You can also change the format at the control level, although this won't affect how data is stored in your table.

Apply formats to controls

1. Open the form or report in Design view.

2. Double-click the control you want to change and open its properties sheet.

3. Display the available formats in the Format property's drop-down list (see Figure 18.7).

4. Select the format you want. Again, the choices in the drop-down list depend on the bound control's data type.

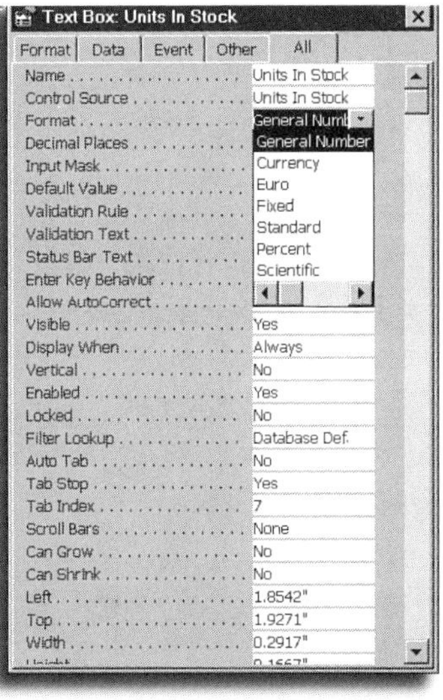

FIGURE 18.7

The formatting options in the drop-down list correspond to the table setting of the field the control is bound to.

VBA's Format property

You can use VBA to change an object's format. Simply add a statement in the form of object.Format = new_format property, where object is the control, form, or property of the object that you're changing. For instance, you could apply the Currency format to a control named **MyControl** on a form named **MyForm** by using the statement Forms!MyForm! MyControl.Format = "Currency".

The wizards don't always explain all the data they display in a form or report. When this happens, you can sometimes use the Format property to display descriptive text. For instance, the Report Wizard displays the current date in the footer. To add descriptive text to the date

- Open the report in Design view, and double-click the date's text box (it should contain a Now() function) in the report's footer to open the control's property sheet.

- Delete the current format (medium Date) and enter
  "Printed on "mmmm d", "yyyy".

In Print Preview mode, the modified property displays a text string similar to Printed on June 1, 1999. This alerts those reviewing the report that the date is only a print date and not a part of the report's data. This works because the mmmm, d, and yyyy are all date formatting symbols that can be used to create custom formats. For a complete list of all the possible formatting symbols, see **Format Property** in the Access help file.

Using the *Format()* Function

The Format property offers many display options, but not every option you might need. When the Format property isn't enough, try the Format() function. You won't apply this function via a control's property sheet; rather, you'll use this function in expression form. You can format the results of a calculated control, or the results of a criteria expression in a query. You also can use this function in a VBA module. This function in the form of

```
Format (entry, "format")
```

displays *entry* as defined by *format*. The *format* argument is a set of characters that define the way you want to display *entry*, which you might have seen referred to as *code characters* or *symbols*. This function is very versatile because the value you're formatting can be a value, string, function, or field. To understand this function, use it to display some values.

Use *Format()* to format values

1. Open the Immediate window by pressing **Ctrl+G** (in previous versions of Access, the Immediate window was known as the Debug window).

2. Enter the statement ?Format(.10,"percent"). As you can see in Figure 18.8, Access applies the percentage format to the value .10. The *percent* argument is a named format. You can use any appropriate data type format in this manner. A *named* format is an existing format—you'll find them in the Format property's drop-down list. You can spell any of these out within a Format() function. In this example I used percent, but you can also use General Number, Currency, Fixed, Standard, Scientific, General Date, Short Date, Medium Date, Long Date, Short Time, Medium Time, and Long Time.

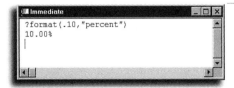

FIGURE 18.8

The Format() function can apply the percentage format to a value.

Working with user-defined symbols

User-defined or *custom* symbols are predefined symbols that you combine to create a unique format. In this example, mmm returns an abbreviated form of the month. Mix and match these many symbols to suit your needs. The function `Format(#6/25/98#, "mmm dd yyyy")` would return `Jun 25 1998`. To add a literal character, enclose it in quotation marks; thus, `Format(#6/25/98#, "mmm dd"", ""yyyy")` would return `Jun 25, 1998`. If you don't want an abbreviated month, use the mmmm symbol. In this case, `Format(#6/25/98#, "mmmm dd"," yyyy")` would return `June 25, 1998`.

3. Enter the statement `?Format(#6/25/98#,"mmm")`. This time, Access displays `Jun` (see Figure 18.9), the abbreviated month component for June 25, 1998. The mmm argument is a user-defined format, otherwise known as a custom format.

The section "Using Expressions in Controls to Display Additional Data," found later in this chapter, explains more about calculated controls.

Using *Format()* to Round Values

Access doesn't have a rounding function as Excel does. Instead, several Access functions have rounding behaviors:

- CInt() returns the rounded integer portion of a value, in much the way you would expect—decimals less than .5 round down and decimals greater than .5 round up. CInt(1.45) returns 1 and CInt(1.5) returns 2. CInt() has a special behavior when the fractional part is exactly .5—it always rounds to the nearest even number. Using CInt(0) with 1.5 and 2.5 yields 2.

- Int() truncates a positive value. When the value is negative, Int() returns the negative integer that's less than or equal to the value. Int(1.5) returns 1, but Int(-1.5) returns –2.

- Fix() is similar to Int() but simply truncates the number and returns an integer, whether it's positive or negative. Fix(1.5) returns 1 and Fix(-1.5) returns –1.

FIGURE 18.9

This time, a date's month component was returned.

As you can see, all these functions have some behavior that keeps them from being an ideal rounding tool. CInt() probably comes close, but only if you want to round to integers—it doesn't let you round to a specified number of decimal places similar to the rounding function in Excel. For display purposes, however, you can use the Format() function for many of your rounding needs. Simply use the # or 0 placeholders. The # symbol displays a blank when no digit exists; 0 displays an 0 when no digit exists. For instance, the function Format(1.5,"##") returns the value 2, as you'd expect. The function Format(1.5,"00") returns the string 02. Both times, Format() rounds the value 1.5 to 2. You can also use Format() to round decimal values, so Format(1.545,"#.00") returns 1.55.

Applying Input Masks

Perhaps one common way to ensure the integrity of the data you enter is to use an input mask. An *input mask* is a pattern that you define and Access applies to limit an entry. For instance, a common phone number input mask is (###) ###-####. This input mask encloses the first three digits (the area code) in parentheses and displays a hyphen between the third and fourth digit in the local number. By applying this input mask, you save your data-entry operator three keystrokes. Table 18.1 lists the input mask characters and their purpose.

Rounding for display doesn't change underlying values

Although using the Format() function to display rounded numbers is convenient, be aware that it rounds them only for display purposes; the underlying number isn't changed. Any calculations that implement this number use the value as actually stored in the underlying table. Sometimes, this lack of precision can lead to problems.

TABLE 18.1   **Input Mask Symbols**

Character	Purpose
0	Forces a digit character (+ or – sign is allowed)
9	Allows only a digit, but doesn't require an entry (no + or – sign is allowed)
#	Allows a digit, + or – sign, or space character, but doesn't require an entry
L	Forces an alphabetic character
?	Allows only an alphabetic character but doesn't require an entry
A	Forces an alphabetic character or digit

continues...

TABLE 18.1   Continued

Character	Purpose
a	Allows only an alphabetic character or digit, but doesn't require an entry
&	Forces an entry but accepts any character
C	Doesn't force an entry and accepts any character
<	Displays characters to the right as lowercase
>	Displays characters to the right as uppercase
!	Fills the mask from right to left
\	Lets you include a literal character by displaying the character that follows

You can also include the separator characters for date, time, decimals and thousands, as defined in your Windows **Regional Settings**.

The mask character determines which character you can enter and how many. To create a mask, enter mask characters as a field's Input Mask property. To illustrate, the following example adds an input mask to the different fields in the Orders table.

Add an input mask

1. Open your table in Design view by selecting it in the Database window and then clicking **Design**. The Orders table opens.

2. Select the OrderDate row in the top panel of the Design View window.

3. Select the Input Mask property in the lower pane.

4. You have many options at this point, but for now, keep it simple and enter a mask that accepts only digits because this is a Date/Time field. Specifically, enter 00/00/00;0;_ (see Figure 18.10). Because the 0 symbol forces a digit entry, any entry must consist of six digits—no more, no less. The mask also displays a slash character between each set of digits. The second section, 0, tells Access not to store the slashes in the underlying table with whatever data you enter. The final character, the underscore, is a placeholder—the mask displays this character until you enter each character in the entry.

Literal characters

You might have noticed that your input mask contains literal characters, namely the slashes, but you didn't preface them with the \ symbol. That's because the backslash character is an acceptable character in a Date/Time field. You need to preface the character with the \ symbol only when that character is totally alien to the field's data type.

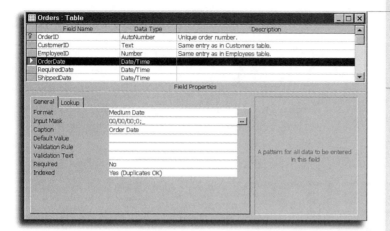

FIGURE 18.10

Enter a date input mask that forces double digits for each date component.

5. Click the **View** button on the Table Design toolbar, and click **Yes** when Access asks if you want to save your changes. Select a new record (the first blank row in Datasheet view).

6. Click the OrderDate field; Access displays the input mask shown in Figure 18.11. (You must click the field; if you just press **Enter** to access this field, it won't display the mask characters until you start to enter data.) As you can see, the mask includes two slashes and displays an underscore as a placeholder.

Quickly selecting a new record

To select a new record, or the first blank row, click the **New** icon on the table's navigational toolbar.

FIGURE 18.11

The mask displays two slashes and an underscore placeholder.

❶ The mask displays a slash between each set of digits it expects.

❷ Until you enter a character, the mask displays the underscore character as a placeholder.

7. At this point, you might try entering some inappropriate entries. For instance, you already know that the 0 symbol forces a character. So, try entering your example date, June 25, 1998, as 62598. The mask should display your entry as 62/59/8 (see Figure 18.12). Then, if you press **Enter**, Access displays an error message telling you the entry isn't appropriate. Click **OK** to clear the message and press **Esc** to delete your entry.

FIGURE 18.12

The result of entering a date that doesn't match the input mask.

1 The mask expects two digits in each section.

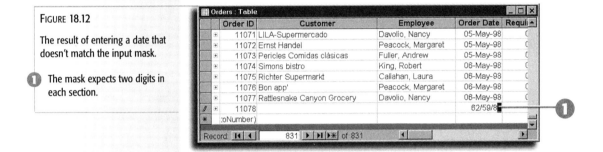

8. Enter a date the mask will accept. Remember, the mask wants two digits for each section, so your month component, 6, needs a leading zero. This time, type 062598 and press **Enter**. Access accepts the entry; however, it doesn't look like you might expect—in mm/dd/yy format. Instead, Access displays the date in Medium Date format, 25-Jun-98. That's because this field already has a Format property, the **Medium Date** format (refer to Figure 18.10).

At this point, you've experimented with only one mask. Table 18.2 displays several example masks and their results with sample data.

Property precedence

The Format and Input Mask properties might seem to conflict with one another, but they don't. Remember, an input mask controls how you enter the data; the Format property controls how Access displays the entry. That means you can enter data in one format and display it in another.

TABLE 18.2   **Input Mask Examples**

Mask	Valid Entry	Invalid Entry	Explanation
>LLLLL	UPPER or upper	9999	Five alphabetic characters are required; displays entry in uppercase
(000) 000-0000	5555555555	5555555 or 555ttt5555	Forces 10 numeric digits
(999) 000-0000	5555555555 or 5555555	5555 or 555tttt	The first three digits are optional; the remaining seven are required
#999	L333 or p33	Y33333	Accepts up to four characters; the first can be a digit, space, +, or –; the remaining three or fewer must be digits
>L<???	p or pl or plew	9kkk or 9kk	Accepts up to four alphabetic characters; at least one is required
\e00?	99e or 99	999 or e99	Displays an e as the first character and requires two digits followed by an optional alphabetic character

One last point to make about input masks is this: Not all data types lend themselves to masks. Although number and currency fields have an Input Mask property, you will generally need to use their Format property only to control how they're displayed; controlling how a numeric field is entered isn't normally as critical as its display. You are more likely to use the Input Mask property with Text or Date/Time fields.

Using the Input Mask Wizard

Input masks can be a little confusing until you've used them a few times. In the beginning, it might be easier to start with the Input Mask Wizard.

Use the Input Mask Wizard to create an input mask

More masks available

The masks shown in Figure 18.13 aren't the only ones available; the wizard is displaying only those masks appropriate for a Date/Time field. In addition to these formats, the wizard offers a mask for zip codes, social security numbers, phone numbers and extensions, and passwords. The wizard works only with Text and Date/Time fields.

1. Open the table you want to change in Design view, and select the field (for example, the Orders table and the ShippedDate field).

2. Select the Input Mask property in the **Field Properties** section and click the **Builder** button 𝄀...𝄀 to launch the Input Mask Wizard.

3. Select the mask you want to apply to the active field in the Input Mask Wizard's first dialog box (see Figure 18.13). I chose Short Date.

FIGURE 18.13

Choose a predefined mask from the Input Mask Wizard.

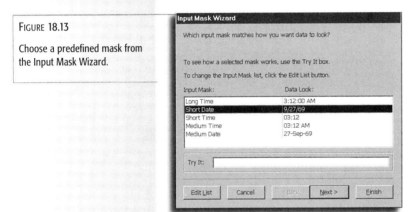

Before going any further, try the predefined mask on data by typing an entry into the **Try It** text box. You can determine then whether the selected mask gives you the limitations you require. If it does, click **Next** to continue to the next window; if it doesn't, select another mask and try it.

The **Edit List** button displays the dialog box shown in Figure 18.14. As you can see, this box displays the selected mask's properties. You can change one or more if you want to create a custom mask; however, all the predefined masks are available by clicking the **Next** button ▶ at the bottom of the Customize Input Mask Wizard dialog box. If you click the **New** button ▶✳, the wizard displays a blank form. At that point, you can create a custom mask that the wizard applies and remembers. You're not going to alter any of the Short Date mask's properties, nor add a custom mask. To return to the wizard's first window, click **Close**.

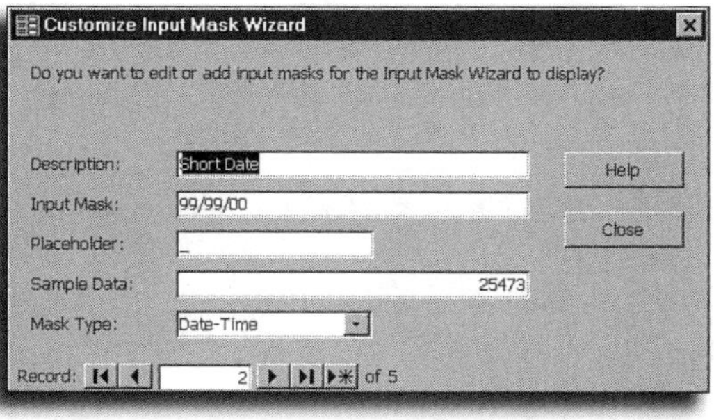

FIGURE 18.14
The Input Mask Wizard lets you customize the mask options.

To continue with the process, click the **Next** button. (If you click **Finish** now, Access assigns the mask and closes the wizard.)

4. The next dialog box enables you to modify the mask and specify the placeholder character (see Figure 18.15). The default is the underscore character. Choose the placeholder you want users to see in the field. After you modify the mask, you can use the **Try It** text box to see the result. You don't have to change a thing, though. Click **Next** when you're ready to continue. Then, click **Finish** in the last dialog box. The wizard enters the mask you chose (see Figure 18.16).

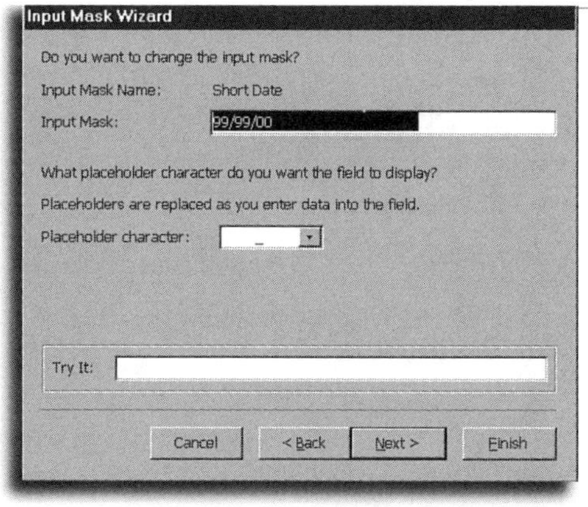

FIGURE 18.15
You can assign a placeholder in this wizard window.

5. Click the **View** button ⊞▾ on the Table Design toolbar, go to the first blank (or **New Record** ▶✱), and then click the field you modified. I chose Shipped Date. Access displays the mask—_/_/_—for you. This is a visual guideline to help you enter the appropriate characters.

If you enter an incorrect entry, such as rabbit, Access just beeps at you because a text string isn't appropriate for a Date/Time field. However, if you enter a value—06898, which represents June 8, 1998—the error message tells you that your entry doesn't conform to the field's input mask. You can determine by looking at the result of your attempt to enter this value that something is missing from the month component because Access doesn't separate the values properly—06/8/98—as you might have expected.

To clear the error message, click **OK**. Then, press **Esc** to delete your entry, and try entering 060898. This time, Access accepts and displays the entry in Medium Date format: 06-Jun-98.

Working with Other Input Mask Components

You might have noticed that most input masks have three sections, separated by a semicolon:

- The first section consists of the mask characters.

- The second component is the value 0 (the default) or 1. This value tells Access whether to store any literal characters you've included in your mask with your data in the table. For example, a date mask might include a slash or hyphen. If you specify the 0 argument, Access won't store these characters in the underlying table. Thus, the mask displays the date 06/25/98 as 062598 in Datasheet view. On the other hand, if you use the value 1, Access stores that same date as 06/25/98.

- The last component denotes a placeholder. You can use most any character you like, but the type of field might lend itself to certain characters. For example, if you're entering values and 0 is an acceptable entry, you can choose to use 0. On the other hand, in your date examples, you used the underscore character as your placeholder. A placeholder character isn't necessary, however. If you leave that section blank, Access won't display anything.

Formatting for the 21st Century

You've no doubt read or heard a lot about Year 2000 compliance. Access, with most PC applications, internally stores all dates with four-digit years. Therefore, your Access application is automatically Year-2000 compliant—well, might be. There is more to accurately handling dates (which is really what Year 2000 compliance is all about) than storing years with the full century.

Access, with the rest of the Microsoft Office applications, makes certain assumptions about dates entered with only two-digit years. The current assumptions are that any date with a two-digit year between 00 and 29 will default to the 21st century. I refer to the "current" assumptions because this functionality is contained in a Microsoft system DLL. Should Microsoft decide that a new "assumption window" is more appropriate, all the company would need to do is issue a new version of the DLL.

What's a DLL?

A DLL (dynamic link library) is a program (without the normal .exe extension) providing functionality that other programs can use. Most of the functionality of Windows itself is contained in various DLLs.

It's entirely possible that this new version of the DLL might be installed on your users' machine (by some other software package) and you and the users of your application might not even realize it—your application would still be an Access 2000 application, but suddenly the dates your users enter might not be the dates they thought they entered. Windows 98 further complicates the issue by allowing users to change the range of the "assumption window," through the Control Panel's Regional Settings tool.

Also, you might need to legitimately enter dates that don't fit the two-digit year assumptions. If you've defined an input mask with a two-digit year, it would prove very difficult to enter someone's birthday if that person were born in 1927.

The easiest solution is to force all date input to use four-digit years and to always display four-digit years. In this way, you can always enter the proper year and won't be required to remember the boundaries of an arbitrary date window (which hopefully has changed because you updated your system).

Force a four-digit year

1. Open in Design view the table with the date you want to restrict.

2. Double-click the date field and enter the input mask `99/99/0000;0;_` in the **Field Properties** section.

3. Click the **View** button [▥ ▾] on the Form Design toolbar.

4. To test the field's entry restriction, select a **New Record** [▸✳] and try to enter the date `06/25/16`. As you can see in Figure 18.17, Access won't accept a two-digit year. Click **OK** to clear the message and press **Esc** to delete the entry

Working with Multiple Input Masks

If the mask characters aren't adequate, you might need VBA. Suppose that you want to force users to enter an area code in the phone number field. You can use the mask \(000\)000\-0000, or you can include a default area code by including the appropriate digits in the mask. For instance, the mask \(555\)000\-0000 displays and stores the area code 555 with each phone number entry. A better solution might be to offer both options. That way, users can accept the default area code or enter a new one when necessary.

Use VBA to define more than one input mask

1. Open the form containing a field that requires more than one input mask in Design view.

2. Click the **Code** button 🔲 on the Form Design toolbar. In the resulting module, select the Phone field from the Object list and the procedure from the Procedure list; in this case, you'll use the BeforeUpdate event to "fix" the entry after checking it. Enter the code for the module. The code shown in Listing 18.1 checks the phone number entry.

The example for this task

You can enter any appropriate VBA code into any form's control when you want to restrict its data entry. This example uses the Northwind Customers form and restricts phone-number entry.

LISTING 18.1 Code for Correcting a Phone Number Entry after the Entry is Made

```
01 Private Sub Phone_BeforeUpdate(Cancel as Integer)
02 Dim strPhone As String
03 strPhone = Me!Phone
04 Select Case Len(strPhone)
05   Case 7
06     Me!Phone.InputMask = "(555) 000-0000"
07   Case 10
08     Me!Phone.InputMask = "(000) 000 0000"
```

Numbering of code lines

Listing 18.1 and other code listings throughout the book include line numbers to make discussion about this code easier to reference. The numbers should not be included as part of any VBA programs.

continues...

LISTING 18.1   **Continued**

```
09   Case Else
10     MsgBox "Please enter an appropriate phone number"
11     Cancel = True
12 End Select
13 End Sub
```

3. Select an additional procedure from the Procedure list and enter the code to check its entry. The following code checks the entry on GotFocus (I chose this event so that VBA will reset the input mask for each record):

```
Private Sub Phone_GotFocus()
Me!Phone.InputMask = "(999) 999-9999"
End Sub
```

4. To test the entry restrictions, click the **View** button [image] on the Form Design toolbar and select a **New Record** [image].

5. Select the field and test the entry with various combinations of data.

SEE ALSO

➢ *To familiarize yourself with the module window, see page 449*

After you select the field you've modified, Access executes the code in the GotFocus event. If you followed the example, Access applies the mask (999) 999-9999 (from step 3) to the current field.

If you type a seven-digit phone number, such as 5555555 (don't type the hyphen character), and press **Enter,** Access launches the AfterUpdate event (from Listing 18.1). This procedure counts the number of characters in your entry. Because there are seven characters, VBA sets the control's Input Mask property to (555)000-0000.

Press **Esc** and enter the 10-digit number 5555555555. Because there are 10 digits, VBA assigns the mask (000)000-0000, which includes no area code and requires 10 digits. (You could use the 9 symbol and it works just as well.) This procedure enables you to specify a default area code, which is convenient when one area code dominates your data but isn't the only code you'll need to enter.

Restoring default values

If you repeatedly enter the same value, you can assign that value as a field's default value by using the Default Value property. During data entry, you can easily overwrite the default value if it isn't appropriate for the current record. But what if you then decide the default value was right after all? Do you retype the default value? Fortunately, this isn't necessary. To restore the default value, press **Ctrl+Alt+Spacebar**.

If your entry doesn't contain seven or 10 digits, VBA displays a warning message prompting you to enter the appropriate number of digits.

Controlling Access

Access displays a bound form's first record when you open the form. Actually, all the records are there and available for review; Access just sets the focus to the first record. This means that anyone who can open the form can review, modify, delete, and even add to your data. Most of the time, you won't want to allow such freedom to all your users.

You can use four form properties to help you limit the access users have to the existing data:

- `Allow Edits` If you set this property to Yes (the default), you can modify saved records.

- `Allow Deletions` When this is set to Yes (the default), you can delete saved records.

- `Allow Additions` Setting this to Yes (the default) enables you to add new records.

- `Data Entry` When set to Yes (No is the default), this property restricts the form to data entry only. You can't view existing records.

To set these properties, open the form's property sheet and choose the appropriate setting from each property field's drop-down list.

Restrict access to existing records

1. Open the form in Design view.

2. Open the form's property sheet by double-clicking the Form Selector or clicking the **Properties** button 🔲 on the Form Design toolbar.

3. Choose **Yes** from the `Data Entry` property's drop-down list. Make sure that the `Allow Additions` property is set to **Yes**.

OpenForm overrides form properties

The `OpenForm` method or action takes precedence over the form's properties, so be careful when using `OpenForm` to open your forms. Use the data mode argument only when you intend to override the form's current settings.

4. To see the result, click the **View** button [icon] on the Form Design toolbar. You can use the blank form to enter new customer records, but you can't access the existing ones. The record navigation buttons shouldn't allow you to go "backward" beyond the new record.

You'll combine the four properties to get the data-entry limits you need. Table 18.4 lists the possible combinations and their effects.

TABLE 18.4 **Limiting Access with Form Properties**

Action	Data Entry	Allow Edits	Allow Additions	Allow Deletions
Enter new records only	Yes	No	Yes	No
Enter and modify new records only	Yes	Yes	Yes	No
Enter, modify, and delete new records only	Yes	Yes	Yes	Yes
Enter, modify, and delete all records	No	Yes	Yes	Yes
Enter new records, delete any record, no edits	No	No	Yes	Yes
Delete records only	No	No	No	Yes
View records only	No	No	No	No
View existing records and add new records	No	No	Yes	No

Using Expressions in Controls to Display Additional Data

If you think forms are just for data entry, you're in for a surprise. Just think about it—most applications display a splash screen when you first launch the application. A *splash screen* identifies the application and the organization. Most of us use switchboard forms to direct the flow of an application, even though you don't realize you're using a form. You also solicit and display information in forms.

On a more traditional note, calculated controls are a good way to display additional information in any kind of form. A *calculated control* is one that contains an expression. An *expression* combines other values and operators to produce a result. *Operators* are the mathematical symbols, such as the +, -, *, and / signs, that you use to perform mathematical operations.

In addition to mathematical operators, Access has several other types of operators:

- Comparison operators allow comparisons: =, <, >, <=, >=, <>, IS, and LIKE.

- Logical operators: OR, AND, and BETWEEN.

- Concatenation operators enable you to combine strings: & and sometimes +.

You use calculated controls to display information that isn't stored in your database. Suppose that you want to show the total sales for a particular product. Or, perhaps you want to show a discounted amount for certain customers. These are values that you won't normally store in your database, but you might need them to conduct business. Calculated controls are just the right tool to get the job done.

For the most part, you'll use text box controls to display the results of expressions. You can use other controls, but the text box is inherently more suitable to the task. Fortunately, adding a calculated control to a form is easy:

- Add the expression as the control's Control Source property

- Precede the expression with the = operator

Now, take a minute to review an existing calculated control. You'll need an existing calculated control, so just open Northwind to explore one.

Review a calculated control

1. Open the Quarterly Orders Subform form in Design view by selecting that form and then clicking **Design View** in the Database window.

Concatenating with &

You should generally use the & operator when you want to concatenate. Although you can safely use the + operator if you're concatenating strings, if other data types are involved in the expression, Access might decide that you want to use the + operator to perform addition and not concatenation. It's a good habit to use only the & operator for concatenation.

Zooming in

If you need more room to type or review your expression, press **Shift+F2** to display the expression in the Zoom box.

2. Double-click the TotalQ1 control (the first control on the left in the totals section). As you can see in Figure 18.18, the field contains the expression =NZ(Sum([Qtr 1])) instead of a field reference. As a result, that control displays the sum of all the first quarter amounts when the form is in Form view.

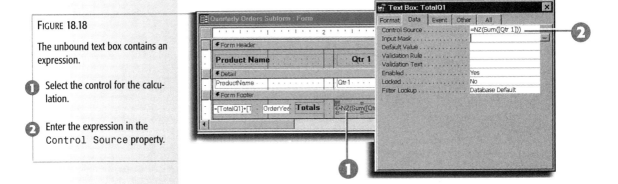

Now, create a calculated control. This example uses the Quarterly Orders Subform form and adds a text box. The expression you'll enter as the control's Control Source calculates the average sale for the first quarter.

Create a calculated control

1. With an existing form (the Quarterly Orders Subform) open in Design view, find or create the space you'll need for the control. You might have to extend the form's footer until there's enough room to insert another text box.

2. Click the **Textbox** tool [abl] on the Toolbox and then click the location to insert a new text box.

3. You can add the expression in two ways: open the new control's property sheet and enter it in the Control Source property field, or click inside the control and just enter it there.

In Figure 18.19, I used the properties sheet method to enter the expression =Avg([Qtr 1]). (To open a control's properties sheet, double-click the control.) I also deleted the control's label.

FIGURE 18.19

Enter an expression into a text box to create a calculated control.

4. Click **View** 🖾 ▾ on the Form Design toolbar to return to Form view. If you've created your own form for this task, save it.

Figure 18.20 shows the results of the new calculated control—the average of the first quarter's sales. (At this point, you haven't formatted the control.)

Quarterly Orders Subform					
Product Name	**Qtr 1**	**Qtr 2**	**Qtr 3**	**Qtr 4**	
Alice Mutton		$702			
Alice Mutton	$312				
Alice Mutton				$1,170	
Alice Mutton	$1,170				
Alice Mutton	$1,123			$2,607	
Alice Mutton		$281			
Totals	$138,289	$143,177	$153,938	$181,681	
Text40:	590.9782				

FIGURE 18.20

The expression you entered returns the average first quarter sale.

Most calculated controls update themselves when the form or the control gets focus. If you want to update all the calculated controls in your form at the same time, you can use the `Recalc` method:

```
form.Recalc
```

In this syntax, `form` is the form object that contains the controls you want to calculate. (Or, with the form open and current, you can press **F9**.)

Using Sum ( ) and DSum ( ) functions

You can't refer to a calculated control in a Sum( ) or DSum( ) function. For instance, you can't use the expression
=Avg([TotalQ1])
because TotalQ1 is a calculated control. Any attempt to enter data returns an error.

The Requery method might be effective in this area, too. Requery updates the contents of a control, however. If you want to calculate the very latest data, you should preface a Recalc method with a Requery method.

Inserting Custom Controls

Want to experiment?

You can view a comprehensive list of third-party ActiveX controls at http://www.download.com/ and check out their development tools. These controls are available for downloading. Be aware, however, that not all ActiveX controls work properly (or the same) in all Office applications.

Access has such a wide variety of controls that you might not need any others. You can insert custom (ActiveX) controls, however, when the native controls aren't adequate. A *custom control* is similar to any other control; it just doesn't come with Access. The Calendar control shown in Figure 18.21 is a popular ActiveX control. (In earlier versions, ActiveX controls were called OLE controls or OCX controls.) You can use the Toolbox or the **Insert** menu to add a custom control to a form or report.

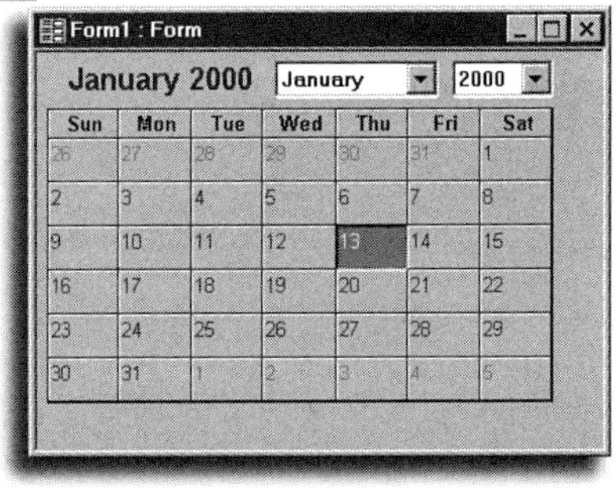

FIGURE 18.21

The Calendar control is an ActiveX (custom) control.

Always insert an ActiveX control on your form—never try to copy an existing ActiveX control.

You can insert a custom control in two ways:

- With a form open in Design view, click the **More Controls** tool [icon] in the Toolbox. Access displays the list in Figure 18.22. Don't worry if yours is different; Access displays the controls available on your system. Click the control you want and then position it on your form.

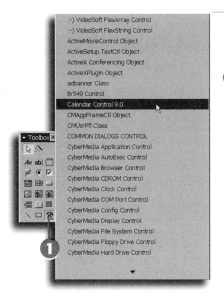

FIGURE 18.22

Access lists the ActiveX controls available on your system.

1 Click the **More Controls** tool in the Toolbox to view the available ActiveX controls.

- With a form open in Design view, choose **ActiveX Control** from the **Insert** menu. Access displays the same list as before in the Insert ActiveX Control dialog box (see Figure 18.23). Select the control you want and then click **OK**. The control appears automatically on the form, but you can move or resize it.

FIGURE 18.23

Or you can choose **ActiveX Control** from the **Insert** menu.

Setting ActiveX Properties

ActiveX controls have two sets of properties:

- The normal control object properties that all controls have in common
- A set of properties unique to the ActiveX control

You can access the control properties by selecting the control and clicking the **Properties** button 🖼 on the Form Design toolbar (or you can right-click the control and select **Properties** from the resulting submenu). To modify the ActiveX properties, double-click the control in Design view. Most ActiveX controls launch a set of tabs from which you can select and modify that control's unique properties.

SEE ALSO

➤ *Learn more about ActiveX controls on page 654*

Registering an ActiveX Control

When you can't find the control to register it

If you can't find a control to register it but know you've installed the control's native application, check the current references. To set this reference, open a blank module and choose **References** from the **Tools** menu. Next, choose the appropriate library in the References dialog box and then click **OK**. After you register the application's library, its controls should also be available to you. Although Access might let you refer to an ActiveX control in a non-referenced library, your application will run faster if you reference the library.

Before you can insert and use an ActiveX control, you must register it. To *register* the control simply means to make Access aware that the control is available and where the files reside. You'll need to register any controls that you purchase, and sometimes you must register controls from other applications.

Register an ActiveX control

1. If you've purchased a control, install it as instructed in the documentation that came with the control.

2. In Access, choose **ActiveX Controls** from the **Tools** menu.

3. Select the appropriate control in the ActiveX Controls dialog box and click the **Register** button. Likewise, click **Unregister** to unregister a control. Click **Close** when you've finished.

SEE ALSO

➤ *For more information on setting a library reference, see page 465*

CHAPTER 19

The World of Subforms

Use subforms with ease and confidence

Learn how to reference subforms correctly

Review a subform alternative: the Tab control

Working with Subforms

Anytime you base a form on a *one-to-many relationship*, you have the potential for a subform. The main form displays one record, and the subform displays the many records that relate to it. For instance, you can use a subform to display open purchase orders for the same customer, or you can display all the items on a particular order.

Set up a subform (general steps)

1. Create a form to represent the one side.

2. Create a form to represent the many side.

3. Make sure that the two forms share a field—the primary key on the one side and the foreign key on the many side.

4. Position the many-side form in the one-side form.

SEE ALSO

➤ *For more information on relationships, see page 13*

A *subform* is a complete form and can generally function separately from the main form. After you place the subform in the main form, Access views the subform as a control of the main form. However, the subform retains its properties and behavior in all but one respect—the purpose of the subform is to support the main form. Thus, the subform displays only those records that relate to the record in the one form. For this arrangement to work properly, the underlying tables or queries must be related, or you must link the two forms.

To ensure that the relationship between the two forms has the effect you want, Access provides two properties at the subform level:

- `Link Child Fields` identifies the foreign key in the subform.
- `Link Master Fields` identifies the primary key in the main form.

After properly assigning these two properties, the subform displays only those records where the *child* field equals the *parent* field.

Creating a Subform

The easiest way to create a subform is to simply create the main form (the one side) and the subform (the many side) as you would any other form. Then, open the main form in Design view and place the subform in the main form.

A perfect example is the Customer Orders form in Northwind (see Figure 19.1). Actually, this form contains two subforms. The main form is based on the Customers table. Customer Orders Subform1 is based on the Orders table and identifies the orders for the current customer in the main form. The second subform, Customer Orders Subform2, is bound to the Order Details Extended query, which is based on the Order Details and Products tables.

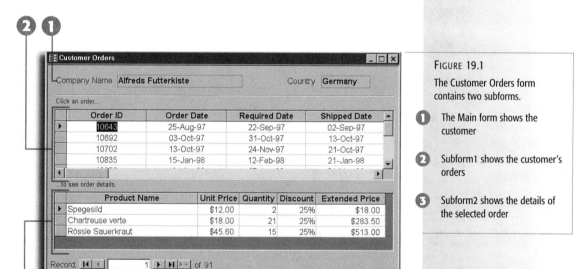

FIGURE 19.1

The Customer Orders form contains two subforms.

1 The Main form shows the customer

2 Subform1 shows the customer's orders

3 Subform2 shows the details of the selected order

Figure 19.2 shows the relationship between the underlying data sources. The Customer Orders form is based on the Customers table. Customer Orders Subform1 displays dates from the Orders table, where the OrderID value is the same as the Customer form's current record. Customer Orders Subform2 displays product data from the Order Details table, matching the ProductID value in the Customer Orders Subform1 to that in Customer Orders Subform2.

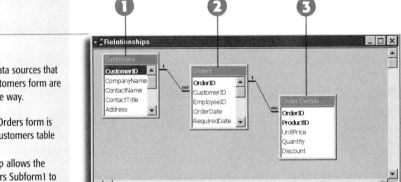

FIGURE 19.2

The underlying data sources that complete the Customers form are all related in some way.

1 The Customer Orders form is based on the Customers table

2 This relationship allows the Customer Orders Subform1 to link and stay in sync with the data in the Customer Orders form

3 This relationship allows the Customer Orders Subform2 to link and stay in sync with the data in the Customer orders Subform1

Inserting subforms

You can add a subform to a main form in two ways through Design view. Use the **Subform/Subreport** tool on the Toolbox to insert another existing form as a subform. Or, you can select the form you want to insert as a subform in the Database window and drag it to the main form.

Create a subform

1. Select the table you want to base your main form on (in this case, the Customers table) in the Database window, choose **Form** from the **New Object** button's drop-down list , and double-click **Form Wizard**.

2. Specify the fields you want to display in your main form (in this case, **CompanyName** and **Country** are added to the **Selected Fields** list box). Then, click **Next** twice. Choose **Standard** as the form style, and then click **Next**. Name the form (this example uses frmMain). Next, choose the **Modify the Form's Design** option (you want to rearrange the controls), and then click **Finish**.

3. In Design view, move the Country field to the right of the CompanyName field. (Doing so has nothing to do with the subform or its links—you're just rearranging the controls.)

4. You don't have to create the subforms because they already exist. Click the **Control Wizards** tool in the Toolbox. Then, click the **Subform/Subreport** tool in the Toolbox and click inside the form below the CompanyName field. Access will launch the Subform/Subreport Wizard.

5. In the wizard's first dialog box, select the **Use an Existing Form** option and then choose **Customer Orders Subform1** from the list box (see Figure 19.3). Click **Next**.

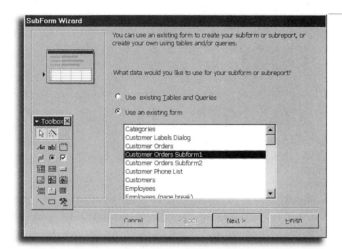

FIGURE 19.3

Select the Customer Orders Subform1 form in the Subform/Subreport Wizard.

6. The next dialog box will attempt to link the subform to the main form. In this example, Access wants to link the two forms by the CustomerID field, so click **Finish**. The relationship between the main form and this subform is based on the CustomerID field. This subform displays only those records that match the CustomerID field in the main form.

7. If you open the subform's property sheet, you can see that Access has already provided the `Link Child Fields` and `Link Master Fields` settings—`CustomerID` (see Figure 19.4).

8. The second subform is a little more complex. Click the **Subform/Subreport** tool in the Toolbox and then click inside the form below the first subform. Click the **Use an existing form** option, choose **Customer Orders Subform2**, and click **Finish**.

You can't use the wizard to set up your child and parent links because you want the second subform to relate to the first subform, not the main form. The wizard will try to link the new subform to the main form.

FIGURE 19.4

The Subform/Subreport Wizard
sets the Link Child Fields and Link
Master Fields properties for you.

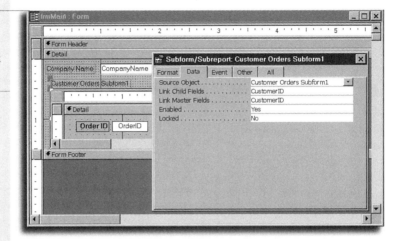

Selecting a subform

Selecting a subform on a main form
can be tricky. First, click an empty
area of the main form. Then select
the subform control by clicking its
horizontal or vertical ruler or the
ruler intersection box in the upper-
left corner of the subform.

9. You have to set the links in the second subform yourself. To
do so, open the subform's property sheet by clicking the
Properties button on the Form Design toolbar. Then,
enter OrderID for the Link Child Fields property because
you want to link the two subforms by the OrderID field.

10. You can't reference the OrderID field on the first subform as
easily. You must also tell Access which form or subform
you're referencing. To this end, enter the reference
[Customer Orders Subform1].Form![OrderID] as the Link
Master Fields setting. (This chapter covers more about referencing subforms in the section "Referring to Subforms
and Their Controls.")

11. To see the completed form, click the **View** button on
the Form Design toolbar. Your form should resemble the
one shown in Figure 19.1. (It isn't critical that all the controls be in the same position.) The first subform displays all
the orders for the customer in the main form. The second
subform displays information about the selected order in the
first subform.

Working with Both Sets of Subform Properties

When you set the linking properties for the subform in the preceding example, you opened the subform's property sheet. If you're unfamiliar with subforms, you might not have recognized those properties and are probably wondering where the subform's form properties are. They're still available. You see, subforms have two sets of properties—properties as a form and properties as a subform control—which affect different behaviors. This chapter won't review each individual property, but it shows you how to access both sets.

Throughout this section, the two sets are referred to as the *form* and *subform* properties. The form properties control the subform as a form—they're the set of properties you're most familiar with. To access them, select the subform control, and then double-click the box in the upper-left corner of the subform—the form properties dialog appears. Rather than double-click, you can also click the **Properties** button on the Form Design toolbar or right-click and choose **Properties** from the shortcut menu. These are the properties that all forms share (see Figure 19.5).

Figure 19.5

A subform has form properties, like all forms.

To display the subform's property sheet, you can click an empty spot on the main form, and then select the subform control. Another, slightly faster way can be a little tougher at first: With the subform's form property sheet showing, if you click exactly the border of the subform (as shown in Figure 19.6), you will select the subform control and display the subform's property sheet. In either case, you will see the property sheet, as shown in Figure 19.7.

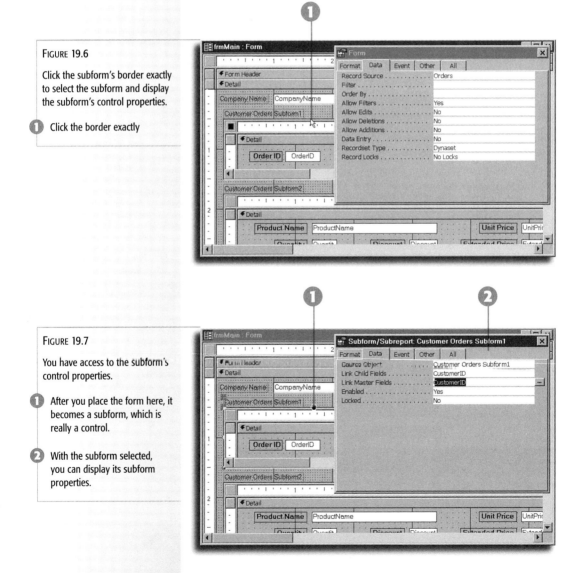

FIGURE 19.6

Click the subform's border exactly to select the subform and display the subform's control properties.

1 Click the border exactly

FIGURE 19.7

You have access to the subform's control properties.

1 After you place the form here, it becomes a subform, which is really a control.

2 With the subform selected, you can display its subform properties.

There's really no trick to it. When the subform is selected as a form, you can modify the form properties. When the subform is selected as a control, you can modify the subform's properties. Just remember that a subform has two sets of behaviors, so it requires two sets of properties.

SEE ALSO

➤ *To learn more about form wizards, see page 115*

Referring to Subforms and Their Controls

Access views a subform as a control, not a form. Unless you're aware of this, referencing a subform's controls can prove very frustrating. To see why, take a step backward. To reference a subform, you use the following syntax:

```
Forms![frmMainForm]![frmSubForm]
```

So it stands to reason that you'd reference a control on a subform by using the following syntax:

```
Forms![frmMainForm]![frmSubForm]![cmdSubFormControl]
```

But it doesn't work that way. Remember, Access sees the subform as a control, and controls don't contain other controls. The proper way to reference a subform's control is to use the Form property in the following format:

```
Forms![frmFormName]![frmSubForm].Form![cmdSubFormControl]
```

To change a subform control's value, you use the following syntax:

```
Forms![frmFormName]![frmSubForm].Form![cmdSubFormControl] =
newvalue
```

To change a subform control's property, use the following form:

```
Forms![frmFormName]![frmSubForm].Form![cmdSubFormControl].
property = newpropertyvalue
```

A Subform Alternative: The Tab Control

There's another way to display one-to-many records, and in some cases it might be more appropriate: the Tab control. A Tab control object allows you to display several controls or multiple pages of data on individual tabs. However, you can also use it to display one-to-many records. Using a Tab control is a good choice when you want to keep one side of the relationship available for quick review, but you don't want it constantly in view.

To see this subform alternative, rework a Northwind subform. Specifically, you need to display the relationship shown in the Quarterly Orders form shown in Figure 19.8 in a Tab control. The main form displays customer information; the subform is based on the Quarterly Orders by Product query.

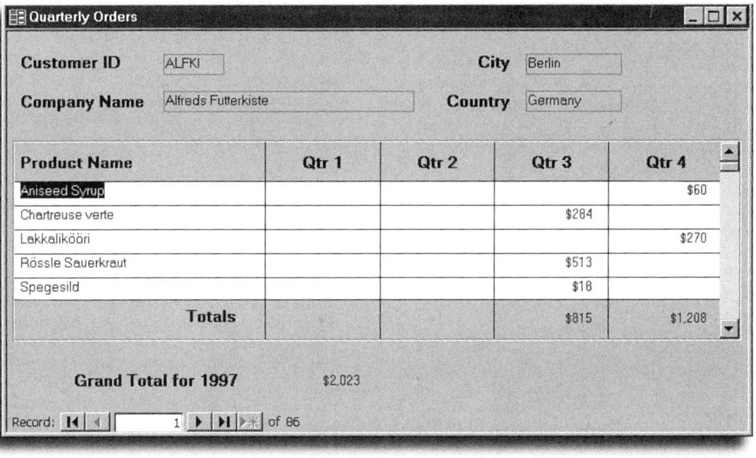

FIGURE 19.8

The main form displays customer information; the subform is based on the Quarterly Orders by Product query.

Display a one-to-many relationship in a Tab control

1. Select the Customers table in the Database window, and then choose **Form** from the **New Object** button's drop-down list. Then double-click **Design View** in the New Form dialog box.

2. Click the **Tab control** tool in the Toolbox and then click inside the blank form.

3. Create page 1 first. To begin, display the field list by choosing **Field List** from the **View** menu or clicking the **Field List** button ▤ on the Form Design toolbar.

4. Double-click the Field List box's title bar to select all the fields. Next, drag all the fields at once to the first page of the Tab control, which is arranged in sections, as you can see in Figure 19.9.

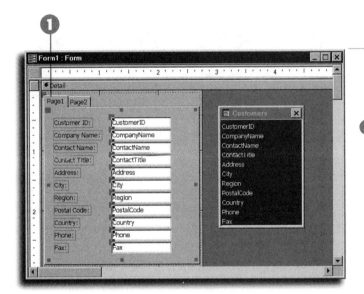

FIGURE 19.9

All the Customer fields have been added to the first page of your Tab control.

❶ Placing extensive information into tabs and sections gives the form a clean appearance, with information available at a glance

5. Double-click the Page1 tab, which displays the properties sheet. Select the properties sheet's **Format** tab and enter the caption Customer Information. This page is equivalent to a subform's main form.

6. Now you're ready to create the subform's equivalent on the Tab control's second page. Click **Page2** to select the second page. Make sure that the **Control Wizard** button 🖎 is selected, and then click the **Subform/Subreport** tool 🖽. Then click anywhere in **Page2**.

7. When Access launches the Subform/Subreport Wizard, click **Next** without making any changes to the first dialog box.

8. In the second dialog box, choose the **Quarterly Orders by Product** query from the **Tables/Queries** drop-down list. Then, add all the fields to the **Selected Fields** list box and click **Finish**. Increase the size of the subform control so it can display more records. Then add the page caption **Quarterly Products** (see Figure 19.10).

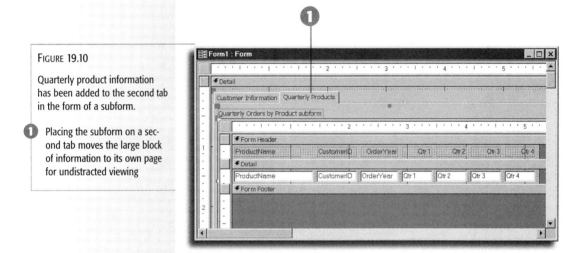

FIGURE 19.10

Quarterly product information has been added to the second tab in the form of a subform.

❶ Placing the subform on a second tab moves the large block of information to its own page for undistracted viewing

9. Click the **View** button on the Form Design toolbar to see the results (see Figure 19.11). As you can see, the first page of the Tab control displays customer information.

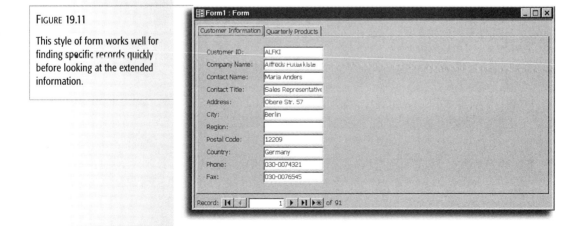

FIGURE 19.11

This style of form works well for finding specific records quickly before looking at the extended information.

10. To see quarterly order data for the current customer (in
Figure 19.12), click the Quarterly Products tab. This page
shows only those orders that pertain to the customer in the
tab's first page. (The subform's default view in Figure 19.12
has been changed to Continuous Forms, and the field sizes
have been adjusted for a better display).

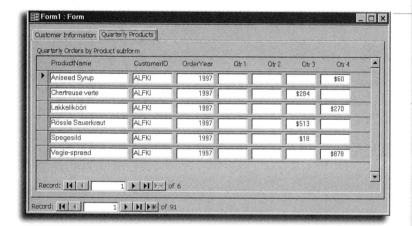

FIGURE **19.12**

Expanding the page with the subform creates an even better view
for navigating through the
detailed information quickly.

Advanced Form Techniques

Learn about form events

Create form event procedures

Open forms from other forms

Link forms with VBA code or a macro

Working with the Form Module

As you've seen in the last few chapters, you can accomplish quite a lot by using the various form properties and controls. What you might not realize at this point is that you can use VBA to program your forms (and form controls) to perform specific tasks not inherent to the form object.

If you want to program your form or controls with VBA code, you need to open the form's module (what's known as a *class module*), choose the appropriate object and event, and enter the procedure code. (All form modules are class modules; all class modules aren't form modules.)

SEE ALSO

> *For more information about class modules, go to page 447*
> *For an explanation of a subprocedure, see page 489*

Figure 20.1 shows a typical form module. If you've used Access 97, notice that Access 2000 now opens your module in a separate application window; the Visual Basic editing environment used by Excel and Word is now used by Access. For the most part, the form (class) module is comparable to the standard module. In appearance, there's little difference. The form module has a title bar, Object and Procedures drop-down lists, and two view buttons (Procedure View and Full Module View), just as the standard module does. However, the title bar does give you a clue—notice that the icon in the title bar is different and the prefix Form_ is added to the form name. Also notice that the Visual Basic editing environment, by default, displays two other windows—the Project and Properties windows. You'll learn more about these windows in Chapter 26, "Introducing Visual Basic for Applications."

Using code in your forms

This chapter looks at the form's module and then shows you some code you might want to use with your own forms. The information about class modules also applies to report modules.

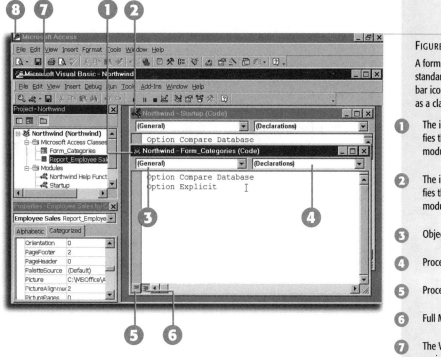

FIGURE 20.1

A form module looks similar to a standard module, except the title bar icon identifies a form module as a class module

❶ The icon in the title bar identifies the form module as a class module.

❷ The icon in the title bar identifies this module as a standard module

❸ Object drop-down list

❹ Procedures drop-down list

❺ Procedure View

❻ Full Module View

❼ The Visual Basic editing environment opens in it's own window

❽ Access is visible in its own window

The main difference between a standard module and a form class module isn't visible. Procedures and subprocedures in a form's module are limited in scope to the form and its controls; procedures and subprocedures in a standard module can be available to the entire application. The code you'll enter in a form module will respond to the form and control events. These procedures are known as events or subprocedures.

SEE ALSO

➤ *Learn more about scope on page 478*

Creating Event Procedures

There's only one way to create an event procedure—open a class module and enter the appropriate code. However, there are a number of different ways to access a form module:

- In the Database window, select the form whose module you want to open and click the **Code** button 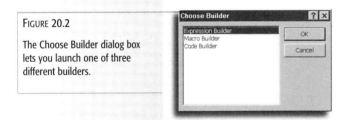 on the Database toolbar.

- Open a form in Design view and click the **Code** button 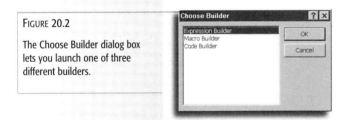 on the Form Design toolbar.

- With a form in Design View, open the form's property sheet. Select a form event (event properties generally begin with the word On) and click the **Builder** button 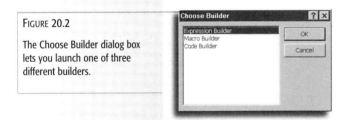 to the right of the property field to display the Choose Builder dialog box (see Figure 20.2). Select **Code Builder** and click **OK** to open the form's module to the appropriate event. For instance, if you select the form's On Open property, the Code Builder opens the module to the Open event (see Figure 20.3). As you can see, the Code Builder supplies the procedure's first and last statements.

What if I always want to go to the module window?

When you click the **Builder** button 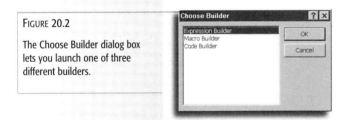, in a default Access installation the Choose Builder dialog box appears. However, if you find that you always select the Code Builder, you can change the behavior of the **Builder** button. From the **Tools** menu, choose **Options**. On the **Forms/Reports** page, select the **Always Use Event Procedures** check box.

FIGURE 20.2

The Choose Builder dialog box lets you launch one of three different builders.

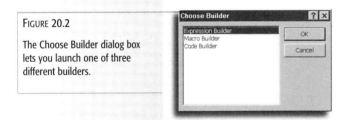

FIGURE 20.3

The Code Builder supplies the procedure's first and last statements.

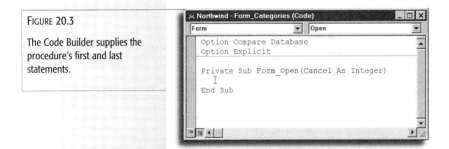

- With the form in Design View, open the form's property sheet and select the appropriate event property. Open the property field's drop-list and choose **[Event Procedure]**. (This drop-down list also displays macros. If you select one of the macros, Access executes that macro in response to the event.) Click the **Builder** button. Access opens the form's module to the appropriate event, bypassing the Choose Builder dialog box.

After you open the form module, you're ready to enter code. If you used a method that opens the module to the appropriate event and supplies the first and last statement, begin by entering your code.

If you've opened the module to the General Declarations section, you need to specify the appropriate object and procedure. The Object drop-down lists all the objects now in your form, including the form itself. In Figure 20.4, the **Suppliers** form module (from the Northwind database) is opened. As you see, this form offers several objects.

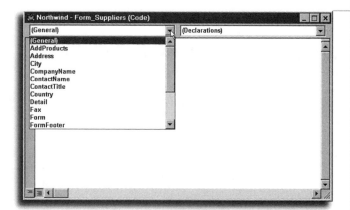

FIGURE 20.4

A form module's Object drop-down list catalogs all the objects in the form.

To attach an event procedure to any of these objects, select the object from the Object drop-down list. When you do, the Procedure drop-down list (to the right of the Object list) defaults to the selected object type's most common event, or the object's first attached procedure. For instance, if you select a command button from the Object drop-down list, VBA selects that button's Click event in the Procedure list. Also, VBA supplies the appropriate beginning and ending statement for that button's Click event. Specifically, the first line names the button and the event as follows:

```
Private Sub buttonname_Click()
```

The last statement is a simple End Sub statement. All procedures require both statements. At this point, enter the appropriate code between the first and last statement. If a Click event already exists, VBA displays it.

If the event offered isn't the one you need, select the appropriate event from the Procedure drop-down list. Figure 20.5 shows the many events available to a form. You might have noticed that some events appear in boldface type. That means these events already have an attached procedure.

FIGURE 20.5

The Procedure drop-down list offers events for the selected control in the Objects drop-down list.

❶ Boldface type means that the event already has an attached procedure.

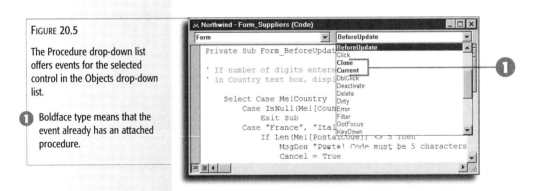

SEE ALSO

➤ *To use the Insert Procedure command to enter a subprocedure, see page 454*

➤ *To use a procedure in reports, see page 388*

Responding to Form Events

Forms have many events. Knowing in what order Access executes these events is important. Table 20.1 lists form events, each event's property, and the order in which Access executes these events.

TABLE 20.1   **Form Events**

Event	Property	Order
Open	On Open	When you open but before Access displays the first record
Load	On Load	After you open the form and load all its records
Resize	On Resize	When you change the form's size with a macro or event procedure
Activate	On Activate	When a form becomes the active window but before Access selects a record
Current	On Current	When a record receives the focus (or the form is refreshed or requeried)
Unload	On Unload	When a form is closed but before Access removes it from the screen
Deactivate	On Deactivate	When the form loses focus
Close	On Close	When Access closes and removes the form from the screen

Beware of cascading events

When writing subprocedures, be careful to consider all the repercussions of the code. You need to avoid including commands in event procures that trigger the same event. For instance, if you include a `Maximize`, `Minimize`, or `Restore` command in a `Resize` event, you'll create what's known as a *cascading event*, which calls itself directly or indirectly and creates a terminal loop or runtime error. The `Maximize`, `Minimize`, and `Restore` commands cause a cascading event because when they execute, they resize the form, which triggers the `Resize` event again. If, while running a VBA procedure, you receive a stack overflow error, there's a good chance that you somehow coded a cascading event.

Timing can be critical to some tasks. Suppose that you want to execute a task when the form displays a record—any record. If you attach the code to any form event other than the Current event, it just won't work as expected. That's because Current is the only event that Access executes every time a record gets the focus. Suppose that you want to set the form's recordset when you open the form, on-the-fly style. In this case, you must attach the code to the form's Open event because it's the only event that Access executes before it loads records.

If your form has a subform, Access loads the subform, its controls, and records before it loads the main form. You'll also want to keep this timing behavior in mind when planning events.

Understanding the Order of Events

Understanding the order of events—especially when subforms are involved—can be difficult at first. One of my favorite techniques that helps me understand what's happening in this type of situation is to use MessageBox functions in my code. Select a form that has a subform and enter a MessageBox function in all events (for the main form and the subform) listed in Table 20.1. When you open the main form, these message boxes let you know exactly which event is firing.

To enter a basic MessageBox function, type the following in each event procedure:

```
MsgBox ("I am now entering the x event in the y form")
```

where *x* is the name of the event and *y* is the main form or subform, as appropriate. You should often find this technique helpful.

Using Form Events to Open Other Forms

You often open additional forms to view additional information or allow additional input. You can trigger a form-opening event from another form in a number of ways—you can use a form event or a control event. A logical form event might be Close. For instance, you might open the application's Switchboard when you close a form, to control the user's choices.

The example forms in this chapter

Several examples in this chapter use the Products and Main Switchboard forms from the sample Northwind database that comes with Access. You can use most any form you like, however.

Open a form from a form event

1. Open the Products form module by selecting it in the Database window and then clicking the **Code** button 🖫 on the Database toolbar.

2. Select **Form** and then **Close** from the **Object** and **Procedure** drop-down lists, respectively.

3. Enter the following code line between the opening and ending statements provided by VBA:

```
DoCmd.OpenForm "Main Switchboard"
```

4. Save the form, and then open it in Form view by closing the module window and then clicking the **View** button ⊞ ▾ on the Form Design toolbar.

5. In Form view, close the form to trigger the Products form's `Close` event. As a result, VBA executes the `OpenForm` method and opens the Main Switchboard form.

6. Delete the `Close` event and resave the form.

Similarly, you can use a control event to open another form without closing the current one. For instance, you could attach the same `OpenForm` command to a command button's `Click` event. Then, when you click it, VBA would open the Main Switchboard form without having to close the Products form. Admittedly, this event is simple, but it's one that's used a lot.

Linking Forms with VBA Code

The preceding section shows you how to open a form by using a command button event. Specifically, you added an `OpenForm` method to the form's `Close` event. This section shows you how to link two forms by using a command button. I don't recommend one method over another; you decide which method works best for you in a given situation.

The easiest way to link two forms is to create the forms and then use the Command Button Wizard to link them. This wizard adds all the code you need and does it quickly. The finished product might need a little tweaking, but the wizard does a very thorough job on its own.

You need two forms: a main form and a linked form. The main form opens the linked form. Use Products as the main form and Main Switchboard as the linked form.

Use a wizard to link forms

1. Open the Products form (the main form) in Design view.

2. Make sure that the **Control Wizard** button is selected, and then add a command button to your form. In response, Access launches the Command Button Wizard.

3. In the wizard's first dialog box, choose **Form Operations** from the **Categories** list and **Open Form** from the **Actions** list (see Figure 20.6). Click **Next** to continue.

FIGURE 20.6

Make the appropriate selections in the Command Button Wizard.

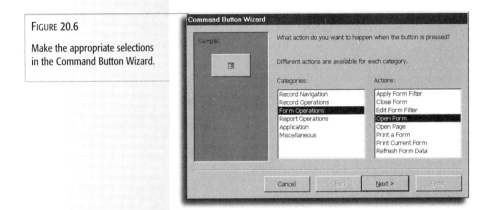

4. The next dialog box asks you to identify the form you want to open. Here, you specify the linked form—in this example, the **Main Switchboard** form (see Figure 20.7). Click **Next** to continue.

FIGURE 20.7

Identify the form you want to open when you click the command button.

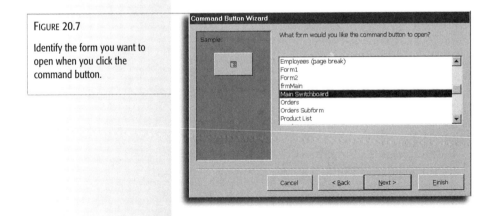

5. The third dialog box lets you choose between a text caption and a picture. Select **Text** and change the default text to `Open Main Switchboard` (see Figure 20.8). Click **Next** to continue.

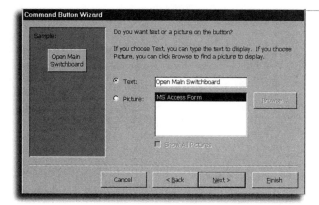

FIGURE 20.8
Display text as the button's text.

6. In the final dialog box, name the button `cmdOpenMainSwitchboard` and click **Finish** to return to the main form.

7. Click the **View** button 📇 ▾ on the Form Design toolbar and click the new **Open Main Switchboard** button on your main form. Doing so executes the code that the wizard added to your command button. That code opens your linked form—the Main Switchboard form (see Figure 20.9).

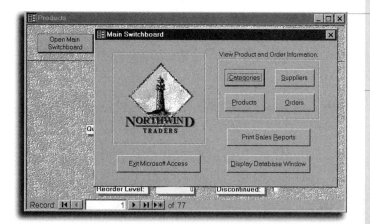

FIGURE 20.9
Clicking the **Open Main Switchboard** button opens the Main Switchboard form.

To review the code added by the Command Button Wizard, open your main form in Design view, select the main form, click the **Code** button 🛠 on the Form Design toolbar, and then choose **cmdOpenMainSwitchboard** from the **Objects** drop-down list and **Click** from the **Procedures** drop-down list.

SEE ALSO

➤ *For more information on using the Command Button Wizard, see page 155*

➤ *Find exact instructions on how to add a control to a form on page 260*

➤ *The Tab control is a good alternative to linking forms. For more information, see page 344*

Linking Forms with a Macro

You don't have to use VBA code to link forms. You can always use a macro, and a simple one at that. The OpenForm macro action has one argument that specifies the form you want to open. Now, re-create the example from the last section, but use a macro instead of VBA code.

SEE ALSO

➤ *For a more complete look at creating macros, see page 421*

Use a macro to link forms

  1. Click the **Macros** button on the Database window object bar, and then click the **New** button to display a blank macro window.

  2. Create the macro shown in Figure 20.10. First, select **OpenForm** from the **Action** column's drop-down list. Then, choose the linked form from the Form Name field property's drop-down list. Following the example, that argument is the Main Switchboard form.

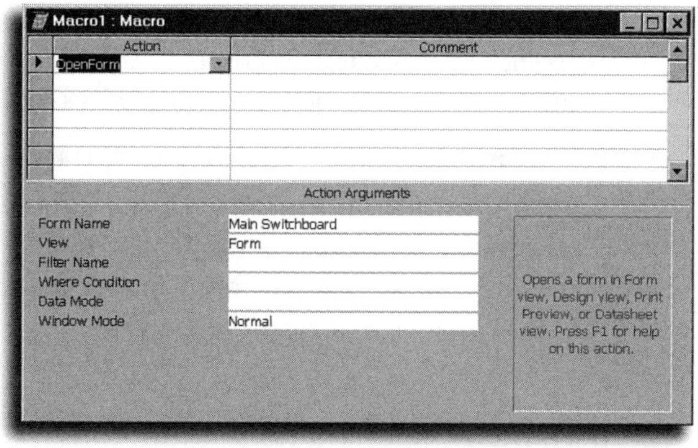

FIGURE 20.10

This macro opens the Main Switchboard form.

3. Save the macro as `macOpenMainSwitchboard` and close the macro window.

4. Open the Products form in Design view. You can use the command button from the preceding exercise, or create a new one. Either way, open the button's property sheet by clicking the **Properties** button ![icon] on the Form Design toolbar or by double-clicking the button. Then, select the On Click property field and select **macOpenMainSwitchboard** from that property's drop-down list. If the field displays [Event Procedure], ignore it—choosing **macOpenMainSwitchboard** overwrites the current entry.

5. Click the **View** button ![icon] on the Form Design toolbar and click the command button. As in the previous example, doing so opens the Main Switchboard form.

Printing Form Data Without the Form

Another frequent form task is printing records. If you choose **Print** from the **File** menu, Access gives you several choices: You can print all the records, the current record, or a selection of records. If you click the **Print** button ![icon] on the Form View toolbar, Access prints all the records.

The forms for this example

This example continues to use the Products form from the Northwind database, but you can use most any form to practice the following technique. This printing solution works best when the form's bound table or query has a primary key field. If there's no primary key field, use the field that contains the most unique entries.

For better or worse, Access prints the record and the form when you execute any print task in Form view. If you want to print the current record without the form, you need VBA.

Create a procedure that prints data without the form

1. Open the form you want to add this printing capability to in Design view and add a command button. For this example, add yours to the Products form's header section. Name the button cmdPrint and enter the caption Print Current Record.

SEE ALSO

➤ *For complete instructions on how to add a control to a form, see page 260*

2. Click the **Code** button 🐞 on the Form Design toolbar to open the form's module. Choose **cmdPrint** and **Click** from the **Object** and **Procedure** drop-down lists, respectively.

3. Enter the procedure shown in Listing 20.1.

LISTING 20.1   Printing a Record Without the Form

```
1 Private Sub cmdPrint_Click()
2 Dim varID As Variant
3 If IsNull(Me![ProductID]) Then
4   MsgBox ("Can't print this record")
5   Exit Sub
6 End If
7 varID = Me![ProductID]
8 DoCmd.OpenReport "rptPrint", , , "[ProductID]= " _
    & varID
9 End Sub
```

4. Close the module window and then click the **View** button 📼▾ on the Form Design toolbar to open the form in Form view.

5. Don't try the new button just yet. Instead, select the table or query on which your current form is based (for this example, the Products table) and create a new report. Then, choose **Report** from the **New Object** button's 🔡▾ drop-down list, and then double-click **AutoReport: Tabular** in the New Report dialog box.

6. Save the report as `rptPrint` and then close it.

7. Return to the Products form and click the new command button, which executes its `Click` event. This event creates a report, using only those records where the table or query's primary key entry matches the current entry in the form. This example relies on the ProductID field. Because the form is now open to a record whose ProductID field contains the value 1, Access prints only that record in rptPrint.

If you don't have a primary key field, this technique prints the current record and any other record that contains a matching entry.

Dealing with Strings

If the field you end up choosing is a `Text` field, you'll need an extra step. Specifically, you must enclose the contents of the text field that you're matching in quotation marks. In these situations, use the code shown in Listing 20.2.

Form tasks

Some techniques discussed in this section might seem more control oriented than form oriented. They're included here because each does consider the form environment in some way.

LISTING 20.2   When the Matching Entry Is a String

```
01 Private Sub cmdPrint_Click()
02 Dim varID As Variant
03 If IsNull(Me![ProductID]) Then
04   MsgBox ("Can't print this record")
05   Exit Sub
06 End If
07 varID = Me![ProductID]
08 varID = Chr(34) & varID & Chr(34)
09 DoCmd.OpenReport "rptPrint", , , "[ProductID]= " & varID
10 End Sub
```

This procedure contains an extra line:

```
varID = Chr(34) & varID & Chr(34)
```

This line inserts a double quotation mark around the contents of the Text field, so the OpenReport method can use the string in its *where* argument. Remember, if the field you're matching doesn't contain unique entries, this technique might print more than the current record.

Reducing Data-Entry Tasks

If you enter a lot of repetitive data, stop and rethink the application's strategy—there might be a way to get Access to enter some of this data for you. For instance, if you enter zip codes, you can use the following technique to enter a code's respective city and state.

This technique is relatively simple. You'll enter the zip code first in one of two ways: by choosing the code from a list box (which you'll enter) or by entering it in the zip-code control. If you choose an entry in the list box, that control's Dbl Click event compares the selected zip code to existing ones in your address table. If a matching code exists, VBA copies that record's city and state to the corresponding form controls. If the zip code isn't in the list box, you have to make all three entries yourself. As soon as you do, VBA adds the new zip code to the list box.

The form for this example

This example uses the Employees form from the Northwind database. You can use any form that contains similar fields—ZIP Code, City, and State.

A technique for reducing data entry

1. Base a Select query, similar to the one in Figure 20.11, on the table that contains your address fields. This query returns all the zip codes now in your address table. (If you need help creating this query, refer to Chapter 6, "Creating Queries.")

2. Double-click in the top half of the query window to display the Query Properties dialog box. Select Unique Values and change it to Yes. Doing so causes the query to return a list of unique zip code entries. (Setting this property adds the DIS-TINCT keyword to the query's underlying SQL.)

3. Save your query appropriately—for this example, name it qryZIP.

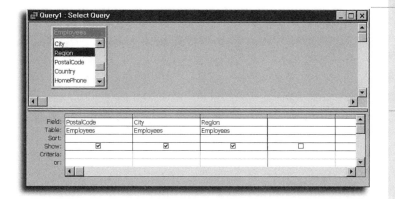

FIGURE 20.11
This query returns all the zip codes in your address table. You haven't set the query properties yet to make it return only unique zip codes.

4. Open your data-entry form in Design view. Remember, you're working with the Employees form, so when you open the form, you have to select the **Personal Info** tab to get to the appropriate section.

5. Add a list box to your form and name it lstZIP. For this example, add it to the right side of the form (see Figure 20.12). Change lstZIP's Row Source property to qryZIP, its Column Count property to 3, and its Column Width property to 1";0";0". The list box technically contains all three of qryZIP's fields but displays only the PostalCode field.

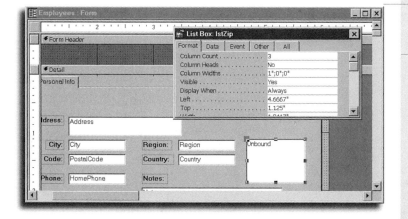

FIGURE 20.12
A list box is added to the form.

SEE ALSO

➤ *See how to insert controls on page 260*

6. Attach the code in Listing 20.3 to lstZIP's Dbl Click event.

LISTING 20.3   *lstZIP's Dbl Click* **Event**

```
01 Private Sub lstZIP_DblClick(Cancel As Integer)
02 Dim varCity As Variant, varRegion As Variant, _
   strZIP As String
03 strZIP = Me![lstZIP]
04 Me![PostalCode] = strZIP
05 strZIP = "'" & strZIP & "'"
06 varCity = Me![lstZIP].Column(1)
07 varRegion = Me![lstZIP].Column(2)
08 Me![City] = varCity
09 Me![Region] = varRegion
10 End Sub
```

---

7. In the module window, select **Form** from the **Object** drop-down list and **Current** from the **Procedure** drop-down list. Then enter the following code:

```
Private Sub Form_Current()
Dim ctrlZIP As Control
Set ctrlZIP = Forms!Employees![lstZIP]
ctrlZIP.Requery
End Sub
```

> **1** This line doesn't use the Me syntax but refers to the form by its fully qualified name. Either way is correct.

This procedure updates lstZIP when you enter new zip codes.

8. Return to the form, select the PostalCode field, and set its Tab Index property to 1. If you need to open its property sheet, click the **Properties** button 🗗 on the Form Design toolbar.

9. Click the **View** button 🖽▾ on the Form Design toolbar, and click the **Personal Info** tab. Immediately, you see that the new list box contains a list of existing zip codes (see Figure 20.13).

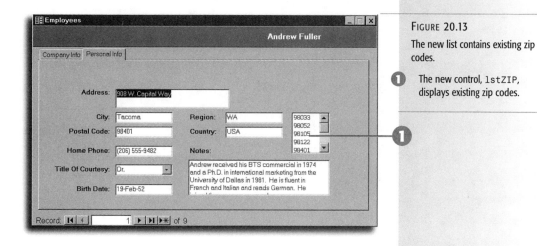

FIGURE 20.13

The new list contains existing zip codes.

❶ The new control, 1stZIP, displays existing zip codes.

10. Select a new record and press **Enter**. Notice that, rather than select the City field, Access skips to the postal code control. If the zip code you need is in the list box, double-click it; the VBA code enters the selected zip code in the PostalCode field and the zip code's respective city and state in the appropriate controls. If the zip code is not in the list box, you can enter the zip code, city, and state information in the appropriate text boxes.

Figure 20.14 shows the result of double-clicking **98033** in 1stZIP. When the zip code you're entering isn't in 1stZIP, enter the code yourself in PostalCode, along with the appropriate city and state. This is where the form's Current event comes in. When you add the new data, the Current event updates 1stZIP, and that newly added zip code is available for the next time.

FIGURE 20.14

Selecting a zip code from
`lstZIP` automatically fills the
value in the PostalCode field.

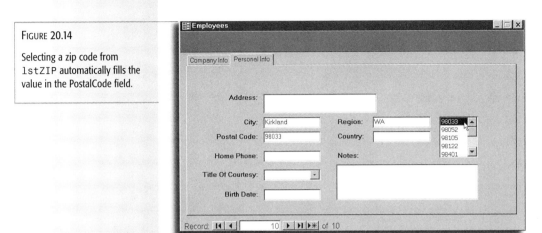

Working with Pop-Up Forms

Occasionally, you might need to display additional information about the current record. Or, you might need to prompt users to take a certain action or provide more information. When this happens, you might want to consider a pop-up form. A *pop-up form* stays on top of all other open or active forms until you react to it. The two kinds of pop-up forms are

- Modal—You can't access any other object or menu command while a modal form is open. Most dialog boxes—even custom ones—are modal. Set the form's Modal property to Yes.

- Modeless—A modeless form remains on top of the current form, but you can access other objects while the form is open. Set the form's Modal property to No.

SEE ALSO

➤ *Create custom dialog boxes on page 112*

By and large, most pop-up forms are modeless, so you can access other objects and menu commands while the form is open. However, you need to take some action to close the form. The Suppliers form in Northwind has a good example of a modeless pop-up form. As you can see in Figure 20.15, this form contains a command button with the caption **Add Products**.

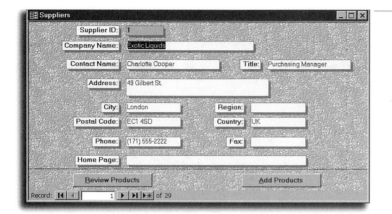

FIGURE 20.15
You can open the Products form from the Suppliers form by clicking the **Add Products** button or by pressing **Alt+A**.

When you click the **Add Products** button, the attached VBA code opens the Products form, as shown in Figure 20.16. You might have noticed that the form is empty. That's because the acAdd argument in the attached statement,

```
DoCmd.OpenForm strDocName, , , , acAdd, , Me!SupplierID
```

temporarily sets the form's Data Entry property to Yes. That setting won't display or allow access to existing records. You can use the form only for data-entry purposes. If you want to see the rest of the code, open the Suppliers form in Design view, and then open the form's module by clicking the **Code** button [icon] on the Form Design toolbar. Then, select **AddProducts** from the **Object** drop-down list. Access automatically displays the button's Click event.

The OpenArgs argument

In case you're wondering, the Me!SupplierID reference in the OpenForm method's arguments copies the value in the SupplierID field of the Supplier form to the Products form's **OpenArgs** property. This is an easy way to keep track of your current position when you open another form. Simply refer to the OpenArgs property in an OpenForm method to return to the exact form and record that had the focus when you opened the Products form.

FIGURE 20.16
Open the Products form so that you can enter new product information.

SEE ALSO

➤ *For more information on Data Entry mode, see page 327*

Linking Forms by Fields with the *OpenForm's where* Argument

In the last example, the Suppliers and Products forms aren't really related. You simply open the Products form to enter new product data, should the need arise. However, you can use the same technique to open pop-up forms that display more information. For example, the **Review Products** button at the bottom left of the Suppliers form opens the form shown in Figure 20.17. As you can see, this form displays information about the current supplier's products.

FIGURE 20.17

Clicking the **Review Products** button opens this form.

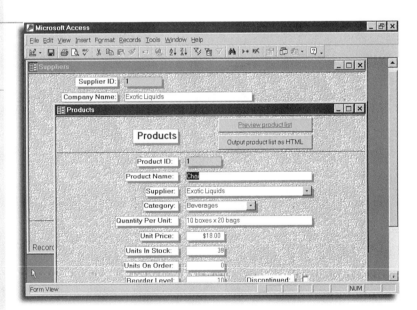

VBA accomplishes this by specifying a *where* argument in an OpenForm method:

```
DoCmd.OpenForm "form", , , "where"
```

The *form* argument specifies the form you want to open; the *where* argument tells Access which records to attach to the form. In this case, the statement

```
DoCmd.OpenForm "Product List", , , "[SupplierID] = _
    Forms![Suppliers]![SupplierID]"
```

opens the Product List form displaying only those records whose SupplierID field contain the same value as the SupplierID on the Suppliers form.

By the way, the Product List pop-up form is another modeless form. All Northwind pop-up forms are modeless. The truth is, you might never need a modal pop-up form, but if you do, you need to know one important fact: The Modal Yes setting doesn't completely inhibit access to all features. To open a form in true modal form, use the OpenForm method:

```
DoCmd.OpenForm "form", , , , , acDialog
```

The acDialog constant opens the form as a dialog box, which by constraints is a modal form.

A common use for a modal form

One common use for a modal form is when you're performing some process and need input from users. You might have a VBA function that's performing various data manipulation, and at a certain point needs users to supply some information (perhaps a name of a file). If you open a form by using the **acDialog** constant in your **OpenForm** statement, all code suspends processing until the user supplies the necessary information to your input form. If you don't use the **acDialog** constant, even if you open a form whose **Modal** property has been set to Yes, your code continues to run without waiting for the necessary input and probably results in a runtime error.

Making Your Point
with Reports

Make your reports attractive and organized

Grouping and sorting in your reports

Page numbering

Calculate totals

Grouping and Sorting Data

Now it's time to make your reports stand out by making them more attractive and better organized. Not only will you see how to group and sort functions to organize your report, but you'll also see how to calculate totals with controls, to number pages, to use graphics, and to add special effects to your reports.

Suppose that you work for one of the top coffee distributors in the country. Your boss has asked you to manage a database of all the current wholesale accounts and create a quarterly financial report sorted by the city in which each account is located. This is a piece of cake if you're using Microsoft Access.

If you want to follow along, you can create a temporary table and include the following fields:

Entry Number (use AutoNumber and make this the primary key)

Customer Number

Name

Street Address

City

State

Zip

Phone

Year-To-Date Sales

Don't forget to save your table. You will use the Report Wizard to create your report.

Create a report with a wizard

1. From the Database window object bar, select **Report** and then click the **New** button. Select the **Report Wizard** and the name of the table/query used as the source for your data (the table you created). Then click **OK**.

2. Select the fields to include in your report: the name, street address, city, state, zip code, and the year-to-date sales amount. You might want to select other information as well, including the phone number, the entry number, the customer

Selecting the record source

In gathering its data, your report looks to the record source you've specified. If all your data is kept in one table, you can select that table as your record source. If your data is kept in multiple tables, you must use a query as your record source. If you have a table with a large number of fields and want only a few of them to appear on the report, you might want to create a query that returns only the required fields and use that as the report's record source. If you create a query that's used only as a report's record source, it's not necessary to sort the output of the query. A report has its own sort order and actually ignores any sorting done by the query.

number, and whatever else you think is important from your table or query. Then click the **Next** button.

This is also your last opportunity before your report is designed to change the source for your data.

3. Choose the grouping levels for your report. You want a report sorted by the city in which each account is located, so select the **City** field. You can have up to four grouping levels. Then click the **Next** button.

4. Choose the sorting options for the report. You can't select the City field because you've already told the wizard that you want to group on this field, so your report automatically sorts by City. Within each city, you want the accounts listed alphabetically from A–Z. Select the **Name** field from the field list drop-down box, and then select the proper order (ascending or descending). Using the Report Wizard, you can have up to four sort levels for your data; in Design view, you can have more.

5. Select a layout option for your report. Because you've selected a number of fields to include on the report, as well as names and addresses, and because some of these fields can be lengthy, select landscape as the orientation to ensure that you have enough room horizontally for your information. Also select the check box that forces all the fields to fit on the page.

6. Select the style for your report. The options given include **Bold**, **Casual**, **Compact**, **Corporate**, **Formal**, and **Soft Gray**.

7. Title your report and click the **Finish** button.

You've created a report that has all your accounts listed alphabetically by city, and alphabetically within each city. Most likely, you will want to go into the design of the report and modify it to better suit your needs.

Another example you can use is contained in the Northwind database. It's titled Sales Totals by Amount. In this report (see Figure 21.1), you can see many similarities to what has been discussed so far in this chapter.

Practicing with this example

For practice, try to re-create this Northwind report. This report has figures grouped into $10,000 sections. It also uses greater than criteria and other restrictive values in its queries. This allows you to test what you've learned.

FIGURE 21.1

The Northwind report Sales Totals by Amount in preview mode shows some samples of grouping and subtotaling.

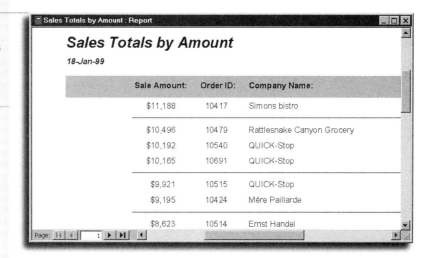

In addition to setting your report's sorting and grouping options while using the Report Wizard, you can also set these properties from within Design view: from the **View** menu choose **Sorting and Grouping** (see Figure 21.2).

FIGURE 21.2

The Sorting and Grouping properties dialog box.

1. Use this area to add fields for sorting or grouping.

2. This symbol indicates that the report is grouped by the City field.

3. Set the sort order for your report here.

4. Set group properties here.

5. Group header for the City field is displayed because the Group Header property is set to Yes.

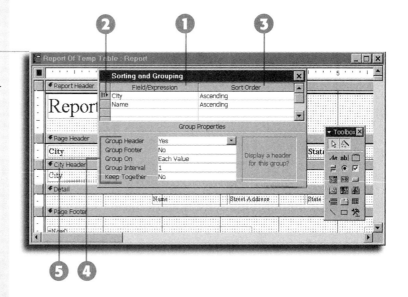

As you can see in Figure 21.2, you couldn't set a number of group properties when you used the Report Wizard. These properties are a big part of the powerful and flexible reporting capabilities provided by Access:

- `Group Header` controls whether your report has a Group Header section.

- `Group Footer` controls whether your report has a Group Footer section. You must have a Group Header or Group Footer if you want your report grouped by a field.

- `Group On` can generally be set to `Each Value` or `Prefix Characters`. The `Each Value` setting groups the field on each unique value; `Prefix Characters` groups based on the first *n* characters indicated by the `Group Interval` property. For fields with a data type other than text, `Prefix Characters` are replaced by a more appropriate selection—a date field allows you to group by month, year, or quarter, to name a few.

- `Group Interval` works with the `Group On` property. When `Group On` is set to `Each Value`, this property is ignored. If `Group On` is set to `Prefix Characters`, `Group Interval` will indicate the first *n* characters to group on.

- `Keep Together` has three possible values: `No`, `Whole Group`, and `With First Detail`. When set to `No`, this property have no effect. When set to `Whole Group`, this property forces a page break to fit the group header, detail, and group footer on one page (assuming that these three sections all fit on one page). When set to `With First Detail`, this property allows only the group header to be printed on a page if at least one line of detail can also be printed.

SEE ALSO

➤ *For information on creating select queries as the basis of your report, see page 213*

➤ *For more help on grouping, sorting, and other criteria within queries, see page 81*

Calculating Totals with Controls

Report controls are considered *bound* or *unbound*. The source of the data that the control displays determines its type. For example, if a text box's Control Source is set to a field in the underlying table or query, it's a bound control. Conversely, if a control's Control Source isn't set to a field in the underlying Record Source, the control is an unbound control.

An example of an unbound control might be a label in which you simply type in the text that you would like to appear. An unbound text box might get its data from a global variable or string literal, assigned by a macro or function run by the report's Open event.

A *calculated control* is a special kind of unbound control derived from a calculation that you define and enter for the Control Source property. An example would be a mathematical equation that inputs an average based on year-to-date sales figures divided by the number of months included in the report. This would be entered into the Control Source's field as =[YTD]/6 (6 being the number of months included in the year-to-date figure).

Another example would be a control that includes a customer's first name and last name separated by a space, regardless of the length of each name. That expression would look similar to this:

[first name]&" "&[last name].

The name contained in the First Name field would be printed first. When it was finished, a space would be inserted. Following the space would be the name contained in the Last Name field.

The Toolbox contains the items needed to set up controls. These include buttons for creating labels, text boxes, option groups, toggle buttons, option buttons, check boxes, combo boxes, list boxes, command buttons, images, unbound and bound objects, forced page breaks, subreports, and special effects such as lines and rectangles.

SEE ALSO

➤ *For details on the Toolbox, see the techniques on page 256*

➤ *For more specific information on placing controls onto forms and reports, see the techniques on page 260*

Are those brackets really needed?

Access uses square brackets ([ ]) to help identify table names, field names, and some special keywords. Actually, if you don't include spaces in the field names, you can get away without using the brackets in most cases; when field names have spaces, the brackets tell Access to view the words as a single unit. If Access really needs the brackets, it actually adds them for you when it checks the syntax of what you entered. Unfortunately, there is no easy rule for when you need to use them—you will learn through trial and error. One place that you need to use them is when referring to the special words [Page] or [Pages] in a report (see the section "The Art of Page Numbering," later in this chapter).

Switching the field order

Many times, you want the last name first. If so, you can sort alphabetically according to last name. This would look similar to [last name]&", "&[first name].

Create a calculated control

1. To begin a calculated control within a text box, you can enter the expression directly into the control. Begin with the = sign.

2. Enter the field you will be calculating from—for example, `=[Unit Price]`.

3. Add the calculation—for example, `=[Unit Price]*.15`.

SEE ALSO

➤ *See page 542 for information on the Expression builder and how to use it for creating calculations*

This calculation gives you the dollar amount in the Unit Price field multiplied by .15, or 15 percent. The following are the most commonly used expressions and calculations:

+	Add
-	Subtract
/	Divide
*	Multiply
[ ]	Enter field name between brackets
=	Calculation control, numerical
<	Less than
>	Greater than
<>	Equal to
!	Follows a table selection
" "	Inserts the amount of spaces between the quotes into a calculation
&	The concatenation character, used to join pieces of an expression

> **Use the Expression Builder**
>
> The Expression Builder is a great help when you're attempting to do more complicated formulas. For information on the Expression Builder and how to use it to create calculations, see Chapter 30, "Using Builders, Utilities, and Add-ins to Increase Efficiency."

The Art of Page Numbering

Page numbering is another expression commonly used in most reports. Page numbers help organize your report and are practically a necessity in your finished product. The page number control box is an unbound control because it doesn't get its data from a single table or query.

Where you put your page numbering and how it looks is a matter of personal preference. Normally, page numbers are placed in the page header or footer. The format of the page number depends on how you've entered the expression.

Entering =[Page] in the Control Source property gives you only the page number. To include the word "page" before it, you must type that in quotation marks before the [page] expression. It would look similar to this:

```
="Page " & [Page]
```

Another example of commonly used page numbering is the "Page 1 of 3" variety. For page numbering to be shown this way, you must use two fields and include two items of text. It would look similar to this:

```
="Page " & [Page] & " of " & [Pages]
```

Figure 21.3 shows the property sheet with this control source for the page number control.

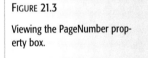
FIGURE 21.3

Viewing the PageNumber property box.

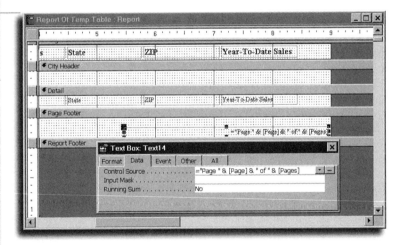

Starting with a Page Number Other Than the First Page

Using the Northwind catalog report as an example, you can see how it makes sense to start your page numbering on a page other than the first. Figures 21.4 and 21.5 show the first three pages of this report.

FIGURE 21.4

The cover and the company blurb obviously don't need page numbers.

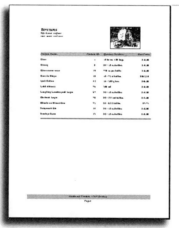

FIGURE 21.5

Page 3 of the Northwind catalog is the first numbered page.

The Northwind catalog report has a clever design and should give you an idea of how to creatively achieve very different-looking reports. The cover and the company blurb are kept in the Report Header section. They're separated by using the page break button on the toolbox. There's no page numbering control in the Report Header section, so the items contained in the header aren't subject to having the page number printed.

The page numbering information for this report is kept in the Page Footer section. A header isn't technically considered a page, so the page numbering won't print on the header unless it's specifically put into each section of the header.

Figures 21.6 and 21.7 show this report in Design view.

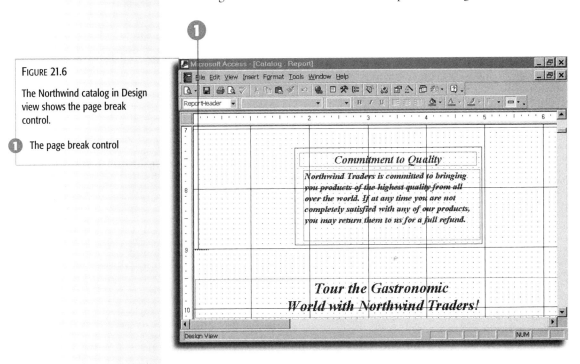

FIGURE 21.6

The Northwind catalog in Design view shows the page break control.

1 The page break control

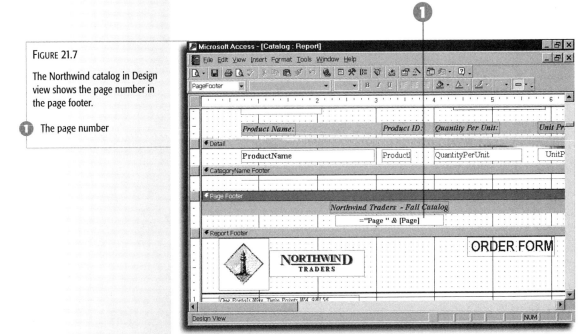

FIGURE 21.7

The Northwind catalog in Design view shows the page number in the page footer.

1 The page number

Inserting Graphics

The use of graphics not only helps your report stand out, but it also can serve a valuable purpose as well. For example, look again at the Northwind catalog report, in Figure 21.8. In Preview mode, notice how each food/beverage section contains a photograph of what's being described. Without the photographs, it would be just another boring list of products and prices. The photographs add a splash of color and make the catalog look much more attractive.

FIGURE 21.8
Stand out from the crowd by inserting graphics.

Another unique way in which graphics can be used is for personalized service. Suppose that you take your cat to your local veterinarian's office for her annual checkup. Back when you took Bunky in for her first visit, her photograph was taken and put into a database. Now, when the vet pulls up Bunky's information on the computer, it not only tells him all of Bunky's medical history and vital information, but it also shows the photo. When you receive your bill (another type of Access report), Bunky's picture is looking back at you. A little personalized service goes a long way.

Graphics limitations

Graphics can adversely affect application performance. They should be used for effect—you wouldn't place a large graphic on a 100-page report that's run every morning for internal use.

You can insert graphics and images into your reports in two main ways—as *bound* or *unbound* objects.

Bound Objects

Bound objects are graphic images actually stored in your database, in a field within a table. They're readily available for you to use in a form or report, just as any other field would be. They must, however, be placed in a bound object frame. Figure 21.9 shows how a bound object field has been defined in the Categories table; Figure 21.10 shows how that field is used in the Northwind catalog.

FIGURE 21.9

A table can also contain images. The Picture field in the Categories table is defined with a data type of OLE object.

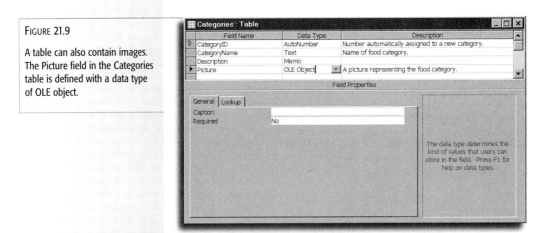

FIGURE 21.10

A bound object frame control is used to display the OLE object in the Categories table.

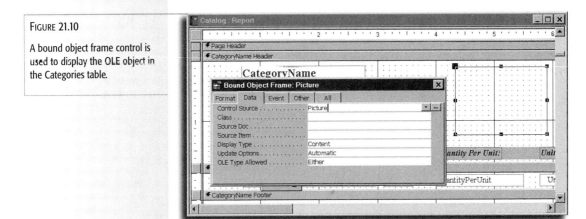

Unbound Objects

The second way to display a graphic or image is to use an unbound object, one not stored within your database. Access gives you two choices for displaying unbound objects:

- Through the use of the unbound object frame control. This control is very similar to the bound object frame control, but it's limited to displaying unbound objects.

- With the image control. This control is very similar to the unbound object frame control, but its limitation is that you can't do in-place editing of the image.

With the bound and unbound object frame controls, you can double-click the image and edit it right on the form or report. The image control, because it doesn't support this in-place editing capability, displays graphics faster than either of the other two controls.

Another difference between bound and unbound objects is that placing a bound object on a form or report allows for the graphic to change as the underlying table record changes; unbound graphics don't change (unless you change them programmatically).

Graphics objects

A complete discussion of all the properties, methods, and events associated with graphic objects and their related controls is beyond the scope of this book. This is just one area where you need to refer to the help file and experiment on your own.

Inserting Graphics in Your Report

Now insert a graphic in a report. For this example, use the image control.

Insert a graphic in your report

1. From the Database window object bar, select **Report** and click the **New** button. Select **Design View**. You don't need to select a table or query for this example.

2. Click the **Image** icon [🖼], and then position and size it on your report. As soon as you release the mouse button, the Insert Picture dialog appears (see Figure 21.11).

FIGURE 21.11

When creating an image control, you need to identify the graphic that the control displays.

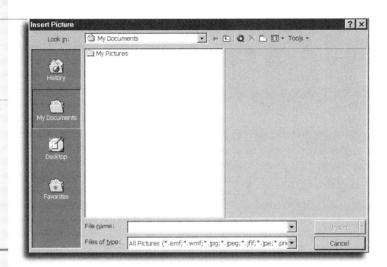

FIGURE 21.11

When creating an image control, you need to identify the graphic that the control displays.

Check the Size property

If your image doesn't look right, try changing its **Size Mode** property. Using the **Stretch** setting for this property conforms the image to the size of the box you've created for it. Using **Zoom** keeps the image proportions intact and resizes the image automatically. Using **Clip** inserts the image at its normal size.

3. Navigate to the Windows directory and select a bitmap file. (I used triangles.bmp for this example.) When you click the **Insert** button, the graphic is placed in the image control. Figure 21.12 shows the image (with the Size Mode property set to Zoom and the control resized for a better fit) in Design view.

FIGURE 21.12

View your image control and its associated property sheet.

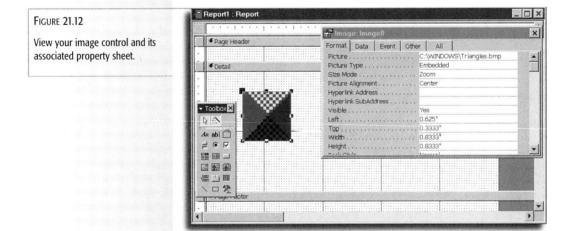

Inserting a graphic with the unbound or bound object frame control is essentially the same process, with some minor exceptions:

- When you insert an unbound object frame control, you won't see the Insert Picture dialog. Instead, you see the Insert Object dialog, which lets you insert an existing file or activate in-place editing to create a new file.

- When you insert a bound object frame control, you won't see any additional dialog boxes because, by definition, the bound control can be used only with a graphic stored in your database. The record source for your report must contain an OLE Object field, which is the source for the control.

To Frame or Not to Frame

The choice of whether or not to frame your images is a matter of personal preference. If the background of your image is the same color as the background of your report, going without a frame would provide a seamless image insertion. This can be useful when you're trying to blend items into a report such as a watermark, logo, or faint background image, or when you want to give your report a very fluid appearance.

The benefit of using a frame is that you can produce a contrasting image insertion. You can make your image stand out on the page by using a special effect, such as Raised or Shadowed. Other special effects available to you are Flat, Sunken, Etched, and Chiseled. You can also adjust the back color, border color, and border style to further alter the appearance of your frame.

To show the difference between a framed and unframed graphic, I used the image from the preceding example, copied it, put a sunken frame around it, and changed the report's background color to help show the effect. You can see the difference in Figure 21.13.

Using Transparent

If your back color style is set to Transparent, no special effects or borders are displayed. If it's set to Normal, the size of your border width dramatically affects the special effect you've selected. Experiment with the other options, such as the color selections and the border style, to come up with creative combinations.

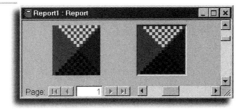

Working with OLE Graphics

Very simply, *OLE* stands for object linking and embedding. One option listed in the property sheet for a graphic or image (OLETypeAllowed) determines whether you want the item linked, or embedded, or either. What's the difference?

When you specify that your graphic is to be linked, you're telling Access that when it prints or views that graphic, it refers to the graphic and uses what's now available. Suppose that you use a graphic that you're designing. You already know the name of the file, but you're constantly making changes to it. By linking the graphic, the most recent edits appear.

When you specify that your graphic is to be embedded, you tell Access to put the object itself into the database. Access always refers to that location when displaying the graphic. It has stored the object information into its memory and always refers to that. An example of this might be a photograph or a logo.

The OLETypeAllowed property specifies the type of OLE object that can be placed in the control. Selecting **Linked** says that the control can contain only a linked object. If you aren't certain what type of object your control can contain, select **Either**.

OLE objects don't need to be pictures. They can be a wide variety of objects, including a Microsoft Excel spreadsheet, a chart or graph, a drawing, or any item from a supported extension, such as .tif, .gif, .bmp, or .jpg.

Adding Lines to a Report

Adding lines and other types of artistic design can go a long way toward making your report look professional and pleasing to the eye. Adding lines to your report can assist in separating data fields, highlighting certain areas of your report, and creating borders. Figures 21.14 and 21.15 are some great examples of how to use lines to separate your data.

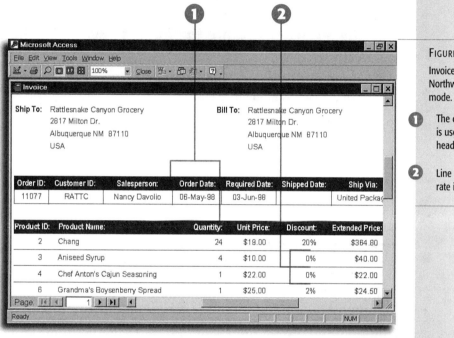

FIGURE 21.14

Invoice report from the Northwind database in Preview mode.

① The colored rectangles control is used to highlight field headers.

② Line controls are used to separate invoice detail lines.

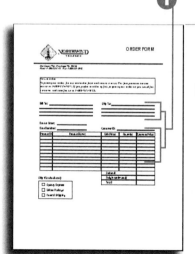

FIGURE 21.15

Hold down the **Shift** key to draw a perfectly straight line.

① Use lines and rectangles to leave blanks or a grid in the report

Creating depth in the report

Sending an item to the back or bringing it forward determines how deep that item is on your page. If you have text on top of a rectangle on top of a square and send the rectangle to the back, the order becomes rectangle, square, text on top. Use the **Format** menu to access this feature.

In the toolbox, notice the buttons for creating lines and rectangles. You can draw a freehand line or rectangle of any size and at any angle you want. You can put text or an image on top of the rectangle by sending the rectangle to the back of the document.

Drawing a Border Around the Report Page

Drawing a border is a little more complicated because you need to create an event procedure (using VBA in the report's On Page event, as shown in Figure 21.16:

```
'Draw a page border around this report.
Me.Line (0, 0)-(Me.ScaleWidth, Me.ScaleHeight), , B
```

This code is executed during the printing process (or preview process) between the time when Access formats the document and when it sends the formatted document to the printer (or screen).

FIGURE 21.16

Adding the event procedure to the Summary of Sales by Year report's On Page property.

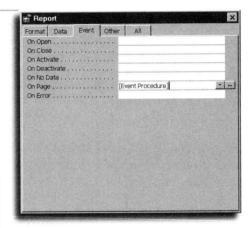

SEE ALSO

➤ *For more information on creating event procedures, see page 352*

Displaying Detailed Data with a Subreport

Learn what a subreport is and when you need one

Link subreports to the data in the main report

Set subreport properties

What's a Subreport and Why Do You Need One?

Lightweight reports and forms

If your report or form loads slowly and has no event procedures attached to it, remove the object's module by setting the **Has Module** property to **No**. Doing so will reduce the object's size and help it load quicker. Of course, if any code is attached to the object, you shouldn't change this property. If you delete the object's module and later decide to add a procedure to the object, simply change **Has Module** to **Yes**.

A *subreport* is a report that you insert within another, or main, report. You'll use subreports to display related—and usually detailed—information about a group or several groups of data in the main report. This relationship isn't necessary, however. You can insert unrelated reports into a main report, which most likely will be unbound. An *unbound* report isn't attached to an underlying table or query.

Many times you'll use subreports to display detailed or summarized data that's related to information in the main report. For instance, you might use a subreport to display quarterly or monthly summaries in a main report that displays specifics about each order. The arrangement could be reversed just as easily.

The Northwind database has two report/subreport configurations you can review. Figure 22.1 shows the Sales by Year report open and maximized in Print Preview. Below the report's title and date is a bordered box with sales information summarized by quarters. The records below that display each order in more detail, however.

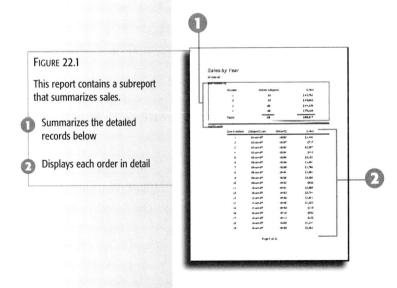

FIGURE 22.1

This report contains a subreport that summarizes sales.

1 Summarizes the detailed records below

2 Displays each order in detail

Figure 22.2 shows this report in Design view. As you can see, the summarized records at the head of the report are actually a subreport. Both reports are based on the Sales by Year query. The only difference is that the subreport uses the Count() function to return just one record for each quarter, rather than display each record. The main report then displays each record.

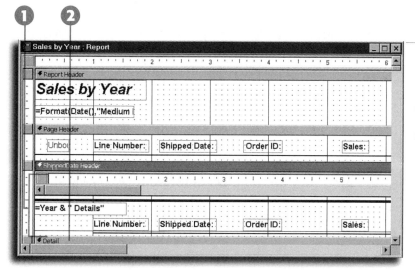

FIGURE 22.2

The summarized data is actually a subreport.

❶ The subreport

❷ The main report's Detail section, which displays each order

Adding a Subreport to an Unbound Main Report

Probably the simplest report/subreport arrangement is a subreport in an unbound report. That means the report is really just a shell, and you can add whatever you like to it. Also, the subreport records probably won't be related to anything in the main report.

You'll probably use this setup when you want to display two or more short but unrelated reports together. This is a simple process: You create all the reports, including the unbound main report, open the main report in Design View, and insert each subreport by using the Subform/Subreport Wizard.

The database in this chapter

During the exercises in this chapter, you'll be working with a number of tables, queries, and reports in Northwind, the sample database that ships with Access. You can use almost any table with the exercises.

Create subreports in an unbound main report

1. Start with the main report by clicking **Reports** on the Database window's object bar and then clicking **New**. Next, double-click **Design View** in the New Report dialog box.

2. Add text or other controls to your main report, such as a label control to the Page Header section.

3. Save the report (this one is saved as rptMain).

4. Make sure that the **Control Wizards** icon is selected, and then click the **Subform/Subreport** tool in the Toolbox. Next, click inside the report's **Detail** section to anchor the subreport and launch the Subform/Subreport Wizard.

5. In the wizard's first dialog box, identify the table, query, report, or form to be added to the main report as a subreport. If you're adding a table or query, choose the **Use Existing Tables and Queries** option; if you're adding a report or form, select **Use an Existing Report or Form** and select the appropriate form or report from the list.

   For this example, you will use the **Category Sales for 1997** query, so retain the default, **Use Existing Tables and Queries** (see Figure 22.3) and click **Next**.

FIGURE 22.3

The wizard's first dialog box asks you to identify the object type you're adding as a subreport.

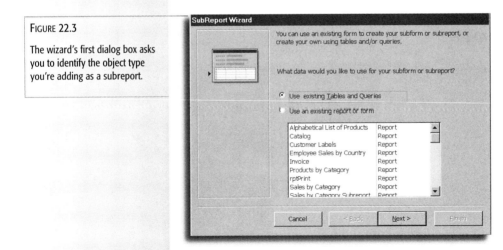

6. Select the appropriate table or query from the **Tables and Queries** drop-down list, and then select the fields you want to include in the subreport from the **Available Fields** list. Select the query **Category Sales for 1997** and select both fields (see Figure 22.4). When you're satisfied with your choices, click **Next** to continue.

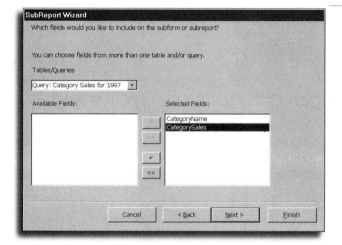

FIGURE 22.4

Choose the table or query and its corresponding fields for your sub-report.

7. In the final dialog box, accept or change the default subreport name and click **Finish**. When you accept the default name, Access adds the subreport to the report (see Figure 22.5).

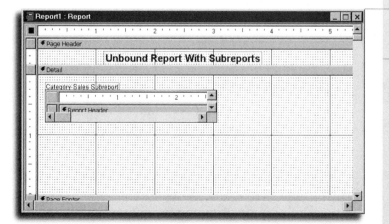

FIGURE 22.5

You've added the first subreport.

8. Repeat steps 4 through 7 to add a second table or query as a subreport—insert it right below the first. Add the **Sales by Category** query. Figure 22.6 shows the completed report/subreport in Design view.

FIGURE 22.6

Add two queries as subreports to this unbound main report.

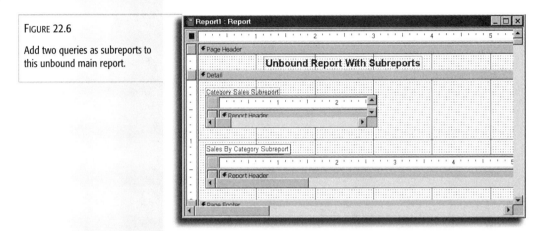

9. Click the **Print Preview** button 🔍. Figure 22.7 shows the report in Print Preview.

FIGURE 22.7

The two subreports are unrelated to one another and to the main report.

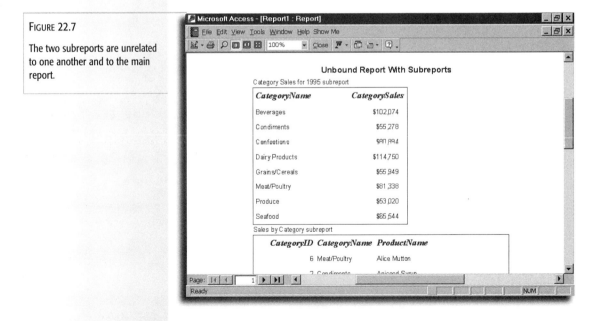

At this point, you need to modify your report or enhance it to suit your needs. You'll probably try several variations before you hit on just the right one. Although this type of report is useful in some situations, you'll generally use subreports linked to the main report.

SEE ALSO

➤ *To learn how to modify reports, see page 131*

Linking a Subreport's Data to the Main Report

Most of the time you'll probably want the subreport to display more detailed information about some group in your main report (or vice-versa). You can do this by linking the two objects. For instance, the Sales by Year report, which you looked at earlier in Figure 22.1, uses the subreport to summarize quarterly sales totals while displaying the detail orders for the year in the main report.

To link the two reports, you specify the linking field in both reports. You don't have to display the linking fields in either report, but you must include them in the underlying table or query. If you want to set these links manually, open the subreport's control property sheet and set the following properties:

- Link Child Fields identifies the linking field in the subreport.

- Link Master Fields identifies the linking field or control in the main report.

"Control" in this sense doesn't mean the controls on the subreport. Rather, the subreport is a control in the main report.

To access the Subform/Subreport property sheet, right-click the subreport control in the main report and choose **Properties** from the resulting shortcut menu. Figure 22.8 shows the subreport's property sheet. As you can see, both linking fields are the Year field. That way, the subreport displays all the order records for the same year for which your main report summarizes quarterly data.

Deleting the border

The wizard displays a subreport with a border around it. If you don't like this format, delete it by setting the subreport control's **Border Style** property to **Transparent**. To access the Subform/Subreport property sheet, right-click the subreport control and choose **Properties** from the resulting shortcut menu.

Another example of subreports linked to a main report

Probably one of the best examples of a main report and linked subreports can be found in an employee information database. In such an application, you might find a main Employees table with all the basic information about an employee. You would probably also have additional tables that contained job history, training course, skills, and so on. To prepare a report that shows all information available for each employee, create a main report that contains all the basic employee information and then a subreport for each table containing additional information. Each subreport would be linked to the main report by the EmployeeID or other similar field.

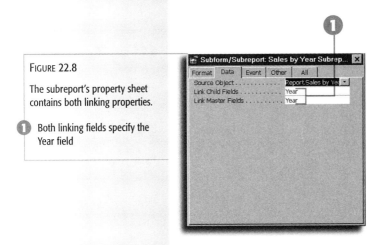

FIGURE 22.8

The subreport's property sheet contains both linking properties.

1. Both linking fields specify the Year field

Automatic linking

Access automatically sets the Link Master Fields and Link Child Fields properties for you when conditions are right: when a relationship exists between the tables on which you base the report and subreport; or when the main report's table has a primary key, and the subreport's bound table or query contains a field with the same name and a compatible data type and field size.

You can link two fields as long as they contain the same kind of data and compatible data type and field size properties. An AutoNumber field is compatible with a Number field if the Field Size property for the Number field is Long Integer.

Assigning Subreport Properties

You've already learned about the two most crucial subreport properties: Link Master Fields and Link Child Fields. What you might not realize is that a subreport has two sets of properties:

- As a control, the subreport has a special list of Subform/Subreport properties, which you saw in Figure 22.8. These properties are consistent with control properties in general.

- As a report, it has a set of report properties similar to any other report.

Subreports as reports also have report events. Subreports as controls don't, however.

You learned how to access a subreport's *control* properties in the last section. To set a subreport's *report* properties, open the main report in Design view. Then double-click the **Report Selector** to open the report's property sheet. Or you can click the

Properties button ⬛ on the Report Design toolbar.

To open the property sheet for one of the subreport's controls, double-click it, or select it and click the **Properties** button ⬛ .

Other Important Properties

There's probably no way you can estimate the size of the subreport. Therefore, it's a good idea to apply the Can Grow and Can Shrink properties. That way, the subreport can grow to accommodate many records, or shrink to save space when there are few or no records to display. You'll find these properties in the Subform/Subreport property sheet.

The Can Grow property's default is Yes, meaning that it stretches to display all its records. The Can Shrink property's default is No because reducing the subreport might have an adverse affect on controls with fixed positions after it.

For more information on subforms, see Chapter 19, "The World of Subforms."

Using the Database window

All these examples use the Subform/Subreport Wizard to insert subreports in a main report. However, you don't need the wizard. Instead, drag the object you want to add to the main report from the Database window. When you're ready to add the subreport, open the main report in Design view, and then display the Database window by pressing the **F11** key or by clicking the **Database Window** button ⬛ . Then select the table, query, form, or report in the Database window and simply drag it to the main report.

Creating Labels and Mail-Merge Documents

Take the work out of printing labels

Use custom-sized labels

Merge Access data with Word documents on-the-fly

Link Access data to Word documents

Using the Label Wizard

You can use Microsoft Word to create mailing labels, but if your data is in Access, you should consider using the Label Wizard instead. You tell the wizard which table or query contains the address data, the size of the labels you're using, and the information you want to include on each label—the wizard does the rest.

SEE ALSO

➤ *Access offers several report wizards. For more information, see page 122*

Create mailing labels

1. In the Database window, select the table or query that contains your address data. For this example, use the Customers table in the Northwind database that comes with Access.

2. Select **Report** from the drop-down list of the **New Object** button, and then double-click **Label Wizard** in the New Report dialog box (or select **Label Wizard** and click **OK**).

3. In the wizard's first dialog box (see Figure 23.1), specify the label size, the unit of measure, and the label type. If the wizard doesn't offer the label size you're using, you need to customize your report by clicking the **Customize** button (but more about this option later). For now, create a report based on a standard size—Avery number 5096. Avery happens to be the default manufacturer, so you don't need to change the **Filter By Manufacturer** setting, which lists each manufacturer's products. Be sure to specify the unit of measure and the type of labels you're using (if necessary) before clicking **Next** to continue. If you're following the Customers table example, retain the defaults.

4. The wizard gives you the option of modifying several format defaults (see Figure 23.2). Use the defaults for the example, but you can modify these options to suit your needs. When you're done, click **Next** to continue.

The flexibility of Access labels

The results of using the Label Wizard on the Customers table in Northwind show one of the more common uses of labels—addresses. You can use these steps with any table or query that contains address data. Access, however, doesn't know or care if you're using addresses for your labels. You can find numerous uses for labels and apply these examples to any table or query with any information. For example, if you're taking a physical inventory count for auditing or moving purposes, you might want to attach a label to each item that displays the item's ID number, name, and the location where you want it moved or stored.

Finding compatible labels

Earlier versions of Access supported Avery labels. Access 2000 supports six different manufacturer labels, drastically increasing the number of labels at your disposal. You can run this wizard in advance to see which label styles are supported before making your purchase. Use the scrollbars to see all the types, and click **Cancel** after you have the label information.

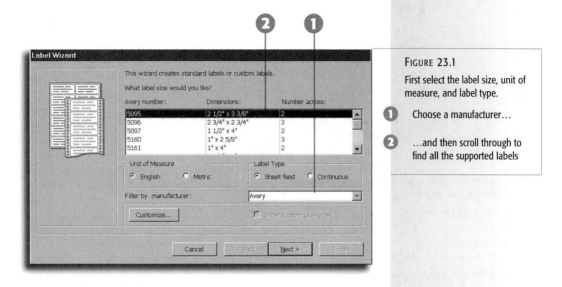

FIGURE 23.1
First select the label size, unit of measure, and label type.

1 Choose a manufacturer...

2 ...and then scroll through to find all the supported labels

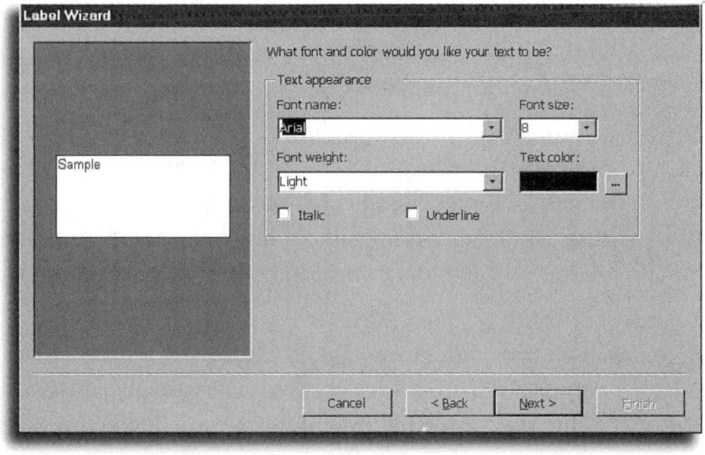

FIGURE 23.2
The second dialog box allows you to specify formats.

5. The wizard asks you to specify the bound fields you want to display on each label, but you're doing much more. You're actually creating the label template. This means you must select each field as you want it to appear on the actual label (see Figure 23.3).

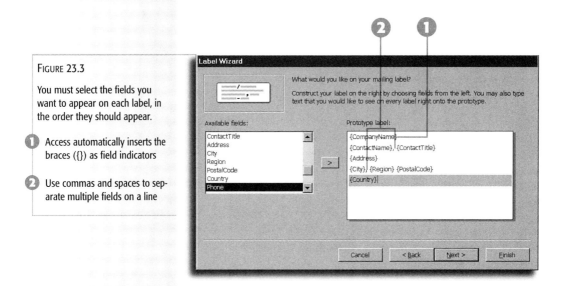

FIGURE 23.3

You must select the fields you
want to appear on each label, in
the order they should appear.

1 Access automatically inserts the
braces ({}) as field indicators

2 Use commas and spaces to separate multiple fields on a line

Options for selecting fields

You can include as many fields as
you want in your label template—
just keep the label's measurements
in mind. Also, if you selected a label
type in the dialog box in Figure 23.1,
such as a label that's 4″ by 6″, you
can continue adding fields on a single line. The wizard's prototype
label-viewing area scrolls over as
you add additional fields to the
right. Access warns you if you're
going too far when you try to click
Next.

Sorting labels

Any type of label can be sorted by
fields that you don't include in the
label. For example, if you don't
want to include the Country field in
an address label but still want all the
labels grouped by country, you can
omit the Country field on the label
but add the Country field to the
Sort by list.

Select the addressee for the first field—in this case, the
CompanyName field. Double-click the field selection or
click the **>** button to move it to the label template. Press
Enter to go to the next line. Then select the address or
remaining fields, and press **Enter** to move to the following
lines. Be sure to insert commas and spaces where appropriate. To delete a field, simply highlight it and press **Delete**.
After you add all the necessary fields, click **Next** to continue.

6. The next dialog box asks you to specify a sort field for your
report. This step isn't necessary, but as you can see in Figure
23.4, you're sorting by the PostalCode field (zip code). This
can speed up sorting if you're following postal regulations to
take advantage of reduced postage. Click **Next** to continue.

7. The final dialog box (see Figure 23.5) prompts you for a
report name. You can use the wizard's default or enter a new
one. (In this example, it's rptCustomerLabels.) You can also
choose whether to view the report in Design view or Print
Preview. If you select **See the Labels As They Will Look
Printed**, the label report opens in Print Preview. After you
make the appropriate selections, click **Finish** to see the completed report (see Figure 23.6).

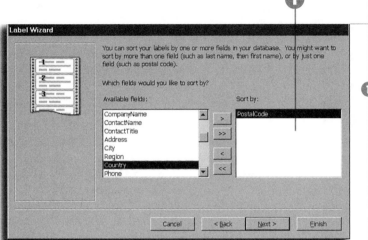

FIGURE 23.4

The wizard sorts your labels by the field you specify.

❶ Sort by any field, even if it's not included in the label

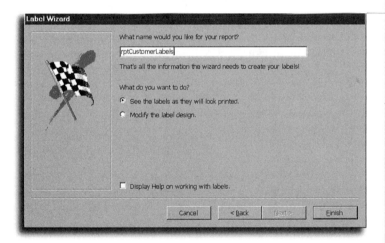

FIGURE 23.5

The last dialog box prompts you for a report name and lets you specify Design view or Print Preview.

8. When you're satisfied with the report, you can print your labels. Be sure to insert your label sheets in the appropriate printer tray, and then click the **Print** button 🖨 on the Print Preview toolbar or choose **Print** from the **File** menu.

Printing tips

If it's too difficult to tell label dimensions from Print Preview, try printing only one page of the report on a set of labels to see if the information fits. Choose **Print** from the **File** menu to print by page rather than use the **Print** icon 🖨, which prints all pages.

FIGURE 23.6

Here's your completed label
report in Print Preview.

If you don't like the way the labels look in Print Preview, you
have two options:

- You can click the **Design View** icon  and adjust the
  report's design.
- You can close Print Preview (eventually delete the report
  from the Database window) and start the wizard over, making your corrections.

Although the latter seems redundant, it's often easier to let the
wizard do the work for you than to try to manipulate or add
fields in Design view. You might print one sheet of incorrect
labels onto plain paper and pencil in your changes for reference
as you rerun the wizard.

Using Custom Labels

Creating a label report is straightforward and simple, as long as
you're using a standard label size. If this isn't possible, you'll

need to customize your report. Although this process takes a lit-tle more time, it's still easy. You'll need to know some precise measurements before you start:

- Label width
- Label depth
- Top, bottom, left, and right margin
- Space between each label column, sometimes referred to as the *gutter* or *ditch*

For the following example, use the Customers table from the Northwind database.

Work with custom labels

1. Select the table in the Database window, select **Report** from the drop-down list of the **New Object** button , and then double-click **Label Wizard** in the New Reports dialog box.

2. In the first dialog box, click the **Customize** button to dis-play the New Label Size dialog box (see Figure 23.7). The list box is empty because you have no custom label reports. If your list box already has an entry, you can click **Edit** to modify it or **Delete** to remove it. Be sure to change the **Unit of Measure** and **Label Type** options before continu-ing, if necessary.

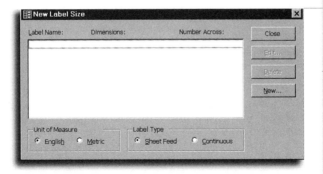

FIGURE 23.7
You're going to base a label report on a custom-sized label.

3. Click **New** to open the New Label dialog box (see Figure 23.8). Enter an appropriate name in the **Label Name** text box. Then choose an **Orientation** setting and specify the number of columns each sheet has.

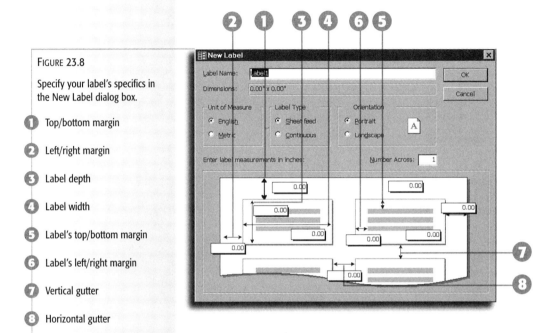

FIGURE 23.8

Specify your label's specifics in the New Label dialog box.

1 Top/bottom margin

2 Left/right margin

3 Label depth

4 Label width

5 Label's top/bottom margin

6 Label's left/right margin

7 Vertical gutter

8 Horizontal gutter

Copying the label layout for reference

Because of the number of dimensions used, you might want to print out the New Label dialog box to use as a reference. After specifying all the label dimensions, press **Print Screen** on your keyboard. Your computer probably won't print automatically, but pressing **Print Screen** copies the screen image onto the **Windows** Clipboard. Open a new document in any image program, such as Paint. Press **Ctrl+V** (the Paste key combination), and Windows pastes this screen image into the blank document. You can print it from there.

4. In the bottom section of this dialog box, you must enter the precise measurements for each specified area. Just highlight the 0.00 setting and enter the appropriate measurement.

5. After you enter all the measurements, click **OK** to continue. Then click **Close** to return to the wizard's first dialog box, which lists your custom label report. Click **Next** to continue.

6. Repeat steps 5 through 8 of the previous exercise to complete the label template.

Printing Multiple Labels

As long as you need to print just one label for each record, the Label Wizard should meet that need. But what if you want to print more than one label for one or more records? The solution is a combination of objects: two tables, one query, and your label report. One table contains your address information and the number of labels you want to print for each addressee (or record). The second table contains a list of consecutive numbers, from 1 to *x*, where *x* equals the maximum number of labels you might ever need to print. (Of course, you can change *x* any time you like by adding to or deleting from this table.)

Print multiple labels

1. Make sure that you have a table that contains complete address information. (It can contain additional data as well—simply ignore what you don't need for your labels.) Open this table in Design View and add a Number field named LabelCount.

2. In Datasheet view, add the appropriate value to each record. In other words, if you want to print two labels for Nancy Davolio, enter the value 2 in the corresponding LabelCount field (see Figure 23.9, which hides several fields in the table). You can update this value any time you need more or fewer labels for someone.

SEE ALSO

➤ *Need help altering your table's design? See page 61*

3. Create a one-field table named tblLabel. Name the lone Number field Label. In Datasheet view, enter a list of consecutive values (see Figure 23.10). Make sure that your list includes all the values, up to and including the largest value you entered into the LabelCount field, you added to your address table. (It's all right to list more values, but not fewer.)

This section's example

The example adds this label-printing utility to the Northwind database. You'll rely on the Employees table because it already contains address data. You can use any database you like, but just remember that you need a table with address information or any other information for which you want duplicate labels.

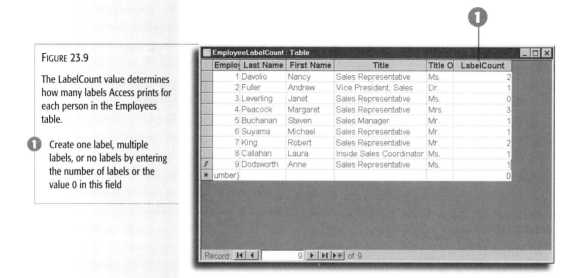

FIGURE 23.9

The LabelCount value determines how many labels Access prints for each person in the Employees table.

① Create one label, multiple labels, or no labels by entering the number of labels or the value 0 in this field

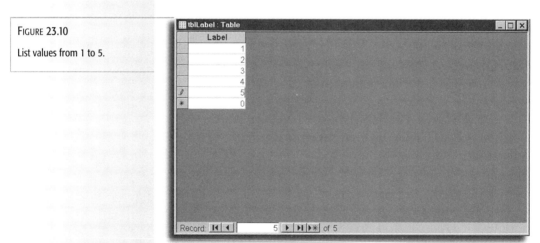

FIGURE 23.10

List values from 1 to 5.

4. Base a query on your address table, and add all the appropriate address information to the design grid. Then add LabelCount to the design grid.

5. Add tblLabel to the design grid by clicking the **Show Table** button on the Query Design toolbar and then double-clicking tblLabel in the resulting Show Table dialog box. Click **Close**.

SEE ALSO

➤ *For help creating the query in this example, see page 79*

6. Enter the expression `>=[tblLabel].[Label]` into the
LabelCount field's **Criteria** cell (see Figure 23.11). Save the
query; I saved mine as `qryLabel`. This expression returns one
record for each requested label. Specifically, the expression
matches each record's LabelCount value to the list of consecutive values in `tblLabel`. When a match is found, the
query displays one record for that match. Furthermore,
Access displays one record for every value in `tblLabel` that's
less than the one that matched.

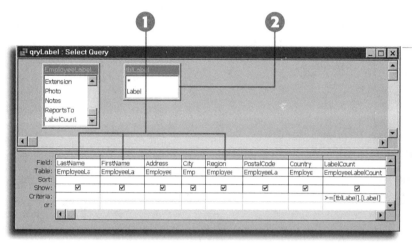

7. Build the label report. Select the query—`qryLabel`—in the
Database window, select **Report** from the drop-down list of
the **New Object** button , and then double-click **Label
Wizard**.

8. In the Label Wizard's first dialog box, select the appropriate
options and click **Next**. This example uses **5260**, **English**,
and **Sheet Feed**.

9. You can change the font formats if you like. Click **Next**.

10. In the next dialog box, add the appropriate fields to the label
template in the appropriate order. When you're satisfied
with the label's structure, click **Next** to continue.
Remember, you don't need to add the LabelCount field to
the label itself; its function should be invisible.

11. In the following dialog box, you can choose a sort order for your labels, but not in this example. Click **Next** to continue.

12. In the final dialog box, name your label report rptLabel and click **Finish**. Figure 23.12 shows the resulting report in Print Preview.

FIGURE 23.12

The wizard displays the label report in Print Preview.

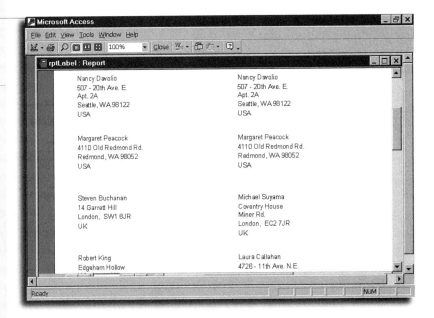

As you can see, the number of labels for each employee matches their corresponding value in the LabelCount field of the Employees table. All you have to do is load your label sheets and print the report. Notice also that a few employees don't have any labels—that's because you entered 0 in their respective LabelCount fields.

Merging Access Data with Word Documents

Access doesn't have a word processor, but you can use the report generator as one if you want. If you have Word, you'll probably prefer to type form letters and such in Word and then merge your Access data into the Word document. An added bonus to this arrangement is the menagerie of formatting tools that Word offers.

The merge process is fairly simple and straightforward. First, you store data, such as address information, in an Access database. Second, you use Word to create a mail-merge document. This document contains the information you want to share, plus special field codes that refer to fields in your Access tables. When you merge your Access data with the Word mail-merge document, Word relies on your Access database to fill the field codes in the Word document.

To successfully complete the process, you need two things:

- An Access table or query
- A mail-merge Word document, which you can create during the merge process

You can merge with an existing Word document, or you can create a new one on-the-fly. If you're sending the same letter over and over, you'll want to use the first method. But the first time you run the merge, you'll create the Word document as part of the merge process. Look at both ways, first creating the document as part of the merge process, and then running a second merge with the existing document.

Create a mail-merge document

1. In Access, choose the table or query that contains the data you need to merge into Word (in this example, the Employees table), and choose **Merge It with MS Word** from the **OfficeLinks** button ![icon] on the Database toolbar. If you want, you can click the **OfficeLinks** button rather than open the drop-down list. Doing so defaults to the Mail Merge Wizard.

2. The Mail Merge Wizard displays the dialog box in Figure 23.13. The **Link Your Data to an Existing Microsoft Word Document** option lets you merge with an existing document. You don't have a document yet, so select **Create**

What you need to merge

This section on merging assumes that you're using Office 2000 or have standalone copies of Access and Word. You must have Word installed to take advantage of the merge feature.

Working with the example

You'll rely on the Employees table in Northwind for your Access table. Because part of the mail-merge process involves adding the field codes to the Word document, you'll create a document as part of this example.

a **New Document and Then Link the Data to It** before clicking **OK**. In response, Word launches and opens a new document. (If not, you can click the **New** button 🗋 on the Standard toolbar to open a new document when Word launches.)

FIGURE 23.13

The wizard wants to know if you're merging with an existing document or creating a new one.

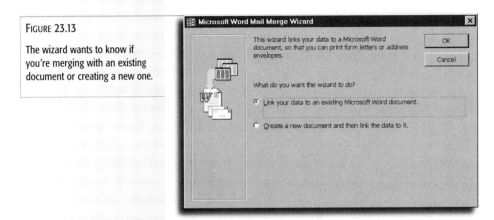

3. The first thing you need in your mail-merge document is the date. Choose **Date and Time** from the **Insert** menu, select the fourth option (month, date, year format) from the resulting dialog box, select **Update Automatically**, and click **OK**. The next time you use this merge document, Word uses the current date.

4. Press **Enter** four times.

5. You're ready to insert the merge fields. In this case, you want to add seven fields: Last Name, First Name, Address, City, Region, Postal Code, and Country. Because you selected the Employees table in Access before you started the wizard, Word links to that table, and all the Employees' fields are available in the **Insert Merge Field** button's drop-down list (see Figure 23.14); simply insert them in the appropriate order. First, open the **Insert Merge Field** button's [Insert Merge Field ▾] drop-down list and select **First Name**. Press the space bar to enter a space between the addressee's first and last name. Then, select **Last Name** from the **Insert Merge Field** button's drop-down list.

FIGURE 23.14
All the Employee table fields are available in Word.

6. Press **Enter** to move the cursor to the next line.

7. Choose **Address** from the drop-down list and press **Enter**.

8. Choose **City**, enter a comma, and then press the space bar. Next, select **Region**. Then press the space bar and select **Postal Code**. Press **Enter** to go to the next line.

9. Select **Country**, the final field.

10. Press **Enter** twice and enter the word **Dear** followed by a space.

11. Choose **First Name** from the **Insert Merge Field** button's drop-down list, enter a space, and then select **Last Name** from the drop-down field. Follow the **Last Name** field code with a semicolon, and then press **Enter** twice.

12. Enter the body of your letter (see Figure 23.15). Remember, you can add field codes to the body of your letter—simply insert the fields in the appropriate spot in your letter.

13. After you finish your letter, add several blank lines to the top margin to better center it. At this time, you should also apply any special formatting you want.

14. If you want to save the document, choose **Save As** from the **File** menu. Name this mail-merge document meeting.doc.

FIGURE 23.15

You'll merge Access data with this letter later.

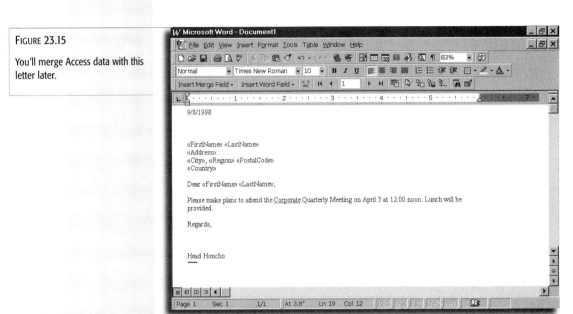

15. When your document is exactly the way you want it and you're ready to merge your Access data, you have two choices:

- **Merge to a new document.** You can view and then save the results of the merge.

- **Merge directly to the printer.** You bypass this step and print all the merged letters.

To merge to a new document, click the **Merge to New Document** button on the Mail Merge toolbar. Word creates one document with the default name **Form Letter1**. Each page of this document contains one of your merged letters. You can view them, print them, or even modify them. If you want to return to the mail-merge document (the document with your field codes), choose that document from the **Window** menu.

To merge to the printer, click the **Merge to Printer** button on the Mail Merge toolbar. This prints all the merged letters automatically without creating a new document.

If you want to merge by using the meeting.doc document, choose the **Link Your Data to an Existing Microsoft Word Document** option in the Merge Wizard's first dialog box. When prompted, locate the meeting.doc mail-merge document in the Select Microsoft Word Document dialog box. When Word launches and opens meeting.doc, click one of the merge options—merge to a new document or merge to the printer—as you did in the preceding example.

Word's mail-merge feature

Word's mail-merge feature is very flexible and powerful, and I haven't attempted to show you all its features. I've concentrated on linking Access data with the mail-merge feature.

Automating the Database

Creating Macros

Use macros for automation

Navigate in the Macro Design window

Use names to organize macros

Use conditions

When to Use Macros

Access macros are powerful tools that provide an easy way for you to automate almost anything you can do with the mouse or the keyboard. By using macros, you can automate many tasks that would otherwise require several separate steps. You also can pull together the collection of tables, forms, reports, and queries that make up your database into a single, easy-to-use application.

Another advantage to understanding how macros can be used is that it will be easier to learn VBA (Visual Basic for Applications). Because so many macro actions mimic VBA functions, when you are ready to move on to VBA, you will be further ahead than someone who refuses to learn about macros. VBA can intimidate most people, but if you are familiar with the macros in Access, using VBA won't seem that hard when it comes to the point where there's no way to do your programming using macros alone.

The best way to start designing macros is to think of some process that you do in your database repeatedly. It might be something you do many times a day, or perhaps it's a daily or a weekly process. Suppose that you receive a comma-delimited text file weekly from an outside party, and you need to append the data in this file to the data already in the particular table in your database. This is a good job for a macro. Or perhaps you have a series of, say, five action queries that you must run, one after the other, every day—another good job for a macro.

The Macro Design Window

Because the Macro Design window is used to create a new macro and to edit existing macros, you first need to look at the window itself.

To open the Macro Design window, click **Macros** in the Object portion of the Database window (see Figure 24.1). A list of any existing macros appears. Select **New** from the Database window's toolbar to open the Macro Design window without displaying an existing macro.

Editing an existing macro

When you want to edit a macro, rather than click **New**, choose an existing macro and then click **Design** on the Database window's toolbar.

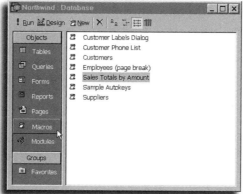

FIGURE 24.1

Select the **Macros** object to see whether an existing database, such as Northwind, has any macros. Then click **New** to open a new macro.

Default display of the Macro Design window

You can control whether the Macro Names or Conditions column displays by default when you open the Macro Design window. From the **Tools** menu choose **Options** while the Macro Design window is open. On the **View** page, select the check boxes labeled **Names Column** and **Conditions Column** to set the defaults as you prefer.

The Macro Design window will then give you a blank sheet for your new macros. Your window should be similar to the one shown in Figure 24.2. Depending on your system defaults, you might need to click the **Macro Names** [⊞] or **Conditions** [⊞] toolbar button to display these columns.

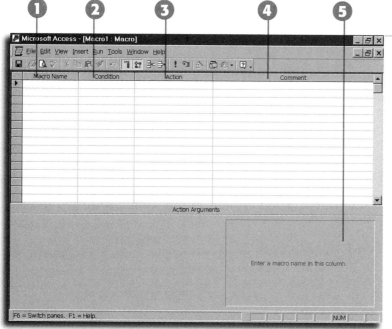

FIGURE 24.2

The Macro Design window has several tools to help you create macros.

❶ The Macro Name column

❷ The Condition column

❸ The Action column

❹ The Comment column

❺ Context-sensitive help message

Edit a macro

1. To open the Macro Design window, click **Macros** in the Object portion of the Database window. A list of any existing macros is displayed.

2. Select the macro you want to edit, and click Design in the Database window toolbar to open the Macro Design window displaying the selected macro.

As shown in Figure 24.2, the Macro Design window has a similar look and feel to the other Design view grids. The Name and Condition columns are for more complex macros that are discussed later in the section "Generating Macros with Multiple Actions."

Notice the Action column. This is where you will tell Access what actions to take in your macro. A macro might consist of a single action or many actions. To add an action to your macro, move the cursor to the Action column and open the drop-down list to access all the actions available. More than 50 actions are listed, with several actions that allow additional subactions. For example, the RunCommand action has more than 300 additional subactions.

Next notice the Comment column. Comments are just that—comments, or notes to yourself. Comments don't affect what the macro does or how. It's always a good practice to include comments. You don't have to put a comment in every line of the macro (unless you are forgetful like me), but if you have to come back and make changes to the macro six months from now, you will thank yourself many times if you've commented it.

Also shown in Figure 24.2, at the bottom right, is a context-sensitive help message panel. This message changes depending on the action picked in the Action column. The help message also gives you hints on a particular action's arguments. If you need more help than what's provided in the short message, press **F1** and Access will give you a help window that goes into more detail for that particular action and its arguments.

Another area of the Macro Design window is the Action Arguments area, at the bottom. To see arguments in this area, select an action in the Action column. To see some arguments, create a simple macro that presents a message box to the user.

Commenting macros

You're allowed 255 characters in a macro comment. You can extend comments over several lines by indenting subsequent lines. You should include such things as the intent, the affected tables, queries, and so on. You might also include other databases where you also use this macro so that you can change all the macros if needed.

Why so many arguments?

Although the term *argument* has a negative connotation in conversations between humans, it's not a negative term in programming macros. Arguments are descriptive terms you add to an action to tell it specifically what to do, when or where to perform the action, and on which objects. In simple terms, if your action is to jump, you'd specify arguments such as the frog, height, distance, and direction. Arguments also take a certain form, or *syntax*, similar to the way sentences are arranged in a certain order. With macros, however, you enter arguments visually in fields and Access writes the syntax for you.

Create a message box

1. In the first line of the **Action** column, click the drop-down arrow. From the list, select **MsgBox** (see Figure 24.3).

When you select MsgBox, the Action Arguments area displays four arguments for the MsgBox action: Message, Beep, Type, and Title.

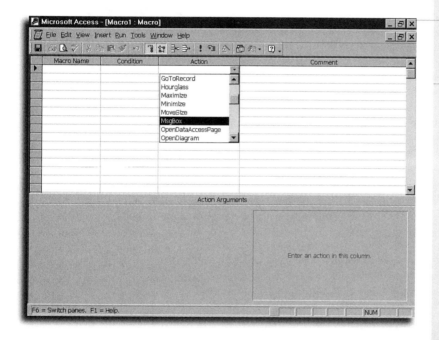

FIGURE 24.3
Select the Macro action from the drop-down list.

2. Place the message you want to display in the Message argument. You can put any text in this argument, such as My first macro.

3. Turn the annoying Beep off by typing No or by selecting **No** from the drop-down list.

4. Select which built-in icon will be displayed next to the message in the Type argument. I usually select Information or Warning, and rarely select Critical.

5. Place the title of the message box, such as Congratulations, in the Title argument area. This appears in the title bar of the message box. The result should resemble Figure 24.4.

Using the selection option in arguments

Similar to options in the **Field** property's Design View, you can click at the right end of the argument space to reveal a drop-down box that shows options available for that field. Also notice that as you fill in the arguments, the help area gives you hints particular to that argument.

FIGURE 24.4

Enter a name to save your
macro to.

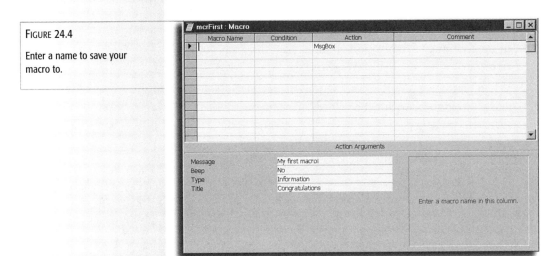

6. Save your macro by clicking the **Save** icon . Use a logical filename, such as mcrFirst, so you can readily recognize
its purpose by name.

7. Run your macro by clicking the **Run** icon .

If you follow the preceding steps, you should see the standard
MsgBox form with your options in it (see Figure 24.5).

FIGURE 24.5

Use a macro to customize and
run MsgBox forms of various
types.

Generating Macros with Multiple Actions

In this simple example, your macro performed only a single
action. But what if you want to perform several consecutive
actions, or steps? No problem. You can define multiple actions
that execute one right after the other by simply adding the
desired action in the next row of the Macro Design window.
When you're working with macros in forms and reports, you'll
see where being able to specify multiple actions comes in handy.

Now that you are more familiar with the basic Macro Design window, move on to something a little harder than a single message box.

Create a multiple-action macro

1. Open the Northwind sample database.

2. Open a new macro window.

3. On the first line of the new macro, select the RunSQL action.

4. In the SQL Statement argument, enter the following:
   ```
   SELECT * INTO tblTemp FROM Customers;
   ```

5. On the second row, select the OpenTable action and enter tblTemp for the Table Name argument. Your macro should resemble Figure 24.6.

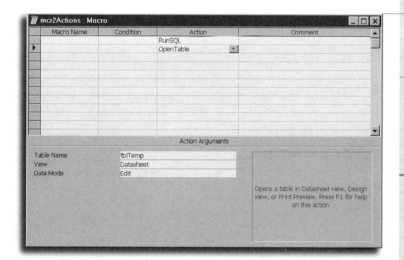

6. Save the new macro under the name mcr2Actions.

7. Run the macro.

This macro executes two actions: it runs a SQL string that creates a new table named tblTemp from the contents of the existing Customers table and then displays the new table.

Take another look at the mcr2Action macro.

Remember Access's Zoom feature

You might find it useful to use the built-in Zoom feature when entering or reviewing the SQL statement. Simply press **Shift+F2** while the SQL Statement argument is selected.

FIGURE 24.6

Use a single macro to perform multiple actions.

Notice any warning message(s)

You might have noticed that Access issued a warning message when you ran macro mcr2Actions the first time. This is typical of any SQL statement that alters your database tables. You are given the opportunity to cancel the action if you choose. If you run the macro a second or third time, you will actually see two warning messages. Because the first action is creating a table named tblTemp, the table already exists when you run the macro a second time, and Access wants to make sure that you really want to delete and replace it.

Update an existing macro

1. Open the `mcr2Action` macro in Design view.

2. Place the cursor on the first row, and click the **Insert Row** icon ⬚ on the toolbar. The new top row should now be empty.

3. Select the action `SetWarnings` for the first row of the macro.

4. Select **No** for the `Warnings On` argument.

5. In the fourth and last rows, again select the action `SetWarnings`.

6. Select **Yes** for the `Warnings On` argument.

7. Save and run the macro.

It's much nicer now that those pesky warning messages are gone.

Macro Conditions

About macro conditions

Expressions entered as a condition in a macro statement must evaluate to True or False. If the condition is True, the corresponding action is executed. If the condition is false, the corresponding action isn't executed.

You can use the Condition column to add a decision-making capability to a macro. Suppose that you want to create a macro that displays one message under certain conditions and another message under other conditions. The Conditions column allows you to do just that.

Want a more complex expression?

To build complex expressions, use the Expression Builder by right-clicking the **Condition** column or by clicking the **Builder** icon ⬚ on the toolbar.

Create a condition

1. Use the `mcr2Action` macro again by opening it in Design view.

2. Make sure that the **Condition** column is displayed. If it isn't, click the **Condition** icon ⬚.

3. In the **Condition** column, on the same row as the `OpenTable` action, enter the following:

   `InputBox("Enter Yes to display the table")="Yes"`

   Your macro should now look like Figure 24.7.

4. Save and run the macro.

SEE ALSO

➤ *For information and practice with using expressions, see page 542*

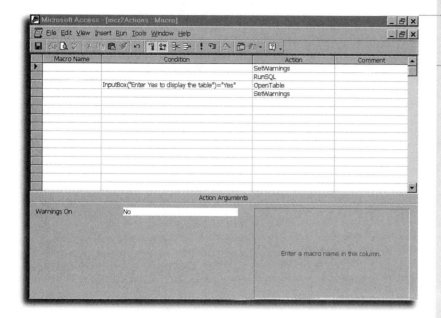

FIGURE 24.7
Enter a conditional expression.

Your macro now opens the table only if you type yes when prompted; otherwise, it simply moves to the action on the next row.

Macro Groups

Yet another section of the Macro Design window is the Macro Name column. If it's not visible, unhide it by clicking the **Macro Name** icon. The Macro Name column makes it much easier to manage your macros as they grow in number. By specifying a name in the Macro Name column of the first row, your macro is now considered a macro group. A macro group allows you to store various related macros, all macros related to a specific form for example, under a single macro name. This can make it much easier to keep things organized and tidy.

Create a macro group

1. In the first row of your mcr2Actions macro in the Macro Name column, enter some text. For this example, use ShowTable.

FIGURE 24.8

The completed macro with group names.

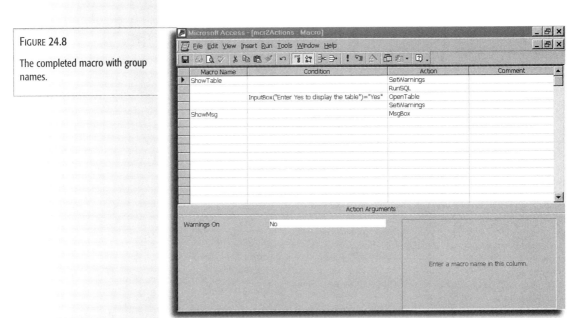

2. On the fifth row of your macro in the Macro Name column, create another macro group named ShowMsg.

3. Select the MsgBox action for the fifth row and enter This runs like a separate macro for the Message argument. Your macro should look similar to Figure 24.8.

4. Save the macro.

Now when you run your macro, it executes only the first macro group. How do you run the second macro group in the same way? The answer is simple: You don't. If you have more than one macro group in a macro, use a RunMacro action, or from the **Tools** menu choose **Macro** and then **Run Macro** to run the other macro groups. Then you can specify which macro group you want to run. You can see how you would execute the other macro groups by selecting the RunMacro action. Under Macro Name, you can now see your other macro groups. Figure 29.9 shows some example macro groups.

FIGURE 24.9
Use the RunMacro command to
run a specific group in a macro.

When you're programming multiple macros for your forms and
reports, being able to group macros will help you manage them.
If Access didn't have macro groups, you would have to create
one macro object for each set of actions that you wanted. With
the macro groups, you can have all the actions that relate to a
form or a report in one macro.

Macro Actions and Their Arguments

As noted earlier in the chapter, you can use more than 50 macro
actions. Many of the more commonly used actions are demonstrated
throughout this book. A complete list of the actions available, as well as
a brief description about what they do and the arguments they require,
is available directly from your PC. Open a new macro and select any
action you might be interested in. All the pertinent information is summarized on one screen. If you want more examples, many are found in
this book. Examples can also be found in Access Help.

Running Macros

Run macros manually

Attach macros to events

Use macros that run when you open your application

Enable startup options

Methods Used to Run Macros

After you create and save a macro, you can run or execute it in several ways.

Manually Running Macros

The first method used to run your macro uses the standard interface that Access provides to all macros.

Run a macro from the Database window

1. In the database window, select the **Macro** object if it isn't already selected.

2. Select the macro that you want to run. Your database window should look similar to Figure 25.1.

FIGURE 25.1

The mcrFirst macro is selected.

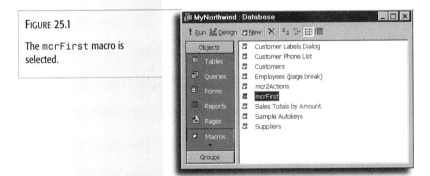

3. Click the **Run** button to execute your macro.

Although all macros that you create can be run in this manner, remember that in the case of macros that contain groups, only the first group of actions are executed. Macro groups other than the first one are ignored.

To execute a particular macro group within a macro, use the menu. For cases where you need to manually run a specific macro within a macro group, you can use the following method.

Run a macro from a macro group

1. From the **Tools** menu, choose **Macro** and then **Run Macro** to open the Run Macro dialog box (see Figure 25.2).

FIGURE 25.2
Use the **Tools** menu to run a
macro from a macro group.

2. Select the macro you want to execute from the drop-down
   list.
3. Click **OK** to execute your macro.

Using the *RunMacro* Action

Another way to execute macros is by using the RunMacro action.
By using RunMacro in a macro, you can tell a macro to run yet
another macro.

Execute a macro from within another macro

1. In the first line of a new macro, select Msgbox for the Action
   argument.
2. Place some text you want to display in the message argument. You can put any text in this argument, such as We made
   it!
3. For the Type argument, select **Information.**
4. Click the **Save** icon 💾 . Use mcrChild as the name.
5. Close the macro design window and open a second new
   macro.
6. Select the RunMacro action.
7. Enter mcrChild as the Macro Name argument.
8. Save this macro as mcrParent.
9. Run the mcrParent macro. You should see a message box
   similar to that in Figure 25.3.

Finding macro group names

The Run Macro dialog box
shows you all available macros
in the database, with any macro
groups available using the
format *macroname.*
macrogroup, where
macroname is the name in
the database window and
macrogroup is the particular macro group within that
macro.

FIGURE 25.3
This message box is displayed
from a macro called by another
macro.

Attached Macros to Events

Probably the most common way to run a macro isn't to run it directly at all, but for it to run in response to an Access event. Remember that events can be triggered by all sorts of things that might happen on a form or a report, or even an individual control on a form or report—for example, a form being opened triggers the form's OnOpen event, when the current record being displayed by a form moves from one to another record the form's OnCurrent event is triggered, or after a user updates the data in a control on a form the control's AfterUpdate event is triggered. These are but a few of the dozens of events built into Access.

You can take advantage of these events by telling Access to run a macro or VBA code whenever a specific event occurs for a specific form, or report, or control (see Chapter 20, "Advanced Form Techniques"). By using events in this manner, you can refine your application so that it can deliver functionality not provided by Access itself, including the ability for users to move between the various objects of your application without ever seeing or even being aware that the database window even exists.

Debugging Macros

Sometimes your macros might not do as you expect. You can define these unexpected results as *errors*—anything that doesn't produce the intended result is an error. Errors can be caused by logic errors, syntax errors, or runtime errors.

Logic errors are probably the most difficult to find or even understand. These errors are hard to find because they represent a misunderstanding or unawareness on your part of what a macro action does or what side effects the action might have. The more difficult logic errors might show no visible manifestation for months. Make sure that you understand all the actions and side effects as you review your macro line by line. Trying to find a logic error can be the most frustrating and time-consuming part of debugging.

Syntax errors are probably the easiest of the three types of errors to find, but they can be just as difficult to fix. Syntax errors usually don't get past Access parser, so you will get immediate feedback in the Macro Design window (see Figure 25.4).

FIGURE 25.4

Run your macro in the Macro Design window before you finish so that you can check for syntax errors.

Some syntax errors make it past the parser in the Macro Design window but show up when you run the macro. These errors, called *runtime errors*, are a little more difficult to resolve than syntax errors because they don't show up until the macro is run. These errors are easier to find than logic errors, however, and you shouldn't have too much trouble correcting them. See Figure 25.5 for an example of a runtime error.

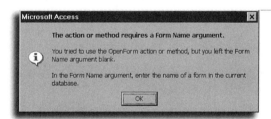

FIGURE 25.5

An action that requires arguments shows an error if you don't include all the arguments.

Some runtime errors are the result of a misspelled control name or any other database object name. For these kinds of errors, learn how to use the Expression Builder and you will eliminate those errors in the future.

SEE ALSO

➤ *For detailed information on using the Expression Builder, see page 541*

In the more complex macros, you will have to resort to stepping through the macro to find the row causing the error. The single-stepping feature can also be a great learning tool because it will help you see how your macro is run.

Step through a macro to learn

If you are curious to learn more about how macros work, use the Northwind database and study the macros it contains. You can find out where the macro is attached to a event by reading the first comment in Macro Design view. Then locate the specific object, call the macro, and follow the steps to step through the macro. This method helps you understand the function and purpose (along with read the comments) of how the macro is designed.

Step through a macro

Documenting your macro with comments

The comments in this macro tell you that the macro is used by the Customers form, and specifically that the section of the macro named `ValidateID` is attached to the `BeforeUpdate` event of the CustomerID control.

1. In the Northwind database, open the Customers macro in Design view.

2. Click the **Single Step** icon 🔳 on the toolbar. Close the macro.

3. The Customers macro supports the Customers form, so open that form. The form should display record 1, with a CustomerID value of ALFKI.

4. Change the CustomerID value to ANATR and press **Tab**. This triggers the `BeforeUpdate` event for the CustomerID control. Because a macro, `Customers.ValidateID`, is attached to that event, Access begins execution of the macro.

5. Because you turned on the Single Step option for this macro (step 2), the Single Step dialog box opens (see Figure 25.6).

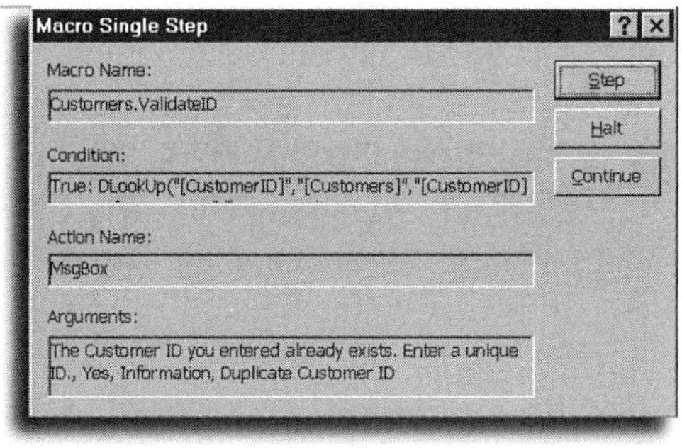

FIGURE 25.6

You can watch each line's execution to find an error or to learn how an existing macro works.

6. When you single step through your macro, the execution is temporarily halted until you select **Step**, **Halt**, or **Continue**:

   - The **Step** button lets you execute your macro one line at a time.

   - **Halt** halts the execution of your macro without going further.

   - **Continue** continues running the macro without single stepping through the rest of it.

   The key information about the macro is displayed, but this row of the macro hasn't yet executed. Click the **Step** button to execute the macro's current row (in this case, the display of a message box) and stop again before executing the macro's second row.

7. Click the **Step** button again to execute the second row, and return to the form.

8. Press the **Esc** key to restore the original content of the CustomerID control, and then close the form.

Working with the *AutoExec* and *AutoKeys* Macros

Access handles two special macros differently because of their names: AutoExec and AutoKeys.

Using *AutoExec*

When you open your database, Access looks to see whether the database includes a macro named AutoExec. If so, the AutoExec macro is executed automatically. This macro can be used to prepare your application for use; typically it's used with the startup options described later in this chapter.

I normally use the AutoExec macro to call a VBA function (using the RunCode action) that has been customized for each particular application. The VBA code might set up my custom security, copy remote data to local tables, and so on. If you've written some code that you want performed when your database opens, use an AutoExec macro to invoke that code.

Using *AutoKeys*

Access gives any macro named AutoKeys special treatment when your database is opened. With the AutoKeys macro, you can assign any key combination available to any macro action that you choose. You can even override the default behavior for certain key combinations.

Bypassing AutoExec

If you need to bypass the AutoExec macro, you can do so by holding down the **Shift** key when you open your database.

An example of an *AutoKeys* macro

1. In the Northwind database, open the macro named Sample Autokeys in Design view.

The Name column on the second row contains the characters ^p. These characters represent the keyboard combination **Ctrl+P.** If this macro were named AutoKeys, this row would tell Access to execute the action whenever the keyboard combination **Ctrl+P** is pressed.

2. From the **File** menu choose **Save As,** and save this macro with the name AutoKeys.

3. Close the Northwind database and then reopen it.

4. Press **Ctrl+P.** The RunMacro action contained in the AutoKeys macro is executed, displaying a dialog box (see Figure 25.7).

FIGURE 25.7

Using a macro named AutoKeys, you can assign hotkeys for use in your application.

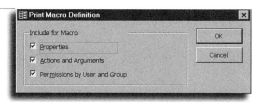

5. Close the dialog box and delete the AutoKeys macro.

Table 25.1 shows the key combinations that you can use.

Use Alt+ key combinations to open menus

Notice that an Alt combination isn't listed, so you can't reassign any key that has Alt as part of the combination. Using the Alt key with other keys is reserved for various predefined actions. For example, **Alt+F** opens the **File** menu, and **Alt+E** opens the **Edit** menu.

TABLE 25.1 **Access Key Combinations**

Text for the Names Column	Keystrokes
^A or ^4	Ctrl+Any letter or number key
{F1}	Any function key
^{F1}	Ctrl+Any function key
+{F1}	Shift+Any function key
{INSERT}	Ins
^{INSERT}	Ctrl+Insert
+{INSERT}	Shift+Insert
{DELETE} or {DEL}	Del
^{DELETE} or ^{DEL}	Ctrl+Delete
+{DELETE} or +{DEL}	Shift+Delete

Using the Startup Options as a Shortcut

Even though this chapter is focused on macros, much of what you can do with the AutoExec macro has been automated (beginning with Access 95) by using the startup options. With the Northwind database open, choose **Startup** from the **Tools** menu. In the dialog box displayed, click the **Advanced** button to expand the dialog box (see Figure 25.8). Table 25.2 summarizes these options.

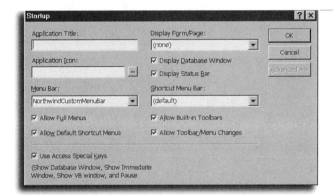

FIGURE 25.8

The Startup dialog box provides some shortcuts for some of the same results as the AutoExec macro.

TABLE 25.2 Startup Options

Option	Description
Application Title	Rather than display Microsoft Access in the upper left, it displays the text that you put here. Also, in VBA, if you don't supply a title for your message box function/statement, it uses this text for the default. Notice that the Msgbox macro action still displays Microsoft Access.
Application Icon	Replaces the "key" displayed to the left of the application title, and is the icon displayed for a minimized application in the status bar.
Menu Bar	The menu that replaces the default menu bar in Access when your application loads. It's global.
Allow Full Menus	When disabled, it takes away the design commands from menus and toolbars, such as Design view. Design commands are still available through the shortcut menus.

continues…

Preparations for the startup options

You want to select the startup options after you build all the forms for your database, including splash, switchboard, and other forms you might use on startup. Setting the Startup options usually is one of the last things to do when preparing to test your application as end users would use it.

TABLE 25.2 **Continued**

Option	Description
Allow Default Shortcut Menus	When enabled, it allows the use of the Access default shortcut menus.
Display Form	Opens a form when your database starts.
Display Database Window	Turns off the display of the database window when deselected.
Display Status Bar	Turns off/on the status bar in the lower left and bottom of the Access window.
Shortcut Menu Bar	Replaces the default shortcut menus and works with **Allow Default Shortcut Menus**.
Allow Built-in Toolbars	Turns on/off the availability of Access default toolbars.
Allow Toolbar/Menu Changes	Can/can't modify default or custom menus and toolbars.

Advanced Option

Use Access Special Keys	Turns on/off allowing users to show the Database window and Debug window, even if they know the shortcut key to do so.

Introducing Visual Basic for Applications

Understand what Visual Basic for Applications is and who needs it

Become familiar with the VBA coding environment

Learn the easy way to write code

Understand why you should document your code

When to Use VBA

What about Visual Basic and Access Basic?

If you're familiar with Visual Basic or Access Basic (version 2.0 and earlier), you will find the language and the coding environment similar. The language itself is very similar because VBA is a subset of Visual Basic. Also, you enter VBA and VB code into a similar module (discussed more later in the section "Using the Visual Basic Editor"). Unlike Visual Basic, VBA doesn't supply its own interface objects, commonly referred to as forms and controls; instead, VBA uses the hosting application's objects. As a result, a VBA project is always attached, or associated with, an application. You can't write a standalone VBA project.

You might be wondering how Visual Basic for Applications (VBA) applies to you as an Access user. After all, even without VBA, Access is a powerful relational database. When you add VBA to the equation, you have a versatile development tool for controlling Access, creating custom applications, integrating other Office applications, and even integrating with non-Microsoft software.

You might think you don't need VBA, especially if you're proficient with macros. The truth is, anything a macro can do, VBA can do better, faster, and more reliably. Plus, sometimes in an application's life macros simply aren't enough—many things can't be done at all by using macros. When this happens, VBA provides more complete functionality, more protection, and faster performance than macros.

Increasing Functionality

You might already be using VBA

You're probably using VBA already and just don't realize it. Have you written an *event procedure*? Have you created a *user-defined function (UDF)*? If you've done either, you've done so using VBA.

Suppose that you want to add a batch reporting feature to an application. In other words, you want your users to choose all the reports they want to print from a dynamic list of reports, click a **Print** button, and then go to lunch. A *dynamic* list updates automatically as you add and delete reports from your application. Unfortunately, you can't accomplish such a task with macros, no matter how many of them you link together. However, VBA can tackle this job with a small amount of code.

Avoiding Errors

You might be a macro master, but do your macros ever crash your application? If so, you're in good company—a system crash can happen to the best of developers. However, VBA is better equipped to handle errors than macros. In fact, Access macros offer no error protection at all—your favorite macros can easily crash your system if everything doesn't go exactly as you planned.

Fortunately, VBA can handle errors with ease. You can tell VBA to handle errors in various ways. Your code can look for a specific kind of error or all errors. You also can decide what to do when errors do occur: ignore it, log it out to a file, or do nothing at all and let Access handle it. It's your choice—you're in control.

Expanding Control

Handling errors is only a small portion of the control you'll have over your application using VBA. At other times, you'll use VBA to pass variables, prompt users for information, and even direct the application on its way. Macros are too limited for this type of interaction.

SEE ALSO

➤ *For more information on variables, see page 471*

Improving Performance

After you have everything under control, speed is an important consideration, no matter how fast your new system runs. Without fail, VBA code is always faster than a comparable macro, but you won't notice the difference when performing simple tasks. If a simple macro gets the job done, don't hesitate to use one; when the task is complicated or manipulates thousands of records, on the other hand, VBA reduces the time you spend waiting for your application to execute its tasks.

Exploiting Compatibility

Another important consideration when choosing between macros and VBA is compatibility. Because most Office applications use VBA, you can share code from one application to the other. You also can manipulate Access from the other Office applications.

A common language across applications means that you need to learn only one language to exercise programmatic control over other Office applications. Furthermore, thanks to OLE Automation, you can fully integrate the Office applications to manipulate data across applications or even run one application from another.

All this programmatic control is just part of a bigger picture. VBA is now available to other software developers by special licensing. This means even more compatibility across the application spectrum as non-Microsoft software begins to use and support VBA in their applications. I won't speculate that VBA will become the standard programming language across the personal computing industry, but it's already becoming a major player. You're likely to find it cropping up in more of your applications. In the end, you benefit because you have only one language to learn and grow with.

SEE ALSO

➤ *To learn more about shared components, see page 600*

You might never need these features, but it's nice to know they're available and, as you might suspect, you can't access those features with a macro.

The truth is that VBA is much more than a macro language. You can use VBA to create custom applications and to extend your application's existing functionality. For instance, by using VBA you can

- Present a custom dialog box
- Control the appearance of a report
- Solicit information from your system regarding users or the state of the current application
- Prompt users for additional information
- Manipulate data in interactive controls
- Manipulate data in other Office applications
- Resolve unique problems with user-defined functions (UDF)
- Customize the menu and toolbar structure

SEE ALSO

➤ *See more about appropriate uses for macros on page 422*

Understanding Modules

Access modules are nothing more than places to store VBA code. They fulfill no purpose whatsoever other than that of a storage container. Look at a typical module and see what's stored there.

Look inside a module

1. Open the sample database named **Northwind**.
2. Click **Modules** on the **Objects** bar of the Database window.
3. Two modules are listed. Select **Utility Functions** and click the **Design** button on the toolbar.

You've just opened the Microsoft Visual Basic Editor (VBE) window. Although your display might be somewhat different, it should be similar to Figure 26.1. The capabilities of this powerful and versatile editor are discussed in more depth later in the section "The VBA Programming Environment."

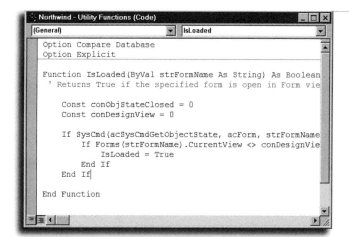

FIGURE 26.1

The horizontal line separates the module's Declaration section from its only procedure, a function named IsLoaded(). If the module contained additional procedures, another horizontal line would follow the End Function statement.

This window displays the content of the module you opened in Design view, Utility Functions. All Access modules consist of a Declaration section and usually one or more *procedures* (what you use to store your VBA code). The Utility Functions module is no exception.

When you create a new module, the Declaration section is automatically created for you, and you can optionally add one or more procedures.

As mentioned earlier, procedures are where you store your VBA code. Each procedure has a beginning line, an ending line, and, if it's going to do anything at all, one or more lines in between. The first line of the procedure IsLoaded(),

```
Function IsLoaded(ByVal strFormName As String) As Boolean
```

consists of four parts, let's look at only two of them for the time being:

- The procedure name—in this case, IsLoaded().
- The type of procedure. There are two types of procedures. IsLoaded is a *function*, denoted simply enough by the first word on the line. The other type of procedure is called a *subprocedure*, denoted as you might expect by using the word Sub as the first thing on the line, instead of Function. (It's not important that you understand the differences right now, only that you are aware that there are two types of procedures.)

Just one other thing about modules before moving on. Did you know that two types of modules are actually found in Access? You've already looked at one type, a standard module, in this chapter. The second type of module is called a *class module*.

Although everything discussed so far has been related to standard modules, it's all equally applicable to class modules as well. Nothing to unlearn! This chapter doesn't discuss what makes a class module different; just be aware of the terminology for now.

The VBA Programming Environment

The programming environment used in Access is the same one used in other Office products and is also used in the Visual Basic application. It's called the Visual Basic Editor (VBE). This name, however, might be a bit misleading in that, as you'll see, the VBE environment includes a number of other very useful tools in addition to the editor itself.

You might have already used a class module without realizing it

If you've added any VBA code to an event procedure of a form, report, or any control on either one, you've already worked with a class module. Although not all class modules are related to a form or report, Access creates a specialized class module whenever you try to add VBA code in an event procedure. You don't really need to be concerned with this because it's all done for you, behind the scenes.

As discussed earlier, there are two different types of modules and you will use the VBE to work with both. The primary difference in terms of the VBE is the way that the environment is opened for the different types.

Open a standard module

1. In the Database window of the Northwind database, select **Modules** from the **Objects** panel.

2. To display any existing standard module, select it from those listed and click the **Design** button on the toolbar.

3. Click the **Close** button ✖ at the upper right of the VBE window to close the VBE.

Open a class module related to a form

1. In the Database window of the Northwind database, select the **Customer Orders** form and open it in Design view.

2. Click the **Code** button 🖼 on the toolbar.

3. The VBE is now displayed. You should see something similar to Figure 26.2.

4. Close the window and the form. If you're prompted to save changes, respond with **No**.

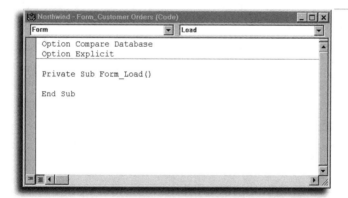

FIGURE 26.2
The Visual Basic editor displays an existing form's class module.

Using the Visual Basic Editor

As you begin to examine some features found in the VBE window, you will do more jumping around, looking at this feature and that, than you would normally do. Therefore, there's some

Making `Option Explicit` the default for a new module

You can choose whether the `Option Explicit` statement is added by default when you create a new module. You can set this default behavior while a module is open by choosing **Options** from the **Tools** menu and selecting the **Require Variable Declaration** check box on the **Editor** page. The `Option Explicit` statement is explained in detail in Chapter 27, "Programming Access with VBA."

possibility of accidentally altering existing code. To prevent that, use the code module for a new form rather than any existing form.

Explore the VBE

1. Open a new form in Design view.

2. Add two or three controls to the form—any type you like, just make it easy on yourself.

3. Click the **Code** button 🖼 on the Form toolbar. You should see something similar to Figure 26.3, but your display could be somewhat different.

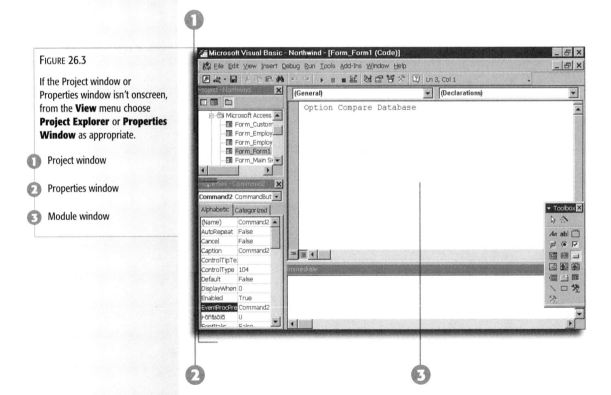

FIGURE 26.3

If the Project window or Properties window isn't onscreen, from the **View** menu choose **Project Explorer** or **Properties Window** as appropriate.

1️⃣ Project window

2️⃣ Properties window

3️⃣ Module window

The Properties Window

The Properties window conveniently displays the properties for each object associated with the open module. In this case, because you opened the class module for a form, the Properties window lets you select the form itself or any form components, including its controls.

Use the VBE's Properties window

1. Click the Properties window and open the list control at the top.

2. All the objects that make up the form are listed, including the form itself. Select **Form1** from the list.

3. The Properties window now displays the current properties for Form1. Scroll through Form1's properties until you find OnLoad. It contains [Event Procedure], which indicates that the event has an associated event procedure and, indeed, that event procedure is now displayed in the module window (see Figure 26.4).

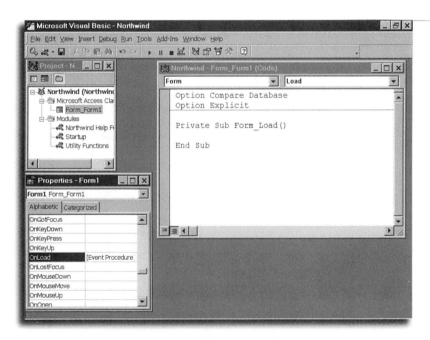

FIGURE 26.4
The Properties window allows you to select an object and display the object's properties.

The Module Window

Now look closer at the module window and examine its components (see Figure 26.5). You might recall from the earlier discussion of modules that all modules consist of a Declaration section and usually at least one procedure. The module shown consists of a Declaration section and a single procedure—the event procedure for the form's OnLoad event.

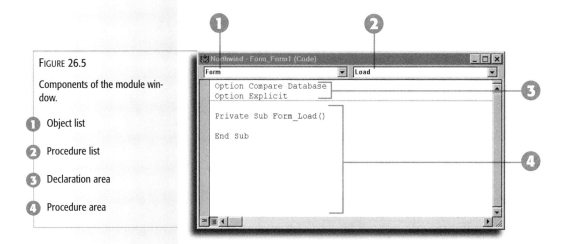

FIGURE 26.5

Components of the module window.

1. Object list

2. Procedure list

3. Declaration area

4. Procedure area

The Object and Procedure lists work as a team. You can select any object that's part of the form from the Object list, including the form itself and a (General) section. The items available for selection from the Procedure list vary, depending on what's selected in the Object list.

For example, when Form is selected in the Object list, the Procedure list is updated to list only those events applicable to a form. If a control such as Text4 is selected in the Object list, the Procedure list contains a list of only those events related to the control Text4. The list of events applicable to a control varies, dependent on the type of control.

Use the Object and Procedure lists

1. Select **Form** from the **Object** list if it's not already selected.

2. From the Procedure list, select **Open.** (You might have to scroll to find it.)

    Your display should now resemble Figure 26.6. An event procedure for the form's Open event has been added.

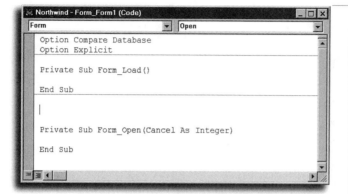

FIGURE 26.6

The event procedure for the form's Open event has been added to the module.

When you drop down the Object list, you should see something similar to Figure 26.7. For this example, I have added three text box controls named Text0, Text2, and Text4 to the form. Each object is included in the list. Also note the Detail item, which represents the Detail section of Form1.

3. Select **Text0** from the **Object** list. Yet another event procedure has been added, this time for the BeforeUpdate event of the Text0 text box (see Figure 26.8).

4. With **Text0** still selected in the **Object** list, look for the Open event in the Procedure list. It's not listed, however; no Open event is associated with Text0 because it's a control, not a form.

The Object list doesn't list all objects

All objects have at least one property–their names. Most have more. However, not all objects have any associated events. Label objects, for example, have properties but no events. Thus, they're listed in the Properties window but not in the module window's Object list. You can't write code for an event procedure that doesn't exist.

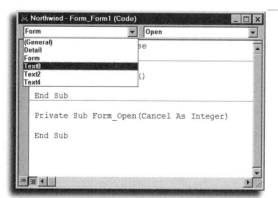

FIGURE 26.7

All the objects associated with the form that could have related event procedures are listed in the Objects list.

FIGURE 26.8

The event procedure for the
BeforeUpdate event of
Text0 is added to the module.

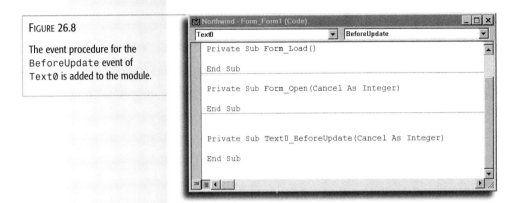

5. Click anywhere in any of the four components displayed
(the Declaration section, the procedure named Form_Load,
the procedure named Form_Open, or the procedure named
Text0_BeforeUpdate). Notice that the Object and Procedure
lists change to indicate the currently active (selected) component.

Entering Code

You enter code simply by typing. Although the VBE provides
some nifty features to assist you, it's still basically typing. In the
next several sections you will enter sample code to see how to
use a few basic VBE features; additional features will be introduced as the need arises. It's not necessary that you understand
the code at this time, so don't worry about it.

Enter code into the VBE code window

1. Enter the following line of code, exactly as shown, into the
Form_Open procedure:

```
MsgBox "Today is " & Date, vbOKOnly, "Sample MsgBox"
```

The result should resemble Figure 26.9.

2. From the **Debug** menu, choose **Compile Northwind.** If
everything goes well, your display should resemble Figure
26.10. If an error message appears instead, click **OK** to clear
it, and try again after correcting the code line.

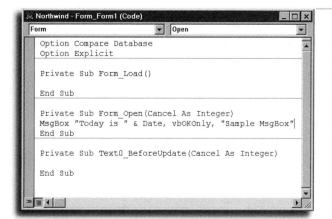

FIGURE 26.9

A single line of code is added to the form's Open event procedure.

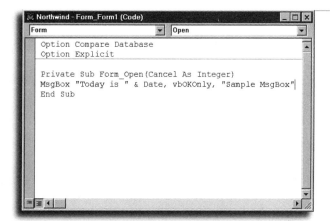

FIGURE 26.10

Form1's class module complied correctly.

Before actually running the code, notice that two of the three procedures you added earlier are now missing. VBA recognized that the two procedures contained no code, and therefore served no purpose, so it deleted them.

Trigger the Open event

1. From the **File** menu choose **Save Northwind**.

2. Name the form **Form1** if prompted to do so.

3. Close the VBE window.

4. With the new Form1 displayed in Design view, click **Form View** 📠 ▾ to open the form. Your display should resemble Figure 26.11.

What happens when I compile my code?

When you choose **Compile** from the **Debug** menu, essentially two things happen. First, VBA reads all the VBA code in the module to look for *compile errors* (errors in which VBA couldn't understand what the code was trying to do). The most common causes are syntax errors—something is misspelled or the punctuation is incorrect. If no errors are found, VBA translates your code into a form that the computer can more easily and quickly process. This translated version of your code is stored away until it's actually needed.

FIGURE 26.11

The Open event procedure displays a message box when Form1
is opened.

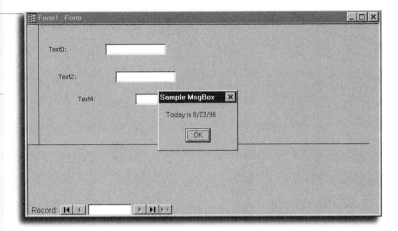

5. Click **OK** to remove the message box.

6. Put the form back into design view by clicking **Design View** 📝 ▾ on the toolbar.

7. Open VBE by clicking the **Code** button 🔧 on the toolbar.

The following steps show you how VBE reacts to several of the more common keyboard keys.

Use VBE to edit an existing procedure

1. Place your cursor before the first character in the line of code you entered earlier.

2. Press **Tab**.

3. Press **Enter** twice, to insert two blank lines.

4. Place your cursor before the first character in the last line of the procedure, which reads

```
End Sub
```

5. Press **Enter**.

6. Move your cursor to the blank line immediately below the first line of the procedure, which reads

```
Private Sub Form_Open(Cancel As Integer)
```

7. Enter the following line, including the leading quotation mark:

```
'Display today's date when Form1 is opened
```

The leading quotation mark denotes this line as a *comment*. Comments perform no function other than to document and explain what the code does.

Your procedure should now resemble Figure 26.12.

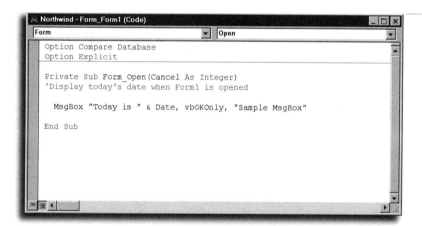

FIGURE **26.12**

Using comments, indentation, and white space makes your code much easier to read.

You will agree that VBE reacts to the keyboard pretty much in the way you expect. No hidden surprises so far. You should also note, using Figure 26.12, that the VBE toolbar includes a number of longtime Office icons used for editing, including icons for **Cut**, **Copy**, **Paste**, and **Undo**.

You probably also noticed that VBE uses color to help users more easily distinguish between the various elements found in any procedure.

The Auto List Members

Perhaps the most difficult coding skill to master is memorizing all the different functions and statements and their appropriate arguments, properties, and methods. Fortunately, Access is loaded with features that remember for you. These features will make you feel right at home with VBE in no time.

VBE options and default behavior

The VBE has a fair number of options available that you can change to fit your own taste and work styles. To view or change the options, choose **Options** from the **Tools** menu. You have a great deal of control over the colors, fonts, indentation, and other behavior of the editor.

Whether you're a developer or a casual user, the *Auto List Members* drop-down list could easily end up being your favorite coding feature because it lists object types, properties, and methods. As soon as you enter a code segment that this feature recognizes as an object, the Auto List Members list displays a corresponding list of choices. But this feature doesn't stop there. After you define the object type, the drop-down list displays a list of appropriate properties and methods. If you aren't an accomplished typist, you'll especially appreciate this feature.

Auto list and naming conventions

Using the Auto List Members list not only saves you typing time, but it also helps by keeping your naming conventions and case similar and consistent.

Using the Auto Members list

1. Open a new module by clicking **Modules** and then clicking **New** in the **Database** window.

2. Position the cursor below the Option statement(s) and enter Dim MyReport As Report. As soon as you type the space character that follows the word As, VBA displays the drop-down list shown in Figure 26.13.

FIGURE 26.13

The Auto List Members list box displays appropriate objects, properties, methods, and constants.

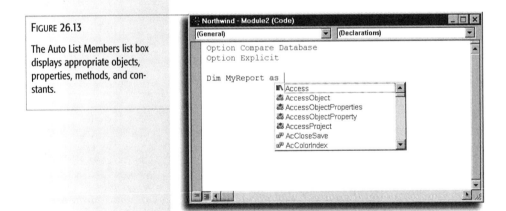

3. Scroll down the list until you find **Report**. Or type an r, and Access skips to the first item that begins with that character. Double-click **Report** to add it to the module window.

4. Press **Enter** to add a new line and then enter `MyReport.` (including the period). As soon as you type the period, VBA displays a second list consisting of properties and methods specific to the Report object.

5. Double-click **Caption** to add it to the module window.

You can use several keyboard combinations to act on the selected item in the Auto List Members list box:

Shortcut Key	Action
Tab or **Ctrl+Enter**	Enters the selected item
Spacebar	Enters the selected item and adds a space character
Enter	Enters the selected item and moves the cursor to the following line
Esc	Closes the list

Visual Coding Tips

The sample code that you've used here has been simple to the extreme. But even simple code, consisting of only a single line, is much easier to read when you make generous use of comments, spacing, and indentation. As the complexity and volume of your code increases, this becomes more apparent, especially when—not if—you have to revisit a procedure months after you last worked on it. You will be most grateful if the code is well documented with comments and is arranged on the page in a manner that makes it as easy to read as possible.

Don't use comments to describe how your code works—the code itself does that. Comments should describe what the code is intended to do. Many sources are available to determine what a piece of code is doing from a VBA perspective, including references like this book and Access Help, but only one source can determine what the code was intended to do at the time it was written—the comments provided by the person who wrote the code. For example, the purpose of the following code line is probably pretty obvious in terms of what VBA does. Certainly, any questions about what it does can be resolved pretty easily.

```
C=A*B
```

In VBA terms, the code is multiplying the value contained in A by the value contained in B and storing the product in C. A comment like the following is of little value:

```
'Multiple A by B and save product in C
```

However, the following comment is useful:

```
'Calculate Gross Pay as the product of Hours worked and
Hourly rate
```

Without this comment, it could take a developer some time studying the surrounding code to understand what even this simple line of code is intended to do.

Another technique to develop easily maintainable code is to use meaningful names whenever possible. The following code line really needs no comment at all:

```
dblGross_Pay = dblHours_Worked * dblHourly_Rate
```

In this case, the code itself is self-explanatory.

Programming Access with VBA

Learn about the Application model's many objects

Speak VBA like a native

Learn everything you need to know about variables and more

Familiarizing Yourself with the Access Applications Model

Microsoft, VBA, and VB

What you learn in this chapter can be adapted to apply to any Microsoft Office application because they all use VBA. Learning VBA will also give you a good inroad to learning Visual Basic, which can lead to many opportunities in program development.

When you purchased Access, it might have seemed as though you acquired two products: a relational database and a development package. In fact, you did. Since the addition of Visual Basic for Applications in Access 95 (and Office 95), Access has matured into a powerful development tool. The good news is that you don't have to be a professional programmer or developer to use it.

If you could open up your Access application and look inside, you would find that it's made up of different elements called *objects*. Each form, each report, each table, and so forth are all separate objects. All objects of a like kind are grouped into a *collection*—thus, you have a collection of forms, a collection of reports, and so on. If this seems a bit confusing, don't worry! It will become clearer as the pieces begin coming together. But key to understanding VBA is to understand a bit about how this structure, called an *object model*, is organized.

Another way to think of the two models

Imagine holding a 3D cube. For the most part, the Applications model covers the flat horizontal and vertical plane facing you; the DAO model covers all the visible and invisible lines, giving the cube depth into your data storage area. The main thing to consider is because Access uses industry standards like these, you can eventually scale your applications far beyond the desktop—even beyond Access itself—and into a larger environment.

Actually, you're probably interested in the two separate object models listed here:

- The Access Applications model gives you programmatic control of the many objects Access offers: forms, controls, queries, and reports.
- The Data model gives you access to the actual data by using Active Data Objects (ADO) or Data Access Objects (DAO).

Understanding Collections

This book doesn't attempt to teach you everything there is to know about VBA, but it gives you the information you need to get started. First, you need a clear understanding of the Access Applications hierarchy. The following collections are among the most frequently referenced elements of the application model:

- The Forms collection
- The Reports collection
- The Modules collection

- The Screen object
- The DoCmd object

SEE ALSO

➤ *Review the difference between standard and class modules on page 29*

As mentioned earlier, each collection contains like objects. For instance, the Forms collection contains forms, and so on.

Three other points about objects need to be mentioned before continuing:

- All objects have one or more *properties*. Properties are nothing more than a way of describing an object's characteristics. An object's name, for example, is a property. Various properties of the form also determine a form's color and size.

- An object can have *methods*. A method is an action of some kind. A query object, for example, has an `Execute` method that causes the query to run, and a form object has a `Repaint` method that causes Access to redraw the form onscreen.

- An object can also have one or more associated *events*. The developer might attach some VBA code or a macro to any particular event of a specific object. One of the many events associated with a form object for example is its `Open` event, which is triggered each time a form is opened. If there's any VBA code or a macro attached to a form's `Open` event, the code or macro executes each time the form is opened.

The Screen object controls your application's appearance attributes.

Where Do All These Objects Come From?

If you assume that all the objects you use in Access are simply part of the Access product, you would be wrong. For example, I've mentioned two distinct sets of objects thus far: the Applications model and the Data model. The objects making up the Applications model are indeed part of the Access product itself; however, the objects made available by the data model aren't. In new applications that you create in Access 2000, the data model is by default provided by ADO. ADO objects can be used by other applications, such as Visual Basic, without even

More about collections and objects

A collection is also an object itself, and an object can contain a collection. Thus, a collection might be nothing more than a collection of other collections. However, the concept really isn't as difficult as it first appears. You've probably already seen some of this structure and not been aware of it. A form, for example, is an object and is part of the Forms collection; a form also contains a collection of controls.

Applications converted from previous releases of Access

If you convert an application from a previous release of Access to Access 2000, you might find that the data model is based on DAO instead of ADO.

The references list is tailored to your system

The actual list you see will almost certainly be unlike Figure 27.1. Don't worry about it. The various lists are caused by different products having been installed on our two different systems and is quite normal. The list of references established for a given database will even be different depending on how the database was created. If, for example, you convert a database that was created using a previous release of Access to an Access 2000 database, it will contain a reference to DAO. If, however, you create a new database using Access 2000, the database will contain a reference to ADO instead of DAO.

having Access installed on the machine. The ADO objects are packaged as a *library*. Your application can use these objects because during the installation of Access, a reference was established to the ADO library. Programs other than Access can establish this same reference and therefore use the ADO objects in the same manner.

New references can be established, or existing ones displayed, by choosing **References** from the **Tools** menu whenever the Visual Basic editor is open.

Notice in Figure 27.1 that three of the four library references established, as indicated by the check boxes, have names that in no way imply that they're part of Access per se—they're part of what you get when you buy and install Access, and they're required for you to use Access, but they're components shared by any number of other products.

FIGURE 27.1

References to four libraries have been established.

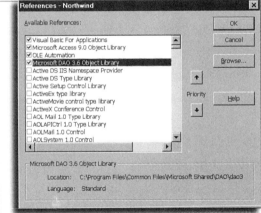

The befuddling MISSING reference

There is a good chance that sooner or later an Access application that has been working perfectly will suddenly fail. When you investigate, you will find that built-in functions such as RTrim, Mid$, Date, and so on are all of a sudden causing compile errors. It this happens, display the list of references for the affected application. Most likely, you will find that one or more of the references have been marked with the keyword MISSING. Most often this is caused by having uninstalled or installed some seemingly unrelated piece of software. Usually the problem can be corrected by unchecking the reference marked as MISSING, scrolling through the list of available references, and finding the same component under a slightly different name.

I've mentioned how VBA is also used by a number of other products. Those products all have established a reference to the Visual Basic for Applications library just as the Access product has.

Using the Object Browser

A more difficult aspect of VBA coding is remembering which objects are members of which collections and which properties and methods pertain to what objects. This dilemma is made more difficult when you consider that objects can be supplied by a virtually unlimited number of sources. The Object Browser helps solve this dilemma by providing a quick reference to all available objects and their respective properties and methods. The browser also displays a brief synopsis of each (see Figure 27.2).

The Object Browser hosts ActiveX

Technically, the Object Browser is displaying ActiveX objects. That's why you can view objects from other applications in addition to the Access objects.

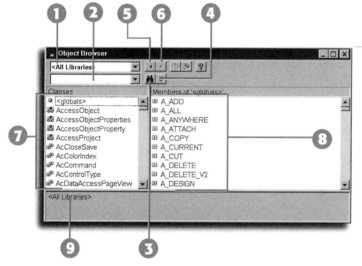

FIGURE 27.2

The Object Browser lists the available objects.

1. Project/Library drop-down list
2. Search Text drop-down list
3. Search button
4. Show Search Results/Hide Search Results toggle button
5. Go Back button
6. Go Forward button
7. Classes list box
8. Members of list box
9. Displays syntax and arguments

You can launch the Object Browser in one of three ways (available only in a VBE window):

- Click the **Object Browser** button.
- Choose **Object Browser** from the **View** menu.
- Press **F2**.

The Object Browser hosts a varied list of object libraries. A *library* is a set of objects available to an application. (Don't be concerned if your list doesn't match mine.) To see a list of available objects, choose a library from the Project/Library drop-down list, and the Browser updates the Classes list accordingly.

Use the Object Browser to display Access objects

1. Open a blank module and press **F2**.

2. Choose Access from the Project/Library drop-down list. The Browser accommodates your choice by displaying only Access objects in the **Classes** list.

3. Select the **Report** object in the **Classes** list. The Object Browser updates the **Members of** list box to display only the object's properties, methods, collections, events, and constants (if any), as shown in Figure 27.3.

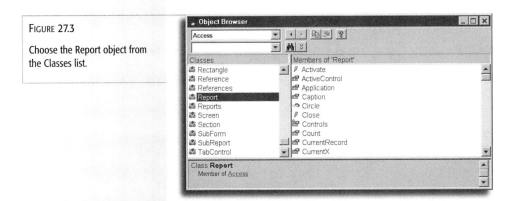

4. To display additional information on the Report object's Circle method, select **Circle** in the **Members of** list box and press **F1**.

When you want more information about a property, method, or constant, select it in the **Members of** list and press **F1** to display the appropriate Help screen. Typically, the bottom section of the Object Browser displays additional information about the item you've selected in the **Members of** list, so you might not need to display a Help screen. For instance, in Figure 27.4, the Report's Circle method is selected in the **Members of** list, and the Object Browser displays pertinent information about that method. Specifically, the browser displays the method's syntax and arguments. This feature alone can save you many trips to the Help section.

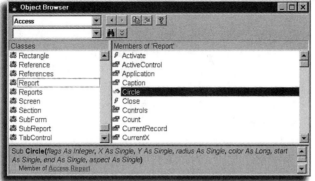

FIGURE 27.4
The Object Browser displays the
Circle method's arguments
and syntax.

At this point, you can easily copy the method and its arguments right into your module. Simply highlight the statement in the bottom section of the Object Browser and press **Ctrl+C**. Return to your module window, position your cursor at the point where you want to paste the statement, and then press **Ctrl+V**.

As you scroll through the items in the **Class** and **Members of** lists, notice that each is prefaced with a small symbol. These symbols indicate each item's type: library, object, property, collection, method, event, or constant. Table 27.1 contains an explanation of each symbol.

Navigating the Object Browser

As you move from item to item, you can click the Go Back or the Go Forward button to navigate between your previous and current selections.

TABLE 27.1   **Object Symbols and Their Objects**

Symbol	Explanation
	Library
	Class (or object)
	Property
	Collection (Property)
	Method
	Event
	Constant

Searching

If you don't want to scroll through the list boxes for a particular object, you can search for it instead. To do so, simply enter the object you're searching for into the **Search Text** control. Then, click the **Search** button. Doing so opens a middle window in the Object Browser, which displays the matching object. At this point, you can select any item from the list of items in the middle window to display that item's properties, methods, and constants. To close this middle window, click the **Hide Search Results** button to the right of the **Search** button.

Search for an object in the Object Browser

1. Enter form into the **Search Text** control and click the **Search** button. As Figure 27.5 shows, a middle window appears to display any object(s) that match the string **form**.

FIGURE 27.5

The Object Browser displays the result of its search.

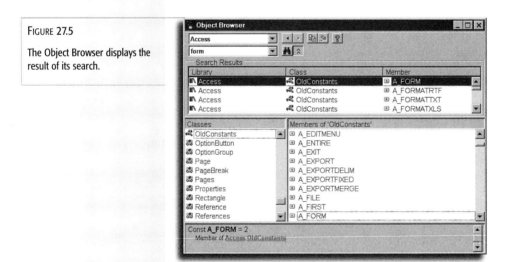

2. Select the A_FORM member (the first item) in the middle section of the Object Browser. Doing so displays even more information—its properties, methods, and constants—about that object.

The Object Browser remembers your searches; if you need to repeat a search, you can select it from the **Search Text** control's drop-down list (see Figure 27.6). After you select the item in the drop-down list, press **Enter** or click the **Search** button.

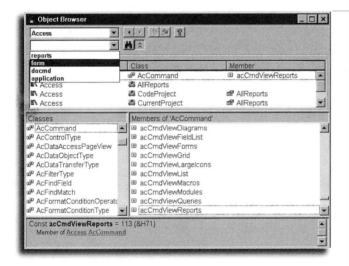

FIGURE 27.6

To repeat a search, select the search item from the **Search Text** control.

After you get the hang of using the Object Browser, you might find it quicker and easier to use than the Help section or a reference manual.

Learning to Speak VBA

It's useful, I think, to examine the similarity between our spoken language and VBA, a programming language. Both rely on *syntax* rules for clear communication.

All sentences in our spoken language consist of a subject (noun) and an action (verb). VBA is the same. A VBA sentence, known as a *statement*, generally contains a subject and an action. In VBA, *objects* can be viewed as a subject and *methods* can be viewed as verbs. The object is the thought's subject; the method is the action.

Some sentences have additional words, called adjectives, that describe the subject's attributes. In VBA, a *property* identifies an object's attributes.

If you're beginning to think VBA isn't so hard to speak, you're right. It really isn't, once you understand a few basic concepts.

Now you need to think about punctuation. When speaking VBA, it isn't enough to know an object's name, properties, and methods. You have to punctuate the components properly, or VBA won't know what you're referring to. Here are a few guidelines:

- Refer to an object by its collection and name.
- Separate the object from its collection with an exclamation point (!), or *bang*.
- Separate the object from a property or method with a period (.), or *dot*.

To properly refer to an object, use the form

`collection![objectname]`

where `collection` identifies the object's collection and `objectname` is the name of the object you're referring to. That's why this component is called the *identifier*. Besides the bang, `objectname` is typically enclosed in brackets. Although not required, it's good practice when referring to any object that you've created.

Now, suppose that you want to refer to a form named `frmMyForm`. To do so, you'd use the statement

`Forms![frmMyForm]`

Forms identifies the forms collection, and `frmMyForm` is the form's name. Notice how the two components are separated with the bang character and the report is enclosed in brackets.

Many Access objects have two levels of structure. For instance, forms and reports can both contain controls. To reference a control, add a third component in the form:

`collection![objectname]![controlname]`

where `controlname` refers to the control on `objectname` that you're referring to, such as

`Forms![frmMyForm]![cmdMyControl]`

Syntax conventions

This book uses the convention that italicized words in a syntax sample are *placeholders*, meaning that you'll fill in your own names without using italic.

Elements in the syntax

Using square brackets isn't necessary unless the object contains special characters (such as a space) or is a reserved word, although use of a reserved word outside of its intended context should be avoided altogether. In the earliest versions, Access Basic required these brackets, so many developers continue to use them for the sake of compatibility.

When to Dot

You learned earlier that most objects have methods and they all have properties. You'll use VBA to execute methods and modify or retrieve properties. You'll attach both references to an object reference, but not at the same time. For instance, to reference an object's property, use the syntax

```
collection![objectname].property
```

where *property* represents the attribute you're referring to. This time, the components are separated with a dot.

For instance, you might want to change the color of a command button's text to red. To do so, you must make reference to the applicable property—in this case, ForeColor. Your statement will be similar to

```
Forms![frmMyForm]![cmdMyControl].ForeColor = 255
```

The syntax for referencing a method is similar to that used to reference a property:

```
collection![objectname].method
```

or

```
Forms![frmMyForm].Refresh
```

SEE ALSO

➤ *Read about referencing a subform on page 343*

Working with Variables and Data Types

After a while, you might find that typing object references is rather tiring. They can grow outrageously long, and most of us aren't ace typists. So the sooner you learn about variables, the better, because you can assign an object reference to a variable, one with a short name, and save yourself time. You also save processing time, because VBA must evaluate each level in every reference. That means Access must evaluate a typical identifier, such as

```
Forms![frmMyForm]![cmdMyControl]
```

In this case, there are three levels before VBA finally finds cmdMyControl.

What's a Variable?

Most likely, you understand the concept of variables. If you're not a programmer, however, you might not know how to apply variables to your code. Generically, a *variable* is a character or symbol that can assume any one of a set of values. In the equation

```
x = 100
```

x is the variable and 100 is the value that x represents.

A variable can equal any one of a set of values. That means you can change the value of a variable, but only within the confines of a particular set. This concept isn't an absolute because you could define your variable to equal anything under the sun if that's what you wanted. But a variable doesn't have a value until you set it. To define a variable simply means to give it a value. Continue by applying this idea to VBA.

In programming terms, a *variable* is a portion of your system's memory where you store a piece of data. Sometime during the run of your application, your code refers to your variable in some way. Generally, you'll use the value in a calculation or you'll update it. Working with a variable has three advantages:

- You can refer to it as often as you like.
- You can change its value.
- It can represent any type of data.

Fortunately, working with VBA variables is easy. Simply create and name the variable, identify the variable's data type, and then use the variable.

Naming Variables

VBA is generous with its variable-naming conventions, but you'll want to remember a few rules:

- Begin a variable name with an alphabetic character.
- Don't use the characters ., %, &, !, #, @, or $ in a variable name.
- A variable name must be unique (within the scope it's used).
- A variable name can be up to 255 characters long.

At this point, you know the rules for naming a variable, but you don't know how to tell VBA that you want to use a variable. To introduce a variable to VBA, you *declare* it by entering a statement as follows:

```
Dim variable As data_type
```

where `variable` is the variable's name and `data_type` defines the variable's set type. (The next section discusses data types.) For instance, the statement

```
Dim strMyVariable As String
```

declares the variable `strMyVariable` as a `String` data type.

What's a Data Type?

Declaring a variable's data type gives you control over the data stored in that variable, which can prevent errors. Suppose that your code uses a variable named `intMyValue` in a calculation and you declare this variable by using the statement

```
Dim intMyValue
```

Because you didn't explicitly assign a data type, VBA defaults `intMyValue` as a `Variant`, which accepts any type of data. As a result, VBA attempts to calculate anything you assign to `intMyValue`, which can cause an error if `intMyValue` equals anything other than a numeric character. A better solution is to declare your variable by using the statement

```
Dim intMyValue As Integer
```

Now VBA stores only integer values in `intMyValue`. If you try to assign anything other than an integer to `intMyValue`, VBA returns a mismatch error.

Applying the appropriate data type to your variables takes a little planning, but it's easy to do and well worth the effort. In doing so, you'll conserve memory resources and prevent errors. Also, your code will run faster. Table 27.2 lists the VBA data types, their memory requirements, and their data sets (limitations).

The origins of Dim

The reserved word **Dim** is short for *dimensions*. In effect, you're saying, "The dimensions of this variable are defined as..." You'll eventually see other ways to declare a variable.

TABLE 27.2 VBA Data Types

Data Type	Memory (in bytes)	Set
Byte	1	0 to 255
Boolean	2	True or false (–1 or 0)
Integer	2	–32,678 to 32,767
Long (long integer)	4	–2,147,483,648 to 2,147,483,647
Single (single-precision floating)	4	–3.402823E38 to –1.401298E-45 for negative values; 1.401298E–45 to 3.402823E38 for positive values
Double (double-precision floating point)	8	–1.79769313486232E308 to –4.94065645841247E-324 for negative values; 4.94065645841247E–324 to 1.79769313486232E308 for positive values
Currency	8	–922,337,203,685,477.5808 to 922,337,203,685,477.5807
Date	8	January 1, 100 to December 31, 9999
Object	4	Any object reference
String (variable)	10 + string length	0 to approximately 2 billion
String (fixed)	Length of string	1 to approximately 2 billion
Variant (numbers)	16	Any number value up to the range of a Double
Variant (characters)	22 + string length	0 to approximately 2 billion

Most VBA data types are straightforward and need little extra explanation. I do want to mention a few points that aren't so obvious:

- The Currency data type is a *scaled integer*. VBA always rounds this value to the fourth decimal place.

- The Date data type stores date and time values as a double-precision floating point number. The integer portion represents the day; the decimal portion represents the time.

- The fixed-length String data type requires less memory, but you must know the actual length of the string you're storing. When the string might vary or when you don't know the exact length, you should use the variable String data type.

- A Variant data type can store any type of data, except for a fixed-length string.

Assigning Data Types

Now, suppose that you want to declare a simple variable, which you'll use in a simple calculation. Search the data type table and see that Byte handles values from 0 to 255—you think Byte should be adequate. Next, open a blank module and enter the function shown in Listing 27.1.

LISTING 27.1   **Testing the Byte Data Type**

```
1 Function ProductTest(x As Byte, y As Byte)
2    Dim bProduct As Byte
3    bProduct = x * y
4    ProductTest = bProduct
5 End Function
```

To test the function, open the Immediate window and enter the statement ? ProductTest(3,5), as shown in Figure 27.7.

Planning and the Currency data type

The Currency data type is a good example of planning ahead for the data type you want to use. Depending on how accurate your data needs to be, you might want to use another more accurate data type (that rounds to more decimal points) for your calculations. For example, calculating averages and percentages often throw off dollar amounts so that your figures don't match to the penny. You might calculate the averages first on a more accurate data type and then perform a procedure to turn the result into a dollar amount.

Numbering of code lines

Listing 27.1 and other code listings throughout the book include line numbers to make discussion about this code easier to reference. The numbers should not be included as part of any VBA programs.

Opening the Module and Immediate windows

To open a blank module, select **Modules** from the Objects panel in the Database window and click **New**. To open the Immediate window, choose **Immediate Window** from the **View** menu.

FIGURE 27.7

Test the function with two one-digit values.

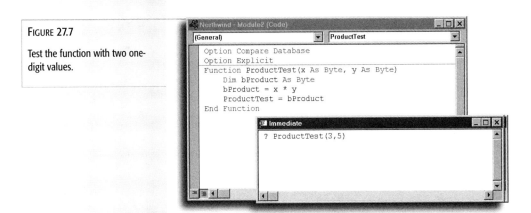

At first glance, everything seems to work fine—your function returns the value 15. To see how the function handles a negative value, enter the following statement into the Immediate window:

```
? ProductTest(-3,5)
```

This time, VBA displays an error message (see Figure 27.3) because you tried to assign a negative value, –3, to a Byte data type. Click **OK** to clear the error.

FIGURE 27.8

A negative value causes an error.

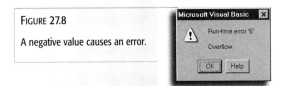

There's one final test for the function. Enter the following statement into the Immediate window:

```
? ProductTest(30,50)
```

Again, the function fails, as shown in Figure 27.9. Click **End** to clear the error. The Byte data type is adequate for 30 and 50, but not the product of these values. Remember, Byte accommodates values between 0 and 255; the product of the two values, however, is greater than 255. In this case, the Integer data type is probably the best choice.

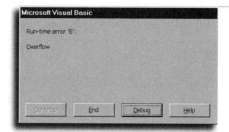

FIGURE 27.9
The `Byte` data type can't handle values over 255.

Choosing data types is a balancing act. You need a data type that will adequately handle every possible value while consuming as little of your memory resources as possible, but if you must err, do so on the large side.

Using *Option Explicit*

You've probably noticed that every module used in this chapter contains the statement

`Option Explicit`

This statement determines your module's declaration mode: *implicit* or *explicit*. `Option Explicit` forces you to declare a variable before you can use it; implicit requires no declarations. It's recommended that you use the explicit option, the default setting. By using `Option Explicit`, you nip many errors in the bud; without `Option Explicit`, you're on your own.

To demonstrate the advantage of using explicit declaration, open a blank Module window and enter some code without it. If your module contains an `Option Explicit` statement, select and delete that statement now. Then, enter the function exactly as shown in Listing 27.2.

Enabling `Option Explicit`

This exercise assumes that you're using the default setting and that your modules include an `Option Explicit` statement. If this isn't the case, you can enter the statement yourself in the Declarations section. To set the default, choose **Options** from the **Tools** menu while VBE is open, and then click the **Editor** tab. In the resulting window, select the **Require Variable Declaration** option in the Coding Options section.

LISTING 27.2 **Testing Implicit Declarations**

```
1 Function VariableTest()
2     intVariable = 10
3     intResponse = intVariable * 10 ──①
4     VariableTest = intResponse
5 End Function
```

① Access defaults the new variable, `intVariable` to a data type a `Variant` and automatically initializes its value as `Empty`.

Practice debugging

If you've followed this example, you know that the failure to define a variable has caused a problem in the calculation. If you were looking at Listing 27.2 as part of your own code, notice something else about the variables—none of them have been declared with a data type in the definition. As stated earlier, this causes a number of different errors because Access defaults to the `Variant` data type, which might not suit your purposes.

You can choose to ignore a function's data type

Declaring a function's data type is something you might not want to bother with at first. In fact, most of the time you can get by just fine by ignoring it and letting Access default to the `Variant` type. Of course, developers all over will groan at this statement; we sometimes forget that real users just need to get their work done. So, don't overwhelm yourself while you're learning.

It appears that you've encountered a dreaded error. The function should have returned a value of 100, but instead it said the answer is 0. As is usually the case, VBA did exactly what it was told. The variable `intVariable` equals 10, but because the variable in line 3 of the code is intentionally misspelled, the variable `intVaraible` is empty. Consequently, `intResponse` equals 0 because nothing * 10 = 0. `Option Explicit` prevents this kind of error.

Giving Your Function a Data Type

This chapter discusses declaring appropriate data types for variables. A function also has a data type and, like a variable, defaults to the `Variant` type if not explicitly declared.

The previous example doesn't declare data types for the functions. This means that VBA is returning the result of each function as a `Variant`. That's not inherently wrong, but not limiting the results can let unknown errors slip by. (Besides, `Variants` require more memory.)

To assign a data type to a function, simply declare it in the function's name statement as follows:

```
Function MyFunction(arguments As data type) As data type
```

For instance, you could declare `VariableTest()` as an `Integer` by using the statement

```
Function VariableTest() As Integer
```

SEE ALSO

➤ *Learn more about preventing errors on page 521*

Understanding Scope

At this point, you know how to declare, define, and assign data types to variables. The next step is to learn about a variable's *scope*. By scope, I mean which application's components have access to a variable. Within Access, VBA has three possible levels of scope: local, module, and public.

Local: Keeping It Specific to the Procedure

A *local variable* belongs to its procedure. In other words, only the hosting procedure can refer to it. All the variables used in this chapter, up to this point, have been local variables.

Use a local variable

1. Open a blank module.

2. Enter code similar to Listing 27.3.

3. Open the Immediate Window and enter ?ScopeLocal().

LISTING 27.3   **Declaring a Local Variable**

```
1 Function ScopeLocal()
2     Dim strScope As String
3     strScope = "This is a local variable"
4     ScopeLocal=strScope
5 End Function
```

As you can see in Figure 27.10, the procedure returns the string This is a local variable. What do you suppose would happen if you try to call this variable from another procedure?

FIGURE 27.10
The function returns a simple string message.

Checking the Dim statement for scope

Notice that this function is similar to Listing 27.3, except that it doesn't contain a Dim statement for the strScope variable.

Test a variable's scope

1. Return to your open module. Type the procedure from Listing 27.4 below the code you just entered.

LISTING 27.4   **Testing for a Variable in a New Procedure**

```
1 Function ScopeModule()
2     strScope = "This is a module variable"
3     ScopeLocal=strScope
4 End Function
```

2. Return to the Immediate window and enter the statement

```
?ScopeModule()
```

In response, VBA displays the compile error shown in Figure 27.11 because Listing 27.4 doesn't declare the variable strScope. At this point, only ScopeLocal() can successfully refer to strScope.

FIGURE 27.11

Referring to a local variable in a function other than the one that declares that variable causes a compile error.

1 A variable declared within a procedure is a local variable and is available only to the procedure where it's declared.

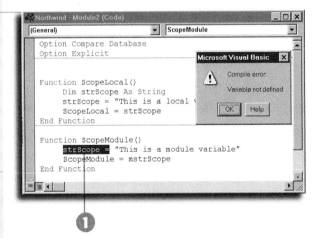

Click **OK** to clear the error message.

Module-Level Variables: Sharing Variables Within the Module

Sometimes it's appropriate to declare a variable once and give all the procedures in your module access to that variable. This is easily accomplished by declaring that variable in the module's Declarations section instead of in a particular procedure. To see how this is done, make the variable mstrScope available to any procedure within the module.

Make a variable available to all procedures in a module

1. Return to the module from the previous example and position your cursor at the end of the Option Explicit statement in the Declarations statement.

2. Press **Enter** and type the statement
    ```
    Dim mstrScope As String
    ```

3. Go to the function named ScopeModule and rename the variable strScope to mstrScope. You should have something that resembles Figure 27.12.

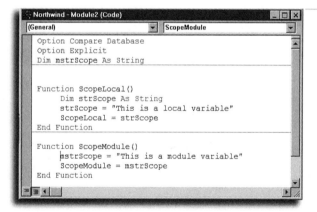

4. Return to the Immediate Window, type again or position the cursor at the end of an existing ?ScopeModule() statement, and press **Enter**.

This time, VBA responds by displaying the string This is a module variable (see Figure 27.13).

Variable naming conventions

Notice that Figure 27.12 uses a different prefix for the module-level variable than for the local variables. This isn't a VBA restriction, but is a convention used only to help document the code. By using this convention, I know that the variable named mstrScope is a module variable and is declared as a String. This kind of convention can save many wasted steps looking around to find this info. A sample set of naming conventions can be found in Chapter 2. This convention is used throughout the book.

FIGURE 27.12

After declaring mstrScope in the Declarations section, that variable is available to all the procedures in the module.

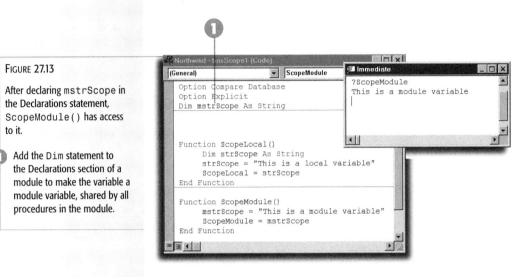

FIGURE 27.13

After declaring `mstrScope` in the Declarations statement, `ScopeModule()` has access to it.

1 Add the `Dim` statement to the Declarations section of a module to make the variable a module variable, shared by all procedures in the module.

Use module variables sparingly and public variables rarely

Overuse of module and public variables is generally a bad practice. Sometimes their use can be the most sensible thing to do, but most of the time there's a better way. For example, if each of several procedures must use a specific piece of data, you might be inclined to put that data into a **Public** variable, and reference that variable in each procedure that uses the data. It's better to pass the data as an argument to each procedure that uses it. The latter approach allows for greater flexibility and is much easier to maintain.

Going Public

At this point, the variable `mstrScope` is available to every procedure in the current module. It isn't, however, available to any procedure in any other module.

Test and create public variables

1. Return to the module containing Listings 27.3 and 27.4 and save it (using the .bas prefix and a descriptive name, such as basScope1), and then close it.

2. Open a blank module and enter the procedure shown in Listing 27.5.

LISTING 27.5 A Module Variable Versus a Public Variable

```
1 Option Explicit
2 Function ScopePublic()
3     mstrScope = "This is a public variable"
4     ScopePublic mstrScope
5 End Function
```

3. Open the Immediate window and enter the statement
```
?ScopePublic()
```

4. The compiler returns an expected error that the variable isn't defined. To clear it, click **OK**.

Fortunately, there's a simple solution to this error: change `mstrScope` to a `Public` variable.

5. Double-click **basScope1** in the Project window. (You might have to move things around onscreen to find this window, or you might have to open it by selecting **Project Explorer** from the **View** menu.)

6. Add the following `Dim` statement to basScope1's Declaration section:
```
Public pstrScope As String
```

Finding the correct public variable

If the Declarations section of the module you're using has no variable, see the preceding section on moving local variables to module variables.

7. Close the window containing basScope1, and select the window containing the code from Listing 27.5.

8. Change the two references to `mstrScope` to `pstrScope`.

9. Save the module as `basScope2` and close it.

You can now refer to a public variable (`pstrScope`) from all procedures, not just those in a module where you've declared that variable as a local or module variable.

To see the results of this application-sharing declaration, simply return to the Immediate window and execute all procedures. As you can see in Figure 27.14, all the procedures in this example work properly—including `ScopePublic()`, which is in a module other than `pstrScope`'s declaration statement.

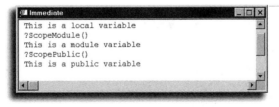

FIGURE 27.14

If you declare `pstrScope` as a public variable, any procedure in your application can refer to it.

Static Variables

There's one last variable type to discuss: static variables. (I've waited until now, because a static variable has a special attribute.) A static variable is *persistent*, meaning that it retains its value beyond the life of the procedure.

Normally, a local variable's lifetime lasts only as long as the procedure runs. As soon as VBA exits the code, the variable ceases to have value. Explore this behavior by running a simple procedure that adds the value 1 to itself.

Test a variable's persistence

   1. Open a blank module and enter the procedure shown in Listing 27.6.

LISTING 27.6   **Testing a Variable's Life Span**

```
1 Function Life()
2     Dim intValue As Integer
3     intValue = intValue + 1
4     Life = intValue
5 End Function
```

   2. After entering the procedure, open the Immediate window and enter the following statement, which returns the value 1 (see Figure 27.15):

```
?Life()
```

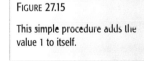

FIGURE 27.15

This simple procedure adds the value 1 to itself.

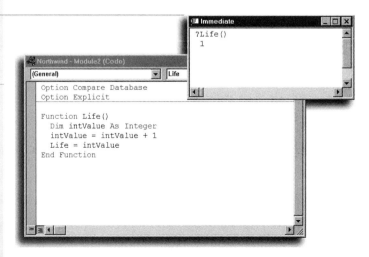

The first time you run this procedure, intValue equals 0. The statement in line 3 then adds the value 1 to 0. As a result, the function returns the value 1. Indeed, the function continues to return 1, no matter how many times it's executed. You can test this by executing Life() a second time.

The life of intValue ends with the End Function statement. As soon as VBA executes that statement, intValue no longer has a value. When you execute Life() the second time, intValue is again equal to 0. Therefore, intValue + 1 equals 1, just as it did the first time you ran the function.

To prolong a variable's life, use the Static statement instead of the Dim statement. Static tells Access not to reset the variable's value when exiting the procedure. To witness this behavior, change intValue's lifetime to Static.

Now return to the Immediate window and run the statement twice. The first time, Life() equals 1, but the second time, Life() returns 2 (see Figure 27.16) because VBA remembers intValue's value beyond the life of its calling procedure. When you run Life() the second time, VBA recalls intValue's last value.

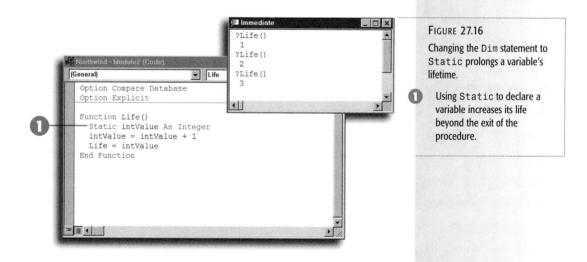

FIGURE 27.16

Changing the Dim statement to Static prolongs a variable's lifetime.

❶ Using Static to declare a variable increases its life beyond the exit of the procedure.

Writing Procedures

Throughout this chapter, the word *procedure* is used quite a bit. A procedure is any task you execute with code. All procedures have two things in common: their first and last statements. Beyond that, procedures are unique to their task.

Each VBA procedure begins by specifying its type, its name, and any arguments its code might need to complete its task. You complete each procedure with an End statement. If you use one of Access's built-in features (for example, see Figure 27.17), VBA provides these lines of code for you.

FIGURE 27.17

The Insert Procedure dialog box enters the procedure's type, name, and End statement for you.

Let Access do the work

To avoid typos, consider letting Access create procedure functions for you. Choose **Procedure** from the **Insert** menu to bring up the Insert Procedure dialog box. Next, enter the function name **FP1**. Then, choose the function type, which in this case is **Function**.

Although you've worked with several function procedures already, try one more—this time from the perspective of setting out to create a function procedure.

Create a function procedure

1. Open a blank module and enter the code in Listing 27.7. (A data type hasn't been declared for the function, but you can easily do so; see the earlier section "Giving Your Function a Data Type.")

LISTING 27.7 A Function That Prompts for a Value Between 1 and 100, and Then Displays the Product of Your Entry and 10

```
1 Function FP1()
2    Dim intResponse As Integer
3    intResponse = InputBox("Enter any value between 1 and 100")
4    intResponse = intResponse * 10
5    MsgBox intResponse
6 End Function
```

The input box

Listing 27.7 creates an input dialog box for interacting with the user. Similar steps are often used when creating an interactive application.

2. To execute `FP1()`, open the Immediate window and enter
`?FP1()`

3. Enter 3 when prompted (see Figure 27.18) and then press **Enter** or click **OK**.

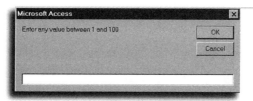

FIGURE 27.18

The function procedure prompts you for a value.

You just used two built-in functions, `InputBox()` and `MsgBox()`, within your own function. You can use `FP1()` to return the product of any value between 1 and 100 by 10.

Although the intent of this function is to return the product of any value between 1 and 100 by 10, it works just fine for user-inputted numbers between –3276 and +3276. I point this out as another example of VBA doing exactly what you tell it to do, but not necessarily what you want it to do. You didn't provide any VBA code to limit input to numbers between 1 and 100; you instructed only the user. Indeed, if users enter a number outside the stated range or a non-numeric character string, the function breaks (that is, Access issues a nasty runtime error message).

What's that function's function?

Don't confuse function procedures with the Access built-in functions, as they aren't the same thing. Built-in functions perform a specific task; they can't undertake the many unique tasks required by a custom application. However, you can include a built-in function in a procedure by assigning the result to a variable.

Calling a Procedure from Another Procedure

Often, you might need to call one procedure from another. This is especially helpful if you repeat the same task or calculation within the context of several larger but different routines. Suppose that the preceding example—multiplying values between 1 and 100 by 10—is a task you repeat often, but in different areas of your application. In this case, you don't have to repeat your calculating code over and over. Instead, enter it as a function and then call it when needed.

Call a procedure from another procedure

1. Open a blank module and enter the procedures shown in Listing 27.8.

① Creating the `CalProduct()` function

② The `CalProduct()` function being called by a subsequent procedure

③ `CalProduct()` function called here as well

LISTING 27.8   A Sample Procedure for Calling Another Procedure

```
01 Function CalProduct(strMsgTxt As String) As Integer     ①
02    Dim intResponse As Integer
03    intResponse = InputBox(strMsgTxt)
04    intResponse = intResponse * 10
05    CalProduct = intResponse
06 End Function
07 Function NeedProduct100()
08    Dim strText As String
09    strText = "Enter a value between 1 and 100"
10    MsgBox CalProduct(strText)                            ②
11 End Function
12 Function NeedProduct1000()
13    Dim strText As String
14    strText = "Enter a value between 1 and 1000"
15    MsgBox CalProduct(strText)                            ③
16 End Function
```

Balance is the key to calling functions

Leaving one function to visit another always slows down your code. It might not be worth your time to create extra procedures unless the repetitive code is complex. This simple example doesn't adequately portray this balance, but it's an important consideration. Another consideration is that it's often simpler to develop and maintain several small pieces of code than it is to develop and maintain a single large piece of code. Again, balance is the key.

Task-wise, the procedures in Listing 27.8 are similar to the earlier FP1() function. However, NeedProduct100() and NeedProduct1000() each sets a variable to contain a string that's passed to CalProduct(). CalProduct() uses the passed argument to solicit the value you want multiplied, does the multiplication, and returns the product to the calling procedure. Finally, the calling procedure accepts the returned result and displays it.

To see these procedures in action, open the Immediate window and enter the statement

```
?NeedProduct100()
```

Line 10 in `NeedProduct100()` calls `CalProduct()`, which displays the same input box shown earlier in Figure 27.18. Enter the value 3 and press **Enter** or click **OK**. At this point, the product is returned to `NeedProduct()` and used in the message box to display the result.

If you're wondering how two functions can be more efficient than one, that's where `NeedProduct1000()` comes in. Enter the following statement into the Immediate window:

```
?NeedProduct1000()
```

The flow through the VBA code is very similar, except that `CalProduct()` is called from line 15. The advantage is that a single piece of code is doing the calculation in both cases.

SEE ALSO
➤ *Learn more about input boxes on page 507*

Using Subprocedures

Most everything you've done in this chapter has used functions, so now look at using a subprocedure. As stated earlier, the two types of procedures have only two differences. A subprocedure can't return a value, and the syntax used to call a subprocedure is slightly different from the syntax used to call a function. Listing 27.9 shows three procedures very similar to those shown in Listing 27.8. The difference is that the procedure `CalProduct()` has been changed from a function to a subprocedure.

LISTING 27.9   A Sample Procedure for Calling a Subprocedure

```
01 Sub CalProduct(strMsgTxt As String)
02    Dim intResponse As Integer
03    intResponse = InputBox(strMsgTxt)
04    intResponse = intResponse * 10
05    MsgBox intResponse
06 End Sub
```

continues...

LISTING 27.9   Continued

```
07
08 Function NeedProduct100()
09   Dim strText As String
10   strText = "Enter a value between 1 and 100"
11   CalProduct strText
12 End Function
13
14 Function NeedProduct1000()
15   Dim strText As String
16   strText = "Enter a value between 1 and 1000"
17   CalProduct strText
18 End Function
```

So, what are the differences?

- Lines 1 and 6 are changed to indicate a subprocedure instead of a function.

- The data-type declaration for the return value has been removed from Line 1 because the subprocedure has no return value.

- Lines 11 and 17 have been changed because the syntax to call a subprocedure is different than for a function.

- The MsgBox built-in function has been moved to the subprocedure (Line 5).

When do you use a subprocedure versus a function? It appears on the surface that the answer is you can use a subprocedure whenever the code doesn't need to return a value, as in the case of CalProduct() in Listing 27.9. Although that's basically true, there could be other considerations regarding a return value. For example, you might decide to add some code to CalProduct() that checks the value entered in response to the InputBox. Such code could check what the user entered and make sure that it's within the range requested. If you were to do that, you should then let any calling procedures know about it in case the user entered an invalid number. So now you are back to providing a return value—therefore, to using a function instead of a subprocedure.

Which should you use?

The choice between using a function or a subprocedure still boils down to whether the procedure returns a value. The questions as to whether a return value is needed isn't always as straightforward as you might expect, however. Luckily, as you've seen, the procedure can be easily changed from a function to a subprocedure and back again if need be.

Using VBA for Interactive Input

Learn how to pass data to your procedures at runtime

Display and solicit information with message and input boxes

Use VBA to make decisions

Know where to go when your code doesn't work

Working with optional arguments

You can also declare an argument as being optional by using the syntax Sub MyWork(intMorestuff As Integer, Optional dteMydate As Date). Here, intMoreStuff is a required argument; if you omit it, VBA returns an error. However, dteMyDate isn't required; you can include it or omit it without creating an error.

Naming convention used in this chapter

This chapter contains a number of references to variable names that use a prefix of dte instead of the dtm prefix used in Chapter 2 for Data/Time data. dte is used to denote that only the Date portion is of interest.

Passing Arguments to Your Code

Built-in functions and the procedures that you write oftentimes require one or more pieces of information to perform their task. Such a piece of information is referred to as an *argument*. The syntax for passing arguments to a built-in function and a function procedure is the same: the function's name and a pair of parentheses. For example, the built-in function Sum(*expr*) has a name (Sum) and one argument (*expr*). You supply the argument, or information, so Sum() knows which field to total.

The same is true with function procedures. For instance, MyCalcPay(EmployeeID) is a user-defined function named MyCalcPay, usually referred as MyCalcPay(), and EmployeeID is the argument. EmployeeID tells MyCalcPay() which employee to work with.

What if the built-in function or user function doesn't require an argument? The general syntax to call the function is still the same, but the argument itself is just omitted—for example,

```
Date()
MyWork()
```

The syntax used to pass an argument to a subprocedure is slightly different; no parentheses are used—for example,

```
MyShowNumber 125
```

If a subprocedure requires no argument, enter the procedure's name, as follows:

```
MyShowFirst
```

or

```
CALL MyShowFirst
```

These two lines are functionally equivalent, but you might find that the use of the CALL statement makes your code more readable.

Letting the Code Make Decisions

Until now, your code tasks have been straightforward. But what if you need more flexibility? Sometimes you need code to make decisions based on the available data; sometimes you want your code to do one thing, and other times you want the code to do something else. VBA provides several powerful statements that provide this decision-making capability:

- If...Then...Else
- Select Case
- IIF() built-in function

The *If...Then...Else* Statement

Now, look at the VBA If statement:

```
If condition Then
        trueaction
Else
        falseaction
End If
```

This syntax can be read as **If** *the condition is true,* **Then** *execute the trueaction,* **Else** *(the condition is false) execute the falseaction.*

The Else portion of the If statement is optional. Thus, if you want your code to do something special when a condition is true but have no special need when the condition is false, you can use the syntax

```
If condition Then
        trueaction
End If
```

Syntax of the If statement

A number of other syntax options are available for the If statement, but I recommend the two syntaxes shown here—they are used in all the coding examples. Also note that the indentation shown isn't really part of the required syntax, but is a very useful aid to readability.

Expressions that evaluate to true or false

You might see examples of VBA code in other publications that use the values −1 and 0 instead of the keywords **True** and **False**. These keywords actually represent the values −1 and 0, respectively. I feel, however, that the keywords are less ambiguous. Using the keywords exclusively also has another potential benefit. In most cases, when VBA evaluates a numerical expression to determine the true/false condition, it treats the result as false if it's equal to 0, and true if it's equal to anything else. This behavior is fine if you are aware of it, but it can also mask what could be an error elsewhere in your code—that is, you might have intended a value to be −1 (true), but it is actually a 6. VBA still evaluates the 6 as true, but if you expected it to be −1, your code isn't doing what you had intended.

Helpful features built in to the VBA editor

As you type code, certain words are automatically highlighted in a different color. Those words might also be changed to begin with a capital letter. This is done to improve readability and to help you avoid errors.

Work with VBA's *If* statement

1. Open a blank module by clicking **Modules** and then **New** in the Database window.

2. Enter the code shown in Listing 28.1, which includes examples of both If syntax styles.

LISTING 28.1   **The *If* Statement, Using Two Different Syntaxes**

```
01 Function RunIf(bolcheckme as Boolean)
02      If bolcheckme Then
03          Debug.Print "Passed argument is true."
04      Else
05          Debug.Print "Passed argument is false."
06      End If
07
08      If bolcheckme Then
09          Debug.Print "Passed argument is true."
10      End If
11 End Function
```

3. Press **Ctrl+G** to open the Immediate window.

4. Enter ?RunIf(True). Because bolcheckme is true, the *condition* of both If statements are true. As a result, VBA executes the corresponding Debug.Print statement in each If statement.

5. Enter ?RunIf(False). This time, bolcheckme equals false. The Else statement of the first If statement is executed because its condition is false. Because no false statements are specified for the second If, VBA exits the If block without doing anything further.

Thus far, you have used a single line of code for the *trueaction* and *falseaction* portions of the If statement. You can, however, include as many lines of code as might be required for either one.

Create a multiple-line *If* statement

1. Open a blank module and enter the code in Listing 28.2.

LISTING 28.2 **An *If* Statement with Multiple Lines in its *trueaction***

```
1 Function RunIfThen(bolcheckme As Boolean)
2   If bolcheckme Then
3     Debug.Print "First statement"
4     Debug.Print "Second statement"
5   End If
6 End Function
```

❶ VBA executes these lines when the If condition is true.

---

2. press **Ctrl+G** to open the Immediate window.

3. Enter the statement `?RunIfThen(True)`. Because `bolcheckme` is true, VBA executes both `Debug.Print` statements.

4. Enter the statement `?RunIfThen(False)`. Because `bolcheckme` is false, VBA skips the *trueaction* statements and quits.

Next, you will practice a technique known as *nesting*. Look at the function `RunNestedIf()` in Listing 28.3. Notice that there are two If statements, but you might not notice that one is contained inside the other. The first If statement begins on line 2 and continues through line 10, but nested inside it is another If statement, beginning on line 5 and continuing through line 9. Take a closer look to see how this technique works.

LISTING 28.3 **An *If* Statement Nested Within an *If* Statement**

```
01 Function RunNestedIf(intcheckme As Integer)
02   If intcheckme = 1 Then
03       Debug.Print "Passed argument is 1."
04   Else
05       If intcheckme = 2 Then
06           Debug.Print "Passed argument is 2."
07       Else
08           Debug.Print "Passed argument is not 1 or 2."
09       End If
10   End If
11 End Function
```

Create a nested *If* statement

1. Open a blank module and enter the code in Listing 28.3.

2. Open the Immediate window and enter ?RunNestedIf(1). Because intcheckme equals 1, VBA executes the true action and prints the string Passed argument is 1.

3. Enter the statement ?RunNestedIf(2). This time, the condition being checked on line 2 is false, so VBA executes the Else action beginning at line 5. The condition being checked for on line 5 is true, so VBA executes the true action and prints the string Passed argument is 2.

4. Enter the statement ?RunNestedIf(3). The condition being checked on line 2 is false, so VBA executes the Else action beginning at line 5. The condition being checked for on line 5 is false, so VBA executes the Else action for this If statement and prints the string Passed argument is not 1 or 2.

Notice the indentation used in Listing 28.3. Specifically, lines 2, 4, and 10 are all part of the same If block and are indented an equal amount—likewise for lines 5, 7, and 9. Now compare that to the following:

```
01 Function RunNestedIf(intcheckme As Integer)
02 If intcheckme = 1 Then
03 Debug.Print "Passed argument is 1."
04 Else
05 If intcheckme = 2 Then
06 Debug.Print "Passed argument is 2."
07 Else
08 Debug.Print "Passed argument is not 1 or 2."
09 End If
10 End If
11 End Function
```

I think you will agree that indentation makes the code much easier to read and understand. It's not terribly important what convention of indentation you adopt for your code—you can choose to have yours look different than what's shown in Listing 28.3. Find a convention you like, and use it without fail.

Figure 28.1 shows the results of passing the RunNestedIf() function each of three different arguments.

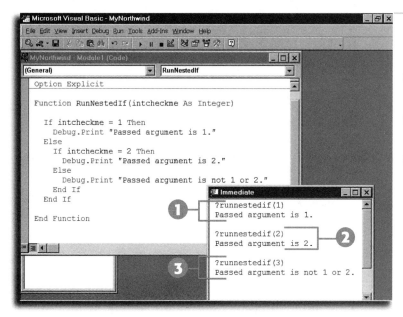

FIGURE 28.1

Using the function containing nested If statements.

1 Line 3 prints this string when `intcheckme` equals 1.

2 Line 6 prints this string when `intcheckme` equals 2.

3 Line 8 goes into action when `intcheckme` is neither 1 nor 2.

Working with *Select Case*

The Select Case statement is similar to the If statement in purpose. However, Select Case provides an easier way of dealing with a situation in which the condition you want to evaluate might have numerous different values. Use the following syntax for the Select Case statement:

```
Select Case condition
    Case a condition
        a action
    Case b condition
        b action
    Case c condition
        c action
    Case Else
        Else action
End Select
```

As with the If statement, the Else statement isn't required, but I recommend that you use it. Select Case's *condition* argument is usually an expression that evaluates to one of several possible values. The subsequent Case statements then specify individual possibilities and the action you want taken when each condition is met.

Use caution when defining Case statements

A Select Case statement evaluates the condition against the value of each Case statement, starting with the first one, until a match is found. When a matching Case is found, no further evaluations take place. Thus, if more than one Case statement meets the condition, only the first one found will be used. Any subsequent Case statements are ignored.

Work with *Select Case*

1. Open a blank module and enter the procedure in Listing 28.4.

Same functionality, different VBA code

The functionality of the code shown in the Listings 28.3 and 28.4 is identical, but the code itself is totally different. In this case, as in almost all cases, there are an almost unlimited number of ways to do the same thing. However, try to imagine how awkward it would be to, in this case, use If statements to handle all numbers from 1–10 differently. It will work, but it would be inefficient. The Select Case solution is more straightforward, with a few more Case statements.

LISTING 28.4   **Using the *Select Case* Statement Instead of Nested *If* Statements**

```
01 Function ShowItemValue(intcheckme As Integer)
02   Select Case intcheckme
03     Case 1
04       Debug.Print "Passed argument is 1."
05     Case 2
06       Debug.Print "Passed argument is 2."
07     Case Else
08       Debug.Print "Passed argument is not 1 or 2."
09   End Select
10 End Function
```

2. Open the Immediate window and enter the statement ?ShowItemValue(1). Line 4 displays the string Passed argument is 1.

3. Enter the statement ?ShowItemValue(2). Line 6 displays the string Passed argument is 2.

4. Enter the statement ?ShowItemValue(3). Line 8 displays the string Passed argument is not 1 or 2.

As you can see in Figure 28.2, using the Select Case statement produces results identical to those produced by using the nested If statements in Figure 28.1. However, as the number of specific conditions that must be handled grows, using Select Case is less awkward than nesting a large number of If statements.

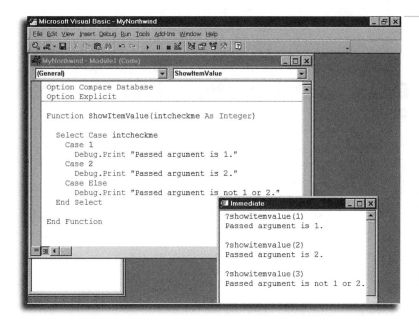

FIGURE 28.2
Select Case makes it
easy it check for many possible
conditions.

The *IIf()* Function

The built-in function IIf() is similar to the If...Then...Else statement, but has one significant difference. Because it's an Access built-in function rather than a VBA statement, you can use it outside a VBA module, such as in a control on a form or report, or in a query.

Similar to the If...Then...Else statement, the IIf() function evaluates a conditional expression and, depending on the true or false result of that evaluation, performs an action. If the condition is true, the function does one thing; if the condition is false, the function does another. The syntax of IIf() is

```
IIf(expression, trueexpression, falseexpression)
```

where *expression* is the condition you're evaluating, *trueexpression* is what you want to return if the condition is true, and *falseexpression* is what you want to return if the condition is false. For example, notice the use of the following IIf() function:

```
=IIf(LastName is null,"unknown",LastName)
```

Exercise caution when using the IIF() statement

Behind the scenes, Access doesn't evaluate the arguments of an IIF() statement in the order you might expect. Both the *trueaction* and *falseaction* are evaluated before the first argument is evaluated, whereas in an If...Then...Else construct, either the *trueaction* or the *falseaction* is evaluated, not both. This makes IIF() a bit slower than using If...Then...Else, and also causes errors you might not have expected. For example, if the *falseaction* evaluates to an invalid expression, an error occurs even if the first argument evaluates to True.

This line returns the string `"unknown"` if `LastName` is null and the value (content) of `LastName` if `LastName` isn't null.

Displaying Information with a Message Box

Most every application needs to pass information to users. The most common way of communicating with the user is implementing a message box by using the built-in `MsgBox()` function. This function displays a message, and users must respond by choosing from the options presented. The options from which users can choose are determined by the arguments used when calling `MsgBox()`. The function has five arguments:

`MsgBox(message, type, title, help, context)`

The `message` argument is the information you want to communicate to your users; `type` defines the choices (command buttons) the message box offers users, and `title` displays a title in the title bar. The `help` and `context` arguments call up help topics (they are optional, but you can't use one without the other). Of the five arguments, only `message` is required. If you omit `type`, Access displays only one choice—**OK**.

Create a simple message box

1. Open a blank module and enter the code in Listing 28.5.

All optional arguments are omitted. Use quotation marks for your message string.

LISTING 28.5   Using the *MsgBox()* Function Without any Optional Arguments

```
1 Function MessageBox1()
2   Dim intResponse As Integer
3   intResponse = MsgBox("Shall we continue?")
4   MessageBox1=intResponse
5 End Function
```
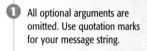

2. Open the Immediate window and enter `?MessageBox1()`. VBA displays the simple dialog box shown in Figure 28.3.

FIGURE 28.3
Microsoft Access is the default value for the title bar argument.

3. Click **OK** to close the box; VBA displays a 1 in the Immediate window.

The built-in MsgBox() function returns a value of 1 to intResponse, which is in turn used to set the return value for MessageBox1().

Using the *type* Argument

If all you need is an **OK** button, omitting the *type* argument is fine. When you need a bit more flexibility, include the *type* argument, which specifies the number and type of buttons to display, the icon style, the default button, and the *modality*. (Modality controls whether the message box suspends only the application or your entire system.) Table 28.1 lists the different button constants and icon values, and gives more information about the modal choices.

TABLE 28.1   Button Setup, Icons, and Modal Choices

Constant	Value	Displays
vbOKOnly	0	OK.
vbOKCancel	1	OK and Cancel.
vbAbortRetryIgnore	2	Abort, Retry, and Ignore.
vbYesNoCancel	3	Yes, No, and Cancel.
vbYesNo	4	Yes and No.
vbRetryCancel	5	Retry and Cancel.
vbCritical	16	Critical Message icon.
vbQuestion	32	Warning query icon.
vbExclamation	48	Warning message icon.
vbInformation	64	Information message icon.

continues…

Built-in VBA constants versus values

Although you can use the constant or the value when specifying the *type* argument, I strongly recommend using the constant. It makes the code much easier to read, and there is nothing to remember (thus less chance of an error). Also, the numbers could change between releases of Access but the constants won't.

No need to memorize all these constants

Remember that VBA provides several tools that can help you select these constants. The Auto List Members feature and the Object Browser are useful in this regard.

TABLE 28.1   **Continued**

Constant	Value	Displays
vbDefaultButton1	0	First button is default.
vbDefaultButton2	256	Second button is default.
vbDefaultButton3	512	Third button is default.
vbDefaultButton4	768	Fourth button is default.
vbApplicationModal	0	The current application is suspended until the user responds to the message box.
vbSystemModal	4096	All system applications are suspended until user responds to the message box.
vbMsgBoxHelpButton	16384	Adds Help button to the message box.
vbMsgBoxSetForeground	65536	Specifies the message box window as the foreground window.
vbMsgBoxRight	524288	Text is right-aligned.
vbMsgBoxRtlReading	1048576	Specifies that text should appear as right-to-left reading on Hebrew and Arabic systems.

SEE ALSO

➤ *For more information on the Auto List Members feature, see page 457*
➤ *Find more information on the Object Browser on page 465*

Button Defaults

The default response button is generally the button on the left. You can change the default button, regardless of the button's relative position to the other buttons, by adding a specific value to the *type* argument. Table 28.2 explains a few possible *type* arguments.

TABLE 28.2   **Determining the Default Button**

Type Argument	Explanation
vbYesNo + vbQuestion	Displays a Yes/No button combination and a question mark icon. Yes remains the default button because you have done nothing to change it.
vbAbortRetryIgnore + vbExclamation + vbDefaultButton2	Displays Abort, Retry, and Ignore buttons with an exclamation mark icon, and makes the Retry button the default.
vbYesNoCancel + vbQuestion + vbDefaultButton3	Displays Yes, No, and Cancel buttons with a warning query icon and makes the Cancel button the default.

Using *MsgBox()* Return Values

The MsgBox() function can display seven different buttons to users. To know which button a user chooses in response to your message box, MsgBox() returns a unique value depending on which button is clicked. Table 28.3 lists the button types available for MsgBox() and their associated return values.

TABLE 28.3   **Button Types and Their Return Values**

Button	Value	Constant
OK	1	vbOK
Cancel	2	vbCancel
Abort	3	vbAbort
Retry	4	vbRetry
Ignore	5	vbIgnore
Yes	6	vbYes
No	7	vbNo

Work with return values

1. Open a blank module and enter the code in Listing 28.6.

LISTING 28.6   **Using the Value Returned from a *MsgBox()* Function**

```
01 Function basStrangeMsg() As Boolean
02   Dim bolResponse As Boolean
03   Dim strMsgTxt As String
04   Dim lngMsgBoxType As Long
05
06   strMsgTxt = "Something strange has happened! " & _
                    "Do you want to continue?"
07   lngMsgBoxType = vbYesNo + vbQuestion
08
09   If MsgBox(strMsgTxt, lngMsgBoxType, "My message box") _
          = vbYes Then
10     bolResponse = True
11   Else
12     bolResponse = False
13   End If
14
15   basStrangeMsg = bolResponse
16 End Function
```

The _ at the end of the line is a continuation character. It tells VBA that the current line of code is being continued on the following line. The continuation character is useful for making your code easier to read than it would be if you had to keep scrolling to the right to read a very long statement on a single line.

2. Open the Immediate window and type `?basStrangeMsg()`. You should have something that resembles Figure 28.4.

3. Press **Enter**. VBA displays the simple dialog box shown in Figure 28.5. Click **Yes** to close the dialog box; VBA displays `True` in the Immediate window.

4. Move the cursor to the end of the `?basStrangeMsg()` line in the Immediate window and press **Enter** again.

5. Click **No** to close the dialog box. VBA displays `False` in the Immediate window.

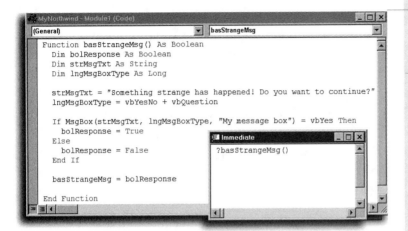

FIGURE 28.4

You can take different actions based on the user's response.

FIGURE 28.5

The message box gives users two possible responses.

The code in Listing 28.6 might look different than what has been used thus far, but it introduces no new VBA statements or concepts not previously discussed. It's simply structured differently. The primary difference is line 9, where variables are used for two arguments for the MsgBox() function. Using variables for arguments isn't limited to MsgBox(), but variables can be used with most built-in functions, VBA statements, and functions and subprocedures that you write. The next example takes this technique one step further to give you a better idea of just how useful it can be.

Look at Listing 28.7. This code is very similar to that used in Listing 28.6, but with several key differences:

- basContinueMsg() on line 1 includes two arguments, one of which, strBoxTitle, is optional.

- Lines 6–8 check to see whether the optional argument was omitted and, if so, set a default value to be used for the title of the message box.

The use of arguments and variables yields reusable code

Although you want to display different messages in your own application than you have here, the function shown in Listing 28.7 is an example of reusable code. basContinueMsg() can be called from any VBA code any number of times. It lets you determine at runtime what message is displayed, but always returns a value so that you know how users respond.

- On line 9, all the arguments used in the MsgBox() function use variables instead of literal values. Two of these variables can be passed to the basContinueMsg() function as arguments.

① vbCrLf is a built-in constant representing the special characters that can cause a carriage return/line feed–that is, cause a new line to be started. The & character is used here as a concatenation operator.

② Len() returns the length of a character string passed as an argument. If no value is supplied for strBoxTitle when basContinueMsg() is called, the length of strBoxTitle will be 0.

LISTING 28.7   **Declaring an Optional Argument in a Procedure**

```
01 Function basContinueMsg(strMsgTxt As String, _
            Optional strBoxTitle As String) As Boolean
02   Dim bolResponse As Boolean
03   Dim lngMsgBoxType As Long
04
05   strMsgTxt = strMsgTxt & vbCrLf & ──────────① 
            " Do you want to continue?"
06   lngMsgBoxType = vbYesNo + vbQuestion
07   If Len(strBoxTitle) = 0 Then ──────────②
08     strBoxTitle = "General Continue Message"
09     ' if optional argument omitted, set default title
10   End If
11
12   If MsgBox(strMsgTxt, lngMsgBoxType, strBoxTitle) = _
            vbYes Then
13     bolResponse = True
14 Else
15     bolResponse = False
16 End If
17
18 basContinueMsg = bolResponse
19 End Function
```

Use a function while omitting its optional argument

1. Open a blank module and enter the code in Listing 28.7.

2. Try this function while omitting its optional argument. Open the Immediate window and enter
`?basContinueMsg("This is cool.")`.

3. VBA displays the dialog box shown in Figure 28.6. Click **Yes** to close the box; VBA displays True in the Immediate window.

FIGURE 28.6
The function uses a default title bar for the message box because the function's optional argument was omitted.

4. Enter the following into the Immediate window:

```
?basContinueMsg("Another job well
done.","Congratulations")
```

5. VBA displays the dialog box shown in Figure 28.7. Click **No** to close the dialog box; VBA displays False in the Immediate window.

FIGURE 28.7
Display a message box by using a title bar passed as an argument.

You can easily modify line 1 of Listing 28.7 so that if the user omits the optional argument, a default will be provided. If you use the following line, for example, the value of strBoxTitle defaults to General Continue Message if the user omits the strBoxTitle argument:

```
Function basContinueMsg(strMsgTxt As String, _
   Optional strBoxTitle As String = "General Continue
➥Message")_
   As Boolean
```

This change makes lines 7–10 useless, so they can then be deleted.

Soliciting Information with Input Boxes

VBA has a built-in function, InputBox(), that provides a quick and easy way for you to solicit input from your application users. The syntax of this function is

```
InputBox(promptstring, titlestring)
```

Full syntax of the InputBox() function

InputBox() has a several other optional arguments not shown in the examples. The discussion is limited here to the two most commonly used arguments. You can refer to Access Help for a more complete description of this function.

where *promptstring* is the text that describes to users what information is being solicited, and *titlestring* is an optional argument you can use to provide your own title bar text when the dialog box is displayed.

Prompt for information with an input box

1. Open a blank module and enter the code in Listing 28.8.

LISTING 28.8   **Soliciting Information from Users with the *InputBox()* Function**

```
01 Function basGetBirthDate()
02 Dim intResponse As Integer
03 Dim strUserInput As String
04 Dim strMsgTxt As String
05
06 strMsgTxt = "Please enter your birthdate " & _
                "in the form mm/dd/yyyy"
07 strUserInput = InputBox(strMsgTxt,"Get Birth Date")
08
09 intResponse = MsgBox("You were born on " & _
                        strUserInput, vbOKOnly)
10 End Function
```

2. Open the Immediate window and enter ?basGetBirthDate(). An input box similar to Figure 28.8 appears.

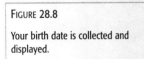

FIGURE 28.8

Your birth date is collected and displayed.

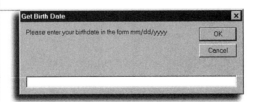

3. Type your birth date and press **Enter**. A simple message box displays your birth date.

Now that you're comfortable with the InputBox() function, use it again, but this time I will introduce several other functions built into VBA. The code in Listing 28.9 uses the same InputBox() function from the previous example, but the rest of the code is more complex. (If you have trouble following along, don't worry—it will become clearer as you go along.)

LISTING 28.9   **Validating User Input**

You can use *comments* (the text following the apostrophes) to denote more clearly which End If statement belongs to which If statement.

```
01 Function basGetBirthDay()
02   Dim intResponse As Integer
03   Dim strUserInput As String
04   Dim intLen As Integer
05   Dim lngDays As Long
06   Dim dteDate As Date
07
08   strUserInput = InputBox("Please enter your birthdate " & _
                     "in the form mm/dd/yyyy", "Get Birth Date")
09   intLen = Len(strUserInput)
10   If intLen > 0 Then
11     If (Mid$(strUserInput, intLen - 4, 1) = "/") And _
          (IsNumeric(Mid$(strUserInput, intLen - 3, 4))) Then
12       If IsDate(strUserInput) Then
13         dteDate = strUserInput
14         intResponse = MsgBox("You are " & _
                       DateDiff("d", dteDate, Date()) & _
                       " days old", vbOKOnly)
15       Else
16         intResponse = MsgBox(strUserInput & _
                       " is not a valid date", vbOKOnly)
17       End If 'IsDate(strUserInput)
18     Else
19       MsgBox "Year not entered in form of yyyy", vbOKOnly
20     End If '(Mid$(strUserInput, intLen - 4, 1) = "/")......
21   End If 'intLen > 0
22 End Function
```

The basGetBirthDay() function in Listing 28.9 solicits the user's birth date and displays the user's age, expressed in days, in a message box. Essentially, these objectives are addressed on two lines of code: Line 8 solicits the user's birth date; line 14 calculates the user's age in days and displays the result in a message box. Most of the remaining code validates the user's input and responds if the input is incorrect or missing. Let's look at this code one step at a time:

- Line 8 solicits the user's input and stores the result in the variable strUserInput.

- But what if the user clicked the cancel button on the input box? Or what if he simply pressed **Enter** without having entered and response? Line 9 saves the length of the user's response into a variable, intLen, and line 10 checks the length to see whether it's greater than zero. The length is zero if the user clicks **Cancel** or fails to respond. If the length is zero, the condition is false (line 10), so you exit the function without further action.

- If the program gets to line 11, you know the user entered something, but it might not be what you asked for. This If statement ensures that the user entered four characters after the last slash in the response, or that they expressed the year as four digits, not just two. The condition portion of the If statement here is checking two different things. Because the And operand is used, both things must be True for the condition to be true. The first part of the condition,

  ```
  (Mid$(strUserInput, intLen - 4, 1) = "/")
  ```

  verifies that the fifth position of the user's response, moving from right to left, is a /. The second portion of the condition,

  ```
  (IsNumeric(Mid$(strUserInput, intLen - 3, 4)))
  ```

  verifies that the last four positions of the user's response is a numeric value.

- In line 12, you need to make one last check. Did the user enter a valid date? The response 1/37/1950 will pass the validation tests you have applied thus far. The built-in function IsDate() returns True if the passed argument is a valid date, False if it's not.

- If the user enters a valid date, line 14 indicates that it's okay to display the message box. Part of the display includes the value returned by yet another built-in function, DateDiff(). The statement

  ```
  DateDiff("d", dteDate, Date())
  ```

The richness and flexibility of VBA

Listing 28.9 includes several built-in functions not yet discussed. Hundreds more aren't mentioned yet. The purpose isn't to scare you away, but to give you a better idea as to the richness of the VBA language. Line 14, for example, demonstrates a coding technique you will often see used in VBA code. Notice that the MsgBox() function has another function, DateDiff(), embedded as part of its first argument. In fact, the DateDiff() function uses yet another built-in function as its third argument, Date().

calculates the difference between the value returned by the built-in function Date(), which is always the current date, and the date contained in variable dteDate, and expresses the result in days, as requested by the first argument, "d".

Looping in VBA

Similar to decision-making is the loop structure. Rather than evaluate a condition and then execute a response based on the result of that evaluation, a loop executes a task as long as a condition is met.

The *For...Next* Loop

VBA's For...Next construct repeats a task a predetermined number of times. You can define the number of cycles, or you can use an expression. The syntax for the construct is

```
For count = start To end [Step step]
    task statements
Next count
```

The *count* argument tracks the number of times VBA has executed the task statements; *start* is the value *count* begins with; *end* is the value of *count* at which you want the loop to stop, and *step* specifies the value by which you want to increase or decrease the value of *count* each time the loop is executed.

Modify multiple controls with a simple *For* loop

1. Open a blank module and enter the code in Listing 28.10.

LISTING 28.10   **A Simple *For* Loop**

```
1 Function basForNext()
2 Dim intX As Integer
3 Dim strMsgTxt As String
4 For intX = 1 To 7 Step 1
5    strMsgTxt = strMsgTxt & intX & " "
6 Next intX
7
8 Debug.Print strMsgTxt
9 End Function
```

1 Optional; if omitted, a default of Step 1 is assumed.

2. Open the Immediate window and enter ?basForNext(). You should see something similar to Figure 28.9.

FIGURE 28.9

Line 5 is repeated seven times.

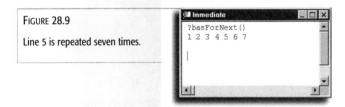

3. Change line 4 of your code to read
```
For intX = 1 To -7 Step -1
```

4. Open the Immediate window and enter ?basForNext().You should see something similar to Figure 28.10.

FIGURE 28.10

You can also decrement the count by using a negative step.

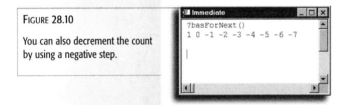

5. Change line 4 of your code to read
```
For intX = 1 To 8 Step 2
```

6. Open the Immediate window and enter ?basForNext(). You should see something similar to Figure 28.11.

FIGURE 28.11

The count can also be changed in increments other than 1.

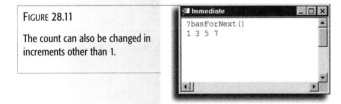

A more practical use of the *For...Next* construct

1. Open a new form in Design view and add three text box controls.

2. Add a command button and change its caption to Change BackColor and its name to cmdChangeBackColor.

3. Add the code in Listing 28.11 to the command button's OnClick event.

LISTING 28.11   Using the *For...Next* Construct to Loop Through All Controls on a Form

```
01 Private Sub cmdChangeBackColor_Click()
02  Dim intCnt As Integer
03  Dim ctlThisControl As Control
04  For intCnt = 0 To Me.Controls.Count - 1
05    Set ctlThisControl = Me.Controls(intCnt)
06    If TypeOf ctlThisControl Is TextBox Then
07      If ctlThisControl.BackColor = 255 Then
08        ctlThisControl.BackColor = 16777215
09      Else
10        ctlThisControl.BackColor = 255
11      End If
12    End If
13  Next intCnt
14 End Sub
```

The phrase TypeOf ctlThisControl Is TextBox on line 6 of Listing 28.11 is worth noting. As you've probably guessed, the phrase evaluates to True if the object represented by ctlThisControl is a text box. The keyword TextBox is only one of many available options, however; you could use the keyword ComboBox, for example, to work with all the combo boxes on the form. The easiest way to find the correct keyword is to simply start typing the If statement, using the TypeOf operator as shown, and after typing the space after the keyword Is, the Auto List Members feature will display a list for you.

4. Change to Form view. Your form should resemble the one in Figure 28.12.

About a collection's Count property and index value

Notice the To argument of the For...Next construct on line 4. The argument is being set to the value of the Count property of the form's Controls collection, minus 1. The 1 is being subtracted so that the count argument, variable intCnt, is also used as an index into the form's Controls collection on line 5. However, the index for a collection starts at 0, not 1. The Count property of the form's Controls collection is 7 (three text boxes, three labels, and one command button). Thus, if you allow For...Next to loop until intCnt reaches 7, an error will occur. The highest valid index into the Controls collection is, in this case, 6 because it starts at 0.

An easy way to find the number corresponding to a color

Notice that lines 7, 8, and 10 of Listing 28.11 all use a number to reference the BackColor property of a control. A quick way to find the number that represents the color you're interested in is to open a form in Design view and either find a control with the background color you want, or copy the number displayed in the properties sheet for the control to the Clipboard (the proper number can then be pasted into your VBA code). If no control can be found that meets your needs, alter one by using the Color dialog box available from the properties sheet.

FIGURE 28.12

The command button changes
the background color of the text
boxes.

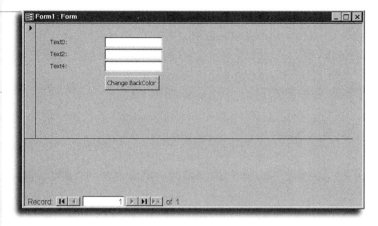

5. Click the command button **Change BackColor.** Each time
   you click the command button, the background color of the
   text boxes change.

6. Save the form as Form1.

The *For Each...Next* Statement

Using the For...Next construct to loop through all the objects in
a collection is fairly common. So, a similar but more specialized
form of the construct was introduced in Access 95—the For
Each...Next statement. The syntax for the statement is

```
For Each element In collection
    task statements
Next
```

where *element* is an object variable of the same type as the
objects in *collection*. You don't have to tell VBA where to start
or how many items there are; VBA will keep track of the items
for you.

The code in Listing 28.12 is functionally identical to that in
Listing 28.11, but it uses For Each...Next instead of the more
general For...Next construct. Listing 28.12 is somewhat
simpler—and faster.

LISTING 28.12   **A Simpler and Faster Way to Examine All Controls on a Form**

```
01 Private Sub cmdChangeBackColor_Click()
02  Dim ctlThisControl As Control
03  For Each ctlThisControl In Me.Controls
04    If TypeOf ctlThisControl Is TextBox Then
05      If ctlThisControl.BackColor = 255 Then
06        ctlThisControl.BackColor = 16777215
07      Else
08        ctlThisControl.BackColor = 255
09      End If
10    End If
11  Next
12 End Sub
```

The following For Each...Next example displays a dynamic list of objects in a combo box. Specifically, it will display a list of all the reports in the application in a combo box.

Display a dynamic list of objects with *For Each...Next*

1. Open a blank form in the Northwind database and add a combo box to it. Name the combo box cboReports. Change the Row Source Type property to Value List.

2. Attach the procedure in Listing 28.13 to cboReports's GotFocus event by clicking the **Code** button 🖼 on the Form Design toolbar. Then choose cboReports and GotFocus from VBE's Object and Procedure controls, respectively.

3. Close the VBE, click the **View** button 🖼 ▾ on the Form Design toolbar, and open the control's drop-down list. As you can see in Figure 28.13, the combo box offers a list of all Northwind reports.

FIGURE 28.13

You used a For
Each...Next loop to fill this
combo box with all the available
reports in Northwind.

If a new report is added, the code in Listing 28.13 dynamically updates
the list for you.

LISTING 28.13   **Code for the *Got Focus* Event**

```
01 Private Sub cboReports_GotFocus()
02 Dim db As DAO.Database
03 Dim obj As Object
04 Dim obj1 As Object
05
06 Set db = CurrentDb()
07 Set obj = db.Containers("Reports")
08
09 For Each obj1 In obj.Documents
10 Me!cboReports.RowSource = Me!cboReports.RowSource & _
                             obj1.Name & ";"
11 Next
12
13 End Sub
```

When Your Code Doesn't Work

Few of us are so proficient at VBA that we don't make mistakes.
In fact, the best developers depend heavily on VBA's debugging
features. During testing, you can count on two types of programming errors you'll need to debug: syntax and logic errors.

Syntax errors are very common and, fortunately, most are caught by VBA when you enter the code. A syntax error simply means VBA doesn't understand the code because you've misspelled something or omitted a required argument. If VBA fails to catch the error as you're entering the mistake, it will stop and point to the offending statement when you compile the code. At that point, you simply correct the highlighted statement.

On the other hand, VBA won't point to your logic errors. Instead, your code doesn't do what you expected. Logic errors can, but usually don't, crash your system. Most often they produce incorrect data or nothing at all. Consequently, logic errors are a bit harder to find and resolve than syntax errors.

Running Code in the Immediate Window

Perhaps the easiest way to find logic mistakes is to use the Immediate window and the Debug.Print statement. You've used these tools in several examples throughout this chapter, so you might already be somewhat familiar with them. The next few examples, however, use them for a somewhat different purpose.

The procedure in Listing 28.14 doesn't do what you want it to do. You should be able to pass it a date and it should return the day of the week for that date, unless the date you use for an argument falls on the weekend. If you use a weekend date, the procedure should change it to Monday. It works for Sundays and Mondays, but not other days.

LISTING 28.14   **Returning Incorrect Results**

```
01 Function basGetDay(dteDate As Date) As String
02   Dim strRetVal As String
03   Dim intDayOfWeek As Integer
04   intDayOfWeek = DatePart("w", dteDate, 2)
05   If intDayOfWeek = 7 Or intDayOfWeek = 1 Then
06     intDayOfWeek = 2
07   End If
08   Select Case intDayOfWeek
09     Case 2
```

continues...

LISTING 28.14 Continued

```
10      strRetVal = "Monday"
11   Case 3
12      strRetVal = "Tuesday"
13   Case 4
14      strRetVal = "Wednesday"
15   Case 5
16      strRetVal = "Thursday"
17   Case 6
18      strRetVal = "Friday"
19   End Select
20   basGetDay = strRetVal
21 End Function
```

The logic of the procedure pretty much hinges on the value of the intDayOfWeek variable. It's therefore probably useful to see what the variable's value is at different points in the procedure's execution. By adding a few Debug.Print statements to the procedure's code, as shown in lines 5 and 9 in Listing 28.15, and then running the procedure from the Immediate window, you can do just that. The Debug.Print statement lets you see what's happening inside the code at the time the code is running.

**Using an identifier in
Print.Debug statements**

Note that Listing 28.15 adds extra characters, **a** and **b**, to each **Debug.Print** statement. This unique value helps you identify which **Debug.Print** statement printed each line in the Immediate window. Although this isn't of much value in this example, because you have only two **Debug.Print** statements, it can be extremely useful when many lines are being sent to the Immediate window.

LISTING 28.15 Using *Debug.Print* to Find Logic Errors

```
01 Function basGetDay(dteDate As Date) As String
02   Dim strRetVal As String
03   Dim intDayOfWeek As Integer
04   intDayOfWeek = DatePart("w", dteDate, 2)
05   Debug.Print "a", intDayOfWeek
06   If intDayOfWeek = 7 Or intDayOfWeek = 1 Then
07     intDayOfWeek = 2
08   End If
09   Debug.Print "b", intDayOfWeek
10   Select Case intDayOfWeek
11     Case 2
12       strRetVal = "Monday"
13     Case 3
14       strRetVal = "Tuesday"
15     Case 4
```

```
16      strRetVal = "Wednesday"
17    Case 5
18      strRetVal = "Thursday"
19    Case 6
20      strRetVal = "Friday"
21  End Select
22  basGetDay = strRetVal
23 End Function
```

A `Debug.Print` statement causes the value of whatever arguments are included in the statement to be displayed in the Immediate window. In this case, you want to know the current value of the `intDayOfWeek` variable at different points during the execution of the procedure, so the added `Debug.Print` statements include that variable as an argument.

A few strategically placed `Debug.Print` statements can help you analyze what's going on (see Figure 28.14). Listing 28.15 passes `basGetDay()` a Saturday, which should equal a 7. However, `basGetDay()` thinks it's a 6. The mistake is right in the code. Listing 28.15 also tells VBA to treat Monday as the first day of the week instead of Sunday, which changes the weekday count by 1. To correct the error, simply replace the 2 argument in the `DatePart()` function (line 4) with a 1:

```
intDayOfWeek = DatePart("w", dteDate, 1)
```

(or omit it, as 1 is the default), and then run the procedure in the Immediate window a second time. Figure 28.15 shows the results of running the corrected procedure with the `Debug` statements still present.

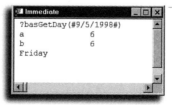

FIGURE 28.14

Using Debug in the function quickly showed you the error.

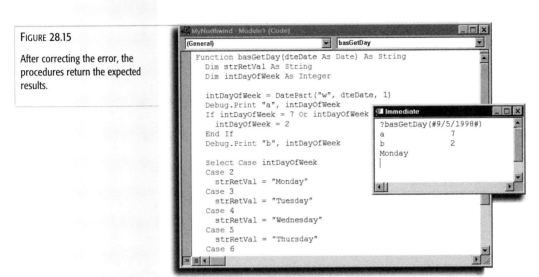

The Immediate window doesn't limit you to functions; you can evaluate any expression. For instance, you can enter ?1 + 3, and the Debug window will return the value 4. Just be sure to proceed each expression with a question mark, or *print indicator*.

It's often very convenient to use the Immediate window to test your use of some built-in function. For instance, by entering

```
?datediff("d",#8/5/1998#,#12/25/1998#)
```

in the Immediate window, you can verify that you understand the function's syntax, and the expected results, without having to deal with other code in a procedure.

Table 28.4 lists other debugging tools. Several of these tools can be invoked in different ways, but they're all available from a Debug toolbar. To display the Debug toolbar, from the **View** menu choose **Toolbars** and then **Debug**.

TABLE 28.4 Debugging Tools

Tool	Icon	Explanation
Toggle Breakpoint		You can set a breakpoint to temporarily halt the execution of your code at a particular statement.
Call Stack		The call stack will list each active procedure in order as they're called, displaying the current procedure at the top of the list.
Quick Watch		This feature displays information about a variable. Simply position the cursor within the variable name and click the icon to display the calling function and the value of the variable. You can also evaluate an expression.
Step Into		This feature will execute your procedure one statement at a time.
Step Over		This tool executes the current procedure only one statement at a time. If the current procedure calls another procedure, VBA executes that entire procedure at once.
Step Out		This tool returns you to the last line in the calling function.

Immediate window shortcut

You don't have to retype a statement each time you want to execute it in the Immediate window. After executing a statement in the Immediate window, VBA retains the statement. To re-execute it, simply position the cursor at the end of the statement and press **Enter**.

Preventing Runtime Errors

When you debug code, you're correcting your mistakes. However, some errors might elude testing. Other errors can occur when your application is used that aren't caused by errors in your code at all, but by something else in the operating environment (an attempt to write to a full disk, for example). These errors are referred to as *runtime errors*. Most often, you can anticipate these errors before they occur—thus, you can design your application to deal with them. The point here is to prevent users from seeing some nasty (and perhaps confusing) VBA or system error message, and any resulting action that might occur (such as the application being closed down). Instead, you want the code to deal with these errors. Three things must be done to properly handle runtime errors:

- You must tell VBA not to process an error if it occurs, but to pass control to your code instead.

- Your code must evaluate and process the error.

- Your code must decide what needs to happen next.

Using the *On Error* Statement

Use the On Error statement to tell VBA not to handle an error if one should occur, but to pass control to your code instead. The syntax for On Error is

```
On Error GoTo pointer-to-error-handler
```

where *pointer-to-error-handler* identifies the code you want to gain control of if an error occurs. The *pointer-to-error-handler* can be a line number or a label, but must be in the same procedure as the On Error statement.

Working with Error-Handling Code

Before your error handler can do much of anything, it must first determine what kind of error occurred. The Err object is used to for this purpose. The Err object has several properties, but this chapter will use just two of them: Err.Number and Err.Description.

After the error is evaluated and any appropriate actions are taken as a result, your error-handling code must then tell VBA what should happen next. Typically, the Resume statement is used for this purpose. You can use any of three syntax:

- Resume   VBA returns to the line that produced the error and attempts to execute it again.

- Resume Next   VBA continues executing at the line immediately following the line that produced the error.

- Resume *other*   VBA resumes at the point specified by *other*.

A second syntax of the On Error statement is also useful here:

```
On Error GoTo 0
```

This statement disables the error handler in the current procedure—that is, it resets any On Error statement that might have been previously executed in the current procedure. Thus, control to handle errors is returned to VBA.

The Scope of On Error Statement

Be careful if you have an **On Error** statement and associated error handling in a procedure and that procedure calls another procedure. If the **called** procedure has no error handling of its own but an error is encountered, VBA will give control to the error handler in the **calling** procedure. Although this isn't necessarily a bad thing, it can be quite a surprise if your code wasn't expecting it to happen. The first procedure's error handler needs to deal with error in all child procedures, or the child procedures need to have their own error handling in place.

Now, suppose that your application tries to save files to disk, which can cause a runtime error if no disk is in the drive or the disk is full. If you omit error handling, such a mishap will stop your application. Instead, you can include a simple error-handling routine to alert users to the problem, give users a chance to correct the problem, and then continue when they are ready. The procedure in Listing 28.16 handles this situation nicely.

LISTING 28.16 **Handling Anticipated Errors Allows Users to Correct the Condition and Continue**

```
01 Private Function DoMyWork() as Boolean
02 On Error GoTo Err_DoMyWork
...
03 DoMyWork = True
04
05 Done_DoMyWork:
06   On Error GoIo 0
07   Exit Function
08
09 Err_DoMyWork:
10   Select Case Err.Number
11     Case 61
12       MsgBox "Disk is full, please insert a blank " & _
                "disk and try again."
13       Resume
14     Case 71
15       MsgBox "Drive isn't ready. Please check and " & _
                "try again."
16       Resume
17     Case Else
18       MsgBox "Undetermined error " & Err.Number & " " & _
                Err.Description
19       DoMyWork = False
20       Resume Done_DoMyWork
21   End Select
22 End Function
```

1 Insert your code for saving to disk here.

2 Without this statement, the error-handling code beginning on line 10 would execute every time the procedure runs. You are all done after line 6, so you need to exit at line 7 without continuing to execute the code that follows.

If any error occurs, VBA passes control to the code at label Err_DoMyWork (line 9). This code is fairly straightforward. If the runtime error is 61 or 71, the code identifies the error and gives simple instructions for correcting it so you can continue. This is where you or your users read the message, correct the error, and then click **OK** to continue. In both cases, VBA will then return to the error-producing line and attempt to execute it again. Everything should be fine as long as you corrected the error.

If the error is anything other than one of the expected errors, the Case Else statement displays the error number and description, and sets the return value of the function to False. The Resume Done_DoMyWork statement (line 20) causes execution to continue at the label Done_DoMyWork (line 5), which is the normal exit point of the function.

A Primer on ADO

Access your data through ActiveX Data Objects (ADO)

Change the source of your data with ADO

Create and use recordsets with ADO

Use ADO to access your data with a SQL string

Understand the key differences between ADO and DAO

The ADO Advantage

Using ADO in Excel, Word, PowerPoint, or VB

All the examples in this chapter can be created or copied into a module in any application that uses VBA, and in most cases VB. You don't need to be in an Access application to work with an Access database, nor are you limited to working with Access data while in an Access application. Remember, however, that to use the ADO objects, the application hosting your VBA code must have a reference to the ADODB Library.

The ADO Library provides a set of objects, properties, and methods that you can use to access and manipulate data stored in a wide variety of data sources, including but not limited to Access (Microsoft Jet) databases, Microsoft SQL Server, Oracle RDBMS databases, or any other data source with an ODBC interface. Although some data sources have characteristics unique to that provider, for the most part ADO allows you to access the data with little regard for what data source is actually being used. Another advantage of using ADO is that it might be used not only from within your VBA code, but also with Visual Basic, VBScript, C++, and other development environments. This all adds up to a set features that lets you build fast, efficient, and portable client/server or Web-based applications.

SEE ALSO

➤ *For information about how to establish a reference to a library, see page 463*

The ADO model includes a rich set of objects, properties, and methods, but this chapter discusses only a few of them. You will be looking primarily at the ADO Connection and Recordset objects, which are all you need to begin using ADO technology to access your data.

The ADO *Connection* Object

As mentioned earlier, you can use ADO to access data from many different sources, including many non-Microsoft products. The ConnectionString property of the Connection object is what you use to tell ADO what kind of data you want to access and where it can be found. The ConnectionString property consists of a series of *argument* = *value* statements separated by semi-colons:

```
"Provider=SQLOLEDB;server=Main; _
        uid=sa;pwd=;database=NorthwindCS"
"Provider=Microsoft.Jet.OLEDB.4.0; _
        Data Source=e:\samples\Northwind.mdb"
```

As you can see, both sample connect strings use the `Provider=` argument, but seem to have very little else in common. This argument is where you tell ADO which OLE DB Provider to use to access the data. (The term *OLE DB Provider* refers to a set of code that serves as an interface between ADO and the actual source data.) A number of OLE DB Providers are available from Microsoft (see Table 29.1), as well as from other commercial sources.

TABLE 29.1   A Sample of the OLE DB Providers Available from Microsoft

Provider Name	Description
`Microsoft.Jet.OLEDB.4.0`	OLE DB Provider for Microsoft Jet
`SQLOLEDB`	Microsoft SQL Server OLE DB Provider
`MSDASQL`	Microsoft OLE DB Provider for ODBC
`MSDAORA`	Microsoft OLE DB Provider for Oracle

The rest of the connect string varies depending on the value of the `Provider=` argument. The first example names the OLE DB Provider for Microsoft SQL Server. In this case, you must supply the name of the server, a user ID and password, and the name of the database you want to access. The second example names the OLE DB Provider for Microsoft Jet (Access), so all you must provide is the path to the database you want to access.

The ADO *Recordset* Object

The actual group of records you want to work with is made available through the `Recordset` object. You use this object and its properties to tell ADO what data source you want to use— that is, what `Connection` and what specific group of data are to be used. The group of data can be an entire table, or only the records returned by a SQL statement—whatever your application requires.

Using ADO Objects

Listing 29.1 shows a procedure that uses ADO to read records from a database table and display a column in the Immediate window. The listing can be viewed as having five different sections: lines 1–5, 6–9, 11 and 12, 13–17, and 19–23.

Why two line 6s?

Listing 29.1 includes lines 6a and 6b. The actual procedure would include only one of these two lines or, if both 6a and 6b are included, one of them should be commented out by starting the line with a single quotation mark. Line 6a is an example of a connect string used to connect to the NorthwindCS database in Microsoft SQL Server. Line 6b is an example of a connect string to connect to a Microsoft Jet (Access) database—in this case, Northwind.mdb. In either case, however, the specifics will probably have to be altered to meet the conditions of your local installation. This general convention is used throughout this chapter.

ADO syntax is extremely flexible

You could have used another syntax on line 11 of Listing 29.1, such as `rstCustomers.Open "Customers", strCnn`. Had this syntax been used, ADO would have created a connection object for you, and you could eliminate lines 2, 8, 9, 20, and 22 from the procedure. However, the use of an explicit connection is recommended, as used here, if three or more recordsets are opened on it, in consideration of time and required resources.

LISTING 29.1   Using ADO to Read Records from a Database Table

```
01 Sub basDemoADO1()
02 Dim cnn1 As ADODB.Connection
03 Dim rstCustomers As ADODB.Recordset
04 Dim strCnn As String
05 Dim strCompanyName As String
6a strCnn = "Provider=SQLOLEDB;server=Main; _
        uid=sa;pwd=;database=NorthwindCS"
6b strCnn = "Provider=Microsoft.Jet.OLEDB.4.0; _
        Data Source=e:\samples\Northwind.mdb"
07 On Error GoTo basDemoADO1_Err
08 Set cnn1 = New ADODB.Connection
09 cnn1.Open strCnn
10
11 Set rstCustomers = New ADODB.Recordset
12 rstCustomers.Open "Customers", cnn1
13 Do Until rstCustomers.EOF
14    strCompanyName = rstCustomers!CompanyName
15    Debug.Print strCompanyName
16    rstCustomers.MoveNext
17 Loop
18 basDemoADO1_Err:
19    If rstCustomers.State <> adStateClose Then _
            rstCustomers.Close
20    If Cnn1.State <> adStateClose Then Cnn1.Close
21    Set rstCustomers=Nothing
22    Set Cnn1=Nothing
23    If Err.Number <> 0 Then _
            MsgBox "An unexpected error occurred"
24 End Sub
```

Lines 1–5 simply name the subprocedure and declare the variables to be used. Notice lines 2 and 3, however—you might not have seen variables defined quite this way before. These lines are declaring variables of a type that will later be set to objects defined in the ADODB Library—specifically, the Connection and Recordset objects. All the ADO objects, properties, and methods (that is, the ADO model) are defined by the ADODB Library.

Lines 6–9 deal with the Connection object. The object is created in line 8 and opened in line 9. It might be helpful to think of the Connection object as being similar to a path to your data source. Notice that line 6 contains a number of arguments that seem as though they might be related to a database, and in fact they are.

Line 6 creates a string that's used as an argument for the Open method of the connection object in line 9. This argument tells ADO what kind of data source you want to connect to and is called the ConnectionString. The ConnectionString is actually a property of the Connection object, but rather than set the property itself, Listing 29.1 passes the string to the Open method as an argument on line 9. ADO uses the argument to set the value of the object's ConnectionString property, but you could have done this yourself by using the following code instead of the code shown in line 9:

```
cnn1.ConnectionString = strCnn
cnn1.Open
```

Lines 11 and 12 define and make available the actual group of records the procedure will be processing. This group of records, referred to as a *recordset*, is made available through the Recordset object. The example uses all the records contained in the Customers table, which in turn is reachable through the connection defined by Cnn1, the connection object defined previously.

Lines 13–17 is a VBA looping structure used to print the CompanyName column in the Immediate window and then move to the next row of the recordset. The code loops between lines 13 and 17 until the condition in line 13 is True—in this case, until the EOF (End of File) property of the recordset is True. ADO sets EOF to True when an attempt is made to read past the last row in the recordset. Thus, when the last available row is printed and line 16 attempts to move to the next row, ADO sets EOF to True and you exit the loop, moving to line 18.

> **Use a global constant to make future changes easier**
>
> The portion of line 6b that reads Microsoft.Jet.OLEDB.4.0 refers to a specific release of the Microsoft Jet OLE DB driver. If references to this driver are made throughout your application, you might want to replace them with a global constant to make maintaining the application much easier. That way, you then have to update only the one constant, as opposed to many references throughout your code, when a newer release of the driver becomes available.

Lines 19–22 are used to clean up after yourself. Lines 19 and 20 close the Recordset and Connection objects so that system resources used by these objects are freed up. The objects themselves aren't removed from memory. Although you can no longer use them to access data, you could change properties and reopen them if you needed to. Lines 21 and 22 actually remove the objects from memory.

Using Recordsets

This chapter discusses recordsets as though they are all the same, but they don't have to be. The Recordset object has properties that you can use to more specifically define how you want the recordset to behave. Typically, you would do this to improve performance of the application.

The first property of the Recordset object you will use is CursorType. Table 29.2 describes the values available for this property.

TABLE 29.2   **The *Recordset* Object's *CursorType* Property**

Constant	Description
adOpenStatic	Provides a snapshot of the data at a point in time. Changes, deletions, and additions made by other users to the source data after the snapshot is taken aren't reflected in the recordset. Improves performance for finding records or producing reports.
adOpenForwardOnly	This is the default. Identical to the static cursor, except that you can only scroll forward through the records by using the MoveNext method. This can improve performance when you need to make only a single pass through the data.
adOpenDynamic	Changes, deletions, and additions made by other users to the source data are reflected in the recordset. All types of movement through the recordset are allowed.
adOpenKeyset	Similar to the dynamic cursor except that you can't see records that other users add, but deletions and changes by other users are reflected in the recordset.

Using adOpenDynamic with a Jet data source

The adOpenDynamic CursorType isn't supported by Jet. CursorType is gracefully demoted to **adOpenStatic** if read-only locking type is used, and set to **adOpenKeyset** otherwise.

Line 9 in Listing 29.2 shows how the CursorType property of a recordset object might be set. You can simply pass your choice as an argument of the Open method. This procedure does exactly the same thing as the basDemoADO1 procedure shown in Listing 29.1, except that in Listing 29.2, you're allowing ADO to create the connection object as described earlier.

LISTING 29.2 Setting the *CursorType* Property of a *Recordset* Object

```
01 Sub basDemoADO2()
02 Dim rstCustomers As ADODB.Recordset
03 Dim strCnn As String
04 Dim strCompanyName As String
05
6a strCnn = "Provider=SQLOLEDB;server=Main; _
        uid=sa;pwd=;database=NorthwindCS"
6b strCnn = "Provider=Microsoft.Jet.OLEDB.4.0; _
        Data Source=e:\samples\Northwind.mdb"
07
08 Set rstCustomers = New ADODB.Recordset
09 rstCustomers.Open "Customers", strCnn, adOpenStatic
10 Do Until rstCustomers.EOF
11   strCompanyName = rstCustomers!CompanyName
12   Debug.Print strCompanyName
13   rstCustomers.MoveNext
14 Loop
15 rstCustomers.Close
16 Set rstCustomers = Nothing
17 End Sub
```

You can set the CursorType property different from how it's done in Listing 29.2. For example, line 9 could be replaced with following two lines as an alternative way of setting the property:

```
rstCustomers.CursorType = adOpenStatic
rstCustomers.Open "Customers", strCnn
```

In the examples thus far, you've used three methods of the recordset object: Open, Close, and MoveNext. Table 29.3 lists several other methods you can use to move from one row to another when working with an ADO recordset.

Use care when formulating the criteria for Find

When the *columnname* used for the Find argument contains text data, most data source providers require that you enclose the *value* portion of the argument in single quotation marks. Because the entire argument must be a string, this can be a little tricky. For example, the expression "MyField = abcd" evaluates to MyField = abcd, which isn't a valid argument for the Find method. The expression "MyField = '" & "abcd" & "'" evaluates to MyField = 'abcd', which is a valid argument because MyField is a text field.

DAO users, beware of the Find method in ADO

In DAO, the Find method supports multiple conditions, joined with the AND operator, in the criteria. ADO allows only a single comparison.

TABLE 29.3   **Methods Used to Move Around in a *Recordset* Object**

Method	Description
MoveFirst	Makes the first row of the recordset the current row.
MoveLast	Makes the last row of the recordset the current row.
MoveNext	Makes the next row in the recordset the current row.
MovePrevious	Makes the previous row in the recordset the current row.
Find	Searches the recordset for a row that matches the criteria passed as an argument. The passed argument is a string with the following syntax:
	columnname operand value
	where *columnname* is the name of any column in the recordset, *operand* is a logical operator such as =, and *value* is the data to be compared to the data in *columnname*. If a matching record is found, the current record of the recordset is set to the match. If no record is found, the recordset moves to the end of the recordset, and its EOF property is set to True.

basDemoADO3, shown in Listing 29.3 and available on the accompanying Web site (http://www.mcp.com/product_support) as Ch29_Samples.mdb, uses several available methods for moving around in a recordset.

Navigate through a recordset by using ADO methods

  1. Open any *.mdb or *.adp file and open an existing module in design mode, or create a new module.

  2. Enter the procedure in Listing 29.3. Note that you should enter either line 7a or 7b, but not both. Whichever one you choose will then have to be modified to meet the conditions of your local installation.

LISTING 29.3   **Using Several of the Methods Available for a Recordset Object**

```
01 Sub basDemoADO3(strBaseName As String)
02 Dim rstCustomers As ADODB.Recordset
03 Dim strCnn As String
04 Dim strSQL As String
```

```
05 Dim strCriteria As String
06
7a strCnn = "Provider=SQLOLEDB;server=Main; _
          uid=sa;pwd=;database=NorthwindCS"
7b strCnn = "Provider=Microsoft.Jet.OLEDB.4.0; _
          Data Source=e:\samples\Northwind.mdb"
08
09 strSQL = "SELECT CompanyName,ContactName FROM Customers"
10
11 Set rstCustomers = New ADODB.Recordset
12 rstCustomers.Open strSQL, strCnn, adOpenDynamic
13
14 strCriteria = "CompanyName = '" & strBaseName & "'"
15 rstCustomers.Find strCriteria
16
17 If Not rstCustomers.EOF Then
18   Debug.Print rstCustomers!CompanyName, _
          rstCustomers!ContactName
19 Else
20   rstCustomers.MoveLast
21   Do Until rstCustomers.BOF
22     Debug.Print rstCustomers!CompanyName, _
          rstCustomers!ContactName
23     rstCustomers.MovePrevious
24   Loop
25 End If
26
27 rstCustomers.Close
28 Set rstCustomers = Nothing
29 End Sub
```

① Creates a recordset based on a SQL statement instead of a table to define the data source.

② Searches the recordset for a record matching the argument passed to the procedure. If a match is found, as indicated by the Find method *not* having set the recordset's EOF property to True, line 18 prints a single line to the Immediate window.

③ Moves you to the last record of the recordset if no match is found, and begins printing each record to the Immediate window, in reverse order. This continues until an attempt is made to read past the beginning of file, at which time ADO sets the BOF property of the recordset to True.

3. Open the Immediate window and enter the line
`basDemoAD03 "Around The Horn"`

The Immediate window is updated as shown in Figure 29.1 because the procedure could find the company named Around the Horn.

FIGURE 29.1

The procedure found the company named Around the Horn.

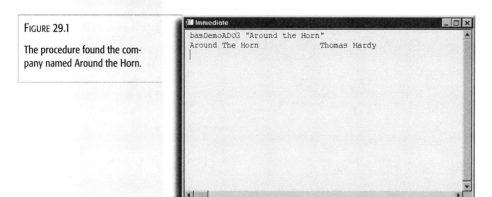

4. Enter the following line in the Immediate window:

```
basDemoADO3 "Around The Corn"
```

This time, because no company named Around the Corn could be found, all the records are printed to the Immediate window, in reverse order.

Thus far, you've used the recordset object only to read the data. You've made no attempt to alter the data in any way. Table 29.4 lists the most common methods used to alter your recordset's data. In addition to these methods, you can edit the data in an existing field by simply assigning a value to the field's Value property.

Value is a field object's default property

When you refer to a field in a recordset with a statement such as rstCustomers!CustomerID, you are actually referring to a specific member of recordset's Fields collection of field objects—In this case, the field object named CustomerID. As with other objects, field objects have a number of properties, and often the case is that the Value property is the default. Thus, the statements rstCustomers!CustomerID.Value = "ACME" and rstCustomers!CustomerID = "ACME" are equivalent. Because no property is explicitly given in the second statement, the default property, Value, is assumed and will be made equal to ACME.

TABLE 29.4 **The *Recordset* Object's Methods Used to Alter Data**

Method	Description
AddNew	Creates a new record in the recordset
Update	Saves any pending changes to the current record
CancelUpdate	Cancels any pending changes to the recordset
Delete	Deletes the current record from the recordset

When ADO recognizes that you've started editing the data (either with an assignment statement or with the `AddNew` method), it changes the value of the recordset's `EditMode` property to indicate that changes are pending. No changes to the actual data source are saved until the `Update` method is called. Indeed, all the pending changes can be cancelled any time before the `Update` method is called by calling the `CancelUpdate` method instead.

However, you must do one more thing before attempting to update the source data. A `Recordset` object has a `LockType` property whose default value can prevent any updates to the recordset. Table 29.5 lists the permissible values of this property. The default value of this property depends on the provider selected for the connection being used.

Explicit and implicit calls to the Update method

ADO calls `Update` itself, without your having done so, under several circumstances. If, for example, changes to the current record are pending and you move to a different record without having called the `Update` method, ADO calls the method to save the changes before moving to the next record. If you are familiar with DAO, this might surprise you, because DAO treats this as an error condition. ADO doesn't treat this as an error, but I suggest that you avoid such implicit calls by explicitly calling the `Update` method whenever appropriate. This can help prevent confusion and helps protect your data by ensuring that updates occur only when your code explicitly causes them to happen.

TABLE 29.5   The *Recordset* Object's *LockType* Property

Constant	Description
adLockReadOnly	Default; you can't alter the data in the recordset.
adLockPessimistic	Record locking is invoked at the beginning of the editing process and is released when the `Update` method is called.
AdLockOptimistic	Record locking isn't invoked until the `Update` method is called.

SEE ALSO
➤ *For more information about locking, see page 603*

Use ADO to alter the contents of a recordset

1. Open any *.mdb or *.adp file and open an existing module in design mode, or create a new module.

2. Enter the procedure in Listing 29.4. Note that you should enter either line 8a or 8b, but not both. Whichever one you choose will then have to be modified to meet the conditions of your local installation.

① These Update sequences aren't preceded by an Edit method as is required in DAO. ADO doesn't support the Edit method.

LISTING 29.4   **Using a Recordset's Methods to Alter Its Data**

```
01 Sub basDemoADO4(strBaseID As String, _
      strBaseName As String)
02 Dim rstCustomers As ADODB.Recordset
03 Dim strCnn As String
04 Dim strSQL As String
05 Dim strCriteria As String
06 Dim strCompanyName As String
07
8a strCnn = "Provider=SQLOLEDB; _
        server=Main;uid=sa;pwd=;database=NorthwindCS"
8b strCnn = "Provider=Microsoft.Jet.OLEDB.4.0; _
        Data Source=e:\samples\Northwind.mdb"
09
10 strSQL = "SELECT CustomerID,CompanyName FROM Customers"
11
12 Set rstCustomers = New ADODB.Recordset
13 rstCustomers.LockType = adLockOptimistic
14 rstCustomers.Open strSQL, strCnn, adOpenDynamic
15
16 strCriteria = "CustomerID = '" & strBaseID & "'"
17 rstCustomers.Find strCriteria
18 With rstCustomers
19   If .EOF Then
20     .AddNew
21       !CustomerID = strBaseID
22       !CompanyName = strBaseName
23     .Update
24
25     strCompanyName = !CompanyName
26     Debug.Print strCompanyName
27
28     strCompanyName = StrConv(strCompanyName, vbUpperCase)
29     !CompanyName = strCompanyName
30     .Update
31
32     strCompanyName = !CompanyName
33     Debug.Print strCompanyName
34
35     strCompanyName = StrConv(strCompanyName, vbProperCase)
36     !CompanyName = strCompanyName
37     .Update
```

①

```
38
39    strCompanyName = !CompanyName
40    Debug.Print strCompanyName
41
42    .Delete
43  Else
44    MsgBox "CustomerID '" & strBaseID & _
              "' already exists.", vbOKOnly
45  End If
46 End With
47
48 rstCustomers.Close
49 Set rstCustomers = Nothing
50 End Sub
```

3. Open the Immediate window and enter the line

   ```
   basDemoADO4 "FRANK","Franks Auto & Computer Repair"
   ```

   You should see a message box telling you that the CustomerID 'FRANK' already exists. Click **OK** to clear the message box.

4. Enter the following line in the Immediate window:

   ```
   basDemoADO4 "FKACR","Franks Auto & Computer Repair"
   ```

   The Immediate window should be updated to resemble Figure 29.2.

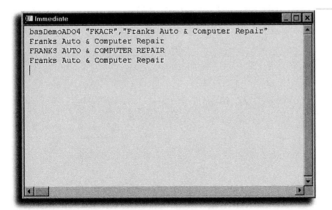

FIGURE 29.2

A new record has been added, updated, changed back again, and then deleted.

Notice line 18 in Listing 29.4. This is the first line of a `With` block that ends on line 46. This `With` statement tells VBA to use the object `rstCustomers` every place where an object is required but omitted. For example, because I used a `With` block, the statements on lines 19–21 are equivalent to

```
If rstCustomers.EOF Then
  rstCustomers.AddNew
    rstCustomers!CustomerID = strBaseID
```

Not only did this save considerable wear and tear on my two typing fingers, but it also improves the efficiency of the VBA code. VBA no longer has to look up the `rstCustomers` object on each of 13 occasions where it's used within the `With` block. Because you used the `With` block construct, it already knows what `rstCustomers` is and where to find it.

Beyond the Desktop

Using Builders, Utilities, and Add-ins to Increase Efficiency

Use the Expression Builder to help create complex expressions

Use database utilities to manage and maintain your database

Use built-in wizards to convert your Access application to a true client/server application

Using the Expression Builder for Complex Expressions

One useful Access tool you've already worked with on occasion throughout the book—the Expression Builder—can be used to construct complicated expressions graphically.

Expressions are any combination of values, functions, constants, fields, and operators that can be evaluated to a single value. You can use expressions in many places throughout Access, but constructing a query is the place where you will probably find the most use for expressions.

You can type any expression that you want directly into the Criteria or Field row of a column in the query design grid. However, you can use the Expression Builder to help build these queries.

Anatomy of the Expression Builder

The Expression Builder is composed of three main parts. You can start the Expression Builder by right-clicking in any criteria or field row of your query open in Design view.

Open the Expression Builder

1. Click the **Queries** tab of your database in the Database window.

2. Select a query to view and click **Design** or start a new query to open that query in Design view.

3. Right-click in the Criteria row of any column and select the **Build** option from the pop-up menu. The Expression Builder window appears (see Figure 30.1).

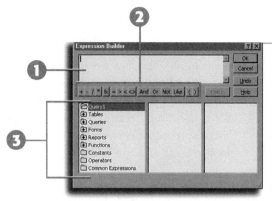

In the Expression Builder, notice the big empty box at the top. This is where the expression you're creating is shown as it's being built. You can use this box to type in any expression that you need, but it's much simpler to build the expression elements that you need graphically by using the components that appear under the empty box.

Directly beneath the Expression box is a row of buttons known as the operator buttons. These buttons are a collection of the most commonly used operators in Access. To use an operator from this collection while constructing your expression, merely click its button. The operator is inserted into the Expression box at the current insertion point.

The bottom half of the Expression Builder contains three list boxes that collectively contain all the expression elements available to you in Access 2000. The list on the left contains a series of folders that contain all the database objects that you can use to create expressions. The folders change depending on the context of the area from which you open the Expression Builder. The database objects that you can use and that are shown in the Expression Elements section of the Expression Builder are as follows:

Tables	User-defined functions
Queries	Constants
Forms	Operators
Reports	Common expressions
Built-in Access 2000 functions	

The middle list box shows the contents of the folder selected in the left list.

The right list box lists the values of the content element selected in the middle list. For example, Figure 30.2 shows the Operators folder highlighted in the left list. The list in the middle shows the various types of operators that you can use to build an expression. And because the Logical element is selected in the middle, the right list shows all the logical operators that can be used to build an expression.

FIGURE 30.2

Select a logical operator from the Expression Builder.

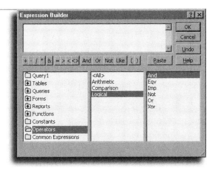

Using the Expression Builder to Build Criteria

You can use the Expression Builder to build quite complicated expressions to use as criteria in your queries. You could calculate a date and use that as a criterion or use part of a field's value as criteria. For the example in this section, you will implement the Expression Builder to build a calculated date for use as criteria for your queries.

Construct a query that uses a calculated date

1. Open a new query, select **Design View**, and click **OK**.

2. Double-click the Orders and Customers tables to add them to your query. Then click the **Close** button to close the Show Tables dialog box.

3. For this example, you're building a query that returns a resultset composed of all customers who had orders in 1996 and whose orders that year took longer than 15 days to process (from receiving the order to shipping the order). Drag the OrderID, OrderDate, and ShippedDate fields down to the design grid from the Orders table. Drag the CompanyName field from the Customers table to the design grid.

4. To assign a criterion to the OrderDate and ShippedDate fields, right-click in the Criteria row of the OrderDate field and select **Build** from the pop-up menu.

5. When the Expression Builder appears, double-click the **Functions** folder in the bottom left list box. Then click the **Built-In Functions** folder that appears within this same list.

6. Click **Date/Time** in the middle list. Then scroll through the right list until you see **Year**. Double-click **Year** to add this function to your expression. Your Expression Builder should resemble the one in Figure 30.3.

Join indicators

Using this expression implies a join between the tables you're querying. If you don't have a join indicator between the two tables in the field listing box, refer to Chapter 11, "Defining and Working with Relationships."

FIGURE 30.3

Build a Date/Time expression with the Year function.

7. Highlight <<number>> and then double-click the **Tables** folder in the left list box.

8. Click the Orders folder underneath the Tables folder, and then click the **OrderDate** element in the middle list. Go to the right list box and double-click <Value> to replace the placeholder in your expression with the value contained in the Orders table's OrderDate field. Your Expression Builder should now resemble the one in Figure 30.4.

Placeholders in expressions

The <<>> brackets enclosing the word **number** in the Expression box indicate that you need to replace that placeholder with a real value.

FIGURE 30.4

The Year function with the
fields and operators for the
expression.

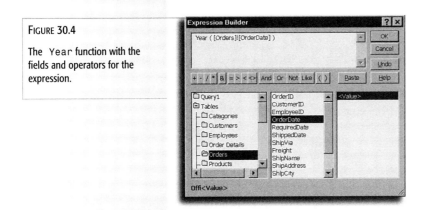

9. Click at the end of the expression you've built so far, and then click the **=** button. Type 1996 into the Expression box and click **OK**.

10. Go to the Criteria row of the OrderDate column in the query design grid to view the expression you just created.

11. If you can't view the expression in its entirety, right-click the Criteria row and select **Zoom** from the pop-up menu. A window appears that contains your newly created expression (see Figure 30.5). This criteria limits the resultset to orders placed in 1996. Click **OK** to return to the design grid.

FIGURE 30.5

Use the Zoom dialog box to view
the whole expression.

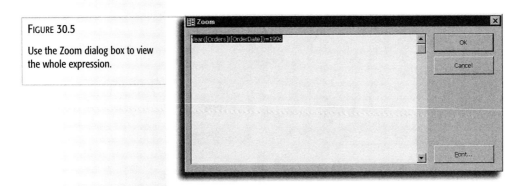

12. To set the criteria for the ShippedDate field, right-click in its Criteria row and activate the Expression Builder.

13. Again, double-click the **Functions** folder in the left list box, and then click the **Built-In Functions** folder. Click **Date/Time** in the middle list box. Double-click the DateAdd function in the right list box to add this function to your expression. Your Expression Builder should appear like the one shown in Figure 30.6.

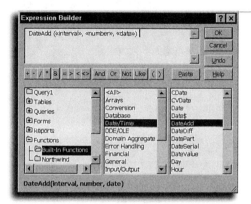

FIGURE 30.6
Again, the placeholders that you need to replace are shown enclosed by <<>> brackets.

14. The DateAdd function enables you to calculate a date by adding a specified time interval. Because you're trying to find all the orders that took more than 15 days to process, you need to use days as your time interval. In the DateAdd function, days are represented by the letter d. Replace <<interval>> with the letter "d" (including the quotation marks).

15. Replace <<number>> with the number 15.

16. Because you're calculating the ship dates that were more than 15 days later than the corresponding Order Dates, you need to use the value contained in the OrderDate field of the Orders table to replace the <<date>> placeholder. Thus, replace <<date>> with the OrderDate field value. (For help with this, refer to step 8.)

17. Because you're trying to find all orders that were greater than 15 days in processing, you need to add a greater than sign to the front of your expression. Click in front of your expression to set the insertion point and click the **>** button.

18. The Expression Builder should now resemble the one in Figure 30.7. Click **OK**.

FIGURE 30.7

Viewing your second expression.

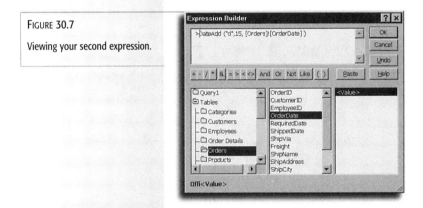

19. Click the **View** icon 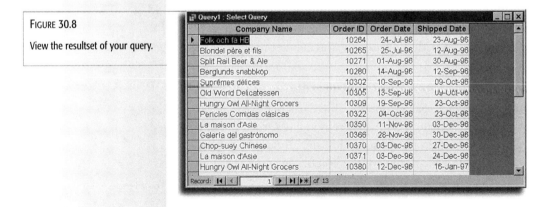. You should see a resultset similar to the one in Figure 30.8. And as you can see, 13 orders were placed in 1996 that took longer than 15 days to process.

FIGURE 30.8

View the resultset of your query.

The query that you just created with the aid of the Expression Builder is equivalent to the following SQL query:

```
SELECT Customers.CompanyName, Orders.OrderID,
Orders.OrderDate, Orders.ShippedDate
FROM Customers INNER JOIN Orders
ON Customers.CustomerID = Orders.CustomerID
WHERE (((Orders.ShippedDate)
>DateAdd("d",15,[Orders]![OrderDate]))
AND ((Year([Orders]![OrderDate]))=1996));
```

Although this isn't the best way to learn SQL, the automatic creation of SQL from a query can be a good starting point. You can understand the basic logic of how these operators work. For example, the query uses a WHERE clause to continue checking through each record until the condition is met for each criteria. The code also shows the JOIN relationship between the related fields in the two tables.

Using Access Database Utilities

Access 2000 includes a number of utilities to help you maintain and manipulate your application. You can find several of these utilities by choosing **Database Utilities** from the **Tools** menu.

The Compact and Repair Database Utility

You might have noticed that as you work with your database, the .mdb file seems to grow, sometimes for reasons that seem a bit mysterious. You would expect the file to get larger as you add records, new forms, queries, and whatnot, but why doesn't it get smaller if you delete objects? And why does the file grow when you haven't intentionally created any new objects or added new data records?

When data records or Access objects are deleted from your database, the disk space they occupied isn't freed up for other use—it just isn't used at all anymore. Also, Access often must create temporary objects that it uses long enough to perform the tasks you requested and then deletes them. This adds to the growth of your database.

The most common use of the Compact and Repair Database utility is to recover this lost disk space, shrinking the size of your .mdb file in the process. The utility also has another function—to repair .mdb files that might have become damaged, perhaps by your computer shutting down unexpectedly.

You can start the Compact and Repair Database utility before or after you open a database by choosing **Database Utilities** and then **Compact and Repair Database** from the **Tools** menu:

- If it's started before your database is opened, you are prompted for the path of the file to be compacted and for the path and name of an .mdb file in which to store the results.

- If it's started after your database is opened, that's all you have to do. The work proceeds without further prompting. The status bar is used to keep you informed of its progress. If all goes well, control is simply returned to you when the work is completed.

Database Splitter

Chapter 33, "Multiuser Considerations," discusses splitting an Access database into two different databases—one to contain the data itself, the other to contain the remaining application objects. The Database Splitter utility provides an easy way to accomplish this task.

Use the Database Splitter utility

1. Open the database you want to split into two databases. For this example, I'm using a database named db3.mdb (created by compacting the Northwind.mdb database into db3.mdb).

2. From the **Tools** menu choose **Database Utilities** and then **Database Splitter**. The dialog box in Figure 30.9 appears.

Do you have a current backup?

Be sure to have a current backup of your file before using your .mdb file as the source and the target file of a compact and repair operation. For example, if you want to compact db1.mdb, save the result into db2.mdb. Then, if all goes well, compact db1.mdb again, but this time save the result into db1.mdb. This protects you in case something goes wrong, and gives you a current backup copy of your database at the same time. Note that this two-step process isn't possible when running the Compact and Repair Database utility while your database is open because it doesn't prompt you for a source or target file name.

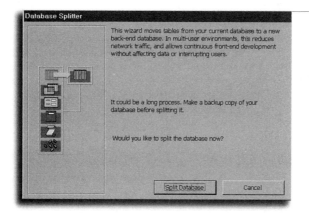

3. Click the **Split Database** button. You're asked to provide a name and location for the back-end database, where all your tables will be stored. For this example, accept the default name, db3_be.mdb. Click the **Split** button when you're done.

4. The utility displays a dialog box when it completes. Click **OK** to return to your database. Notice in Figure 30.10 that the icons for all the tables indicate that they are now linked tables, not local tables.

FIGURE 30.10

All the local tables have been deleted, and links have been established to the new tables in db3_be.mdb.

Linked Table Manager

In the preceding section, you split the db3.mdb database and linked to a set of tables located in the newly created db3_be.mdb database. The information Access requires to manage these links is maintained in the properties of the local objects representing the tables. Figure 30.11 shows this for the Customers table.

FIGURE 30.11

The properties of a local table object for a linked table includes the path to the actual table containing the data.

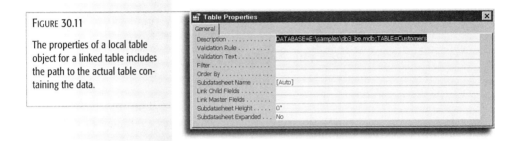

This is all fine and dandy as long as the database containing the linked tables stays put. But if you want to move it, that's where the Linked Table Manager comes in. This utility makes it easy to re-establish links to tables if the stored path isn't valid. In the following example, assume that the path to db3_be.mdb has changed from E:\Samples\db3_be.mdb to e:\Samples\temp\db3_be.mdb. Thus, Access can no longer find the tables where it expects them. If you try to open a table, an error message appears (see Figure 30.12).

FIGURE 30.12

The linked tables are no longer where Access expects to find them.

Use the Linked Table Manager

1. From the **Tools** menu choose **Database Utilities** and then **Linked Table Manager**. The dialog box in Figure 30.13 appears. Because you need to relink all the tables shown, click the **Select All** button and then **OK**.

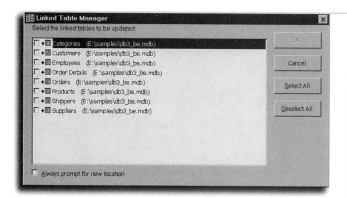

FIGURE 30.13
The Linked Table Manager displays a list of all table objects that represent a linked table.

2. Use the next dialog box to point to the path to the back-end database. The Linked Table Manager issues a message when it has completed. Click **OK**.

3. The dialog box shown in Figure 30.13 reappears, but this time simply click the **Close** button. All the tables are now linked correctly again.

Switchboard Manager

The Switchboard Manager creates and manages forms for your database application that contain buttons to open forms, reports, run macros or code, go to other switchboards, and exit Access. When you create a database by using the database wizards, Access makes switchboards similar to the ones you can create in the Switchboard Manager.

Create a new switchboard

1. Open the database in which you want to create a switchboard. For this example, I'm using a database named db3.mdb (created by compacting the Northwind.mdb database). From the **Tools** menu, choose **Database Utilities** and then **Switchboard Manager**.

2. A dialog box appears, asking if you would like to create a switchboard. Click **Yes**.

3. Another dialog box appears (see Figure 30.14), listing any switchboard forms that might exist in your database. In this example none exist yet, so the only one shown is the default name for a new switchboard. Accept the default name, and begin building your new switchboard by clicking **Edit**.

FIGURE 30.14

FIGURE 30.14

The Switchboard Manager lists all switchboard forms it finds in the database.

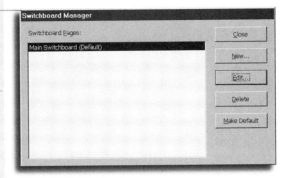

4. The dialog box in Figure 30.15 is where the real work to build the switchboard takes place. Because the new switchboard is still empty, the only available options are to add a new item or to close the dialog box. Add several items to the switchboard by clicking **New**.

FIGURE 30.15

The Edit Switchboard Page dialog box allows you to add new items to the switchboard or to edit existing items.

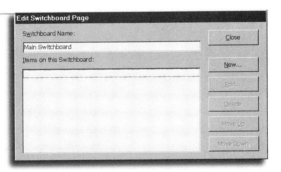

5. Use the Edit Switchboard Item dialog box to add several command buttons to the switchboard. Begin by adding a command button that opens the Customers form. First, you need to give the button a name, which is displayed on the actual command button when it's created. In the **Text** box, enter Review Customers.

6. Select **Open Form in Edit Mode** from the **Command** combo box, and select **Customers** as the form name from the **Form** combo box. Your dialog box should resemble Figure 30.16. Click **OK** when you're finished.

FIGURE 30.16

A command button to open the Customers form has been defined.

7. Continue the process of adding command buttons to the Main Switchboard by clicking **New** again, or edit any buttons that you've already added. Often, however, the resulting switchboard becomes very cluttered if you simply continue to add more command buttons. To avoid such clutter or to help you organize your application, the Switchboard Manager Wizard provides an alternative. You can create additional switchboards that can be invoked by other switchboards. To demonstrate this, click **Close** in the Edit Switchboard Page dialog box to return to the Switchboard Manager dialog box (refer to Figure 30.14).

8. In the Switchboard Manager dialog box, click **New**. The Create New dialog box appears. Enter Reports as the **Switchboard Page Name** (see Figure 30.17). Click **OK** to continue.

FIGURE 30.17

Add a second switchboard page, named Reports, to the Main Switchboard.

9. You now have a second switchboard page named Reports. Edit the page by using the same basic technique in steps 3–7. Begin by selecting **Reports** and clicking **Edit**.

10. The Edit Switchboard Page dialog box reappears. Because you want to add a new command button, click **New**.

11. Use the Edit Switchboard Item dialog box to create a command button labeled **Sales by Category** that opens a report by the same name. The result should resemble Figure 30.18. Click **OK** when you're done, and then click **Close** in the Edit Switchboard Page dialog box.

FIGURE 30.18

Add a command button to open a report.

12. Add a button to the Main Switchboard that opens the Reports switchboard page. Select **Main Switchboard** in the Switchboard Manager dialog box and click **Edit**.

13. Because you want to add an item to the Main Switchboard, click **New**.

14. Update the Edit Switchboard Item dialog box until it resembles Figure 30.19.

FIGURE 30.19

Add the Reports switchboard page to the Main Switchboard.

15. When ready, close the Edit Switchboard Item, Edit Switchboard Page, and the Switchboard Manager dialog boxes.

16. To try out your new switchboard, open the form named Switchboard. Your switchboard should resemble that shown in Figure 30.20.

FIGURE 30.20

Your new switchboard, with two entries.

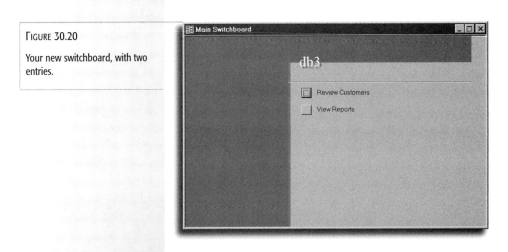

The Upsizing Wizard

The Upsizing Wizard performs a function similar to that pre-formed by the Database Splitter, except that the Upsizing Wizard moves your tables to a Microsoft SQL Server database or to the new Microsoft Data Engine instead of another Jet database or .mdb file. This makes it much easier to upgrade your application to a client/server environment. See Chapter 33, "Multiuser Considerations," for additional information on client/server.

SQL 7

With the purchase of Office Premium or Developer edition, you will receive a desktop version of MSSQL 7, known as MSDE—Microsoft Data Engine. You can find the program on your CD in the SQL\X86\ SETUP\MSDE directory. MSDE is now optimized for five connections.

Use the Upsizing Wizard

1. From the **Tools** menu, choose **Database Utilities** and then **Upsizing Wizard**. A dialog box similar to the one in Figure 30.21 appears. In this example accept the default, a new database. Click **Next** when you're done.

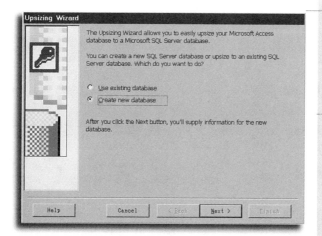

FIGURE 30.21

You can use the Upsizing Wizard to upsize your application to an existing or new SQL Server database, or to a Microsoft Data Engine database.

2. In the next dialog box (see Figure 30.22), provide the name of an available SQL server, the user ID and password of a user with authority to create new databases on the server, and the name of the database that holds your data. Click **Next** when you're ready to go on.

FIGURE 30.22

Provide the name of the SQL server, a user ID and password, and the name of the database to be created.

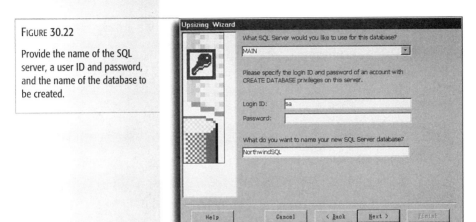

3. Select the tables you want to export to the server. In this example, I selected all the tables. Click **Next** when you're done to display the dialog box shown in Figure 30.23.

FIGURE 30.23

All tables are selected for export to the SQL Server database.

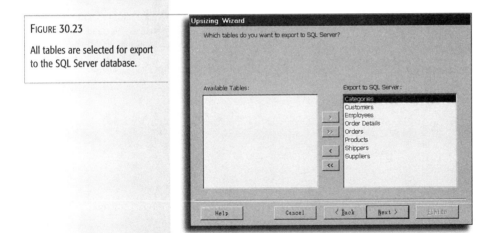

4. The wizard now gives you several choices about how much information from your existing tables should be converted and exported to the server (see Figure 30.24). Make your selections or accept the defaults, and then click **Next**.

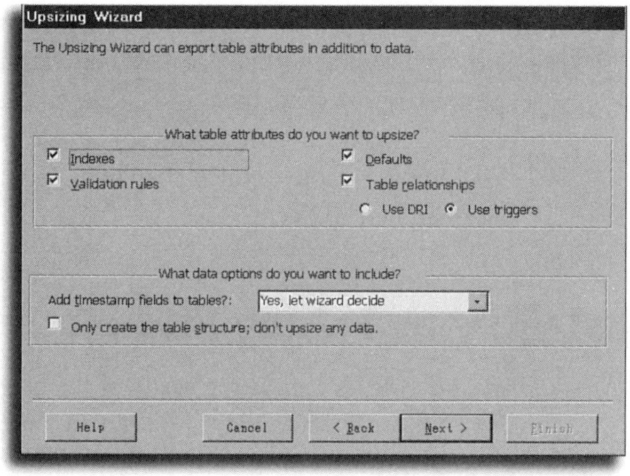

FIGURE 30.24

Select which properties of your existing Access tables should be exported to the new server tables.

5. The dialog box in Figure 30.25 lets you choose an application design. The first option doesn't change your existing application at all, but just copies your table to the SQL Server database. The second and third options let you choose between using your existing application and linking to the new server tables, or creating a completely new client/server application or an Access Project (an .adp file). (For more information about linked tables or Access Projects, see Chapters 33 and 34, respectively.) For this example, select the third option (the default) to create an Access Project. Click **Next**.

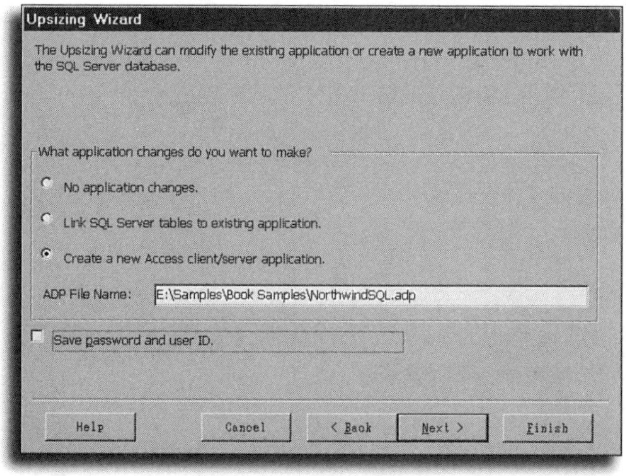

FIGURE 30.25

Select the organization of your application.

6. The wizard has collected all the information it needs. Click **Finish** to complete the upsizing. This step might take several minutes, so be patient. When the wizard is done, a report is displayed with details of the actions taken. You should now be able to open your new Access Project, in this case named db4CS.adp.

Installing and Using Add-ins

Add-ins are utilities that weren't part of the original core functionality of Access. They add to the functionality of the database. Some functionality that had previously been an add-in has since been added to the core functionality of Access 2000. An *add-in* is a library with its code and database objects stored in a database file that usually has an .mda extension.

Add-ins are available from Microsoft, third parties, and even other individuals who have made small utilities that make developing and designing in Access a little easier.

Managing Add-ins with the Add-in Manager

The Add-in Manager provides a user interface to install or uninstall any add-in written for Access.

You can start the Add-In Manager from the **Tools** menu by choosing **Add-Ins** and then **Add-In Manager**. If you look at Figure 30.26, notice the list of add-ins available through the menu. If you haven't installed any add-ins yourself, the list is empty except for the Add-In Manager.

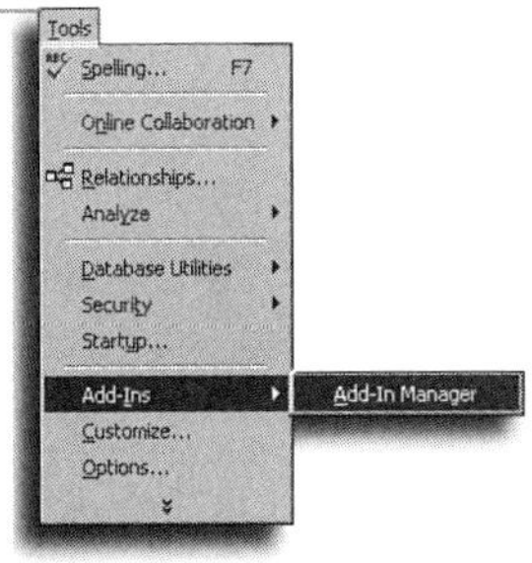

FIGURE 30.26

The menu shows the list of available menu add-ins, including any that you've downloaded and installed.

When you start the Add-In Manager, a dialog box appears with a list of available add-ins. These can be add-ins that you installed at an earlier date; in some cases, nothing will be in the list, as shown in Figure 30.27.

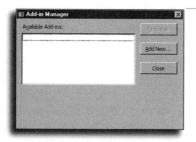

FIGURE 30.27

The Add-in Manager keeps track of what's installed or uninstalled.

If an add-in is installed, an × will be on the same line as the add-in name. By the same token, if an add-in isn't installed, no × will be next to the name.

Install a new add-in

1. From the **Tools** menu, choose **Add-in Manager** and then **Add-ins** to open the Add-in Manager dialog box.

2. Click the **Add New** button. An Open dialog box appears, prompting you for the location of the add-in that you want to make available.

3. Find the file that you want to add. The new add-in is installed and added to the list of available add-ins.

When you install an add-in, it generally inserts a menu item under the **Tools** menu's **Add-Ins** submenu. This is how you start the add-in. The add-in list shows all available add-ins as mentioned before.

Access on the Internet

Add hyperlinks to your databases

Use Access to create static Web pages from your data

Create live-data Web pages with Access

Export data to the Web

How Access and the Web Unite

The original intent of the World Wide Web (commonly referred to simply as "the Web") was to provide scientists with a mechanism for sharing documents across various computer systems. A scientist could publish a *hypertext document* (which contains links to other documents or to sections within the document itself, allowing the viewer to quickly move from one document to another) on a server machine connected to a network; others could then view this document on their own machines. These hypertext documents are written in a format called *Hypertext Markup Language (HTML)*, a text-based encoding of documents that uses tags to specify how the contents should be displayed to viewers. To view an HTML page, the users employ a specialized browser application that interprets the HTML and displays a representation of the page onscreen.

Interchanging terms

Although not technically correct, I use the terms *Web* and *Internet* interchangeably in this chapter.

Although most people equate the Web with the Internet, the Internet actually predates the Web by a number of years. The Internet, developed initially as a government resource, eventually found its way to the academic world. It was only with the development of HTML and the birth of the Web that the Internet world became generally known to the public. Many people still are unfamiliar with such Internet features as FTP, Gopher, Archie, Veronica, and Finger.

The Web quickly gained acceptance after its public introduction in 1991 and is now an essential element of most businesses. Almost all medium- and large-sized companies today have at least a presence on the Web through a home page, if not a dedicated Web server hosting hundreds of HTML pages. The number of Web pages in place today is astronomical. This isn't to say that all these pages serve a useful purpose—in fact, the vast majority probably don't.

Hyperlinks Within Access

Access lets you create fields and set up form controls that can provide hyperlinks to documents on your computer, on a machine accessible across your LAN or intranet, or on the Web. The steps required to create a link to a document don't change no matter where the linked document resides (on your machine, on the LAN, or on the Web). The address or path you use to specify the location of the document will change, of course, but the methods used will be the same.

Working with Document Addresses in Hyperlinks

While we're on the subject of document location, take a quick look at the various ways you can specify the address (or location) of an object on a networked computer. Table 31.1 describes the three most common methods. Notice that your computer is lumped into the group of networked computers. With Internet Explorer, even a detached, standalone computer is considered to be network-addressable by the operating system.

TABLE 31.1   **Document Addressing Methods**

Location	Method	Example
Your computer	Local path	`c:\My Documents\sales.doc`
LAN	UNC	`\\FileServer\marketing\sales.doc`
Intranet Web server	URL	`http://FileServer/marketing/sales.htm`
Internet Web server	URL	`http://www.myco.com/marketing/sales.htm`

A *uniform resource locator* (URL) specifies an object's location on the Internet. It typically takes the form `protocol:address`, as shown in Table 31.1. The `//` portion indicates that what follows is the *hostname* (a unique name identifying the computer on a network) for the server on which the object is located. Some forms of URLs don't specify a hostname, such as `mailto:craig.eddy@cyberdude.com` or `news:microsoft.public.access.internet`.

A *uniform naming convention* (UNC) specifies the location of an object (typically a file) on a PC network. The format is typically `\\servername\sharename\document`, where *servername* is the host-name of the network server, *sharename* is the name given to the shared (or networked) directory, and *document* specifies the exact name of the object in question.

Creating Hyperlink Fields

To link records in an Access database to objects on a network, you create hyperlink fields to hold the addresses of the linked objects.

Add a hyperlink field to an existing table

1. From the Database window, select the table to which you want to add the hyperlink data and click **Design**. For example, to add a Web address field to the Customers table in the Northwind database, select the table on the Tables view of the Database window and click **Design**.

2. Scroll the Design window until you come to an empty row.

3. Enter a name for the field, such as `WebPage`, in the **Field Name** column.

4. Click in or tab to the **Data Type** column. From the drop-down list of field data types, select **Hyperlink**.

5. Press **Tab** again to move to the **Description** column. Enter a description if appropriate (and it usually is).

6. On the General Properties section at the bottom, enter a **Caption**.

7. Save the new table design by choosing **Save** from the **File** menu or by clicking 🖫 .

When you're finished, your screen should resemble Figure 31.1.

Setting a default address

Setting a default value for the address usually isn't applicable, but in certain cases—such as a product catalog in which all addresses begin the same way—it can reduce the number of keystrokes. At other times, you might want to set a default to a home page so that if no specific address is entered, your user won't click a dead link, or can at least start from a general beginning point rather than have no link at all.

Limitations of the Hyperlink data type

You can't index tables by using hyperlink fields. Also, the Lookup page is blank, meaning that you can't retrieve the data for a hyperlink field from another table or query.

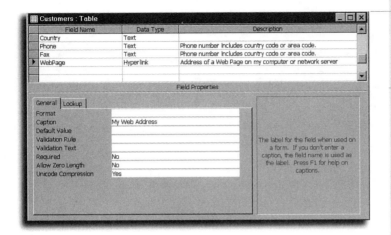

FIGURE 31.1

A hyperlink field added to the Customers table of the Northwind Traders database.

SEE ALSO

➤ For more information about creating fields, see page 63

➤ For more information about using naming conventions for your fields, see page 31

Adding Hyperlink Data

Now that you have a hyperlink field in a table, look at the various ways you can get data into that field. As usual, Access provides several means of accomplishing the same end.

The simplest method for adding the address to a hyperlink field is to just type it into Datasheet view. As soon as you start typing in a hyperlink field, the data appears as a hyperlink (usually underlined text with a blue foreground color—the actual color is determined by your browser options), as shown in Figure 31.2.

Until you save the updated row, the cursor remains the I-beam (text edit) cursor. If you allow the cursor to hover above a hyperlink after the row is saved, it changes to the hand cursor. Any clicking you do causes Access to "follow" the hyperlink, loading the referenced object into its default browser or application. To edit the data at that point, you need to use the keyboard to set focus to the field and then press **F2** to edit the data.

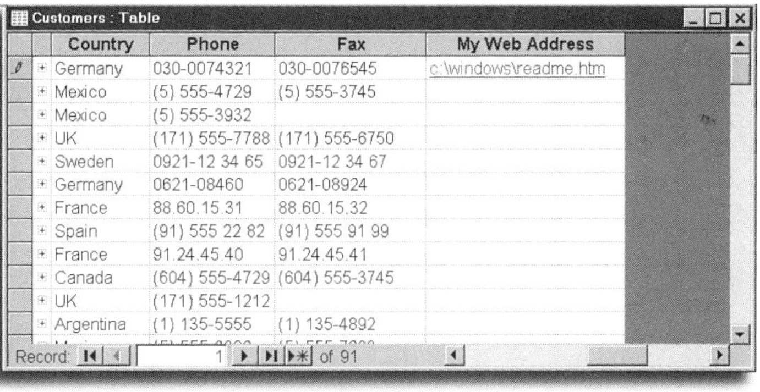

<!-- Figure 31.2 screenshot -->

FIGURE 31.2

Entering hyperlink data using the table's Datasheet view.

Using hyperlink data in VBA and SQL

Access provides a function named `HyperlinkPart` that returns a specific portion of the hyperlink field's data. You can use this function in Visual Basic for Applications code or in a SQL query. For example, to work with the displayed value of a hyperlink, you would use `HyperlinkPart(Customers.WebPage,acDisplayedValue)`.

You can enter a hyperlink strictly as an address, or you can enter a displayed value portion and an address. Hyperlink data takes the form of

displaytext#address#subaddress

The *displaytext* portion is the text that you see when the data is displayed in a field or control, the *address* is the address of the document or object, and the *subaddress* points to a specific location within the file or page referenced in the *address*.

To enter hyperlink data for Microsoft's Home Page, for example, you can enter Microsoft Home Page#http://www.microsoft.com (see Figure 31.3). After you enter this data and save the record, the field displays only Microsoft Home Page (see Figure 31.4).

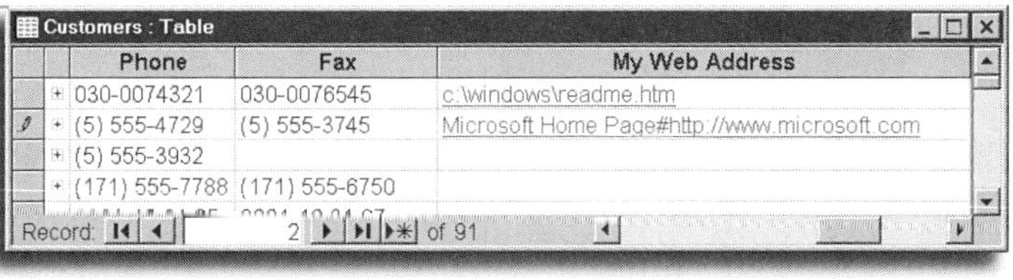

FIGURE 31.3

You can see the *displaytext* and *address* portions because this record is still being edited.

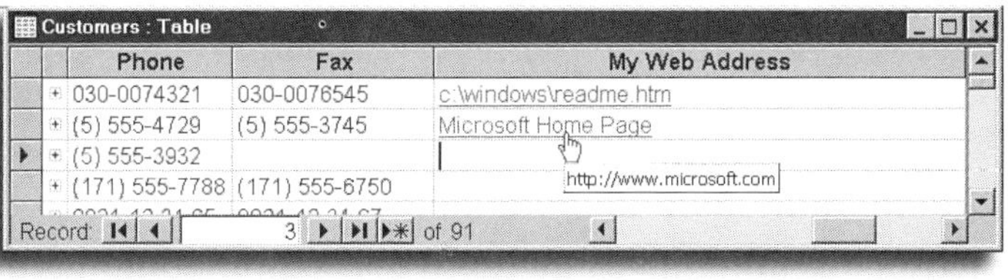

FIGURE 31.4

Access abbreviates the *displaytext* portion of the address. The hand cursor activates the link rather than lets you edit the address.

To edit the hyperlink in Figure 31.4, you can use the keyboard to set focus to the field and press **F2**, or you can use the following steps.

Edit hyperlink field data

1. Right-click the hyperlink you want to edit and choose **Hyperlink**. The fly-out menu shown in Figure 31.5 appears.

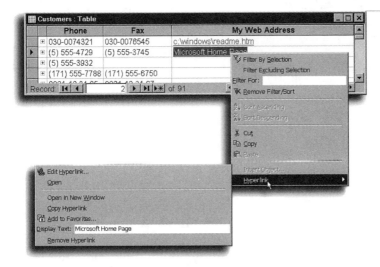

FIGURE 31.5

The menu for editing hyperlink field data.

2. To edit the *address* and *subaddress* portions or to remove the hyperlink altogether, choose **Edit Hyperlink**. The Edit Hyperlink dialog box appears (see Figure 31.6).

3. In the topmost text box, you can edit the display portion of the hyperlink. The dialog box offers a large number of choices for locating the proper address to link to.

4. Use the **Remove Link** button to empty the field's data completely. Use this to delete the hyperlink, displayed text and all other data.

Edit the displayed text of the hyperlink field

To edit the displayed text (Microsoft Home Page), click in the text box next to **Display Text** and edit the text as you would in any text box. To make the changes stick, click outside the menu or press **Enter**. To revert back to the original text, press **Esc**.

FIGURE 31.6

In the Edit Hyperlink dialog box, you edit the *address* and *subaddress* portions of a hyperlink.

Browsing for hyperlink data

If you're using Internet Explorer, you can browse to the Web page whose address you're interested in storing and insert it directly into your hyperlink field. Simply go to a record with empty hyperlink data. From the **Insert** menu choose **Hyperlink** to open the Edit Hyperlink dialog box. Switch to Internet Explorer, browse to the page whose URL you want to insert into the field, and switch back to Access. The hyperlink data will be filled in for you!

The other menu items on the Hyperlink fly-out menu perform various functions, such as launching the default Web browser with the selected hyperlink, adding the hyperlink to your Favorites list, and copying a shortcut to the hyperlink to the Windows Clipboard.

You can also use the Edit Hyperlink dialog box to enter hyperlink data into an empty field. Simply use the Hyperlink fly-out menu and choose **Edit Hyperlink**. The same dialog box appears, except that the caption will change to Insert Hyperlink and the **Remove Link** button won't be visible.

Adding Hyperlinks to Forms and Reports

Datasheet view isn't the only place where you can edit and view hyperlink data. You can link form controls to hyperlink fields, allowing form users to launch their browsers pointing to the address specified in the record. You can also manipulate the Hyperlink Address property available on many controls, allowing you to link those controls to a specific (or programmatically controlled) document. For example, you might link the label control on a form to an HTML document describing the form. (The label control that's placed on a form when you add a bound field to it doesn't support the Hyperlink Address property, though, so you must manually add such a control with the techniques discussed here.)

Add a bound hyperlink field to a form

1. Select the form to which you want to add the hyperlink and open it in Design view. For example, to put the WebPage field added earlier to the Customers table onto the Customers form, select that form in the Database window and click the **Design** button.

2. Open the Field List window (if it's not already opened) by choosing **Field List** from the **View** menu or clicking ▣.

3. Drag the hyperlink field from the **Field List** onto the form, dropping it in the appropriate location. Resize and position the form control to match the rest of the form.

Figure 31.7 shows the Design view results of adding the WebPage field to the Customers form. You can tell that it's a hyperlink field because the field name text box is the typical hyperlink text (blue foreground and underlined).

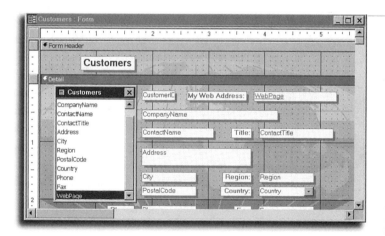

FIGURE 31.7

A form in Design view with a bound hyperlink field added.

SEE ALSO

➤ *To see how to resize controls, see page 267*

To see the link in action, switch to Form view. From there, you can right-click the hyperlink field and have access to the same **Hyperlink** fly-out menu described in the preceding section.

The following steps describe how to add unbound hyperlink controls to your forms. The first is a label control linked to a specific bookmark in an HTML page describing the form. The second is a button linked to that same HTML page, but not to a bookmark on the page.

Add unbound hyperlink controls to a form

1. Open the form (in this case, the Customers form) in Design view.

2. To add the hyperlink to a label for an existing bound control, first delete the label control that was inserted with the bound control. For example, link the label attached to the CustomerID field to a Web page describing the fields on this form. Delete the Customer ID label control.

3. If necessary, open the Toolbox by choosing **Toolbox** from the **View** menu or clicking ![icon]. Click ![Aa] in the Toolbox, click the form where you want to place the label, and drag the label into shape.

4. Type a caption for the label (such as Customer ID:), committing your new caption by pressing **Enter** or clicking elsewhere on the form. Position and size the label appropriately.

5. Click the **Properties** icon ![icon], and select the **Format** or **All** tab to edit the hyperlink data for the control. The Hyperlink Address and Hyperlink SubAddress properties are the ones in question (see the section "Editing Hyperlink Data" for the format of these properties). You can type directly into the text boxes or use the **Builder** button to launch the Insert Hyperlink dialog box.

6. In the Hyperlink Address property, enter C:\MSOffice2000\Office\Samples\Customers.htm, replacing the URL with the one appropriate to your situation.

   In the Hyperlink SubAddress property, enter the bookmark in the page appropriate for the field to which you're attaching the label. For example, in my Web page I have a bookmark for each form field that matches the field name in the Customers table. So for the CustomerID field, I have a bookmark named CustomerID. I'll enter CustomerID into the Hyperlink SubAddress property. Figure 31.8 shows the results so far.

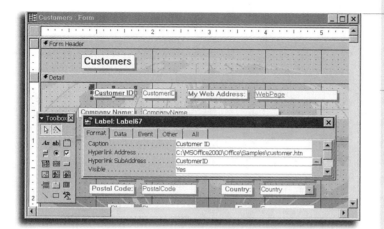

FIGURE 31.8

A form in Design view with an unbound label control that has its hyperlink properties set.

7. Repeat steps 2 through 6 for any other controls you want to provide with this capability. The simplest way to do this is to copy and paste the label control, editing the caption and hyperlink properties. To edit the hyperlink without using the Properties sheet, right-click the control and use the standard Hyperlink fly-out menu.

8. Add a hyperlink command button to the form. This button launches the Web page without specifying a bookmark. Click the **Command Button** control ◻ in the Toolbox, click the form where you want to place the button, and drag the control into place on the form.

9. Give the command button an appropriate caption, such as Help, and press **Enter**. Return to the Properties sheet and enter the URL for the page in the Hyperlink Address property. Because this is intended to be help for the entire form, don't bother with the Hyperlink SubAddress property. For the Customers form, I entered http://localhost/customers.htm.

10. Save the form.

Figure 31.9 shows the results of the preceding steps in Design view. Clicking a hyperlink label causes the Web page in Figure 31.10 to appear at the appropriate bookmark. Clicking the button launches the same page, but the browser positions the display at the top of the page.

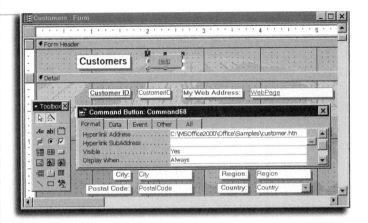

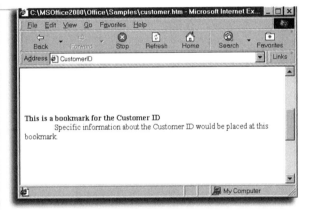

SEE ALSO

➤ *Learn more about the Toolbox on page 256*

➤ *Get more information on positioning and sizing controls on pages 265*

➤ *Learn more about working with forms in Design view on page 108*

➤ *See how to set properties on page 111*

➤ *Learn more about working with reports on page 130*

Web-Publishing Basics

In Access, you can publish your data to the Web in several ways. You can publish *static* or *dynamic* data. Static pages never change—they always display the same data. Dynamic pages, however, generate queries against your Access databases and produce Web pages on-the-fly, using current data from the database.

You can create static Web pages from a single database object by exporting. You can create *Data Access Pages*, the new term for dynamic pages, by using a wizard, using AutoPage, or creating one from scratch. Data Access Pages can use more than one database object as their record source.

Creating an HTML Template File

When you create Web content by using any Access exporting tool, you can specify an HTML template file to be used as a starting point when creating the Web pages. This template file allows you to use your own standards for the Web page to be created. You can add graphics, such as company logos and backgrounds, as well as specify text colors, link colors, and background colors.

You can use any text editor or even a specialized HTML editor such as Microsoft FrontPage to create the HTML template file. Store it in a common directory so that you'll have no trouble locating it when it's time to publish some Web content. A sample template for the Northwind Traders database is installed in the same directory as the .mdb file. Named NWINDTEM.HTM, it can be opened through Internet Explorer (see Figure 31.11) or Notepad.

In addition to HTML code, template files can also contain tokens that Access replaces with appropriate material (see Table 31.2).

Create your own template file for consistency

If you'll be using the Export to HTML features often, you should probably create a template file or two to provide a consistent look and feel across all your Web pages.

FIGURE 31.11

The Northwind Traders HTML
template displayed in Internet
Explorer.

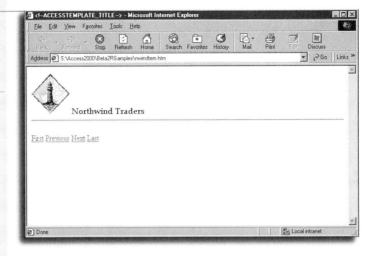

TABLE 31.2   **HTML Template File Tokens**

Token	Replacement
`<!--AccessTemplate_Title-->`	The object name is placed in the Web browser's title bar
`<!--AccessTemplate_Body-->`	The exported data
`<!--AccessTemplate_FirstPage-->`	A link to the first page
`<!--AccessTemplate_PreviousPage-->`	A link to the previous page
`<!--AccessTemplate_NextPage-->`	A link to the next page
`<!--AccessTemplate_LastPage-->`	A link to the last page
`<!--AccessTemplate_PageNumber-->`	The current page number

Exporting Static Web Pages

The simplest, quickest way to create a static Web page from a
database object is to use the Export method. This creates a Web
page based on a single table, query, form, or report in the current database. You can use a template file here as well, but typically this feature is used as a one-shot, quick-and-dirty
mechanism for producing an HTML file containing the current
contents of the database.

Export a database object to an HTML file

1. In the Database window, select the table, query, form, or
   report that you want to save in HTML format.

2. From the **File** menu, choose **Export**.

3. In the Save dialog box, select **HTML Documents (*.html;*.htm)** from the **Save as Type** drop-down list.

4. Select the location and name to save the HTML file to. If you want to use an HTML template file, select the **Save Formatted** check box. Click the **Export** button.

5. If you selected the **Save Formatted** box in step 4, a dialog box appears in which you specify the location of the template file. You can type the filename or use the **Browse** button to locate the template through the familiar file dialog.

6. The HTML file is created in the location you specified. You can use Internet Explorer to view its contents.

Figure 31.12 shows the Customers table from the Northwind Traders database exported without using a template file. Figure 31.13 shows the same table, but this time using the NWINDTEM.HTM template file. Notice that the template-created file has a better look and feel than the straight export. The most important difference is the column headings displayed when using the template file.

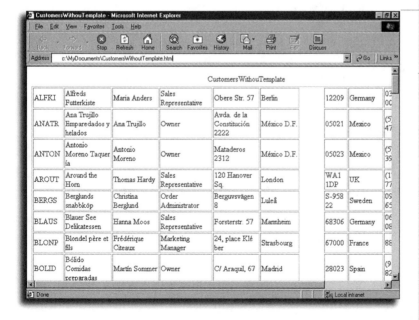

FIGURE 31.12

The Customers table exported to HTML without a template.

FIGURE 31.12

The Customers table exported to HTML using the Northwind sample template.

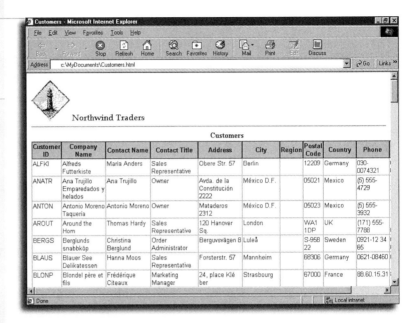

Working with Data Access Pages

A new type of object in the Database window is the Pages object (see Figure 31.14).

FIGURE 31.14

The new Pages Object in the database container.

Access provides two easy ways to create Data Access Pages (dynamic data) for the Web:

- You can use AutoPage, which creates a Web page that uses all the fields from a record source.

- You can use a wizard, which lets you have more control over what your pages will look like.

With either method, you can always change the resulting page in design mode.

Although similar to the manual process, using the Page Wizard gives you greater flexibility. You can select multiple tables, queries, forms, and reports to export, and you can automatically launch the Page Wizard to transfer your HTML pages to a Web server.

The following sections describe how to use AutoPage or the wizard to create Data Access Pages.

Using AutoPage

AutoPage allows you to quickly create a dynamic Web page for displaying and entering your data on the Web.

Create a dynamic data page with AutoPage

1. Select **Pages** in the Database window and then click the **New** button.

2. In the New Data Access Page dialog box, select your record source (a table or a query), select **AutoPage: Columnar**, and then click **OK**.

3. AutoPage creates a Data Access page, using all the fields contained in the selected record source, and then displays it in Page view. Figure 31.15 shows the result of using AutoPage with the Categories table.

New in Access 2000

Data Access Pages are the easiest way to create dynamic Web pages for displaying and entering data. However, there are three important caveats when using Data Access Pages. First, your users must be using Internet Explorer 5; Data Access Pages won't work with earlier versions of Internet Explorer. Second, your users must have a license for Office 2000 (although they don't have to have it installed) if you're using Data Access Pages to display data on the Web, outside an Access database or project. Third, even though Data Access Pages appear in the database container, they aren't stored within the Access .mdb file. The pages are actual HTML files stored external to the .mdb file; the objects in the database container are really shortcuts to the actual file.

FIGURE 31.15

The results of using AutoPage
with the categories table, shown
in Page view within Access.

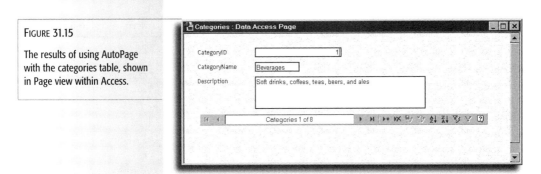

4. If you aren't happy with the page's design, switch to Design
   view and change it just as you would a form or report.

   If you don't like the default theme for the page, choose
   Theme from the **Format** menu. A dialog box appears that
   lets you select a different theme. You can use the **Set
   Default** button to make your selected theme the default for
   all your Data Access Pages.

5. When you are happy with your design and want to save the
   page, select **Save As** from the **File** menu. (Using **Save As**
   lets you choose where to save the file and what name to give
   it. If you just use **Save**, the page is saved with the name
   given to it by AutoPage and in a folder that you will have no
   control over.)

Launch Internet Explorer and use the **File** menu's **Open** command to locate the HTML file created. It will be placed in the
folder specified in step 5. Figure 31.16 shows the Categories
page in Internet Explorer; compare this to Figure 31.15, which
shows the same page opened in Access.

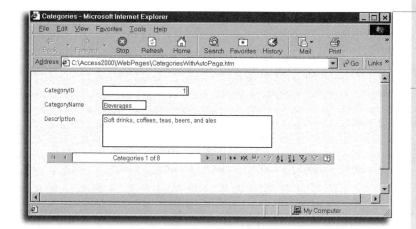

Creating Data Access Pages with the Wizard

Using the wizard to create your Data Access Pages is very similar to using AutoPage, but you have more flexibility. You can use multiple data sources and select the fields you want displayed.

Create Data Access Pages with the wizard

1. Select **Pages** in the Database window and click the **New** button.

2. In the New Data Access Page dialog box, select **Page Wizard**, and then click **OK**. (You also can select a data source at this time, but it's not required.)

3. In the Page Wizard dialog box, select your data source (a table or query) and then select the fields that you want to display. When finished, click **OK**.

4. In the next dialog box, select any grouping options. (Note that if you select a grouping option, the page becomes read-only.) When you're done, click **OK**.

5. The next dialog lets you specify a sort order. When you're done, click **OK**.

Data Access Pages are shortcuts

The objects you see when you click **Pages** in the Database window are only shortcuts to the actual files. If you place your mouse over the object's name, a tool tip appears that shows the full path to the object. If you rename a page object in the Database window, you don't change the object's filename, only its name in the database container. When you delete a page object, you can choose to delete only the link to the object from the Database window or delete the object as well.

6. The final dialog box allows you to give your page a name, select a theme, and open the page in Design or View mode. If you open the page in View mode, Access saves it in the default folder; therefore, if you want to specify the file's location, it's recommended that you first display the page in Design mode. Click the **Finish** button to view your page.

7. When you are happy with your design and want to save the page, choose **Save As** from the **File** menu so that you can specify the file's location.

Figure 31.17 shows a Data Access Page for the Customers table. Although it looks very similar to a page created with AutoPage, notice that all the fields from the Customers table aren't included in the page.

FIGURE 31.17

Microsoft Internet Explorer displays a Data Access Page created with the wizard.

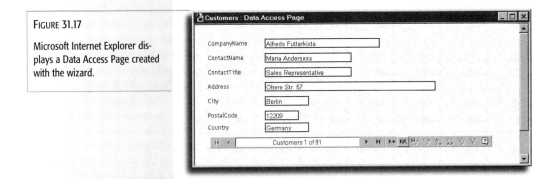

Applying Security to the Database

Understand why database security is important

Use the User-Level Security Wizard

Create users and groups

Set permissions for database objects

Set a database password

Why Have Security?

In today's business world, corporate espionage is a bigger problem than most people realize. Your competitors will always snoop around as much as they can in an attempt to find out what your latest projects are, who your customers are, and what your potential weaknesses are. For these reasons, among others, corporate Information Systems (IS) staffs have started taking desktop data security very seriously. As more and more data and application assets are pushed out to mobile employees—particularly salespeople who travel with laptops—there's a greater need for securing those assets.

Securing Native Access Databases (*.mdb)

Practice safe security—make a backup first

Whenever you're working with database security in Microsoft Access, it's best to have a backup of the original database stored in a safe place. This way, you can easily re-create your database if you ever lose the password information or make your database unreadable.

Microsoft Access provides several handy methods for securing your databases and their contents:

- User-level security
- Setting a database password
- Encrypting the database
- Locking down form, report, and module design through creation of an .mde file

This chapter covers all four methods, with special emphasis on user-level security because it's the most comprehensive.

Implementing User-Level Security

To truly secure your database, you need to implement user-level security, which provides three main benefits:

- You can limit who can open the database.
- You can restrict user access to specific database objects on a per-user and per-object basis.
- You can create groups of users and restrict access on a per-group basis.

User-level security hinges on the ability to define users and to grant or deny each user permission to work with the specific objects in your database. For example, you could give Tom the ability to read data in two of your six tables but deny him the ability to change the data in any of those tables; Kathy, meanwhile, has permission to read or change the data in any of the six tables.

Because you might have many users and many objects in your database, Access provides a feature that allows you to place individual users into groups. You can then grant or deny permissions to a group and thereby affect all the users that have been assigned to that group. Using groups can greatly reduce the effort required to administer your security process.

You already know that the objects discussed are all stored as part of your database (.mdb) file. Information about permissions for each object are also stored in your database, but definitions for any groups and users that you create aren't stored there. A separate file is used to store this information, along with a password for each defined user. This information is stored in a *workgroup information file*.

The default workgroup information file, system.mdw, is installed when you install Access. This file contains one user, Admin, and two groups, Admins and Users. The Admin user doesn't have a password set for it. Unless you specify otherwise, Access uses the default system.mdw as the workgroup information file each time it starts.

Also by default, Access attempts to log on as a user named Admin with no password. If this logon succeeds—and it will until you do something to change it—you never see any logon dialog box requesting you to enter a user and password. In reality, you're already using user-level security but probably didn't realize it. You're actually logging on as a user called Admin with a blank password. Because the Admin user defaults to have all available permissions, it appears as though there's no security.

More on objects and collections

Chapter 27, "Programming Access with VBA," discusses objects and collections. The group and user information outlined here is actually stored as a set of objects and collections. Collections called Groups and Users and objects named Group and User are available through ADO (actually, an extension of ADO, whose reference is Microsoft ADO Ext. 2.1 for DLL and Security) or DAO. You might find it interesting to use the Object Browser to examine this structure.

Implementing User-Level Security

The steps to securing a database can be rather daunting when done manually. However, the User-Level Security Wizard makes the task quite manageable. This wizard has been expanded and much improved in Access 2000.

Use the User-Level Security Wizard

1. Open the database you want to secure. From the **Tools** menu choose **Security** and then **User-Level Security Wizard**. A dialog box similar to that shown in Figure 32.1 appears. Click **Next**.

FIGURE 32.1

The Security Wizard dialog box.

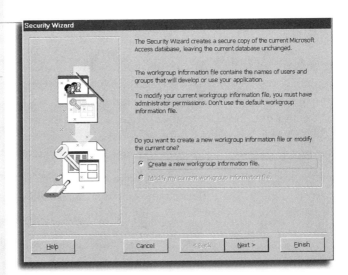

2. Use the **Browse** button to select the path and name where you want the wizard to store the new workgroup information file. Select **I Want to Create a Shortcut to Open My Secured Database** (see Figure 32.2). Click **Next**.

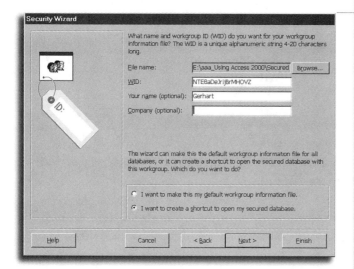

FIGURE 32.2

Define a new workgroup information file.

3. The next dialog box (see Figure 32.3) allows you to selectively secure your database objects. To secure all objects, click the **All Objects** tab, and then click the **Select All** button. Click **Next**.

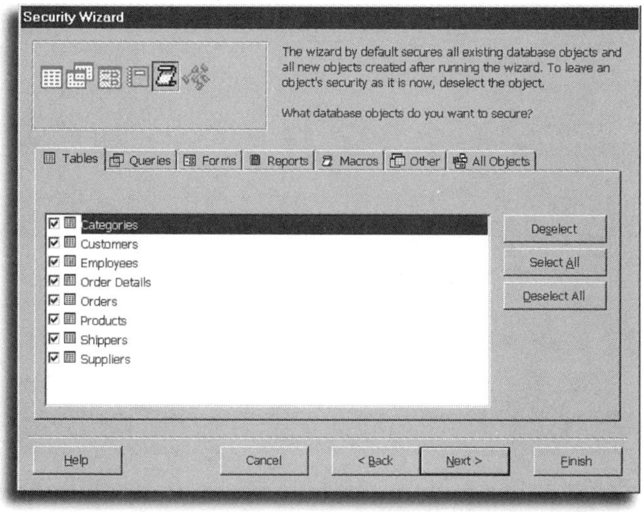

FIGURE 32.3

You can secure all objects in your database (the default) or selectively exclude objects.

4. Select any number of the predefined groups listed (see Figure 32.4). Click the text portion of any group to see a description of the permissions associated with that group. When you're done, click **Next**.

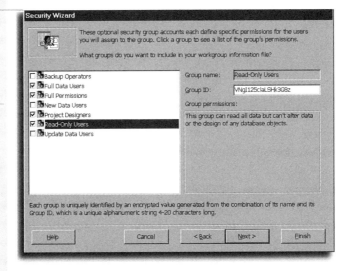

5. Select **No, the Users Group Should Not Have Any Permissions** (see Figure 32.5). Click **Next**.

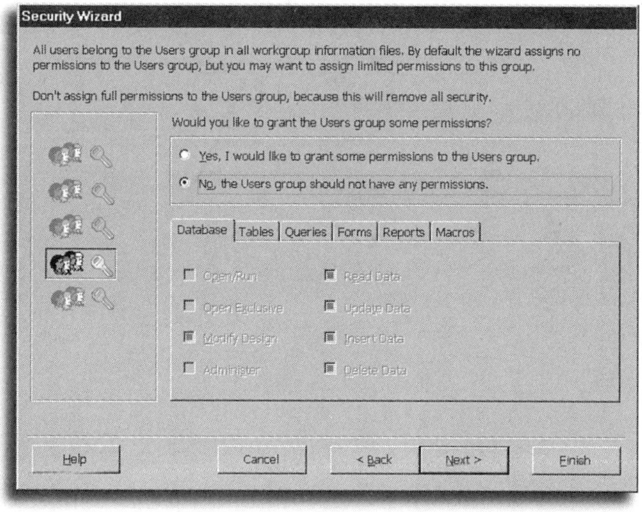

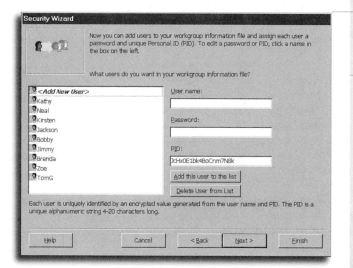

FIGURE 32.5

You can assign permissions to the Users group, but that's not recommended.

6. Figure 32.6 shows the dialog box after a number of users are added. To add your own users, select **<Add New User>**, enter a username, and click **Add This User to the List**. When all your users are added, click **Next**. (Later in this chapter in the section "Adding, Deleting, or Modifying a User or Group," you see how to add or delete users whenever you need to.)

FIGURE 32.6

Nine users have been added to this list of application users.

What if a user is assigned to more than one group?

If you assign a user to more than one group, the least restrictive group (that is, the most permissive option) is applied.

7. In the next dialog box, you can assign your users to groups (see Figure 32.7), although you don't have to do this now. When you're done, click **Next**.

8. For the dialog box in Figure 32.8, enter or use the **Browse** button to provide a name and path to the new, secure database. Click **Finish**.

FIGURE 32.7

You can select a user and assign him or her to groups or select a group and assign users.

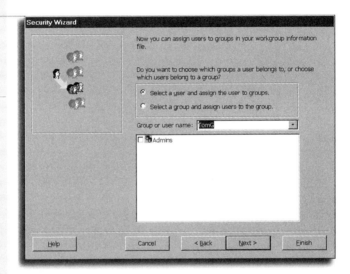

FIGURE 32.8

Before securing the database, provide a name and location of an unsecured copy as backup.

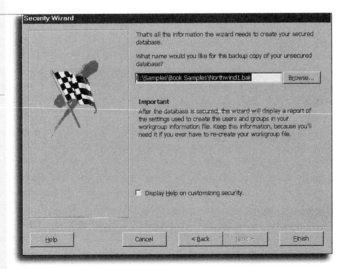

A report containing the information collected by the Security Wizard is displayed. This report should be printed and saved, because the information it contains is required to rebuild your workgroup information file should it ever become corrupted.

Using Workgroup Information Files

The workgroup information file contains information about users in a workgroup: the list of users, their passwords, and their group membership.

Access provides the Workgroup Administrator application, which you can use to change workgroups and create new workgroup information files. To start the application, execute wrkgadm.exe, which is installed into your windows\system (for Windows 95/98) or winnt\system32 folder (for Windows NT).

Join an existing workgroup

1. From the **Start** menu, select **Run** and then enter wrkgadm to start the Workgroup Administrator application. Figure 32.9 shows the Workgroup Administrator's main dialog box.

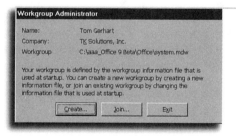

FIGURE 32.9

In the Workgroup Administrator, you can join different workgroups or create a new workgroup information file.

2. To join a workgroup, click the **Join** button.

3. Type the path to the workgroup information file you want to join, or use **Browse** to locate the file. When you have the correct path, click **OK**. A message box appears, informing you that you've successfully joined the workgroup.

Although it's possible to create a new workgroup by using the Workgroup Administrator, I recommend that you don't do so. The Security Wizard provides so much functionality and is so easy to use that it's the preferred method.

Adding, Deleting, or Modifying a User or Group

Manage user and group accounts

1. Log on to a secured database by using a user ID that's a member of the Admins group.

2. From the **Tools** menu, choose **Security** and then **User and Group Accounts**. You should see a dialog box similar to that shown in Figure 32.10. With this dialog, you can add new users, delete an existing user, clear the password of any existing user, or change the password of the user account now logged on.

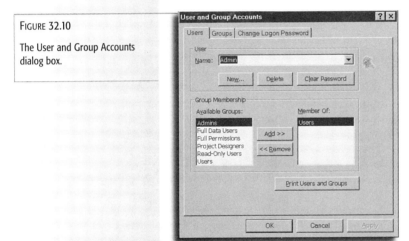

FIGURE 32.10

The User and Group Accounts dialog box.

Changing the Permissions of a User or Group

Manage user and group permissions

1. Log on to a secured database by using a user ID that's a member of the Admins group.

2. From the **Tools** menu, choose **Security** and then **User and Group Permissions**. The dialog box in Figure 32.11 appears. You can use this dialog to change the permissions of any group. Although you can also give permissions directly to users, I recommend that you don't do so because it makes properly administering the database more difficult.

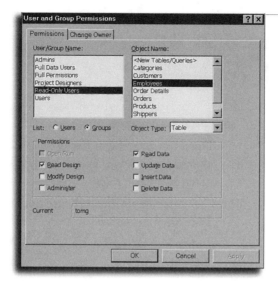

FIGURE 32.11
The User and Group Permissions
dialog box.

Setting a Database Password

The simplest means of securing a database is to set a database password. This way, anyone who doesn't know the password can't open the database with Microsoft Access. However, it doesn't protect the database against someone using a simple hex-dump viewer to browse the database file. Nor does a database password give you the flexibility of user-level security; if a user knows the database password, that user can do most anything he or she chooses.

If you apply user-level security to your database properly, setting a database password is unnecessary and annoying; users will have to enter two passwords, one for their user account and one for the database.

When a database password is established, the dialog box shown in Figure 32.12 appears whenever anyone tries to open the database. Users must enter the correct password, or they receive an incorrect password message box. Unlike many password-protected systems, however, there is no maximum number of retries. Users can keep trying passwords until they eventually get it right; Access won't lock them out after a certain number of failed attempts.

Hex-dump viewing can still be prevented

Encrypting your database makes it inaccessible to programs other than Access. If you encrypt your database after you apply the other user-level security measures, you can prevent someone from snooping through the database with a simple hex-dump viewer. Encrypting is discussed in the next section.

FIGURE 32.12

This database password prompt appears after a database password is established and someone tries to open the database.

Verify your password status

To verify that the password has been set or unset, close the database and reopen it. You should be prompted for a password if you just set the password, or not prompted if you just removed (unset) the password.

Set a database password

1. Open the database in Exclusive mode (from the **File** menu choose **Open** and then select **Exclusive** from the drop-down list to the right of the **Open** command button).

2. From the **Tools** menu choose **Security** and then **Set Database Password**.

3. Enter the password in the **Password** text box. Reenter it in the **Verify** text box.

4. Click **OK** to set the password. (You receive no message indicating this.)

Remove a database password

1. Open the database in Exclusive mode.

2. From the **Tools** menu choose **Security** and then **Unset Database Password**.

3. Enter the current password in the **Password** text box.

4. Click **OK**; the password has been removed. (You receive no message indicating this.)

Close all objects before encrypting

To encrypt or decrypt the database, Access must be able to open it in Exclusive mode. Therefore, you must make sure that no other users have the database opened when you try to encrypt or decrypt it. (This also means that you can't encrypt the database if you have it open in Access.) The good news, though, is that you don't have to open a database at all to get to the encrypt/decrypt menu items; they're available whether or not a database is opened.

Encrypting and Decrypting the Database

Encrypting alone doesn't prevent unauthorized access to your data. In fact, if all you do is encrypt your database, you haven't really secured it at all because anyone with Microsoft Access can open it. In addition to encrypting the database, you should follow the user-level security procedures outlined earlier in this chapter in the section "Implementing User-Level Security."

You also must be logged on as the database owner to encrypt/decrypt it. If you've enabled user-level security and aren't logged in as the database owner, Access fails when you attempt to encrypt or decrypt the database.

Access creates the encrypted database as a copy of the original database. Therefore, you must have enough free disk space available on the target drive you select to support a copy of the database.

Encrypt a database

1. Start Microsoft Access, but don't open the database you want to encrypt.

2. From the **Tools** menu choose **Security** and then **Encrypt/Decrypt Database**.

3. In the Encrypt/Decrypt Database dialog box (a standard File Open dialog box), locate the database you want to encrypt and click **OK**. (The database you select must not have been previously encrypted, or Access attempts to decrypt it as opposed to encrypt it.)

4. In the next dialog box, specify the name and location for the encrypted copy of the database. Click **Save** when you're finished.

Assuming that all the conditions outlined earlier are met, Access encrypts the database and returns to a steady state. You will not get a message box unless something goes wrong; this is one of those "no-news-is-good-news" situations.

Decrypt a database

1. Start Microsoft Access, but don't open the database you want to decrypt.

2. From the **Tools** menu choose **Security** and then **Encrypt/Decrypt Database**.

3. In the Encrypt/Decrypt Database, a dialog box appears; locate the database you want to decrypt and click **OK**. (This must be a previously encrypted database; otherwise, Access attempts to encrypt it as opposed to decrypt it.)

4. In the next dialog box, specify the name and location for the decrypted copy of the database. Click **Save** when you're finished.

Assuming that all the conditions outlined earlier are met, Access decrypts the database and returns to a steady state. You won't get a message box—this also is one of those "no-news-is-good-news" situations—unless something goes wrong in the process.

Creating an .mde file

Creating an .mde file from your existing Access database (.mdb) provides limited protection for several types of objects in your database. The .mde file is similar to an .mdb file except for two differences:

- The **Design** and **New** options are disabled for all forms, reports, and modules, and the **New** option is disabled for pages.
- Any source code that you've created has been removed; only the compiled version is kept.

Your application operates exactly as it does in .mdb format, but the design of your forms, reports, and modules is protected from prying eyes and alteration.

Create an .mde file

1. Open your database (.mdb). From the **Tools** menu, choose **Database Utilities** and then **Make MDE File**. (You can instead make the same selection from the menu while the Access window is open but before a database is opened.)

2. The standard file dialog box appears. After selecting a folder and name for the new file, click **Save**. Access creates the new .mde file without further notice.

Securing an Access Project

An Access project is the front-end portion to a client/server configuration. Because server products, like Microsoft SQL Server, have their own extensive security mechanisms, Access needs to protect only the objects contained within the project itself. Such protection is provided by creating and distributing an .ade file. (Chapter 34, "Using Access Projects," provides more information about projects.)

Keep a copy of your .mdb file

When creating an .mde file, be certain to keep a copy of your original database. Without the original .mdb file, you can't make any changes to your application.

The .ade file contains all the functionality of the original project file (.adp), except for two differences:

- The **Design** and **New** options are disabled for all forms, reports, and modules, and the **New** option is disabled for pages.
- Any source code that you've created has been removed; only the compiled version is kept.

Your project operates exactly as it does in the .adp format, but the design of your forms, reports, and modules is protected from prying eyes and alteration.

1. Open your project (.adp). From the **Tools** menu, choose **Database Utilities** and then **Make ADE File**.
2. The standard file dialog box appears. After selecting folder and name for the new file, click **Save**. Access creates the new .ade file without further notice.

Keep a copy of your original .adp file

When creating an .ade file for distribution, be certain to keep a copy of your original project. Without the original .adp file, you can't make any changes to your project.

Multiuser
Considerations

Learn how to split your database into two pieces: a front end and a back end

Manage the potential for two or more users trying to update the same data at the same time

Choose the best application architecture, client/server or file server, for your environment.

Select the best alternative method for accessing your back-end data from your application's front end

Sharing Your Data

Very often, database applications are intended to be used by several people, not just a single user, and most often these various users all need to share the same data.

Splitting Your Database

It might appear that the easiest way to give all your users access to the same set of data would be to simply copy your application's .mdb file to some shared directory on your network. This would certainly be the quickest way, but it's not recommended. This method sometimes works but can potentially result in poor performance, not only for the users of your application but also for everyone on the same network. Each time a user opens a form, for example, the form must first be read across the network, along with any related subforms and queries, before any real work can even begin. This can result in a significant increase in network traffic.

The ramifications of several users sharing the same applications when the application isn't specifically designed for that environment can go well beyond a hit on network and application performance issues. Very often, the application simply won't work as intended. For example, it's not unusual to use a table as a staging area for data in preparation for its display in a report. If, however, several different users all run the same report at the same time, using the same shared application, the results would be unpredictable. The table used as a staging area could have some records that reflect one user's request and other records that reflect another user's request. Not a pretty sight.

References to .mdb files in this chapter

In this chapter, I refer to the .mdb file containing only the tables as the "data .mdb," and the one containing everything else as the "application .mdb."

A much more efficient approach is to split your application into to separate .mdb files: one to hold only the tables and the other to hold all your forms, reports, and other objects. After splitting your application in this manner, the data .mdb can then be placed in a shared folder on the network and, after linking the application .mdb to the tables in the data mdb, it can be copied to each user's local hard drive. This is very often all that's required, but if the path to the data .mdb is different on various users' machines, you will also have to reestablish the link to the data .mdb for each user's machine.

Split your database

1. Make two copies of your existing application's .mdb file. A convenient way of doing this is to open Access and, from the **Tools** menu, choose **Database Utilities** and then **Compact and Repair Database** before opening a database. Compact your existing .mdb into a new .mdb, named something similar to *applicationname*_Data.mdb. Repeat this operation, naming the new .mdb something like *applicationname*_Code.mdb.

2. Open *applicationname*_Data.mdb and delete all forms, queries, reports, macros, and modules, leaving only the tables. Close the database when you're done.

3. Copy *applicationname*_Data.mdb to a shared folder on your network and delete it from your hard drive.

4. Open *applicationname*_Code.mdb and delete all the tables. From the **File** menu choose **Get External Data** and then **Link Tables**. Use the dialog box to point to *applicationname*_Data.mdb from Step 3. Select all the tables and click **OK**. All the application's tables are now available for use by *applicationname*_Code.mdb, even though they physically exist only in *applicationname*_Data.mdb.

If you prefer, an add-in is available to help with splitting your database. From the **Tools** menu, choose **Add-Ins** and then **Database Splitter**.

Regardless of which method you use to split your database, it's now ready for distribution to your users. You can copy *applicationname*_Code.mdb to a disk or to a shared folder on your network. In either case, it needs to be added to the hard drive of each user's machine.

At this point, *applicationname*_Code.mdb is using the same path to the linked tables, *applicationname*_Data, as was used when the links were established. Depending on your installation's standards, this might be the same path on all your users' machines, or it could be different. If the paths are different, the table links must be reestablished. An add-in is available for this purpose or you can do it manually. To use the add-in, choose **Add-Ins** and then **Linked Table Manager** from the **Tools** menu with *applicationname*_Code.mdb open.

Consider a VBA function to relink attached tables

Very often an application that will be used by a number of users includes a user-written VBA function that checks the links to the application's back-end data and relinks the tables if required. Typically, this function is invoked each time the application is started. This technique avoids several potential pitfalls that might be encountered if your end users must relink the tables themselves.

Data/User Collisions

In any multiuser database environment, your application will likely be exposed to situations where one user's actions on the data has an impact on other users working with the same data. Several scenarios can cause data collisions between users, two of which are shown in Figures 33.1 and 33.2.

FIGURE 33.1

User A starts editing a record, but before he saves the results, User B edits and saves the same record.

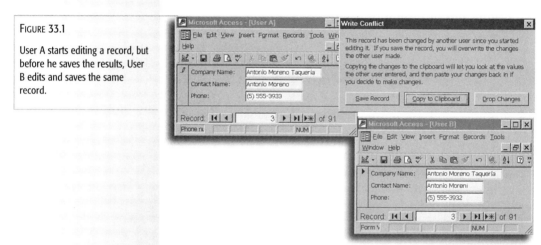

FIGURE 33.2

While User A has a record displayed for review, User B edits and saves the same record. User A, unaware that User B has just edited the data, now attempts to edit the record.

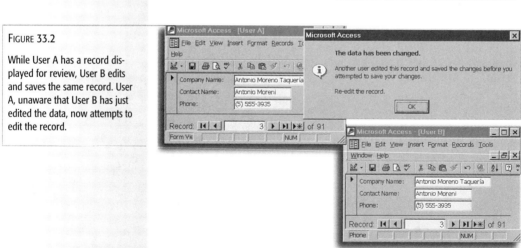

I'm sure that you can see that neither condition is desirable. These messages can be confusing and scary to end users, especially the one in Figure 33.1. Although both conditions can be trapped, they're equally difficult to deal with—it's best just to avoid them, if possible. Fortunately, Access 2000 includes built-in functionality to help deal with or prevent these kind of collisions.

Page/Record Locking

Most relational database management systems (RDBMS) employ some sort of mechanism to help protect against data collisions. This functionality is often called *locking*. The system places a lock on the data and releases it after the data is saved. If a second user tries to save the same data while it's still locked, that user is said to be locked out, and a trappable error occurs. If there's no active error handling code to deal with the error, an error message is displayed to the user. Generally, these locks are placed and released behind the scenes without the developer or user necessarily even being aware that it's happening—at least, not until a collision between users occurs.

Access provides several options that govern how locking is handled (see Figure 33.3).

Processing errors caused by data collisions

The conditions shown by Figures 33.1 and 33.2 are both trappable errors. Although the error numbers aren't displayed in the message boxes, they represent errors 7787 and 7878 respectively and can be trapped by using the form's **On Error** event.

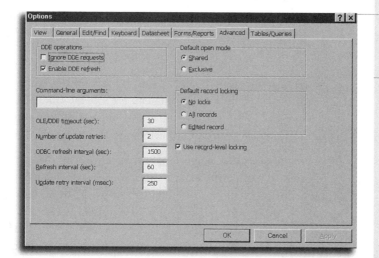

FIGURE 33.3

Available options to control the behavior of locking.

The **Default Record Locking** options provide three approaches to locking:

- **No Locks**—This is the default, but it doesn't mean what you might expect. Locks are still issued, but they remain in effect only during the brief time it takes to actually save the data. This approach is often called *optimistic locking*.

- **All Records**—This setting locks all the records in a record-set.

- **Edited Record**—The affected data is locked as soon as editing begins and remains locked until the data is saved. This approach is often called *pessimistic locking*.

When users alter the data displayed by a form, we say that they're editing the data. But as they move from one control to another and make their changes, the real data—that stored on disk—hasn't yet been affected. The changes made by users don't affect the source data until the record is saved back to disk. This happens when they move to a new record or perhaps click a command button provided by the application. Although several minutes (or possibly even several hours) could pass between the time a user started editing the data and when the data is actually written to disk, the write itself—the saving of the changes—typically takes only a fraction of a second. The point in time when a lock is placed on the data is determined by the approach to locking being used. If the **Edited Record** approach (pessimistic) is used, the lock is placed as soon as the user begins editing, even though the data on disk isn't otherwise affected yet. If **No Locks** (optimistic locking) is being used, the lock isn't applied until the actual save operation begins. Thus, it's possible, when using pessimistic locking, to lock up the data for several minutes or hours, whereas the optimistic locking approach generally results in locks that last for very brief periods.

In previous Access releases, locks were always applied and released to a page of data at a time. In Access 2000, a page of data consists of a block of 4,096 bytes (4K). If the actual data records are less than 4K, a single page might include several data records. In these cases, locking a page results in locking several records at the same time. Access 2000 now has record-level

The All Records option is seldom used

The **No Locks** and **Edited Record** approaches are probably the only options you will ever use. The **All Records** approach is used primarily for utility-like functions, such as a mass update to many/all records in a table.

(row) locking as an available option—in fact, this is the default option and is recommended. (See the **Use Record-Level Locking** check box in Figure 33.3.)

Because page locking might cause many records to be locked at a time and record locking locks only a single record at a time, using record locking reduces the chances of a locked-out condition occurring.

Again referring to Figure 33.3, the four options in the lower left also have an indirect effect on locking strategy:

- **Number of Update Retries**—If an attempt is made to save a record locked by another user, Access retries the save operation the number of times specified here. Acceptable values are 0 through 10.

- **ODBC Refresh Interval (Sec)**—This option is similar to the refresh interval, but pertains only to data being accessed through ODBC. Acceptable values are 1 through 32,766 seconds.

- **Refresh Interval (Sec)**—When records are being displayed in a form or datasheet, they are automatically refreshed from disk at the frequency provided here. Acceptable values are 0 through 32,766 seconds.

- **Update Retry Interval (Msec)**—This option specifies how long Access waits before retrying a save operation. Acceptable values are 0 through 1,000 milliseconds.

All the options described thus far in this chapter, as well as other environmental considerations, must be included when developing your locking strategy. For example, if you set the **Refresh Interval** to 1 sec, the types of collisions shown in Figures 33.1 and 33.2 would be much less than if the interval were set to 1,000 seconds; however, the network traffic would be much higher as well. This might be okay if three people are using your application and are the only three people connected to your network. As the number of people on the network increases, however, so does network traffic. The network itself can become a bottleneck. You could end up with 100 users of the network, all irate about network performance, and all caused by three people using your application.

Experiment with record locking on your own

The examples used in this chapter can be found in Ch33_Samples.mdb and Ch33_Data.mdb at the Web site for this book (`www.mcp.com/ product_support`). The Ch33_Samples.mdb application contains several pairs of forms with similar names, where one form in the pair represents User A and the other form in the same pair represents User B. The example in Figure 33.4 can be created by opening the form `frmUserA_EditedReco rd` and then, in a second instance of Access, open `frmUserB_EditedReco rd`. The two forms are identical except their captions have been changed to make it easier to identify the user they represent. Also note that the `RecordLocks` property of these forms is used to change the behavior of the individual forms. The forms property setting overrides the option settings discussed previously.

Exercise caution when changing any options discussed here

As you might have guessed, most of these choices are trade-offs—you gain something at the expense of something else. There is therefore no magic formula or set of choices that will fit everyone's needs. The best approach is to proceed cautiously when altering the available options. Remember, "If it ain't broke, don't fix it." If you do encounter locking or performance problems, try to determine the most likely cause before adjusting various options at random. Also, your environment is almost certainly not static. Therefore, what was a great set of choices yesterday might not be very good at all today.

There are some absolutes here. If you select the **Edited Record** option, the types of collisions depicted by Figure 33.1 can be eliminated completely. Because pessimistic locking places the lock as soon as editing begins, a second user trying to edit the same data won't be prevented from doing so (see Figure 33.4). In this example, User A started editing a record as depicted by the pencil-like symbol displayed in the Record Selector portion of the form. Before User A saved the record, User B tried to edit the same record but was prevented from doing so. The international "no" symbol on User B's form indicates that the record is now locked by another user, in this case User A. User B also gets an audio indication that she's locked out.

Although the use of pessimistic locking eliminates the most confusing and difficult collision types (the collision in Figure 33.1), your application is still exposed to a user being locked out (collisions of the type shown in Figure 33.2). As mentioned previously, these two situations can be reduced by using record-level locking and adjusting the **Refresh Interval**, but they still won't be eliminated. The forms shown in Figure 33.5 do address the latter of these two, however, by ensuring that users are editing the most current data.

FIGURE 33.4

User A started editing a record and has locked out User B, as depicted by symbols in the Record Selector of their respective forms.

FIGURE 33.5

Forms `frmUserA` and `frmUserB` have been modified to ensure that current data is being edited.

The On Click events for the two command buttons on the forms shown in Figure 33.5 include code to ensure that users are viewing a current copy of the data if they decide to edit the record. Listing 33.1 shows this code.

LISTING 33.1   *On Click* **Event Procedures for the Edit and Save Command Buttons**

```
01 Private Sub cmdEdit_Click()
02 Dim ctl As Control
03 Dim varValue As Variant
04 varValue = Me!txtCompanyName ───────────── ❶
05 On Error Resume Next
06 Me!txtCompanyName = varValue ───────────── ❶
07 If Err <> 0 Then ─────────────────────┐
08    On Error GoTo 0                     │
                                          ❷
09 Else
10    For Each ctl In Me.Controls ──────────┐
11       If ctl.ControlType = acTextBox Then │
12          ctl.Locked = False               ❸
13       End If                              │
14    Next ─────────────────────────────────┘
```

continues…

❶ These lines work together to force the record to be locked. By assigning a value to `txtCompanyname` (even though the new value is the same as the old value), you're putting the form into edit mode, thus locking the record. This ensures that no changes can be made to this record by other users.

❷ Checks to see if line 6 caused an error. Line 6 causes an error if a second user tries to edit the same record that another user has already locked. If this happens, line 8 resets the error and no further processing occurs.

❸ Set the `Locked` property of the text boxes to allow editing by the user.

❹ Refreshes the form to ensure that the user is working with the most current data.

❺ Set the `Locked` property of the text boxes to prevent their being edited.

❻ Saves the record, releasing the lock.

Listing 33.1   Continued

```
15    Me.Refresh                              ────────── ❹
16    Me!cmdSave.Enabled = True
17    Me!txtCompanyName.SetFocus
18    Me!cmdEdit.Enabled = False
19 End If
20 End Sub
21
22 Private Sub cmdSave_Click()
23 Dim ctl As Control
24
25 For Each ctl In Me.Controls
26    If ctl.ControlType = acTextBox Then
27       ctl.Locked = True                    ────── ❺
28    End If
29 Next
30 DoCmd.RunCommand acCmdSaveRecord           ────────── ❻
31 Me!cmdEdit.Enabled = True
32 Me!cmdEdit.SetFocus
33 Me!cmdSave.Enabled = False
34 End Sub
```

Code available on Web site

The database designed for this chapter (Ch33_Samples.mdb) and available from the book's companion Web site (`http://www.mcp.com/ product_support/`) includes examples of using unbound forms or VBA to edit recordsets. When you get to the site, enter the book's ISBN into the Search box and click the Search button. You will find the code on the book's information page.

The approaches described here provide a good working strategy for many applications using bound forms. The primary remaining issue relates to user training. Your users must be told that they might occasionally experience a locked-out condition and, if this happens, to simply try again after a short wait. They must also be trained not to leave a record/form in edit mode for extended periods. They need to edit the record and save it, as opposed to starting an edit and taking a coffee break before saving it.

If, however, your application uses unbound forms or VBA to edit recordsets, be sure to include code in your error-handling process that addresses the various types of data collisions.

The Client/Server Database Environment

In a client/server database environment, application-processing requirements can be shared between the client computer (your local machine) and the server computer. Under ideal conditions, the client does all the work required to display the data, responding to user requests and determining what data is needed, but all the actual database work itself is done by the server. This sharing of work might result in significant performance gains, but not necessarily.

The server machine likely will be a more powerful, faster machine than the client machines, and the database server software is tuned specifically to take advantage of this power. It need not worry about displaying data and nice user interfaces, but is concerned with the rapid manipulation of the data. In a well designed client/server arrangement, the client can take advantage of this by passing short requests to the server in the form of SQL statements; the server processes those requests, passing back only the data in the resultset. Not only does this reduce the processing burden of the client, but it also can greatly reduce network traffic.

The environment created when you're using an .mdb on your hard drive, which is linked to tables in a separate .mdb on the network server, is sometimes mistakenly thought of as being a client/server environment. It's not—it's a file-server environment. In a file-server environment, the server is providing little function beyond acting as a file repository. All data manipulation is performed by the client hardware/software. If, for example, your application executes a select query that uses an non-indexed field as a selection criterion, every record in the table must be passed across the network, examined on the user's machine to see if it meets the specified criterion, and added to the resulting set of records if it does. The result might consist of only a single record, but you might have to read and examine thousands of records to determine that. Not only might this require a lot of processing by the user's computer, but it also generates a lot of network traffic.

Use indexes to improve performance

Liberal use of indexes improves the performance of many applications. In general, consider indexing any field that's used to join one table to another or used as the object of a search criteria. Although indexing will have a negative impact on performance when adding new records or changing existing records, this is usually offset by the performance improvements gained when retrieving the data.

Yet another consideration for a client/server environment

If you're using a Microsoft SQL Server database as a back end, consider using the Access Project feature introduced with Access 2000 instead of a standard .mdb file as the front end. This provides a more natural and direct link to a fuller set of Microsoft SQL Server functions. See Chapter 34, "Using Access Projects," for a discussion of this feature.

Access can be used, however, as a client front end to database server products such as Microsoft SQL Server or Oracle. You might want to do this for several reasons, in addition to the potential for improved application and network performance:

- Improved reliability—In a file-server environment, the risk to your data increases as the number of users increase. If, for example, any of your Access users were to lose power during the middle of an update, your data file on the server could be destroyed. Although this isn't likely, and your site might have normal backup procedures in place to help protect the data stored on the network servers, it might not be a risk you want to take. Major database server products, such as Microsoft SQL Server, include transaction logs and other facilities that make it possible to recover from almost any kind of failure. The failure of any given client, or even the server itself, is almost always recoverable with little or no loss of data.

- Improved scalability—It's possible for even the best designed application to outgrow a file-server environment. As the number of users or records increase, the application that once performed well might begin to run at a snail's pace.

- Usage of existing data—Very often the data you need is already available in an existing database server product's database.

Having said all this, the move to a client/server environment shouldn't be taken lightly, especially if the primary motivation is to improve performance. If you're not careful, you could be disappointed. A well designed and implemented Access application can perform very well in its file-server environment. The existing application's operation needs to be compared to the capabilities and features of the target client/server product to determine if a performance gain is in fact likely to be realized. For example, if your application usually needs to locate a single record in a database containing many thousands of records, the client/server approach might be a good option. If, however, your application is used for analysis of some kind, where it must use thousands of records itself, proceed with caution.

Although moving from a file server to a client/server environment can be done with relatively little pain and effort, it should be viewed more as a conversion effort than a move. Major changes to your Access client might be required to fully benefit from the new environment. The next few sections address some key issues to consider.

To Link or Not to Link

The primary advantage to linking an Access front end to a server database back end is simplicity. It feels very natural for Access developers to work with the data in this manner. This simplicity usually exacts a significant performance price, however.

Although this technique might appear to be very natural, it's anything but. Linking to non-Access tables places several additional layers of software between your application and its data. This additional code directly and indirectly affects performance—directly because executing more code takes longer, indirectly in more subtle ways. Your Access front end might include what seems to be a straightforward query that joins a couple of tables and returns some records. The code between you and your data, however, must translate this query to the server's native SQL language and decide what SQL statements are passed to the database server. Your single SQL statement might result in several separate SQL statements being passed to the server, and might cause thousands of records to pass over the network, even though only a few records are eventually returned to your application. Much of the advantage of the client/server environment has been overridden and lost.

In general, using linked tables is usually the least desirable way to access your data. For example, assume that an application has a form to view employee data and that the form is bound to an employee table. If there are 200,000 employees, Access might attempt to read as many as 200,000 records every time the form is opened, even though only a single employee record can be displayed at any one time. With this many employees, the form will probably have a control into which users can enter an employee number or name to display a record.

When using linked tables in a client/server environment, a better approach is to create a new form that's not bound to any table at all and make the employee form a subform of this new form. Remove the control used to search for an employee from the original employee form and add it to the new main form. Link the main form and the subform by using the content of this search control. Through this technique, Access reads only the specific record you request, not the entire table, thus improving performance of both the application and the network.

Passthrough Queries

A passthrough query allows you to bypass much of the software between your application and your data. Because the passthrough query must be written in the back-end server's native format, no translation is performed. The SQL statement is passed through directly to your server. This has two primary advantages over the use of linked tables:

- Performance is almost always faster.
- Because these queries use the database server's SQL syntax and language, you can use statements that might not be available to you within an Access query.

Stored Procedures

Stored procedures are similar to Access queries, except instead of being stored in Access, they're stored in the back-end database server. Oftentimes, however, the database server product allows functionality in a stored procedure that goes well beyond just SQL statements alone. Microsoft SQL Server, for example, allows you to build very powerful logic into a stored procedure, which might involve many separate SQL statements with other kinds of processing interspersed.

Very often, a single stored procedure can perform the work that would have otherwise required a series of separate SQL statements and perhaps even some VBA code. This not only reduces the processing required of the Access client, but can also reduce network traffic by many thousands of records.

Using stored procedures can be a very powerful tool to ensure that your back-end database server returns only the exact information that your front end needs.

If your front-end client is an Access .mdb file, you will invoke a stored procedure by using a passthrough query. For example, the following line could be used in a passthrough query to execute the stored procedure named sp_Example in a Microsoft SQL Server database:

```
Execute sp_Example
```

Chapter 34 provides information about using stored procedures if your front end is an Access project (.adp) file.

Use of ActiveX Data Objects

ActiveX Data Objects (ADO) provides yet another, recommended way of accessing your back-end database data. By using ADO, you can tap into the benefits afforded by stored procedures as well as server-executed SQL, similar to passthrough queries. As an added benefit, the techniques using ADO to access a client/server database are very similar to those used to access a file-server database. Because these techniques are executed from within VBA, any solution you build by using ADO is very easily ported to other applications, including other Microsoft Office products as well as applications written in VB. Chapter 34 includes examples of using ADO to access a back-end database.

Performance of ADO Versus DAO

Many examples in this book use ADO instead of DAO; ADO is often faster. Generally, ADO is faster than DAO when accessing a data source other than the Jet engine. Although DAO might have a performance advantage when accessing a Jet data source, as new refinements to ADO become available, DAO might lose this advantage.

Performance Issues

Few performance issues or practices are unique to the multiuser environment. Basically, all the things important to good performance of a standalone Access application are even more important in multiuser applications:

- Consider hiding commonly used forms rather than repeatedly have the users open and close them.

- Use queries to retrieve only the records and fields that you will be using.

- Use combo boxes and list boxes judiciously.

- Index all table columns that take part in a join within a query or are used as part of a search criteria.

Many of these techniques are aimed at reducing to the amount of data that must pass over the network. Toward that same end, you should also consider keeping data that seldom changes in local tables. A common example of this are the two-character abbreviations for the 50 U.S. states. In other cases, you might want to have data in local tables as well as on the server. In this case, you would load the local tables from the server data when the application starts up; the local data would then be available for fast local lookup. Don't forget, however, that both sets of data must be updated when necessary.

Consider using unbound forms instead of bound forms. In this case, you would also want to drop any linked tables and access the data directly. If you're connected to your back-end database through ODBC, use passthrough queries wherever possible and, if your back-end database product supports stored procedures, use them.

If you're using a Microsoft SQL Server database as a back end, you should probably be using the Access Project feature introduced with Access 2000 instead of a standard .mdb file as the front end. This provides a more natural and direct link to a fuller set of Microsoft SQL Server functions.

Using Access Projects

Understand what an Access Project is and how it varies from an Access database

Learn how to create, edit, and use a stored procedure

Learn how to create, edit, and use a view

Learn about the new security feature used by Access Projects

Understanding Access Projects

Introducing the Microsoft Data Engine

The Microsoft Data Engine (MSDE) is a new data source that provides data storage that's compatible with Microsoft SQL Server 7. Because MSDE is based on the same data engine as SQL Server, most Access Projects will run on either version unchanged. However, MSDE has a 2GB database size limit and doesn't support all the functionality of SQL Server. You can use MSDE on a single user computer or small workgroup server. You can think of MSDE as a client/server alternative to the file server Microsoft Jet database engine. MSDE runs under Microsoft Windows NT 4 or later and Windows 95 or later.

A new feature introduced by Access 2000, the Access *Project* builds on the concept of using an application front end that's connected to and uses the data found in a back-end database. An Access Project can use a special data engine included with Access 2000, the Microsoft Data Engine (MSDE), as its data store, or it can use a Microsoft SQL Server 6.5 or 7.0 database.

Regardless of the back end used, however, the Access Project, unlike an Access *.mdb file, is constructed as a real client/server type application. The back-end database contains all the database components: tables, views, stored procedures, and relationships. The front end contains all the macros and modules, as well as all user interface objects (forms and reports).

This description of an Access Project might sound similar to a standard Access database (*.mdb file) linked to a back-end database, but the two are in fact quite different. For example, an Access Project (stored as an *.adp file) contains no local tables or queries, nor can it be linked to data in other external sources. Indeed, local tables and queries aren't even an available option with an Access Project.

Although an Access *.mdb file can connect to tables hosted by Microsoft SQL Server through linked tables, such a connection is also provided by the Jet Database Engine. In this environment, however, the functionality and visual interface to the back-end objects is limited. For example, although you can open a linked table in Design view, you can't alter its design. In fact, what's displayed as the design of such a table is only an approximation expressed in terms the Jet Database Engine normally uses. At least equally limiting is that this environment provides no visibility at all to the views and stored procedures available on the server. However, an Access Project doesn't rely on the Microsoft Jet Database Engine for its connection to the back-end database. Not only are tables displayed in terms of the hosting SQL Server product, but you also can alter their design, create new tables, or both. You can even view and create views and stored procedures directly from the Project's interface.

Why Use an Access Project?

The Access Project provides a more natural environment to develop and use a client/server type application. It allows you to operate directly on views and stored procedures located in the back-end server, and even to establish relationships within the server database. All these operations previously required that developers temporarily leave Access and invoke a utility or other service provided by the server product; now the work can all be done without leaving Access.

SEE ALSO

➤ *For more information about the client/server environment, see page 609*

The environment provided by the new Access Project isn't just easier to use from a development perspective, but it's also more efficient than was previously available. Because the environment doesn't rely on the Jet engine to provide the connection, it's more direct and natural, thus more efficient.

If your application will be operating in a client/server environment, you should seriously consider building it as, or converting it to, an Access Project.

Creating a Project

A new Access Project is created in much the same way a new Access database is created.

Create a new Project that uses an existing data store

  1. Be sure that MSDE is running and ready for use. If not, start it from the **Start** menu by choosing **Programs**, **Msde**, and then **Service Manager**. This opens a dialog box similar to Figure 34.1. After selecting the **Server** and **Services** appropriate to your location, click the **Start/Continue** button.

Access Project data source

Before attempting to create a new Access Project or use an existing one, one of the three supported data sources—Microsoft SQL Server 7, Microsoft SQL Server 6.5, or Microsoft Data Engine—must be available and started. All examples in this chapter are based on the use of an MSDE data source; however, if you are using either SQL product, everything will be very similar.

FIGURE 34.1

Using the SQL Server Service
Manager to start MSDE.

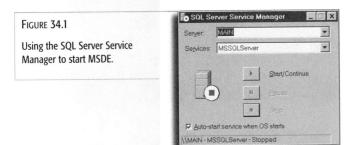

FIGURE 34.1

Using the SQL Server Service
Manager to start MSDE.

   2. Open Access 2000 and choose **New** from the **File** menu. A
   dialog box similar to the one in Figure 34.2 appears. You can
   elect to create a project that uses an existing database as its
   back end, or you can create a project that uses a new back-
   end database. For this example, you will create a project that
   uses the existing NorthwindCS database back end, so select
   the **Project (Existing Database)** icon on the General page
   of the dialog box. Then click **OK**.

FIGURE 34.2

Creating a new Access Project
based on an existing database.

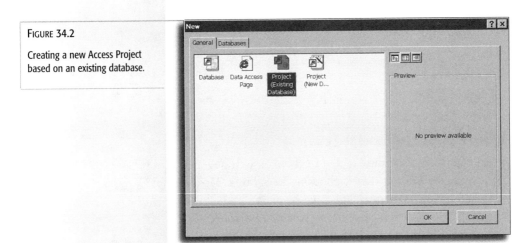

   3. Name your new Project when prompted to do so. (For this
   example, I named mine SampleProject.adp.) After naming
   the Project and clicking **Create**, you see the Data Link
   Properties dialog box (see Figure 34.3).

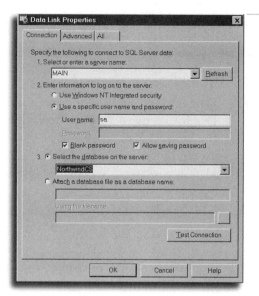

FIGURE 34.3

The values shown here are different than those required on your machine.

4. Whereas I entered Main as the name of my server, you must enter whatever name is appropriate to your installation. Notice, however, that NorthwindCS is selected as the database name.

5. Test your selections by clicking the **Test Connection** button. When you're done, click **OK**. The new Project is opened in the Database window (see Figure 34.4).

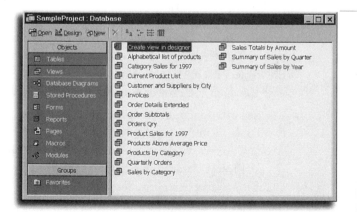

FIGURE 34.4

Database window of the new project named SampleProject.

Comparing an Access Project and a Database

The first and perhaps most obvious difference between an Access Project (*.adp) and an Access database (*.mdb) is seen in the Database window. As you can see in Figure 32.4, three entries in the Project's Database window—Views, Database Diagrams, and Stored Procedures—aren't present in a normal Access database's Database window, and one, Queries, is missing.

As stated previously, an Access Project contains no tables or queries. The Tables view in the Database window provides a visual interface to the tables contained in the back-end database, but because the back-end database has no singular functional equivalent to the Access query, no such interface to queries is provided. Views and stored procedures together do provide the function found in Access queries and more. Views can be thought of as being equivalent to a Select query in an Access database; stored procedures can be thought of as being similar to, but more powerful than, Access Action queries. You look at these a bit closer in the next few sections, but first look at some other differences found in an Access Project.

Other key differences include the following:

- The functionality available by choosing **Get External Data** from the **File** menu. Notice first that unlike a standard Access database, no option to link to external data is presented, only an option to import data. Even the Import option is different, however, in that it doesn't import into the Project itself (the .adp file), but into the back-end database to which the Project is connected.

- The security functionality found by choosing **Security** from the **Tools** menu is completely different than that found in a standard Access database. See the section "Securing an Access Project" later in this chapter for more information about the available security features.

- The rules and syntax required for back-end objects are defined by the hosting data source—that is, Microsoft SQL Server—not by Access or the Jet Database Engine.

Database diagrams in a Project replace relationships in an Access database

The Database Diagrams view in the Database window is similar to the function found by choosing **Relationships** from the **Tools** menu in an Access database.

Working with a Project's Objects

The next few sections outline the visual tools found in an Access Project used to work with the objects located in its back-end database. I won't attempt to describe the various rules and syntax requirements of those back-end products, however.

Tables

Again, don't be misled by the icons used in the Database window in Figure 34.4. In a standard Access database, external tables to which the .mdb file is connected are indicated with a special icon. This isn't the case in an Access Project. When you open a Project's table in Design view, however, you see a display quite different from that of a standard Access (Jet) table (see Figure 34.5).

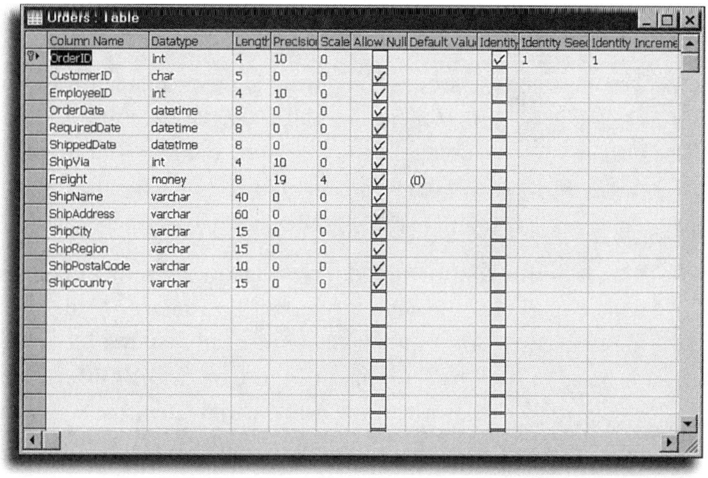

Column Name	Datatype	Length	Precision	Scale	Allow Null	Default Value	Identity	Identity Seed	Identity Increment
OrderID	int	4	10	0			✓	1	1
CustomerID	char	5	0	0	✓				
EmployeeID	int	4	10	0	✓				
OrderDate	datetime	8	0	0	✓				
RequiredDate	datetime	8	0	0	✓				
ShippedDate	datetime	8	0	0	✓				
ShipVia	int	4	10	0	✓				
Freight	money	8	19	4	✓	(0)			
ShipName	varchar	40	0	0	✓				
ShipAddress	varchar	60	0	0	✓				
ShipCity	varchar	15	0	0	✓				
ShipRegion	varchar	15	0	0	✓				
ShipPostalCode	varchar	10	0	0	✓				
ShipCountry	varchar	15	0	0	✓				

FIGURE 34.5

SampleProject.adp's Orders table, opened in Design view.

Although the Project's view of the Orders table has many similarities to that found in the Northwinds.mdb version in Figure 34.6, it's distinctly different. These differences are the result of the Project's tables residing in a Microsoft SQL Server type database, whereas Northwind's version resides in a Jet database.

FIGURE 34.6

SampleProject.mdb's Orders
table, opened in Design view.

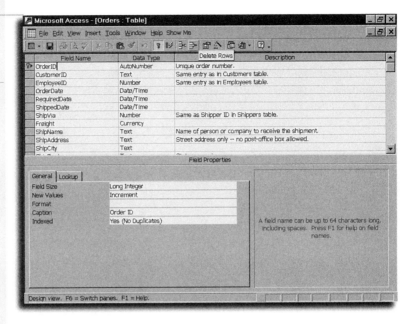

FIGURE 34.6

SampleProject.mdb's Orders
table, opened in Design view.

The first key difference to address is the available options in the
Datatype column. Open SampleProjects.adp's Orders table in
Design view and click in the Datatype column of any row. Scroll
through the list of datatypes available. The list is longer and
more precise than is available with a Jet-based table.

The Identity, Identity Seed, and Identity Increment columns
work together to provide functionality similar to, but more flexible than, the AutoNumber datatype available in a Jet table. In
the case of the Orders table in Figure 34.5, the OrderID row
began with 1 when the table was created (Identity Seed) and is
increased by 1 (Identity Increment) each time a record is added.

Views

A Project view is similar to a Select query, as might be found in
an Access .mdb file. Like a Select query, a view is used to select
specific columns or rows from the data in a single table, or it
might combine several data columns from each of several tables
together and present the result as a single set of records.
However, the interface used to create or modify a view is quite
different from the QBE grid used with a standard Access Select
query. (If you aren't familiar with how to use or create a Select
query, review Chapters 6, 13, 14, and 15.)

Explore the tools used to create/modify a view

1. Open the SampleProject database created earlier in this chapter and select **Views** from the Database window (see Figure 34.7).

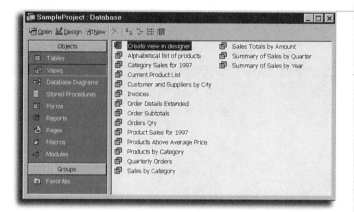

FIGURE 34.7
A list of views in SampleProject.adp.

2. Open a new view. Choose **Show Table** from the **View** menu. Your display should resemble Figure 34.8.

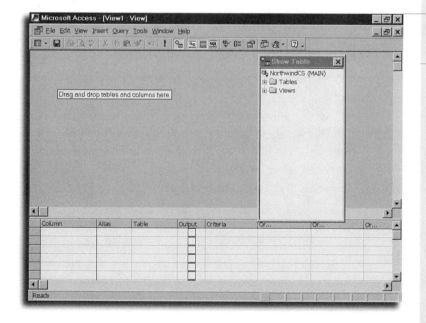

FIGURE 34.8
A new view in Design mode.

3. To create the new view, first decide which table(s) contain the data you want to use. To add each table to the view, select it from the list in the Show Tables window and drag it to the upper part of the View Design window. In this case, add the Products and Order Details tables. After adding these tables, close the Show Tables window. Your view should now resemble Figure 34.9.

FIGURE 34.9

The new view uses two tables.

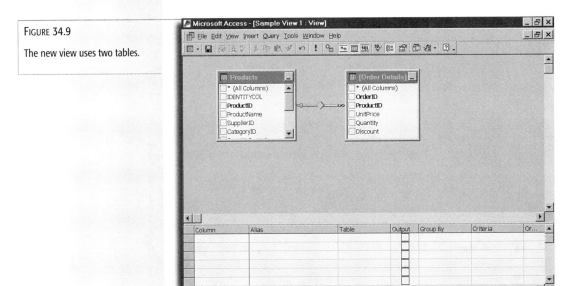

4. Select the columns of data to be included in the view by simply clicking the box to the left of each column name. (To remove a selected column, click the box again). For this example, select **ProductName** from the **Products** table, and **Quantity** from the **Order Details** table.

5. Select **Group By** from the **Query** menu. Click the Quantity row's Group By column in the grid at the bottom of the window. Open the drop-down box and select **Avg**. In the Quantity row's **Alias** column, enter Average Qty Ordered. Your view should now resemble Figure 34.10.

Automation provided by the View editor

Notice that the editor placed brackets around the words *Average Qty Ordered* in the Alias column because the name contains embedded blanks.

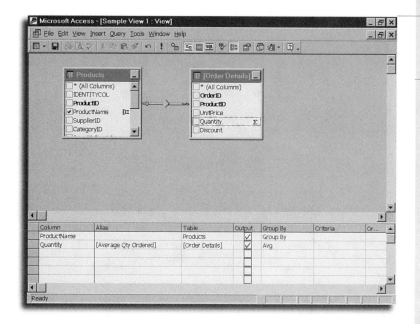

FIGURE 34.10
The view using the Group By
functionality.

6. Click the **View** toolbar icon to display the recordset defined by the view. Name the view Sample View 1 when prompted to do so. Your view should now display the average quantity ordered for each product (see Figure 34.11).

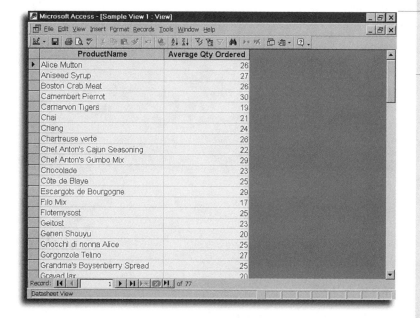

FIGURE 34.11
List of the average quantity
ordered of each product.

7. Return to Design view by clicking the **View** toolbar icon 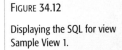.

8. To display the SQL created for this view (see Figure 34.12), click the **SQL** toolbar icon. You can modify this SQL directly, without using the visual tools you've used thus far.

9. Select **Verify SQL Syntax** from the **Query** menu. You should see a dialog box which tells you that the syntax of the SQL statement is verified against the data source. This functionality allows you to ensure that the SQL statements are valid without actually saving them or executing them. For example, change the fourth line of the SQL statement that now reads [Order Details] ON to [Order Detailsx] ON, and again verify the SQL. This time you're informed that an error is found (see Figure 34.13).

Modifying SQL: An example

Try changing the SQL line that now reads AS [Average Qty Ordered] to AS [Average Number Ordered]. Change to Datasheet view and notice the column name has changed to Average Number Ordered. Return to Design view and notice that the grid is also updated to reflect the change made to the SQL statement.

FIGURE 34.12

Displaying the SQL for view Sample View 1.

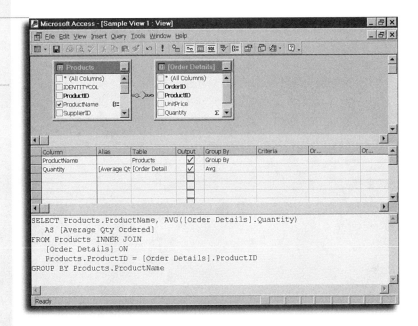

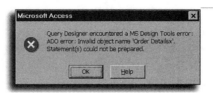

FIGURE 34.13

The reference to ADO gives you some insight about how the connection between the Access Project and its back-end data source can be managed.

Stored Procedures

A *stored procedure* is similar to, but far more powerful than, an Action query in a standard Access database. There are several major differences, however:

- A stored procedure takes full advantage of the sharing of processing work available in the client/server environment.

- Unlike an Access Action query, a stored procedure can return a set of records.

- A stored procedure can consist of any number of actions, each one being the equivalent of a standard Access query.

Explore stored procedures

1. Select **Stored Procedures** from the Database window of the SampleProject project created earlier. Run the stored procedure named **Employee Sales by Country** (this procedure can also be found in the sample database NorthwindsCS) by double-clicking its name. You are prompted to supply a beginning and an ending date; respond with 1/1/1997 and 12/31/1998. As you see, the results look like any standard datasheet.

2. Open the same stored procedure in Design view. The display is totally different than that provided by the visual tools used with an Access query or a Project view. Figure 34.14 shows Employee Sales by Country in Design view. (In the interest of readability, I have formatted it differently from what you will see on your machine.)

FIGURE 34.14

Design view of the stored procedure Employee Sales by Country.

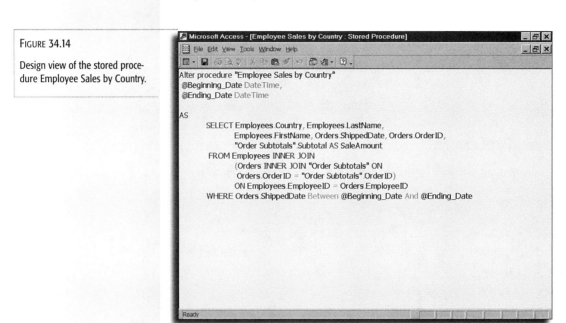

Examination of the actual SQL statements found in the stored
procedure named Employee Sales by Country and the query
Employee Sales by Country found in the Northwind database
reveals that the SQL statements themselves are very similar (see
Figure 34.15).

FIGURE 34.15

The Employee Sales by Country
query from the Northwind
database.

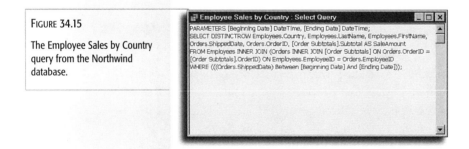

The most significant difference between the design tool for a
stored procedure in an Access Project in Figure 34.14 and the
design tool for a query in a standard Access application is the
lack of visual tools. There's no drag-and-drop functionality here,
nor is the design grid available. The stored procedure must be
entered using the procedure language of the database host.

On the other hand, although not evident in the Employee Sales by Country procedure, you can create far more powerful stored procedures than is possible with the single SQL statement approach used in the standard Access application.

Although the stored procedure in Figure 34.16 contains only a single SQL statement, it provides another example of the power of a stored procedures. In this case, the SQL used contains a clause not supported by the Jet engine—the WITH CUBE clause. Without that clause, the SQL would be pretty similar to a query you might find in an Access database—a query that shows the number of orders submitted grouped by customer and employee.

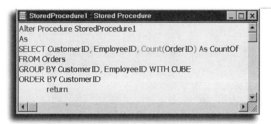

FIGURE 34.16

A stored procedure using the WITH CUBE clause.

However, as you can see in Figure 34.17, the WITH CUBE clause adds another dimension to the query. The first 10 rows are a result of the WITH CUBE clause. The first two rows tells you that the data contains 830 orders, 123 of which were sold by EmployeeID 1. Rows 2–9 show the number of orders for each of the other employees. Finally, rows 11–563 show how many orders were sold for each customer by each employee.

CustomerID	EmployeeID	CountOf
		830
	1	123
	2	96
	3	127
	4	156
	5	42
	6	67
	7	72
	8	104
	9	43
ALFKI	1	2
ALFKI	3	1
ALFKI	4	2
ALFKI	6	1
ALFKI		6
ANATR	3	2
ANATR	4	1
ANATR	7	1

Record: 14 ◄   10 ► ►1 ►* 🗷 ►1 of 563

FIGURE 34.17

Output using the WITH CUBE clause.

Securing an Access Project

The only security available for the Project (.adp) file is to create an .ade file. Choose **Database Utilities** and then **Make ADE File** from the **Tools** menu. Like the .mde file described in Chapter 32, "Applying Security to the Database," an .ade file has had all its source code removed. Thus, the objects contained in it can't be opened in Design view or modified.

The security of a back-end database is delivered by the data store being used (Microsoft SQL Server, for example). However, a dialog box is provided to interface with this functionality. From the **Tools** menu, choose **Security** and then **Database Security** to open the SQL Server Security dialog box (see Figure 34.18).

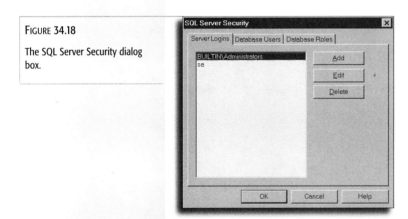

FIGURE 34.18

The SQL Server Security dialog box.

Taking the Next Step

Learn about class modules and when to use them in your applications

Create your own objects by using class modules

Extend your application's impact with ActiveX technologies

What's a Class Module?

Class modules were first made available to Access developers in Access 97. This exciting feature of Office 2000 for aspiring developers is the addition of standalone class modules in Visual Basic for Applications (VBA).

A *class* is the definition (or blueprint) of an object. A *class module* is where you define the class, or object. It's useful to think of a class as a cookie cutter and the objects it creates as the cookies. Until the cutter is applied to the dough, it represents only what the cookie looks like and isn't the cookie itself.

To understand the makeup and power of classes and class modules, review the following definitions:

- *Class module*—A module that can contain the definition for a new object. Procedures can be defined in the module to represent the properties and methods of the object.
- *Encapsulation*—The process of wrapping (or tying together) a number of elements into a single process.
- *Instantiation*—When you create a new instance of a class, you create a new object. The Set keyword (normally in conjunction with the New keyword) assigns a variable to represent the new object—that is, a new occurrence of a class.

When a class is defined, you can create a new object (instantiation) by creating a new instance of the class. You've probably already used classes and associated objects without knowing it. For example, the modules associated with a form or report are class modules, whereas the form or report itself is the instantiated object. Another example of object definition (class) and its instantiated result (object) is the ComboBox class and a ComboBox object (control) on your form.

Create a multiple instance of a form

1. In the Northwind database, open the Customers form in Design view.

2. Change the HasModule property to Yes and close the form.

3. In a new module, enter the code in Listing 35.1.

Which applications use class modules?

Applications that use VBA can use class modules. This includes but is not limited to Access, Excel, Word, and Outlook. For more information on VBA, see Chapters 26–28.

Not all classes have a visual interface

Although a form, report, and combo box all have a visual user interface, not all objects do. An example of a class with no visual interface when instantiated would be the recordset object in ADO or DAO.

LISTING 35.1 **Instantiation of a Second Copy of a Form**

```
01 Option Compare Database
02 Option Explicit
03 Private frm2 As New Form_Customers
04
05 Sub basOpenFrm2()
06 DoCmd.OpenForm "Customers"
07 frm2.Caption = "Second instance of Customer form"
08 frm2.Visible = True
09 End Sub
```

4. Enter basOpenFrm2 in the Immediate window.

5. Close your module, saving it at your option.

6. Two instances of the Customer form are now open, but one is probably hidden behind the other. Use the mouse to move the visible form so that your display resembles Figure 35.1.

   The two forms can be used independently to display different records in the Customers table. In fact, you can even edit data through either form and the result is reflected in both forms.

7. By using the navigation buttons of either form, move the form to display any record you like. Change the phone number displayed to some other number. Save the changes by pressing **Shift+Enter**.

8. Move the second form to the same record selected in step 7. Both forms will display the new phone number.

The default instance of a form

When a form is opened from the database window or by using the `DoCmd.Open Form` statement, Access opens the default instance of the form. If the form is already opened and visible, nothing happens except that the referenced form is made active. If the form is already opened with its `Visible` property set to `False`, the property is changed to `True` so that the form is made visible. A second instance of the default instance can't be opened.

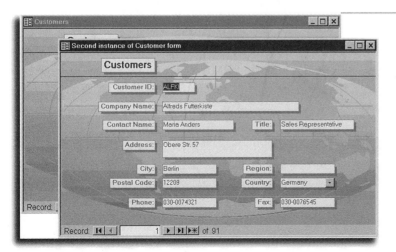

FIGURE 35.1

Two instances of the Customers form are now open.

When to Use Class Modules

As you develop your own solutions, you undoubtedly will run into scenarios where the same set of processes must be applied whenever your application deals with a certain kind of data. These circumstances lend themselves perfectly to *encapsulation*. By creating a class that encapsulates your data with all the associated business rules (which govern how your data should be saved or presented), you can hand over applications to other less knowledgeable developers without worrying that your code or the data it manipulates is being misused or corrupted. This is because they can reference only the properties and methods they need, rather than wade through pages of your code.

You could benefit from using classes for various reasons and in different cases:

- If you use the same type of form, such as an invoice form, you can review multiple invoices simultaneously in separate windows.

- If you need to speed up your multiuser environment in a low-cost manner, you can create class modules that represent your records as reusable objects.

- If business rules are associated with your data, you can ensure that the rules are enforced by encapsulating the rules and the associated data into a single class.

- If complex file-handling processes (low-level text-file handling) require redundant processes, you can encapsulate those processes into a single reusable object.

- You can encapsulate Windows API procedures into plain-English methods and properties. (For those of you who have ventured down that road, you know what an arduous task it is.)

- You can encapsulate the complex inner workings of other applications that expose themselves as type libraries. An example might be a class that provides a simple and controlled interface between your Access 2000 application and Microsoft's Outlook 2000.

Creating Your Own Objects

By thinking of your data as real entities, you will find designing classes easy. The actions they take, the decisions they make, and the characteristics they display are the methods and properties that make up the business rules your application needs to function properly.

To see just how easy it is to create a class of objects, look at a very simple hypothetical application to keep track of telephone numbers. In the example application, a data record consists of ContactID, FirstName, LastName, Phone, and ContactType fields. The ContactType field distinguishes between personal contacts and business contacts. For this example, you create a class so that each object represents one record of this data, and each field is a property of the object.

Create a new class

1. Create a new module in any database.

2. From the **Insert** menu choose **Class Module**. A new module is opened and displayed.

3. Add the module-level variables shown in Listing 35.2 to your module.

LISTING 35.2   The Class Module After the Module-Level Variables

```
01 Option Compare Database
02 Option Explicit
03 Private mlngContactID As Long
04 Private mintContactType As Integer
05 Private mstrFirstName As String
06 Private mstrLastName As String
07 Private mstrPhoneNbr As String
```

---

4. Save your class module by using the name `clsContact`.

Two added events in the class module

Everything that you've learned about modules and VBA programming can be used in class module development. The only difference between regular modules and class modules is the addition of two events, `Initialize` and `Terminate`, that execute code on the instantiation and destruction of the class. This subject is discussed in greater detail later in this chapter.

Naming conventions

Note the **m** prefix used with each of the private variables. This prefix is commonly used to denote that the variable is private to the class.

Use of `Private` versus `Public` variables to store properties

Although you could store a property's value in a `Public` variable, thereby allowing VBA code to set and retrieve its value directly, you would lose much of the benefit to be gained from the use of class modules, primarily the loss of control. The class module would have no way of knowing who set a value or when and would have to perform any required validity checking every time the property is used within the module. Any other VBA code that might be using the property's value would also have the same exposure—that is, the value might not meet all the business rules intended. So again, validity checks would have to be included before each and every use. By making the variables `Private` and using the `Property Get` and `Property Let` procedures, you can apply all the business rules all the time, thus ensuring that the property contains only valid data.

A property's `Private` and `Public` attributes

When you create a property for your object, you can choose to make it public or private. The effect is the same as for a private or public variable. Public properties can be referenced in any procedures in the project; private properties can be referenced only by procedures in the same module.

Creating and Using Properties

Most objects have at least one property. Properties are the way your objects store their attributes or characteristics. The example has five properties, each stored in one variable shown in Listing 35.2. Notice, however, that the variables are defined as Private and therefore cannot be referenced from outside the module itself. How can you assign or retrieve values to or from the properties? VBA provides some special procedures for this very purpose. These procedures are called `Property Let` and `Property Get` procedures. A `Property Let` procedure allows you to assign a value to a property, and a `Property Get` procedure allows you to retrieve a property's value.

Add properties to a class

1. Open the `clsContact` class module.

2. From the **Insert** menu, choose **Procedure**. The dialog box in Figure 35.2 appears. Select **Property** as the **Type**, **Public** as the **Scope**, and enter `ContactID` as the **Name**. Click **OK**. The result should resemble that shown in Listing 35.3.

LISTING 35.3   The Class Module After Inserting the _ContactID_ Property

```
01 Option Compare Database
02 Option Explicit
03 Private mlngContactID As Long
04 Private mintContactType As Integer
05 Private mstrFirstName As String
06 Private mstrLastName As String
07 Private mstrPhoneNbr As String
08
09 Public Property Get ContactID() As Variant
10
11 End Property
12
13 Public Property Let ContactID(ByVal vNewValue As Variant)
14
15 End Property
```

FIGURE 35.2
The Add Procedure dialog box.

3. Repeat step 2, creating properties named ContactType, FirstName, LastName, and PhoneNbr.

4. Save and close the module.

You've probably noticed that VBA has created Property Let and Property Get procedures for each property inserted, but right now they don't do anything. VBA built the framework for you; now you must provide the VBA code that actually does the work.

Add substance to the properties

1. Open your clsContact module.

2. Update each procedure as shown in Listing 35.4.

LISTING 35.4   *clsContact* with the *Property Let* and *Property Get* Procedures
Completed

```
01 Option Compare Database
02 Option Explicit
03 Private mlngContactID As Long
04 Private mintContactType As Integer
05 Private mstrFirstName As String
06 Private mstrLastName As String
07 Private mstrPhoneNbr As String
08
09 Public Property Get ContactID() As Variant
10 ContactID = mlngContactID ━━━━━━━━━━━━ ❶
11 End Property
12
```

❶ Notice the usefulness of the m prefix here. Without any prefixes at all, the resulting statement,
ContactID=ContactID,
would clearly be useless.

continues...

LISTING 35.4   Continued

```
13 Public Property Let ContactID(ByVal vNewValue As Variant)
14 mlngContactID = vNewValue
15 End Property
16
17 Public Property Get ContactType() As Variant
18 ContactType = mintContactType
19 End Property
20
21 Public Property Let ContactType(ByVal vNewValue _
      As Variant)
22 mintContactType = vNewValue
23 End Property
24
25 Public Property Get FirstName() As Variant
26 FirstName = mstrFirstName
27 End Property
28
29 Public Property Let FirstName(ByVal vNewValue As Variant)
30 mstrFirstName = vNewValue
31 End Property
32
33 Public Property Get LastName() As Variant
34 LastName = mstrLastName
35 End Property
36
37 Public Property Let LastName(ByVal vNewValue As Variant)
38 mstrLastName = vNewValue
39 End Property
40
41 Public Property Get PhoneNbr() As Variant
42 PhoneNbr = mstrPhoneNbr
43 End Property
44
45 Public Property Let PhoneNbr(ByVal vNewValue As Variant)
46 mstrPhoneNbr = vNewValue
47 End Property
```

3. Save the module.

4. From the **Insert** menu, choose **Module**.

5. Add the code shown in Listing 35.5 to the new module.

LISTING 35.5 **Sample Code to Exercise the Class Module**

```
01 Sub basUseYourClass1(strFstName As String, _
      strLstName As String)
02
03 Dim objYourObject As New clsContact
04 Dim strName As String
05
06 objYourObject.FirstName = strFstName
07 objYourObject.LastName = strLstName
08 strName = objYourObject.LastName & ", " _
      & objYourObject.FirstName
09
10 Debug.Print strName
11 End Sub
```

The new class is included in the Auto List choices

As you enter this procedure, notice that VBA has added your new class and its properties to the list presented by the Auto List feature. This is visible as you enter lines 3, 6, 7, and 8. VBA is treating your class, object, and properties just like any other.

6. Enter the following line in the Immediate window:

    basUseYourClass1 "*yourfirstname*","*yourlastname*"

Your name should be displayed in a format similar to Doe, John.

7. Save this module as Module1.

The clsContact class isn't very useful yet, but it does work and shows that it can already be used to create an object with its own properties. In the next several sections, you expand this class to make it more useful.

Guidelines for Property Procedures

To eliminate some possible conflicts, VBA incorporated some guidelines for the creation of property procedures:

- The data type passed to a Property Let procedure must exactly match the data type being returned by the corresponding Property Get.

- To pass a variable of type Object, you use a Property Set instead of the normal Property Let; for example,

```
Property Set (oItem as Item)
    'Passing an Item Object
    mobjItem = oItem
End Property
```

■ You can use Property Let, Property Set, and Property Get alone or together to achieve Read-Write, Read-Only, or Write-Only properties. For example, to make a property read-only, simply delete its Property Set procedure.

Creating and Using Methods

For your object to interact further with the outside world, you use methods. Methods are Public Sub or Public Function procedures contained in a class module.

Add a method to your class module

1. Open your module named clsContact and add the following new procedure:

```
Public Sub ShowName()
MsgBox Me.LastName & ", " & Me.FirstName
End Sub
```

2. That's it—you just defined a method named ShowName for the class clsContact. To use the new method, open Module1 and replace lines 8, 9, and 10 of the basUseClass1 procedure (refer to Listing 35.5) with the following line:

```
objYourObject.ShowName
```

3. Enter the following line into the Immediate window:

```
basUseYourClass1 "yourfirstname","yourlastname"
```

The new method, ShowName, displays a message box, as shown in Figure 35.3.

Using Me within a class module

Notice the way the keyword Me is used in this method. It works within the object you created just as it does within the class module of a form or report. That is, Me refers to the currently active instance of clsContact, or in this case the object named objYourObject defined in the procedure basUseYourClass1.

FIGURE 35.3

The ShowName method of the clsContact class displays a message box.

An expanded version of the class module can be found in the files Ch35.mdb and Ch35_BE.mdb. The next few pages refer to the sample found in these files. Ch35.mdb includes several forms and class modules, but the form named frmContacts and the class module named clsContacts are the ones related to this section. Ch35_BE.mdb contains a table with the data used by Ch35.mdb.

The class `clsContact` has been expanded to include several new properties and methods. Table 35.1 outlines a summary of these additions. Listing 35.6 shows the completed class.

Files available on the Web

You can find `Ch35.mdb` and `Ch35_BE.mdb` on this book's related Web site at www.mcp.com\ product_support/. Enter the book's ISBN into the Search box and then click the Search button to go to the book's information page, where you can find the code.

TABLE 35.1   New Properties in *clsContact*

Item	Description
	Properties
ContactTypeList	Contains a list of valid `ContactTypes`. Fills the row source of `cboContactType` on the form `frmContacts`.
ContactList	Contains a list of `Contacts`. Used to fill the row source of `cboContact` on the form `frmContacts`.
	Methods
Load	Reads the requested contact record from `tblContacts` in Ch35_BE.mdb and assigns the field values to the appropriate class property.
Save	Writes new or changed records back to table `tblContacts` in Ch35_BE.mdb based on the values of the class properties.

LISTING 35.6   Properties and Methods of *clsContact*

```
01 Option Compare Database
02 Option Explicit
03 Private mlngContactID As Long
04 Private mintContactType As Integer
05 Private mstrFirstName As String
06 Private mstrLastName As String
07 Private mstrPhoneNbr As String
08 Private mstrContactTypeList As String
09 Private mstrContactList As String
10 Private mstrCnn As String
11 Private mCnn As ADODB.Connection
12
13 Public Property Get ContactID() As Variant
14 ContactID = mlngContactID
15 End Property
```

continues…

Nz ( ) function returns the value given as the second argument if the first argument is null.

LISTING 35.6 Continued

```
16
17 Public Property Let ContactID(ByVal vNewValue As Variant)
18 mlngContactID = Nz(vNewValue, 0)
19 End Property
20 Public Property Get ContactType() As Variant
21 ContactType = mintContactType
22 End Property
23
24 Public Property Let ContactType(ByVal vNewValue _
     As Variant)
25  mintContactType = Nz(vNewValue, 0)
26 End Property
27
28 Public Property Get FirstName() As Variant
29 FirstName = mstrFirstName
30 End Property
31
32 Public Property Let FirstName(ByVal vNewValue As Variant)
33 mstrFirstName = Nz(vNewValue, "")
34 End Property
35
36 Public Property Get LastName() As Variant
37 LastName = mstrLastName
38 End Property
39
40 Public Property Let LastName(ByVal vNewValue As Variant)
41 mstrLastName = Nz(vNewValue, "")
42 End Property
43
44 Public Property Get PhoneNbr() As Variant
45 PhoneNbr = mstrPhoneNbr
46 End Property
47
48 Public Property Let PhoneNbr(ByVal vNewValue As Variant)
49 mstrPhoneNbr = Nz(vNewValue, "")
50 End Property
51
52 Public Property Get ContractTypeList() As Variant
53 ContractTypeList = mstrContactTypeList
```

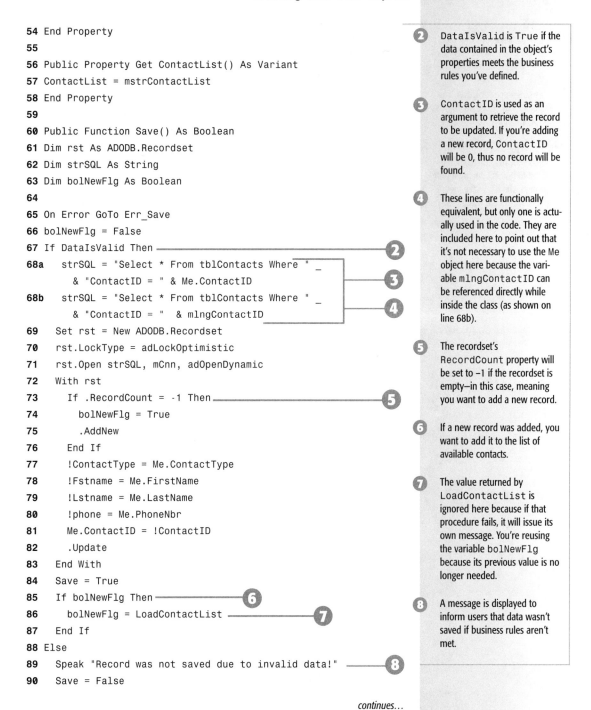

```
54  End Property
55
56  Public Property Get ContactList() As Variant
57  ContactList = mstrContactList
58  End Property
59
60  Public Function Save() As Boolean
61  Dim rst As ADODB.Recordset
62  Dim strSQL As String
63  Dim bolNewFlg As Boolean
64
65  On Error GoTo Err_Save
66  bolNewFlg = False
67  If DataIsValid Then
68a     strSQL = "Select * From tblContacts Where " _
           & "ContactID = " & Me.ContactID
68b     strSQL = "Select * From tblContacts Where " _
           & "ContactID = "  & mlngContactID
69     Set rst = New ADODB.Recordset
70     rst.LockType = adLockOptimistic
71     rst.Open strSQL, mCnn, adOpenDynamic
72     With rst
73       If .RecordCount = -1 Then
74         bolNewFlg = True
75         .AddNew
76       End If
77       !ContactType = Me.ContactType
78       !Fstname = Me.FirstName
79       !Lstname = Me.LastName
80       !phone = Me.PhoneNbr
81       Me.ContactID = !ContactID
82       .Update
83     End With
84     Save = True
85     If bolNewFlg Then
86       bolNewFlg = LoadContactList
87     End If
88  Else
89     Speak "Record was not saved due to invalid data!"
90     Save = False
```

② DataIsValid is True if the data contained in the object's properties meets the business rules you've defined.

③ ContactID is used as an argument to retrieve the record to be updated. If you're adding a new record, ContactID will be 0, thus no record will be found.

④ These lines are functionally equivalent, but only one is actually used in the code. They are included here to point out that it's not necessary to use the Me object here because the variable mlngContactID can be referenced directly while inside the class (as shown on line 68b).

⑤ The recordset's RecordCount property will be set to −1 if the recordset is empty—in this case, meaning you want to add a new record.

⑥ If a new record was added, you want to add it to the list of available contacts.

⑦ The value returned by LoadContactList is ignored here because if that procedure fails, it will issue its own message. You're reusing the variable bolNewFlg because its previous value is no longer needed.

⑧ A message is displayed to inform users that data wasn't saved if business rules aren't met.

continues...

⑨ Check to make sure that the recordset `rst` now exists before trying to close it.

⑩ Close the open recordset. You should always close all objects that you open.

⑪ Destroy the `rst` object. Any object that you create should be set to nothing when you are through with it, to save memory and other system resources.

LISTING 35.6   **Continued**

```
 91 End If
 92 Done_Save:
 93    On Error GoTo 0
 94    If Not rst Is Nothing Then ──────────⑨
 95       rst.Close ──────────────────────────────⑩
 96    End If
 97    Set rst = Nothing ──────────────⑪
 98    Exit Function
 99 Err_Save:
100    Speak "Record was not saved due to unknown error!"
101    GoTo Done_Save
102 End Function
103
104 Public Function Load() As Boolean
105 Dim rst As ADODB.Recordset
106 Dim strSQL As String
107
108 On Error GoTo Err_Load
109 strSQL = "Select * From tblContacts Where ContactID = " _
           & Me.ContactID
110 Set rst = New ADODB.Recordset
111 rst.LockType = adLockOptimistic
112 rst.Open strSQL, mCnn, adOpenDynamic
113 With rst
114    If Not .EOF Then
115       Me.ContactType = !ContactType
116       Me.FirstName = !Fstname
117       Me.LastName = !Lstname
118       Me.PhoneNbr = !phone
119       Load = True
120    Else
121       GoTo Err_Load
122    End If
123 End With
124 Done_Load:
125    On Error GoTo 0
126    If Not rst Is Nothing Then
127       rst.Close
128    End If
```

```
129   Set rst = Nothing
130   Exit Function
131 Err_Load:
132   Load = False
133   Speak "Requested record could not be loaded."
134   GoTo Done_Load
135 End Function
```

The module also includes several `Private` procedures used to encapsulate some simplistic business rules within the class. These rules are

- 1 and 2 are the only valid `ContactTypes`. They represent Personal and Business contacts, respectively.

- A Personal contact (type 1) must include a first and last name.

- A Business contact must include a last name but must not include a first name.

- All contacts must include a phone number in the form of *(nnn) nnn-nnnn*.

These business rules are incorporated in the code shown in Listing 35.7.

LISTING 35.7 Procedures That Define Business Rules Within *clsContact*

```
01 Private Function DataIsValid() As Boolean
02 DataIsValid = True
03 If TypeIsValid(Me.ContactType) Then
04   If NameIsValid Then
05     If Not PhoneIsValid Then
06       DataIsValid = False
07     End If
08   Else
09     DataIsValid = False
10   End If
11 Else
12   DataIsValid = False
13 End If
14 End Function
```

continues...

① Attempt to convert the passed value to an integer. If the value isn't an integer, an error will occur, which will cause the code at line 30 to gain control. (This error won't happen with this particular example, but is shown here only to demonstrate the technique.)

② Built-in InStr() function lets you search a string to see whether it contains another string value. In this case, mstrContactTypeList is being searched to see whether it contains the passed ContactType. If the passed ContactType is found, its starting position within mstrContactTypeList will be assigned to the variable intVal. If it's not found, intVal is set to 0. Because mstrContactTypeList is used by the example form to fill the RowSource property of the ContactType combo box, the error being checked for here (an invalid ContactType) never occurs. It's shown here only to demonstrate the technique.

LISTING 35.7   **Continued**

```
15
16 Private Function TypeIsValid(varType As Variant) _
      As Boolean
17 Dim intVal As Integer
18
19 On Error GoTo Err_TypeIsValid
20 TypeIsValid = True
21 intVal = CInt(varType) ───────────────── ①
22 intVal = InStr(mstrContactTypeList, CStr(varType)) ─── ②
23 If intVal = 0 Then
24   TypeIsValid = False
25   Speak "Please select a ContactType from the list."
26 End If
27 Done_TypeIsValid:
28   On Error GoTo 0
29   Exit Function
30 Err_TypeIsValid:
31   TypeIsValid = False
32   Resume Done_TypeIsValid
33 End Function
34
35 Private Function NameIsValid() As Boolean
36
37 On Error GoTo Err_NameIsValid
38 NameIsValid = True
39 If TypeIsValid(Me.ContactType) Then
40   Select Case Me.ContactType
41   Case 1
42     If Len(Me.FirstName) = 0 Or Len(Me.LastName) = 0 Then
43       Speak "Both a first and last name must be " _
              & "included for a personal contact."
44       NameIsValid = False
45     End If
46   Case 2
47     If Len(Me.FirstName) <> 0 Or Len(Me.LastName) = 0 Then
48       Speak "A last name must be included for a " _
              & "business contact, and the first name " _
              & "must be omitted."
49       NameIsValid = False
```

```
50      End If
51    End Select
52 Else
53    NameIsValid = False
54 End If
55 Done_NameIsValid:
56    On Error GoTo 0
57    Exit Function
58 Err_NameIsValid:
59    NameIsValid = False
60    Resume Done_NameIsValid
61 End Function
62
63 Private Function PhoneIsValid() As Boolean
64 Dim intI As Integer
65
66 On Error GoTo Err_PhoneIsValid
67 PhoneIsValid = True
68 If Len(Me.PhoneNbr) <> 14 Then
69    GoTo Err_PhoneIsValid
70 End If
71 If Mid$(Me.PhoneNbr, 1, 1) <> "(" Or _
      Mid$(Me.PhoneNbr, 5, 1) <> ")" Or _
      Mid$(Me.PhoneNbr, 6, 1) <> " " Or _
      Mid$(Me.PhoneNbr, 10, 1) <> "-" Then
72    GoTo Err_PhoneIsValid
73 End If
74 If CInt(Mid$(Me.PhoneNbr, 2, 3)) = 0 Or _
      CInt(Mid$(Me.PhoneNbr, 7, 3)) = 0 Or _
      CInt(Mid$(Me.PhoneNbr, 11, 4)) = 0 Then
75    GoTo Err_PhoneIsValid
76 End If
77 Done_PhoneIsValid:
78    On Error GoTo 0
79    Exit Function
80 Err_PhoneIsValid:
81    Speak "A phone number in the form of (nnn) nnn-nnnn " _
          & "must be included."
82    PhoneIsValid = False
83    GoTo Done_PhoneIsValid
```

continues…

LISTING 35.7   Continued

```
84 End Function
85
86 Private Sub Speak(strMsgTxt As String)
87 MsgBox strMsgTxt, vbOKOnly, "Contact Object Error"
88 End Sub
```

clsContact is also updated as shown in Listing 35.8 to use the Initialize and Terminate events mentioned earlier in this chapter. This procedure is executed each time a new instance of the clsContact class is instantiated. In this example, it performs two tasks.

LISTING 35.8   Initialize and Terminate Procedures in *clsContact*

❶ Establishes an ADO connection to the data. The Connection object is saved in a module-level variable, mCnn, so is available to other procedures within the module. The procedure GetCurADOPath() returns the path to the current database. It's therefore assumed that the sample database and the database containing the data are in the same folder. If they aren't, a trapped error occurs.

❷ Fills two module variables with a list of available contacts and valid ContactTypes. These variables supply the data to the read-only class properties used by the form to fill the RowSource property of the ContactID and ContactType combo boxes.

```
01 Private Sub Class_Initialize()
02
03 On Error GoTo Err_Initialize
04 mstrCnn = "Provider=Microsoft.Jet.OLEDB.4.0;" & _
      "Data Source= " & GetCurADOPath() & "Ch35_BE.mdb"        ❶
05 Set mCnn = New ADODB.Connection
06 mCnn.Open mstrCnn
07 If LoadContactList Then
08    mstrContactTypeList = "1;Personal;2;Business"             ❷
09 End If
10 Done_Initialize:
11    On Error GoTo 0
12    Exit Sub
13 Err_Initialize:
14    Speak "An error has occurred during class " _
         & "initialization."
15    Resume Done_Initialize
16 End Sub
17
18 Private Sub Class_Terminate()
19 Set mCnn = Nothing
20 End Sub
```

The code in Listing 35.9 includes two procedures:
LoadContactList (lines 1–33) and GetCurADOPath (lines 35–57).
LoadContactList seeds a combo box on the sample form with a
list of contacts. The function is called during initialization of the
class and whenever a new contact is added. GetCurADOPath, which
is also called during initialization of the class, determines the
path of the currently executing application.

LISTING 35.9   **Miscellaneous Procedures in *clsContact***

```
01 Private Function LoadContactList() As Boolean
02 Dim rst As ADODB.Recordset
03 Dim strSQL As String
04 Dim strMsgTxt As String
05
06 On Error GoTo Err_LoadContactList
07 strSQL = "select contactID,fstname,lstname from " _
           & "tblContacts Order By lstname"
08 mstrContactList = "ID;Name;0;" & "' Add a New Record';"
09 Set rst = New ADODB.Recordset
10 rst.Open strSQL, mCnn, adOpenStatic
11 With rst
12   Do While Not .EOF
13     mstrContactList = mstrContactList & !ContactID & ";"
14     mstrContactList = mstrContactList & "'" & !Lstname _
                         & ", "
15     mstrContactList = mstrContactList & !Fstname & "'" _
                         & ";"
16     .MoveNext
17   Loop
18 End With
19 LoadContactList = True
20 Done_LoadContactList:
21   On Error GoTo 0
22   If Not rst Is Nothing Then
23     rst.Close
24   End If
25   Set rst = Nothing
26   Exit Function
27 Err_LoadContactList:
```

① This function builds a string of names that's available outside the class as the property named ContactList. This property is used in the On Load event of form frmContacts to seed a combo box with a list of available contacts.

② This line inserts text that serves as column headings for the combo box as the first entry in the string, and a line that indicates that the user wants to add a new record as the second line.

③ Read each record in the recordset and add the first and last names found to the end of the list of contacts.

continues…

④ This function returns a string containing the path to the application that's now running.

⑤ Get the complete ADO connect string to the current application.

⑥ Extract the complete path to the current application from the ADO connect string.

⑦ This code extracts the directory path (excluding the application file itself) to the application from the complete path.

LISTING 35.9   **Continued**

```
28  LoadContactList = False
29  strMsgTxt = "An error has occurred during " _
                    & "initialization"
30  strMsgTxt = strMsgTxt & " of the class clsContacts."
31  Speak strMsgTxt
32  GoTo Done_LoadContactList
33 End Function
34
35 Private Function GetCurADOPath() As String ── ④
36 Dim strCnn As String
37 Dim strDataSource As String
38 Dim intStart As Integer
39 Dim intEnd As Integer
40 Dim intWork As Integer                         ⑤
41
42 strCnn = CurrentProject.Connection
43 intStart = InStr(strCnn, "Data Source=") + 12
44 intEnd = InStr(intStart, strCnn, ";")                    ⑥
45 strDataSource = Mid$(strCnn, intStart, intEnd - intStart)
46 intStart = 1
47 intWork = 1
48 Do While intWork > 0
49   intWork = InStr(intStart, strDataSource, "\")
50   If intWork > 0 Then
51     intStart = intWork + 1                              ⑦
52     intEnd = intWork
53   End If
54 Loop
55 strDataSource = Mid$(strDataSource, 1, intEnd)
56 GetCurADOPath = strDataSource
57 End Function
```

Form `frmContacts` allows users to display an existing contact by making a selection in the `cboContactID` combo box. The remaining fields of the contact record can then be altered and saved by using the **Save** command button. You can add a new contact by selecting the first available entry in `cboContactID`, by simply leaving `cboContactID` empty, or by clearing its current selection with the **Delete** key and tabbing to the next field. To see how the interface between the form and `clsContact` works, examine the form's module in Listing 35.10.

LISTING 35.10   *frmContacts*'s **Module**

```
01 Option Compare Database
02 Option Explicit
03
04 Private Sub Form_Load()
05 Dim objContact As New clsContact
06 Me!cboContactType.RowSource = objContact.ContractTypeList
07 Me!cboContactID.RowSource = objContact.ContactList
08 Set objContact = Nothing
09 End Sub
10
11 Private Sub cboContactID_AfterUpdate()
12 Dim objContact As New clsContact
13
14 If IsNull(Me!cboContactID) Or Me!cboContactID = 0 Then
15     cbfClearForm
16 Else
17   With objContact
18     .ContactID = Me!cboContactID
19     If .Load Then
20       cbfDistribute objContact
21     Else
22       cbfClearForm
23     End If
24   End With
25 End If
26 Set objContact = Nothing
27 End Sub
28
29 Private Sub cmdSave_Click()
30 Dim bolNewFlg As Boolean
31 Dim objContact As New clsContact
32
33 If IsNull(Me!cboContactID) Then
34   bolNewFlg = True
35 Else
36   bolNewFlg = False
37 End If
```

① The RowSource for the two combo boxes is loaded from properties of the class.

② If the combo box cboContactID is cleared or contains a zero, call the procedure cbfClearForm to clear all controls on the form. Otherwise, use the class's Load method to read the requested record and, if successful, call cbfDistribute to fill the form's controls with data from the requested record.

continues...

③ Call cbfCollect to set the class's properties based on the content of the form's controls.

④ This procedure collects the data from the form's controls and uses it to set the class's properties.

⑤ This procedure distributes the class's properties to the form's controls.

LISTING 35.10   **Continued**

```
38 cbfCollect objContact ─────────── ③
39 If objContact.Save Then
40    Me!cboContactID = objContact.ContactID
41 End If
42 If bolNewFlg Then
43    Me!cboContactID.RowSource = objContact.ContactList
44 End If
45 Set objContact = Nothing
46 End Sub
47
48 Private Sub cbfCollect(objContact As clsContact)
49 With objContact
50    .ContactID = Me!cboContactID
51    .ContactType = Me!cboContactType           ④
52    .FirstName = Me!txtFstName
53    .LastName = Me!txtLstName
54    .PhoneNbr = Me!txtPhone
55 End With
56 End Sub
57
58 Private Sub cbfDistribute(objContact As clsContact)
59 With objContact
60    Me!cboContactType = .ContactType
61    Me!txtFstName = .FirstName                 ⑤
62    Me!txtLstName = .LastName
63    Me!txtPhone = .PhoneNbr
64 End With
65 End Sub
66
67 Private Sub cbfClearForm()
68 With Me
69    !cboContactType = Null
70    !txtFstName = Null
71    !txtLstName = Null
72    !txtPhone = Null
73 End With
74 End Sub
75
76 Private Sub cmdExit_Click()
77 DoCmd.Close acForm, Me.Name
78 End Sub
```

If you open the `frmContacts` form in Design view, notice that all its controls are unbound. Although binding your form and controls to a table or query is simple, it's also limited in that it gives you, the developer, less control.

You're probably thinking that the example might be a lot of trouble to go to for such a simple application—and you're right. But in the real world, things are seldom that simple. More likely you will have several forms—often, several different applications—all sharing the same data. In that environment, it can become very difficult to ensure that your data is always handled correctly. By encapsulating your data interface logic into a class module, this task can become much more manageable and easier to achieve.

One great challenge facing any developer is keeping Access running quickly and efficiently in a multiuser, networked environment. With multiple people entering or editing information, you will run into record locking and perhaps performance issues as well. One of the best ways to ease the burden of multiuser life is to use unbound forms. "But how do I populate the form?" you might ask. Although alternative ways exist, class modules do offer the cleanest and arguably the fastest way to maintain your information.

Understanding ActiveX Technology

ActiveX technology provides a means by which the capability of any application that can use this technology can be expanded to include capabilities beyond the product itself.

Although ActiveX does represent the current state of evolution of several older technologies, it's not just a pretty new face for an older technology. It's a specification for interoperability between components, applications, the operating system, and the network to which the host computer is attached. Although the push for an object-oriented operating system has taken a back seat to object-oriented application development, ActiveX controls are more important than ever because they serve as the infrastructure on which future desktop and networked (client/server) applications will likely be built.

ActiveX standard is here to stay

Although Microsoft instigated ActiveX and ActiveX controls, it has turned over the standard to an independent body, The Active Group, also known as the ActiveX Working Group. (Its Web site is at `http://www.activex.org`.) This means that ActiveX is and will remain an open standard for developing component-based solutions. For Access developers, it means a continuing flood of useful ActiveX controls and components.

Functionality can be made available through ActiveX technology in either of two forms: as an ActiveX control or as an ActiveX component.

ActiveX Controls

Finding additional ActiveX controls

If you want to experiment with some ActiveX controls, you can view a comprehensive list of third-party ActiveX controls at www. download.com and www.activex.com.

In addition to the wide variety of controls Access already provides, many ActiveX controls are also available for use in your forms and reports. These controls perform all kinds of functions, from displaying data graphically to providing a calendar with which users can enter dates. Some can even be used to add animation to your forms. A control is available for just about every purpose imaginable.

Several interesting ActiveX controls are available through Microsoft, and hundreds more are available from third-party developers.

Registering an ActiveX Control

You must *register* an ActiveX control before you can use it within Access. The registration process involves placing entries in the system Registry to provide the control's location and startup properties.

You can register a new ActiveX control on your system in two primary ways. In order of preference, they are

- Run the control's installation application, if available.
- Use Microsoft Access to register the control.

Most commercial ActiveX controls come with an installation application. This application creates new folders for the control's support files (such as a Windows Help file and sample code), copies the control's OCX file to your system directory, and registers the control. If available, you should use this method.

If you've found an ActiveX control in the form of just an OCX file on the Web somewhere or had one developed for you but didn't receive an installation program with it, all isn't lost. You can use Access to register the control for you.

Register a control within Access

1. Start Access.

2. From the **Tools** menu choose **ActiveX Controls**. The dialog box in Figure 35.4 appears.

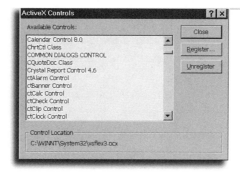

FIGURE 35.4

The ActiveX Controls dialog box lists the controls registered on your computer.

Tip for accessing ActiveX controls

A database doesn't have to be opened to access the ActiveX Controls dialog box. Also, even if you want to register a new ActiveX control for use with some other application, you can still use Access to register it.

Getting to the network from here

If you need to get to a network folder that's not available in the **Drives** list, from the **Tools** menu choose **Map Network Drive** to display the Map Network Drive dialog box. From there, you can locate the network file share that contains the OCX file. On my system, it sometimes takes a minute or more for the Map Network Drive dialog box to appear. If Access seems to go blank and be off in la-la land, give it a minute or two before you panic and press **Ctrl+Alt+Delete**.

3. Your list of registered ActiveX controls will probably look very different because you'll have different controls installed on your computer. If the control you're interested in isn't among those listed, click the **Register** button. (Even if the control is in the list and you just didn't see it, there's no harm in registering a control multiple times.)

4. The Add ActiveX Control dialog box appears. This is a simple File Open dialog box in which you specify the folder for the file, click the file's name, and click **Open**.

5. After the control is registered, the dialog box returns control to you. The control you just registered won't, however, be the selected item in the **Available Controls** list. If the registration process fails, you'll be told that. If you're finished, click the **Close** button; otherwise, return to step 3 to register another control.

Adding an ActiveX Control to a Form

Your forms aren't limited to the built-in controls provided by Access. You can add any ActiveX control to your forms with a few simple steps. When you're finished, that control will behave similar to a built-in control such as the textbox control.

Add an ActiveX control to a form

1. Open the form to which you want to add the control in Design view.

2. The form opens in the Design View window. If the Toolbox isn't visible, choose **Toolbox** from the **View** menu or click the **Toolbox** icon 🛠.

3. From the Toolbox, click the **More Controls** button 🛠. If this is the first time you've used this tool since entering Design view, Access churns for a bit, locating the ActiveX controls installed on your system. This tool is really a pop-up menu, as you can see in Figure 35.5. Your menu will most likely look different.

FIGURE 35.5

The More Controls list, displaying an extensive list of registered ActiveX controls.

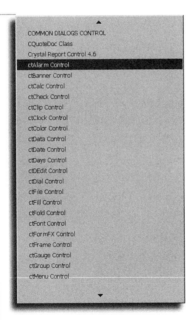

4. Find the control you want to add to the form and select it from the menu. (Be careful to single-click and not double-click. Also, don't attempt to drag from this menu.)

5. Move the mouse pointer over the Form Design window. Notice that the pointer changes to a little hammer with a plus sign. Click the form where you want to insert the control and start dragging. A rectangle appears, showing you the location and shape that the control will have on the form. When you're close to the desired size and shape, release the mouse button.

The control draws any design-time user interface it provides and is available for the Properties and Module windows provided in the Form Design view. Figure 35.6 shows the Calendar Control 9.0 control added to an otherwise empty form.

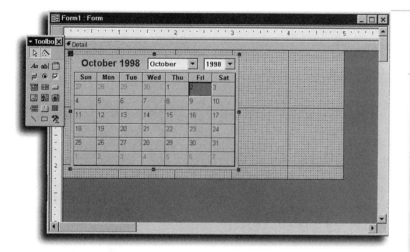

FIGURE 35.6

The Calendar Control 9.0 ActiveX control added to a blank form.

ActiveX Properties

ActiveX controls have two sets of properties:

- The normal control object properties that all controls have in common.

- A set of properties unique to the ActiveX control.

You can access the control properties by selecting the control and clicking the **Properties** button ![properties icon] on the Form Design toolbar. Or, you can right-click the control and select **Properties** from the resulting submenu.

To modify the ActiveX properties, double-click the control in Design view. Most ActiveX controls launch a property sheet from which you can select and modify that control's unique properties.

The sample database, Ch35.mdb, found at the Web site for this book, contains a more complete example of how to use Microsoft's Calendar control. The example includes the form frmGetDate and the module modGetDate. The best way to see the sample in operation is to open modGetDate in Design view and enter a line similar to the following into the Immediate window:

```
?basGetDate("10/27/98")
```

The date passed as an argument tells the Calendar control what date to use when it's displayed, and the basGetDate() function returns the date selected from the control.

ActiveX Components

ActiveX components are pieces of code that are packaged in such a way as to expose their Object Model to any application that can use an ActiveX component. In this manner, the functionality provided by the component is made available to other applications. So what does all this mean to you? Well, potentially, it could mean a great deal. For example, the Microsoft Office product family is packaged so that most functionality of any one product can be used by other applications. This means that just about anything you can do within Word, Excel, PowerPoint, or Outlook you can do within Access by using one or more of the components exposed by the other applications. These products alone expose hundreds of classes, each with their own properties and methods.

Expose available classes

1. Open any module in any Access database (I'm using Ch35.mdb in this example), and choose **References** from the **Tools** menu. The References dialog box appears (see Figure 35.7). This dialog box lists the component libraries found on your machine. The check marks indicate that a reference to the library is already established.

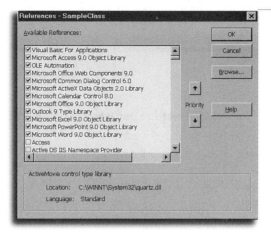

FIGURE 35.7
The list displayed on your machine will be different from that shown here because you probably have different products installed on your system.

2. You can add a new reference simply by scrolling through the list and checking any line you want to add. If references to Microsoft Office, Excel, Word, and PowerPoint 9.0 Object Library's aren't checked, select them now. Also add the reference to the Outlook 9 Type Library if it's not already checked. When you're done, close the References dialog box.

3. Open the Object Browser by choosing **Object Browser** from the **View** menu. Open the upper-left combo box and select **Excel**. The classes exposed by Excel are now available for examination. You might want to look at other libraries as well, such as Word or Office. When you're done, close the Object Browser and the VBA Editor.

I won't try to describe all the different classes that the Office products have exposed for your use. That would require several volumes all by itself. I do, however, want to refer you to the form `frmOutLookCal` in Ch35.mdb (see Figure 35.8). This is about as simple a form as you will find. In fact, the command button has only one line of code:

```
basOpenCal
```

As shown in Listing 35.11, the procedure `basOpenCal`, found in the module `modOutLook`, is also fairly short. If you count only the lines that do the real work, there are only five lines of code.

Adding a reference doesn't immediately update the list

Adding a reference won't move the item to the beginning of the list with the other references. You must first close and reopen the dialog..

Don't let the sheer number of objects overwhelm you

As you can see, a very large number of objects are exposed by these products. And similar to the products themselves, they are all unique. This can be pretty overwhelming at first because of the sheer numbers. However, in most cases you will be interested in only a few of these objects at any one time, just as when writing VBA code you often chose a single built-in function from the many available. It really doesn't matter what the `Eval()` function does if all you want to do is display a message box.

FIGURE 35.8

The sample `frmOutLookCal` form.

① One of these lines, depending on whether Outlook is now open, creates an object, `objOutlook`, representing the Outlook application.

② This is where the real work is done to display the Outlook calendar

LISTING 35.11   **Procedure *basOpenCal* Found in Module *modOutlook***

```
01 Public Sub basOpenCal()
02 Dim objOutlook As Object
03 Dim objNameSpace As NameSpace
04 Dim objFolder As MAPIFolder
05 Dim objCal As Explorer
06
07 ' Resume to the next line following an error. This is
08 ' necessary because "GetObject" will cause an error
09 ' if Outlook is NOT open
10 On Error Resume Next
11 Set objOutlook = GetObject(, "Outlook.Application")
12 If Err.Number = 429 Then
13     Err.Number = 0
14     ' Create a new instance of Outlook
15     Set objOutlook = CreateObject("Outlook.Application")
16     If Err.Number = 429 Then
17         MsgBox "MS Outlook is not installed."
18     End If
19 End If
20 On Error GoTo 0
21 If Not objOutlook Is Nothing Then
22     Set objNameSpace = objOutlook.GetNamespace("MAPI")
23     Set objFolder = _
           objNameSpace.GetDefaultFolder(olFolderCalendar)
24     Set objCal = _
           objFolder.GetExplorer(olFolderDisplayNoNavigation)
25     objCal.Display
26     Set objCal = Nothing
27     Set objFolder = Nothing
28     Set objNameSpace = Nothing
29     Set objOutlook = Nothing
30 End if
31 End Sub
```

Although the code in Listing 35.11 might appear to be totally foreign to you at first glance, it's really quite similar to code used elsewhere in this book. Granted, the names are different, but the syntax is the same as you've used before. Line 22, for example, sets an object variable to represent the object returned by Outlook's `GetNamespace` method. The next three lines all use methods of the objects created by the line preceding them. Line 23, for example, uses a method of the object created in line 22 to create a new object, and so on. Finally on line 25, the `Display` method actually displays Outlook's Calendar object.

To see the end result, open the `frmOutLookCal` form and click its **Open Calendar** command button. Figure 35.9 shows the result. The form in Figure 35.9 isn't just an empty shell, it's the complete working functionality of the calendar provided by Microsoft Outlook. You can do everything here that you could do if you opened the calendar from within Outlook. Try to imagine how much code you would need and the complexity that would be required to provide this functionality yourself. But when using ActiveX components, there's no need. It's there, waiting for you to incorporate it into your own applications. Now think of how you might use the nifty stuff in Word, Excel, and PowerPoint in your own applications.

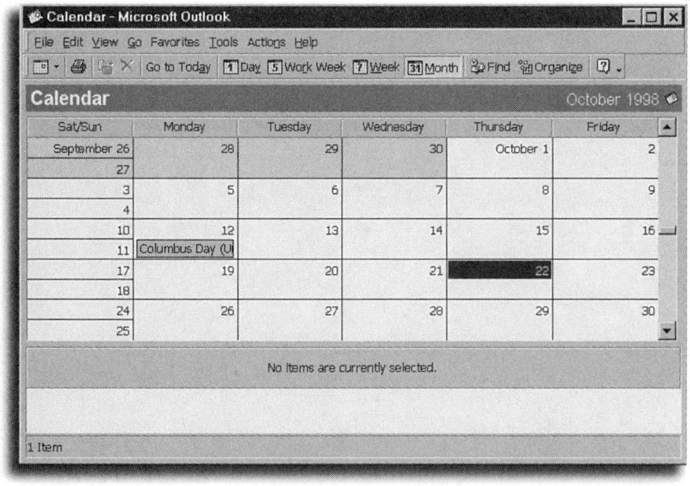

FIGURE 35.9
Microsoft Outlook's calendar, invoked from within Access.

Glossary

? A VBA code indicator used to begin each expression when testing so that the result appears in the Debug window; also an *input mask* character that calls for a letter from A to Z and is optional; also a *wildcard* character used to indicate a single, unknown character. The ? is also used as a print indicator in VBA's Immediate window.

action A macro instruction.

action query A category of four types of queries that can change records within your database with a single action when the query is run. The four types of action queries are *Make-Table*, *Update*, *Append*, and *Delete*.

Active Server Pages (ASP) Web pages that contain scripting language, such as VBScript, which executes on the Web server. After the script executes, it returns a Web page to the requesting browser but doesn't return any of the script code that has executed.

add-in A library with its code and database objects stored in a database file that usually has an .mda extension. An add-in performs a specific function that Access can't handle on its own.

aggregate function One of two types of functions that returns information about a set of records. Domain aggregates can be used in a VBA module, but not a SQL statement. SQL aggregates are used within a SQL statement, but can't be called in a VBA module. However, you can use both in a calculated control.

anomaly An error that occurs while adding, updating, or deleting data because of incorrectly normalized tables. See also *delete anomaly*, *insert anomaly*, and *update anomaly*.

Append query An action query that adds records to the end of an existing table. This can be used to combine databases or to combine tables that match only a subset of fields.

applications model One of two object models used as a basis for programming in Access. The Access Applications model gives you programmatic control of the many objects Access offers: forms, controls, queries, and reports. The *Data model* is the other of the two methods.

argument   Descriptive term used in code. Arguments provide additional information to an action (*function* or *procedure*) to tell it specifically what to do, when or where to perform the action, and on which objects.

ASP   See *Active Server Pages.*

atomic   Term used in *normalization*; data divided into the smallest possible units for separation into fields.

Auto List Members list   An intuitive feature of the Modules window that displays a drop-down list of object types, properties, and methods related to the objects you are coding. Use this shortcut to find available options and avoid typing errors.

AutoReports   A specific report wizard that uses all of a table's or query's fields in the resulting report.

background   The blank palette of a form or report; used in Design view to deselect objects.

bang   An exclamation point (!) used to separate the object from its collection in code.

bound object/control   A form, a report, or a control that's attached to a data source. Data sources include tables, queries, or fields, depending on the type of object that is bound. The bound object reflects changes in its data source.

calculated control   A control that uses an expression as its data source instead of a bound field or query.

call   Refers to the use or activation of a variable or procedure. For example, a procedure calls a variable for use in a function.

cascade   A process in which changes to a primary key value are updated accordingly for all related foreign key values. Also, if you delete a primary key value, Access deletes any related foreign key records.

cascading event   A logical flaw in code where a procedure or subprocedure either directly or indirectly calls itself and creates a terminal loop or a runtime error.

child   The table or field that contains the *foreign key*; used in association with the related table or field (the *parent*), which holds the *primary key*. More than one table might be the child to a single parent table or child to multiple parent tables. A child to one table might be the parent to another.

class   The definition (or blueprint) of an object, as defined in a *class module*. Once defined, you create a new instance of the object (instantiation).

class module   A module that can contain the definition for a new object. Any procedures defined in the module become the properties and methods of the object. Class modules in Microsoft Access exist both independently and in association with forms and reports. See also *scope*.

collection   An object that contains related elements. For example, the Forms collection contains all the open forms.

color matrix   The large rectangle of colored squares used to select or customize colors.

columnar form   A form with all the fields in the underlying table arranged in a single column, one record at a time.

comment   Text that documents and explains code.

condition   A logical expression.

conditional formatting   Allows you to set a value's font, styles, and color depending on set conditions.

constant   Represents a value that doesn't change.

control source   The data source in the underlying table or query, usually a field, that provides information to a *bound control*; available through the respective object's property sheet.

Crosstab query   A complex query that summarizes data in rows and columns (similar to a spreadsheet). A Crosstab query must contain three elements: a column heading, a summary field, and a row heading.

custom   See *user-defined*.

custom codes   Predefined codes or symbols you combine to create a unique format. For example, mmm returns an abbreviated form of the month. If you want to add a literal character, simply enclose it in quotation marks.

custom control   Additional or third-party ActiveX controls not included with Access. These must be loaded and registered before use.

custom dialog box or **pop-up form**   A customized form for applications whose modal property determines its type and whether it stays on top while other forms are active: If the form's modal property is No (or Modeless), the form is known as a pop-up form; you can access other forms in your application while it is active. If the form's modal property is Yes, the form is known as a custom dialog box, and you cannot access other forms in your application until you either close the form or hide it from view.

Data Access Pages   An object that allows you to view and work with data from an Internet or intranet.

data type   Predetermined set of aspects for information kept in a space of memory, such as a variable or field type. These aspects include its allocation of memory space, number and type of characters allowed, and printable format. For example, a Boolean data type for a VBA variable has only two forms: Yes/True and No/False; a Text data type for an Access field has a default size of 50 and can contain numbers and letters, but the field size can be changed.

database   A software application that stores data, usually in the form of *tables*, *records*, and *fields*.

datasheet   A format style for forms, reports, and table information; also a view in Access. The columns and rows look similar to a spreadsheet, with fields as cells.

Declarations section   The section in each module where you *declare* global variables and constants. You make VBA aware that the variable or constant exists by naming it. When you declare a variable or constant in the Declarations section, you make that variable or constant available to all the procedures in the module.

declare   To make VBA aware that the variable or constant exists by naming it. When you declare a variable or constant in the Declarations section, you make that variable or constant available to all the procedures in the module; usually includes setting the data type.

For instance, if inserting a new record causes a calculated control to return incorrect data, you have what's called an *insert anomaly*. An *update anomaly* occurs when updating a single field produces a ton of additional updates.

delete anomaly   Incorrectly deletes additional data based on a single delete action. See *anomaly*.

Delete query   An action query that deletes records in one or more tables specified by criteria. This can be used on related tables if the relationship supports the cascade delete option.

delimited file   One of two types of text files, which you might import; uses a defined character to separate fields of data, such as a tab character.

delimiter   A character, such as a tab or comma that separates fields of data; also used in code as a predefined character, such as ' that separates one component or value from another.

design master   Term used in replication; the design master is the only place that structural changes to the database can be made in order to affect a *replica's* database structure. However, the replica might have additional objects unaffected by the design master.

Design View Grid   The grid-like, Access 97 graphical interface for creating queries; consists of an upper pane where tables are placed and a lower pane, sometimes called the QBE or query by example grid. Actions here automatically generate code. Other objects, such as tables and macros also have a grid-like appearance.

dialog box   A specific form style that displays no navigational toolbars or record selectors, and contains a Close button in the title bar.

dialog box template   Refers to a generic form, which might or might not have some code attached, that you use as a starting point for other forms.

ditch   See *gutter*.

dock   The process that anchors a toolbar anywhere onscreen.

domain   In programming, a defined set of records used as the source for a function, such as the DLookUp() function.

dot   The period character (.) used to separate the object from a property or method in VBA code syntax.

driver Software that is a set of instructions for a specific task or device.

dynamic A list or output that updates automatically as its source changes. For example, a bound list box on a form adds a new item if its underlying table is changed or a Web site report changes as its underlying data changes and requires a live connection to the database. Some dynamic features are built-in to Access; others must be coded.

encapsulation The process of wrapping (or tying together) a number of elements into a single process.

entity integrity A rule that states that a primary key must contain data. See also *referential integrity*.

error Anything that doesn't produce the intended result.

event A database action, either user- or application-generated, such as clicking a button or opening or closing an object; can also trigger code actions.

event procedure Code that VBA executes in response to an object event such as a mouse click.

explicit A code declaration option that means you must declare a variable before you use it; recommended to help catch errors.

expression A formula that combines other values and operators to produce a result.

field A column within a table and the smallest unit of data in the entire database. A field might contain a customer's name, phone number, or zip code; one set of fields comprises a record.

fixed-width file One of two types of text files you might import; the fields are aligned in columns, and space characters—not tabs—are used to arrange the data.

foreign key The result when you relate two normalized tables that have an identical field; specifically it is the field in a related (*child*) table that refers back to a primary key in another (*parent*) table and is used to ensure referential integrity. The table with a foreign key might have another field as its primary key.

form An Access object that displays information stored in a table in nontable (rows and columns) format; used for data entry and viewing.

function procedure As a general rule, a procedure that returns a value, as opposed to just performing an action.

grid Lines and dots on a form or report in Design view that help in positioning controls more easily.

gutter Space between columns.

handle The small squares (in contrasting color) that appear in a frame-like box around a control or label; used in moving or resizing and indicates the control is selected.

hostname Part of a Web address that follows the // indicators; a unique name identifying the computer's address on a network.

HTML See *Hypertext Markup Language (HTML)*.

Hungarian convention A type of *naming convention*.

hypertext document Contains links to other documents or to sections within the document itself, allowing viewers to quickly move from one document to another.

Hypertext Markup Language (HTML) The series of tags used for the text-based encoding of documents to specify how the contents should be displayed to a Web browser and to create hypertext links so that the document does not have to be read in a linear fashion.

IDC See *Internet Database Connector*.

identifier A part of VBA syntax that identifies the object's collection and the name of the object, as in `collection![objectname]`.

implicit Code declaration option in which no declarations are required; not recommended.

inner join A type of join between two tables where only those records from both tables that have a matching value in the related field are selected. In other words, if one table has a value in a related field that doesn't exist in its joined table (and vice versa), that record isn't included in any query results.

input mask A pattern that you define and Access applies to limit a field's entry; the mask character codes determine which characters you can enter and how many.

insert anomaly A situation in which inserting a new record causes a calculated control to return incorrect data. See *anomaly*.

instantiation The creation of a new instance of a class, resulting in a new object.

interface The application elements that tell Access what you want to do, including dialog boxes, command buttons, menus, and toolbars.

Internet Database Connector (IDC) A specialized application that can be installed on either the Personal Web Server or the Internet Information Server; used to produce Web pages that display live data through an ODBC connection to your database.

intranet An internal network that operates identically to, but is not necessarily connected to, the global Internet.

intrinsic constant Reserved word that ensures compatibility with other VBA-enabled applications; represents a value that doesn't change. VBA intrinsic constants always start with the letters ac.

join Determines how the relationship between two tables affects the result of a query that's bound to those tables. Specifically, the join decides which records are selected or acted on. There are two types of joins: *inner join* and *outer join*.

keyword   A reserved word with a specific task, such as the `If()` and `Format()` functions.

left outer join   A join that includes all the records from the one table and only the matching records from the many table.

library   A set of objects and procedures that are available to an application; use the Object Browser to view the contents of a library.

limit to list property   A property that can limit the combo box text to only those items in the list; used to restrict data entry.

list index value   The value, beginning with 0, used to denote a selected list box item's position; represents its value by storing the integer associated with the selected item rather than the item itself.

local variable   A variable that belongs to its procedure; only the hosting procedure can refer to it.

locking   A mechanism to help protect against data collisions, in which the system places a lock on the data and releases it after the data is saved. If a second user tries to save the same data while it's still locked, that user is said to be locked out, and a trappable error occurs.

lookup task   Returns a value or list by referring to coordinates. Those coordinates can be index values or matching criteria. For instance, a combo box with three columns from a table or query would use the `Column` property to return data from any of the three columns; also used with the `DLookUp()` function.

Make-Table query   An action query that generates in a new table from one or more other tables. The new table can be stored in the database.

many-to-many relationship   A complex relationship that requires a third table. In a many-to-many relationship, one table can contain many records for each record in the other table.

method   The action part of a VBA statement, which the specified object is to perform.

modality or **modal value**   A property that controls whether a message or dialog box suspends just the application, or your entire system. See also *custom dialog box*.

module   Window used for entering code; the resulting code module is an object.

named range   A section of the spreadsheet that you've given a specific name to; used for importing partial spreadsheets.

naming conventions   The rules applied when naming application objects.

native controls   All the controls used in the Toolbox, and included with Access.

native object   One that exists within a hosting application.

natural primary key   A data field (not an AutoNumber) that provides a unique entry for each record, such as a social security number; eases the selection of a primary key.

nesting The process of basing a statement or object on another, as in using an IIf statement as the argument for another IIf statement, or running a query from another query.

normalization The process of creating and relating tables according to a fixed set of rules; used to design databases where referential integrity can be readily enforced.

Null The value assigned to a field or variable that contains no data.

object An Access component—the database itself, tables, forms, queries, reports, modules, and so on. In VBA statements, the "actor" that performs the method.

Object Browser An Access interface utility that enables you to view all the objects, classes, modules, methods, properties, and so on, that are available to an application.

Object Linking and Embedding (OLE) A technology that provides the interfaces necessary for one application to be embedded into or linked to another application's data; one of the options listed in the Property Sheet for a graphic or image that can be linked or embedded.

object model A way of describing the properties, methods, and events provided by an application.

OLE See *Object Linking and Embedding*.

OLE Automation A technology by which applications can communicate with one another when running on a Windows-based operating system (Windows 95, Windows 98, and Windows NT). Most of the applications can function as both an *OLE server*, which provides data to another application, or an *OLE container*, which acts as a host for an instance of an OLE server.

OLE container See *OLE Automation*.

OLE DB Provider A code set that serves as an interface between ADO and the actual source data.

OLE server See *OLE Automation*.

one-to-many relationship The most common relationship between two tables, where the one table contains only one record for a given unique value, such as a CompanyID; this relates to any number of records in a related, many table, where the unique value can be repeated if necessary, such as the same CompanyID for numerous CompanyProducts.

one-to-one relationship Each record in either table is related to only one record in the other table.

operators Usually refers to the mathematical symbols, such as the +, -, *, and / signs, used in expressions for query criteria and calculated controls; might also apply to some code symbols.

orphaned record A record that has unmatched foreign key values.

optimistic locking A locking mechanism in which locks are still issued, but they remain in effect only during the brief time it takes to actually save the data. See *locking*.

Parameter query   A query that allows you to prompt users for information to finish providing necessary information interactively.

parent   The table holding where the related field is the primary key in a relationship between two or more tables; the *child* table uses the same field as a *foreign key*.

persistent   Retaining value beyond the life of the procedure.

pessimistic locking   A locking mechanism in which the affected data is locked as soon as editing begins and remains locked until the data is saved.

pivot table   A resultset that's similar in structure to a *Crosstab query*; lets you produce different viewpoints of the same data.

placeholder   A representative word in code that must be filled in with the actual name or object, such as `variable-name`, which can be replaced by `intMyValue`. Placeholders are denoted by *`italic monospace`* in syntax samples throughout this book.

pop-up form   See *custom dialog box*.

primary key   A field selected because it contains a unique value for each record, such as a telephone number; Autonumber is often used as the data type for a generic ID number if the table doesn't have a *natural primary key*.

print indicator   See *?* at beginning of glossary.

procedure   A set of VBA statements that complete a defined task; all procedures begin and end with the same set of lines.

Project   An Access file that provides access to a Microsoft SQL Server database through OLE DB.

property   In a VBA statement, identifies an object's attributes. In Access, an attribute that modifies an object.

query   An Access object that stores questions about the stored data and returns a resultset or can be used as *record source* for a form or report.

query design grid   A graphic tool for creating a query; formerly known as Query by Example.

record   One row or one complete set of data, consisting of related fields; for example, one address in a *table* of contact information.

record source   A bound form or report's underlying table or query; available through the respective object's Property Sheet.

recordset   The collection of records that's attached to an object at any given time and depends on the underlying table or query and any criteria specified; similar to resultset, which might be partial records also.

referential integrity   A set of rules that Access uses to protect the relationships and the data between related tables; controls the ability to add and delete records.

register   A process that involves placing entries, such as new ActiveX controls, in the system Registry, which tells an application the location and startup properties for the control; this must be done before using a new control.

relationship   An association (link) between two fields (usually with the same data) in different tables. For example, using a related CustomerID in both a Customer information table (as a *primary key*) and in an Orders table (*foreign key*). Relationships help enforce referential integrity.

replica   In replication, each database that took its structure and original data from the *design master*; a replica can contain its own set of local objects that will not be replicated to the other members of the set.

replica set   The related group of databases in replication, one of which is the *design master*.

replication   A configuration of servers, networks, databases and rules that enables data to be shared and updated among users in different locations.

report   An Access object that stores the design of a printed report; reports might consist of data from more than one table or query and calculated controls, and might be changed and exported into HTML format.

right outer join   A join that includes all the records from the many table and only the matching records from the one table.

runtime errors   Internal errors that occur when the application doesn't find the conditions it needs to continue.

scaled integer   A data type, such as Currency, where VBA rounds the value to the fourth decimal place to conserve memory requirements.

scope   Code language rules that determine which application's components will have access to a variable depending on its designation as either Local, Module, or Public. Also applies to access of modules depending on whether the module is designated as a Class module (such as for a form) or a standard module (available to all applications).

Select query   A query that retrieves data that meets conditions, groups records, and displays calculations based on your data; probably the most common query.

simple query   A query that retrieves data from specific fields and is usually generated either by a wizard or the *Design View grid* without complex criteria or calculations.

splash screen   The initial screen used when an application is first launched; identifies the application and the organization and might contain initial user selections.

SQL query   A type of query that uses SQL commands to query your data. The SQL-specific queries are *Union*, *Pass-through*, *Data-definition*, and *Subquery*.

standard module A module that isn't attached to any particular object (such as a form or report) and is available to the whole application. See also *scope* and *class module*.

statement A VBA sentence or set of commands, generally consisting of components such as *objects* and *methods* and following a set of syntax rules.

Static A variable data type that is a *persistent* variable, meaning the variable retains its value beyond the life of the procedure. *Scope* refers to a variable's accessibility; persistence refers to a variable's *lifetime*.

static data Data that doesn't change very often or data, such as a report, that doesn't require a live connection to the database; typically used in reference to data on Web pages.

Sub procedure A programming task that's attached to an object.

subdatasheet A datasheet that creates a hierarchical display of your data in Datasheet view. See *datasheet*.

subform or **subreport** A complete form or report that can function separately from the main form/report on which it is used; after placement in the main form/report, Access views the subform/report as a control of the main form/report. These usually display data related to the data shown on the main object. You can insert unrelated reports into a main report, which most likely will be unbound.

switchboard A type of form that ties an application interface together by offering menu options that direct the end user to specific tasks.

symbolic constant A variable whose value remains the same but can be changed.

synchronization In replication, the process of updating two members of a replica set by exchanging all updated records and objects in each member. Two replica set members are synchronized when the changes in each have been applied to the other. Microsoft Jet implements incremental synchronization, which means that only the modified data is exchanged between replicas.

syntax Coding language rules that specify the order and structure of statements and their various components; with macros and queries, components are entered visually, and Access writes the code syntax. Incorrect syntax results in an error.

system-defined constant A type of constant with set values such as True, False, and Null.

table An Access object that stores data as a collection of related data in rows (*records*) and columns (*fields*).

table/query list box A list box (usually on a form) that refers to a table or query (specified in the Row Source property) for its members list; changes in the underlying source update the list box.

tabular   A type of form or report similar to Datasheet view—displaying all the fields in the same row; works well for displaying multiple records.

template   A generic form that you use as a starting point for other forms. See *dialog box template*.

Totals query   A query that performs calculations on groups of records.

turnkey   An application that's ready to use—all you have to do is launch it and go to work.

type argument   An optional component of the syntax for a message box; specifies the number and type of buttons to display, the icon style, the default button, and the modality; also used as a parameter for some controls and command bars. See also *modality* or *modal value*.

unbound   A control or report that isn't attached to an underlying table or query.

unbound object frame   A control that can hold embedded or linked OLE data for a form or report.

UNC   See *Uniform Naming Convention (UNC)*.

Uniform Naming Convention (UNC)   A set of conventions for the addressing method that specifies the location of an object (typically a file) on a PC network.

uniform resource locator (URL)   A set of conventions used to specify the location of an object on the Internet, commonly associated with a Web address.

update anomaly   Occurs when updating a single field produces a ton of additional updates. See *anomaly*.

Update query   An action query that uses criteria to update specified records in one or more tables.

update-latency   In replication, the amount of time it takes to update data between all replicas in a set.

URL   See *uniform resource locator (URL)*.

user-defined   Any value that is selected by either the programmer or end user, usually from within a set of predefined or available options. Synonym for *custom*.

user-defined function (UDF)   See *function procedure*.

user-defined function (UDF) procedure   A type of *function procedure* that, as a general rule, returns a value.

variable   A coding character or symbol that can assume any one of a set of values, usually determined by its *data type* or *declaration*; its value can change within the confines of a particular set.

Visual Basic eXtension/VBX control   A type of *OLE Automation server*; 16-bit OLE servers that could be placed onto Visual Basic forms.

widowed record   A record that doesn't have a foreign key record when required.

wildcards   Characters or symbols that are typically used as placeholders for unknown values or to cover a range of possible values. In Access 97, wildcard characters are only to be used with `Text` data types.

wizard A specific program design to rapidly and more easily create an object or perform a task by presenting the user with a series of dialog boxes step by step.

workgroup information file A file that contains information about the users in a workgroup and the groups of which they are members. The file contains the list users, their passwords, and their group membership. Access reads this file each time it starts in order to determine whether to display the Login dialog box.

zero-length string An actual string that contains no characters—the equivalent of the " " string. A zero-length string isn't the same as a *Null* value, which indicates there is no entry or result.

Index

controls

creating

listings

recordsets

X-Z

Using

Simple Solutions, Essential Skills™

Using is a thorough, simple reference for beginning to intermediate users. It is the series that supplies the answers before users run into problems, and helps them along the way.

Using Microsoft SQL Server 7
Brad McGehee, et al.
ISBN: 0-7897-1628-3
$29.99 USA/
$44.95 CAN

Other Using Titles

Using Windows NT Workstation 4, Second Edition
Paul Cassel
ISBN: 0-7897-1648-8
$29.99 USA/$44.95 CAN

Using HTML 4, Fourth Edition
Lee Anne Phillips
ISBN: 0-7897-1562-7
$29.99 USA/
$44.95 CAN

Using PCs
ISBN: 0-7897-1454-X
$19.99 USA/$29.95 CAN

Using Quicken Deluxe 99
Stephen O'Brien
ISBN: 0-7897-1723-9
$29.99 USA/
$44.95 CAN

Using Visual Basic 6
Bob Reselman
ISBN: 0-7897-1633-X
$29.99 USA/$44.95 CAN

Using Windows 98
Kathy Ivens
ISBN: 0-7897-1594-5
$29.99 USA/
$44.95 CAN

que®